D0481881

THE DANCE IN MIND

▰▱▰▱▰▱▰▱▰▱▰▱▰▱▰▱▰▱▰▱▰▱▰▱▰▱▰▱▰▱▰▱▰▱▰▱

PROFILES AND REVIEWS 1976–83

PHOTOGRAPHS BY LOIS GREENFIELD

793.3
J839

THE
DANCE
IN MIND,

DEBORAH JOWITT

WITHDRAWN

LIBRARY ST. MARY'S COLLEGE

DAVID R. GODINE, PUBLISHER, BOSTON

173445

THE DANCE IN MIND

was set by American–Stratford Graphic Services, Inc., Brattleboro, Vermont, in Bodoni Book, a face named after Giambattista Bodoni (1740–1813), the son of a Piedmontese printer. After gaining renown and experience as a superintendent of the Press of Propaganda in Rome, Bodoni became head of the ducal printing house of Parma in 1768. A great innovator in type design, his faces are known for their openness and delicacy.

The display is set in Gill Sans Bold.

The book was printed and bound by Halliday Lithography, West Hanover, Massachusetts. The paper is Warren's #66 Antique, an entirely acid-free paper.

Book design by Kathleen Westray.

First edition published in 1985 by David R. Godine, Publisher, Inc.
306 Dartmouth Street, Boston, Massachusetts 02116

Copyright © 1985 by Deborah Jowitt
Photographs copyright © 1985 by Lois Greenfield

All rights reserved. No part of this book may be used or reproduced in any manner whatsoever without written permission, except in the case of brief quotations embodied in critical articles and reviews.

With one exception, all the articles in this book were originally published in *The Village Voice* and are reprinted by permission. Copyright © *The Village Voice*, 1976–1983.
"Back, Again, to Ballet" copyright © 1974 by The New York Times Company.
Reprinted by permission.

Library of Congress Cataloging in Publication Data
Jowitt, Deborah. The dance in mind. Includes index. 1. Dancing—Reviews.
2. Dancing—Addresses, essays, lectures. I. Title. GV1599.J66 1985 793.3 84-47654
ISBN 0-87923-534-9

First edition
Printed in the United States of America

CONTENTS

~~~

THE PAST REKINDLED   129

THE NEW GENERATION   165

MODERN, TRADITIONAL, AND VERY

POPULAR 195

TRADITIONS OF OTHER COUNTRIES 239

SOME OTHER VISTAS 263

INDEX 293

PREFACE

꙳

"**D**on't you ever get sick of going to dance?," people ask. Almost seventeen years of two to five nights a week, over eight hundred articles logged in. . . . Do I get sick of it? Of course. Well, no.

There are nights when I'd rather go to bed, have friends over, take in a movie. There are mornings when the words won't come, and there are sloughs of depression over the large amounts of mediocre dance I have to comment on. But when the dancing is wonderful or the ideas bright and fresh, or even, sometimes, when the performance is electrifyingly bad, I'd rather be watching dance and writing about it than doing anything else.

Over those seventeen years, I've done a lot of thinking and talking about criticism—how others practice it, the kind that I'm interested in writing. It all hinges on how the writer (and the editor and the public) views his/her role. I don't see myself as an arbiter of taste, a press agent for dance companies, a teacher to artists, or a consumer guide for audiences—even though I'm aware that what I write may be put to those uses. I may, on occasion, assume the historian's role, or the reporter's, but these aren't always appropriate.

So what do I think I'm doing? Some years ago, in Philadelphia, at a conference on Dance and Philosophy, Alan Kriegsman of the *Washington Post* articulated more lucidly than I ever had a concept of the critic's role that he and I share: he spoke of contributing to the "hum" surrounding a work. We all acknowledge the ephemerality of dancing—an ephemerality that the advent of video has modified, but not conquered. Critical writing, along with the responses (public and private) to what is written, lobby conversations, interviews, dancers' tales, and so on cling to a dance performance, making it resonate in the memory, prolonging its life. To add to that "hum" by stimulating thought, and perhaps dissent—that's what continues to interest me.

But my opinion alone isn't much of a contribution. Reading the works of even the best critics of the nineteenth century, and those of many of the twentieth century, I burn for more details. Did the sylphs dance in unison—an impersonal white veil drawn over the stage? Or did they always cluster in groups of three and four—taking on the semblance of spirit-girls at play?

I'd like my words to be a bridge to the work, a window opening on it. (By that I don't mean I wish to stand between the spectators and the work, only that I offer my perspective for people to compare with their own, if they're interested in doing that.) It's this goal that accounts for the amount of space I give to description. You can't report a dance as if it were a fire, and the essence of a work may utterly vanish in an earnest listing of what body part did what. But there is a kind of descriptive writing that evokes the dance, without pretending to account for every minute of it. The writings on dance I most admire—whether these are by my contemporaries or lions of the past, like Edwin Denby or H. T. Parker—conjure up vivid images of dancers and what they are doing on stage. Opinion is supported by examples or emerges through description. Some of my favorite pieces of dance writing are highly "critical," others are not; but none is without the strong flavor of an individual's vision and an individual's feelings.

Of all the kinds of criticism likely to harm dance, dull criticism tops the list.

My own approach to criticism, however, depends as much on my own taste and background as on any high-minded goals I may set for myself. For the first ten years of my writing career, I continued to perform, and I have never quite given up choreography. My inside perspective on dance has been an asset at times, a liability at others; it is always a fact of life. It keeps me fresh and it keeps me humble. My respect for the labor that even the most self-deluding of choreographers, the most imperfect of dancers, must do has often (but not always) arrested my fingers at the brink of a witty put-down. It may be my background, too, that encourages me to *try* to consider a work on its own terms, rather than to refer to an absolute scale of values. Long ago, I decided that it was pointless to use heavy artillery on small targets.

All but one of the articles in this book were written between 1976 and 1983. They begin where my previous collection, *Dance Beat,* left off. In selecting them, I've tried to suggest the diversity of dance activity that's gone on in New York during those eight years. Many names are missing: Bill Irwin, Molissa Fenley, the José Limón Company, Deborah Hay, Antony Tudor, Jiri Kylian, to name just a few. This is no reflection on the importance of the artist, only on the value of my writings about them.

I owe an enormous amount of gratitude to my husband, Murray Ralph, who began the process of selecting articles for this book by reading, almost unblenchingly, about four hundred of them. Deanne Smeltzer, my editor at David Godine, also read far more articles than appear in the book and sustained me at every turn with her encouragement, advice, and wise decisions.

The Village Voice has provided me with more than generous print space. The various editors, over the years, have encouraged me to develop my own approach and style—a rare policy in the newspaper business. Since the mid-seventies, I have turned my column in to Burt Supree, a prince among editors, who always manages to make me feel that the infelicities he's obliged to point out arise from my fatigue, or misplaced benevolence, or a temporary (but justifiable) aberration, or an understandable slip of the finger.

Since 1974, Lois Greenfield's photographs have graced my articles— sometimes illustrating my points with uncanny aptness, always providing vibrant images of the body in motion.

I'd also like to pay tribute to my fellow critics, whose writing stimulates me and keeps me on my toes, and, above all, to the dancers and choreographers—since without them this book would most definitely not exist.

SOME MASTERS

Paul Taylor and Rudolf Nureyev, rehearsing *Aureole*

The term "master" is likely to cause trouble. Isn't Frederick Ashton a master? Of course, but I don't see his ballets often enough to write convincingly about his style. What about Trisha Brown and Meredith Monk? Aren't they masters? To me they are, but for the purposes of this book I preferred to consider them in relation to the new ideas about dancing that developed during the sixties and seventies, to their comrades in innovation. Alwin Nikolais? Erick Hawkins? I wouldn't dispute their right to be considered masters of their craft.

The artistic bloodlines of the choreographers discussed in this section are intriguingly intertwined, but haven't resulted in many similarities of style. Jerome Robbins danced in a couple of musical comedies that George Balanchine choreographed, long before Robbins became associated with Balanchine's New York City Ballet as a choreographer. When the Balanchine/Kirstein company was operating under the aegis of the Ballet Society, it commissioned Merce Cunningham's *The Seasons.* In 1959, Martha Graham and George Balanchine each choreographed one half of *Episodes* (Webern) for the New York City Ballet, and Paul Taylor appeared as a guest soloist in Balanchine's half. In 1984, Jerome Robbins and Twyla Tharp collaborated on *Brahms/Handel.* Cunningham and Taylor were, at different times, in Graham's company. Briefly, Taylor danced for Cunningham, and Tharp for Taylor. Balanchine is the choreographer that Tharp, who began her career as a maverick radical some forty years later in the mid-sixties, most admires.

Robbins and Taylor were never quite the groundbreakers that Graham was, that Cunningham was and still is. Of these five choreographers, none has Balanchine's range, although in Tharp and, to some degree, in Robbins, we see his brilliance in adaptability translated into an appetite for new challenges.

As a family tree, then, this section is a mess. As a very limited profile of twentieth-century dance, it's not uninteresting. In any case, neither innovation, nor breadth of vision, nor expertise account for great choreography, although they certainly may figure in it. Many bad choreographers have novel ideas, grandiose views of life, skill to burn. In the end, personal taste plays the considerable role many critics are at pains to deny. The five choreographers represented by articles in this section are ones whose work I've had the opportunity to see and write about often. They are among the few who have affected the way I perceive the world, who are able with some consistency to give form to inchoate thought and feeling—to those sensations of living for which, as Balanchine said, ". . . there are no names. . . ."

BACK, AGAIN, TO BALLET

The New York Times, December 8, 1974

⌐┐⌐

The name Jerome Robbins, to most theatergoers, is stuck like an indelible label onto a variety of surprisingly designed and brilliantly made packages. Some people remember Robbins as the man who choreographed the intricate, hilarious Mack Sennett ballet in *High Button Shoes;* others think of the sophisticated naïveté of the Small House of Uncle Thomas sequence in *The King and I;* still others associate him with the nostalgic warmth of *Fiddler on the Roof.* His TV "Peter Pan," starring Mary Martin, delighted millions of American children-at-heart. Everyone knows his first produced choreography, the ballet *Fancy Free;* everyone knows that *West Side Story* opened up new possibilities in American musical theater. It didn't have an upbeat ending, its characters were tough and contemporary, and a lot of them didn't have hearts of gold. *West Side Story* not only stitched acting, singing, and dancing into an almost seamless whole, but all of its irritable, edge-of-violence atmosphere seemed produced by the tensions between movement and stillness. Like a dance.

But since 1968, Robbins has turned away from the commercial theater. He has choreographed no musicals or movies of musicals, directed no plays or television specials, doctored no shows; instead he has made ballets—nearly a dozen of them. Robbins is back with the New York City Ballet, where between 1949 and 1959 he served as George Balanchine's associate artistic director and, for part of that time, as a leading dancer with the company. At least two of his recent ballets, *Dances at a Gathering* and *The Goldberg Variations,* instantly acquired masterpiece status (both are being performed during the City Ballet's current season); and one, *Watermill,* generated the battle between boos and bravos that usually ushers in importantly controversial works.

You could say that Robbins has come home to ballet—except that he's never really been away. His *Fancy Free,* given its premiere in 1944 by Ballet Theatre while Robbins was a twenty-five-year-old dancer with the company, startled and delighted audiences and critics by its wit, vigor and theatrical clarity. Robbins expanded this vignette about three sailors on shore leave into a musical, *On The Town,* and spent the next sixteen years rocketing back and forth between the ballet world and the worlds of so-called commercial dance. Almost every year, he produced a ballet *and* either a musical, a movie, or a television show. In the early sixties, he directed a couple of plays, *Oh, Dad, Poor Dad, Mamma's Hung You in the Closet And I'm Feelin' So Sad* and *Mother Courage and Her Children.* He has abandoned projects or had them fall through, but I can't think of a failure he's been associated with. He must have a special closet just for his awards—Oscars and Emmys and Tonys and all.

Robbins's return to the New York City Ballet came about almost by chance. The way he tells it, he'd stopped off at the NYCB office one day and was asked if he wanted to choreograph something for an upcoming gala. "I had rehearsed Eddie Villella and Patty McBride in *Faun,* and I was so impressed by them that I said well, I'll do a pas de deux for them, to Chopin music (which I love) and I don't know which pieces, but, yes, I *think* I'll do a pas de deux. . . . And that was the beginning." The music kept entrancing him with new possibilities; he added a few more dancers. He says he was ready to stop after he had about a half-hour's worth of dancing, but Balanchine returned from Europe, took a look, and said, "Make more. Make it like peanuts." (Robbins, in telling this, expertly mimes Balanchine greedily popping imaginary nuts into his mouth.) The result was the marvelous *Dances at a Gathering,* almost an hour's worth of astonishing dancing.

In the perpetually impoverished dance world, Robbins stands out as a mogul, an empire builder. While he was performing with the NYCB—just one of the gang—he was also taking time out to do things like choreograph "The Small House of Uncle Thomas" ballet in *The King and I* or co-direct *The Pajama Game* with George Abbott. As a random example of the kind of finances Robbins has been involved with: at one point in 1965, the three-quarters of one per cent of his share of the profits from *Fiddler on the Roof* that he generously donated to help found the film archives of the New York Public Library's Dance Collection amounted to $500 a week. Robbins's income from ballet has never amounted to more than a minuscule fraction of his earnings. So when he mentions that someone remarked to him, "Well, you've retired and are doing what you want now," he's not simply talking metaphorically.

If you hadn't heard what a driven man he can be when he choreographs, you'd think that, for him, making new ballets and remounting old ones was the equivalent of a Mediterranean cruise. Once Robbins was a skinny guy with receding dark hair and a bony, impudently clever face. Now, at fifty-six, he radiates a well-cared-for vitality: his tanned face, shining bald head and crisp gray beard, his tuned-up body, his clothing that has creases in all the right places and none in the wrong ones. Sitting in the study of his East Side townhouse, he looks alert and happy, even though he doesn't much like interviews and mutters ruefully, "I always said I didn't want to be served up Sunday for people's breakfast."

He says that he's loved doing nothing but ballets for five years and feels that he may simply have reached a point when, for a time at least, he's had enough of the multiple collaborations that working on Broadway entails. Not that he doesn't find them stimulating: "In fact, the better the heads (Stephen Sondheim or Leonard Bernstein, for instance), the fiercer the going—and the more exciting. But right now I want to work on my own materials with only the dancers, the studio, the music, and myself." (I laugh because when Robbins's housekeeper brings us tea, he and she struggle together to open a small, recalcitrant folding table. Suddenly Robbins withdraws from the clumsy maneuver and says firmly, "One of us should do it.")

Robbins has never much liked working on tight deadlines either. At the ceremony where he was presented with the Dance Magazine Award of 1958, he mentioned his extreme gratitude to the producers of *West Side Story* for allowing him an unprecedented eight weeks of rehearsal. His disenchantement with expedient solutions must have reached some kind of climax with *Fiddler on the Roof* (1964). Although the show was a great success and satisfied Robbins to a degree, the final compromises he'd had to make were heart-breaking—perhaps because the Russian-Jewish material was so much his own heritage. Robbins applied for and (in 1966) received a grant from the National Endowment for the Arts to experiment with "lyric theater." "I wanted to see," he says, "if I could make theater pieces the way I make ballets. I mean, I'd bring some actors and singers and dancers together and see what would happen. Without time pressures, without *having* to produce; if something comes up, let it develop. What I wanted from the American Theatre Laboratory was the kind of freedom you have in the ballet studio while you're creating. Unknown things come out of you. I have maybe some vague idea of the territory I hope a ballet will land in, but the details of that territory I never know. I really don't."

The performers picked by Robbins for the ATL experiment worked together for two years from ten in the morning until six at night ("The hardest work I've ever done, bar none," says Robbins). Sworn to secrecy, the group explored a variety of fascinating projects—everything from Shakespeare to Japanese tea ceremonies, from pure movement improvisations to material drawn from the Warren Commission report. At the end of two years, everyone was very tired and slightly edgy—perhaps from working together for so long without a fixed goal; perhaps, say some of the participants, because only Robbins knew why one project would be dropped and a new one begun. Although none of the work done at ATL was ever seen by the public, the project had a profound influence on those involved. Robbins is unable to say yet precisely what it did for him, but it's possible that it sharpened his appetite for a high degree of artistic freedom. Which may have something to do with why, these days, he's making not musicals but ballets.

Robbins's importance as a choreographer is undisputed. Not everyone may believe with Clive Barnes that he is "the greatest American-born classicist," but even those who snarl and pick at his works, and reject some of them completely, always hurry to see and talk about his latest ballet. Yet it's difficult to expound on the body of his work because everything he's done is different from everything else he's done. (This is how he explains the astonishing range of his dance work: simply "I've done this; now I want to do that.") You don't think of a Robbins style of dancing the way you think of a Balanchine style. He hasn't created a revolution in dance today—although some might argue with that—he has simply studded it with impressive works.

In a Robbins ballet, there is rarely anything that seems extraneous to what he conceives the spine of a particular work to be. His ballets are so succinct, so polished that they have a way of seeming to sum up or to epitomize an idea, a form, a moment in time. He has the last word; no one will have to do a ballet on that theme again. And in his most exquisite ballets—*Afternoon of a Faun,* for instance—you can't imagine that it could be better done.

Fancy Free wasn't the first ballet with contemporary American subject matter; it wasn't even the first sailor ballet. But its brilliant pacing and the clever ways in which Robbins blended ballet virtuosity with recognizable natural gestures with vernacular dance styles of the period made it a little masterpiece. Still in the American Ballet Theatre repertory, *Fancy Free* now seems quintessentially "forties." Robbins took one of the favorite romantic concepts of the World War II era—the brash camaraderie of servicemen on leave, looking for action—and treated it with unsentimental warmth.

His second ballet, *Interplay* (now in the repertory of the Joffrey Ballet) is a play-party of bumptious, apple-pie-fresh teenagers; their jazziness has a "white America" precision. They're not so much real teenagers of the forties; they're teenagers as America then wanted to see them. Uniformly vigorous, but not contentious. They'd never gang-rape a girl—an act that's implied in one of the sections of *New York Export: Opus Jazz* (1958) a ballet peopled by tougher *West Side Story* types, who thrust fists into the air and herd together, perhaps against invisible aggressors from the adult world.

Moves (1959), a ballet with no music, which bears a stylistic kinship to Anna Sokolow's "lonely crowd" dances, articulates the consciousness of the fifties in a less specific way. The dancers move warily: all of a sudden they've changed position, are somewhere else. Throughout, the ballet contrasts sound with silence, emptiness with presence. The gestures are like high-intensity light beams and the pauses between them create black holes. In one mosaic of carefully sculptured duets, some of the people dance unsuppported by partners; others unconcernedly manipulate the air.

Afternoon of a Faun (1953) is *the* ballet about ballet. The boy and girl who dance together briefly in the white studio are delicately careful with each gesture. They ponder the effect of their dancing in the invisible mirror erected between them and the audience, as if they couldn't feel anything they couldn't see. There's something ineffably poignant about their narcissism.

In Robbins's *Les Noces* (1965), all elements combine eloquently to intimate how barbarously the social aspects of weddings contrast with the privacy of mating. The dancing has a clumsy vigor that's produced not just by the heel-and-toe peasant steps but by a kind of bearish forcefulness in the dancers' torsos that makes the hearty way the celebrators shove the bride and groom together almost shocking. *The Cage* (1951) is probably the most viciously concise "castrating female" ballet ever made. The covey of women jab and whip their legs around like knives as they induct a young novice into the routine business of mating and devouring the male. They're presented as insects, but critic Edwin Denby long ago pointed out that their gestures have a horrifying resemblance to those of important Broadway people at parties.

In the 1946 work *Facsimile,* when an artificial flirtation between two men and a woman turned violent, the woman stopped the action with an anguished cry. I still remember how shocking it was to hear someone scream in a ballet and yet how appropriate it seemed.

The Concert (1956), Robbins's gentle Thurberesque ballet about things people fantasize while listening to music, is the first piece you think of when someone asks if there's ever been a really satisfying comedy ballet. And *Watermill* has become "that ballet with no dancing in it." In this

1972 work, a man watches meditatively while people intent on their own activities move slowly past him—a boy in a boat, a girl spreading a beach towel, men with paper lanterns, women making bundles of dry grasses. Perhaps the people belong to the man's past, perhaps to the present reality of the moonlit place. Everything takes a very long time. Yet ballet-goers who avoid oriental theater or Meredith Monk or Robert Wilson will accept the vanguardism of *Watermill* because of the cohesive beauty of its images.

It's evident from Robbins's ballets—indeed, from all his work—that he loves immersing himself in different worlds and discovering how people in those worlds behave toward each other. Interesting that one of the many things Robbins particularly admires about Balanchine is the latter's ability to evoke specific eras: "His choreography for a Mozart piece or a Gershwin piece or whatever is so *those* worlds and no others. . . . The Mozartean world of *Divertimento No. 15* is so exquisitely Mozartean, it couldn't be any other time." Change the names and he might be talking about himself. I think of Robbins as a choreographer who—consciously or unconsciously—articulates social conventions through dance structures.

Many of his dances—*The Guests, Les Noces, The Cage, Evening's Waltzes, The Concert, Fancy Free*—take place at gatherings. At one time choreographers used social events as pretexts for sparkling dancing; at the wedding of a princess or the coming-of-age of a prince, any number of divertissements are in order. Robbins, I think, centers some of his ballets around social occasions because they tend to heighten tensions or to clarify relationships between people. There is already a built-in element of performance.

These gatherings may not always have been planned by Robbins. They may arise with mysterious spontaneity while a ballet is being created. One of the few "directions" he gave the ten dancers who perform *Dances at a Gathering* was, "Forget the audience and dance the piece for yourselves and each other." This might be the key to the work. The dancers look like themselves—dancers dancing—but they also could be friends or relatives come together to celebrate. They deal with each other sweetly, trustfully, with a kind of grave playfulness, but seldom passionately. And the big wind-blown space they dance in clearly belongs to them.

If you search among memories and accounts of Robbins's thirty-one ballets (he also collaborated with Balanchine on two or three others), you find that, despite his eclecticism, it's possible to pin down a few Robbins characteristics. One is his ability to blend vernacular styles and everyday gestures with ballet steps—without making the former look out of place or the latter appear to be slumming. Another is his "simplicity"—a quality you find mentioned in almost every favorable review of his work. Even the most intricate of his ballets rarely look ornate or cluttered, and their forward impetus never stalls.

The illusion of simplicity (I call it an illusion, because if you use the word *simple* with any dancers who've ever worked with Robbins, they will either stare at you pityingly or begin to foam at the mouth) is heightened by Robbins's frequent use of unadorned motions like walking and running, or by the way he points up quiet gestures—someone reaching out and taking someone else's hand. And in most of his dances there are pockets of stillness in which he shows you dancers sitting or standing, watching each other or the space they inhabit. As Lincoln Kirstein says, he displays a "canny instinct for the artificed use of the apparently accidental."

In keeping with this, the dancers in Robbins's ballets look very "human"; despite all the craft and virtousity involved, the people onstage retain a kind of spontaneity. Their bodies look vulnerable, susceptible to change. You often hear it said that in ballets by Robbins, the dancers look at home—as if they were playing themselves. Part of this is a result of scrupulous casting: Robbins often has several dancers learn a role before he decides who is to play it. (It escapes no one that this procedure also makes shrewd use of the element of competition—keeping all the dancers crackling with alertness.)

But Robbins has something more than a clever casting director's knack for typecasting. He seems to see innate qualities in dancers, qualities that they may not emphasize or even be aware of. Erin Martin, who worked with him in *Ballets: U.S.A.*, in the ATL experiment, and as the Bride in *Les Noces,* remembers how rewarding, how almost collaborative, early stages of Robbins's rehearsals used to be: "Whatever it was that made him choose you for this thing, he was drawing out of you: he'd feed things into you, and you'd give them back. He was very generous, always, during that period."

And Tanaquil LeClercq, once one of the wittiest and most elegant dancers in the New York City Ballet, notes that in her day a dancer could be a superb technician and yet not suggest anything to Robbins. She thinks now that when she was young and unserious and Robbins picked her to do a leading role in his *Age of Anxiety* in 1950, "one of the reasons he used me was that maybe he liked the way I sat down or stood up or chewed gum."

After I had seen Robbins's *In the Night,* I remarked to Edwin Denby that Peter Martins, in a charming duet with Violette Verdy, had the air of a young military officer, and Denby said, "Well, you know, he did wear a sort of hussar's jacket at the first performance, but then Jerry changed the costumes." The jacket came off, but the illusion of the jacket persisted, and it arose not only from the choreography but from Robbins's perceptiveness about Martins as a dancer—his erect bearing, perhaps—something both manly and decorous about his personal style. A military coat would have constitued an overstatement.

With the same sensitivity, Robbins stressed Nora Kaye's forcefulness and capacity for anguish in *The Cage*, Tanaquil LeClercq's wild young legs and wit in *Pied Piper*, Erin Martin's combination of vulnerability and earthy strength in *Les Noces*. More recently in *In the Night*, he emphasized Patricia McBride's budding grandeur and in *Watermill* showed us Edward Villella as the mature and thoughtful man he is instead of the brash boy he must often play. He has pointed up dancers you never noticed before—not by directing them to act boldly, or anything like that, but by selecting movements that enhance them.

When you see a new Robbins ballet, you almost don't notice whether a particular performer does a role well or badly; you feel that performer and role have developed together. The dancers give themselves to Robbins to be manipulated, even bullied. In a sense, they give him his ballet, and he in return is capable—whether they believe this or not—of making them a gift of themselves.

Robbins recently saw *Fancy Free* again and says, laughing, "I could [read: would] never do that ballet now. It's such a *story*!" Robbins has changed. As he himself says, his characters are looser now, less strictly defined. His ballets are less explicit, more open to differing interpretations. Beginning with *Dances at a Gathering*, he has appeared willing to place more trust in the innate expressiveness of the ballet vocabulary. When you dislike something about one of his works, it usually seems that he has been tripped up by his own theatrical expertise, that an effect may be too calculated, or too arch, or too pat, but these days the devices don't call so much attention to themselves. In his best recent ballets, his craft has become almost transparent. In *The Goldberg Variations*, even Robbins's cleverest compositional devices appear to evolve, to be pressed out by shifts in the balance of human relations. A man, his back to the audience, leads a group in what looks almost like a ballet class; suddenly you notice (how did that happen?) that one of the girls has come unstuck from the group and become the man's partner. The change is accomplished so rapidly and unemotionally that you can notice it as pure dancing or interpret it according to your predilections. Once she was one of the gang; now she's flying off with the leader. So what? So, perhaps, nothing. Later, two men and two women dance together with unobtrusive tenderness. They keep changing partners; men dance with women; men with men, women with women. The ambiguous sexuality isn't emphasized the way it is at one point in *Moves;* it's just there. Maybe.

Robbins may not be able to say what the American Theatre Laboratory experience did for him, but since then he has avoided the speedy, pushy vigor that was one of his hallmarks years ago. His musicality has become more subtle—so subtle, in fact, that several critics disliked his recent duet, *Four Bagatelles,* on the grounds that it was abrupt and tricky and violated the music's flow; but musicians point out that the little Beethoven pieces are actually as perverse and as packed with "what-if-I-tried-this?" as the ballet.

Most important, Robbins now conceives of space more fluidly. He used to organize his dances in relation to the framing proscenium arch with almost architectural prec'sion. Now the space in his dances is more elastic. Sometimes you even imagine that only some of the dancing is spilling onto the stage, that there's lots more going on in the wings. Perhaps it's because he's accustomed people to this spaciousness that many are not fond of his latest ballet, *Dybbuk* (now astutely retitled *Dybbuk Variations,* presumably to free it of the burden of plot). In this ballet, Robbins has made the dances appear to occur in a limbo of space, as if they had been cut out and printed onto the stage.

Talk to anyone who's ever worked with Jerome Robbins, they all say the same thing: "Jerry is a perfectionist." Some say it admiringly; others pucker their brows and shake their heads in perturbation; still others surround the term "perfectionist" with a bloom of four-letter words. In search of perfection he spares no one, least of all himself. Balanchine's ballets occasionally hit the stage looking slightly disheveled. (Most New Yorkers have gotten used to this: you can forgive a little sloppiness when you're experiencing a marvelous language spoken by those who articulate it best.) Robbins's ballets never look anything less than scrupulously polished. Seldom is a gesture unfulfilled, a light awkwardly aimed, a dress unbecomingly fitted. You get the feeling that any such imperfections in execution would be taken by Robbins as a personal affront, capable of muddying the impact of his ballets.

He drives his dancers hard. (The New York City Ballet is, as he says, "a wonderful instrument"; why should there be anything its component parts can't do?) Some dancers like being pushed; others emphatically do not. Those who tolerate it best seem to be those who translate Robbins's demands into personal challenges. Ten years ago in an interview, Nora Kaye said the same thing that current NYCB corps member Delia Peters told me last summer in Saratoga. Which is the same thing that Rebecca Wright of the Joffrey Ballet yelled enthusiastically over the roar of the "F" train

---

we were riding. "He makes you do things you didn't think you were capable of." By cajoling? Explaining? "No," says Wright, "more like: 'do it.' "

Robbins has always kept in shape himself even though he stopped performing in the mid-fifties. According to William Glassman, who danced in several Robbins ballets, not only does Robbins never give dancers things they really can't do—only things they *think* they can't do—but when Robbins was still taking ballet classes in the sixties, he didn't give them anything *he* couldn't do. Glassman admires Robbins intensely, but if anyone might have an excuse not to be understanding, it might be he. Once, while rehearsing a difficult lift in *Les Noces,* in which he portrayed the groom, he was dropped on his head (the two fathers whirl the groom through the air). While he lay on the floor waiting for an ambulance to arrive, the rehearsal gradually and nervously recommenced around his recumbent form—Robbins working first with a chair, then with an understudy to try to figure out what had gone wrong. Later, Robbins sent a football helmet full of flowers to Glassman's home. When Glassman returned to work, Robbins let him skip the lift until the very last possible rehearsal; but it stayed in, and it worked. The story has become part of the body of ballet scuttlebutt, but it tells quite a lot about Robbins. In a lot of ways.

Choreographers have their own methods and their own idiosyncrasies. Robbins rarely fumbles around in front of his dancers but, according to them, when he's working his way through a tough place, he's been known to produce over a period of several days three or four perfectly articulated versions of the same sequence before deciding which to use. Or which parts of which. ("Only four?" says one dancer drily. "Only in rehearsal? I've performed eight different versions of the same ballet in as many performances.")

The difficulty for Robbins, as for all choreographers, is that each completed fragment of choreogaphy may alter the picture that he is gradually evolving in his head or shift the balance until a previously made section looks wrong. The difficulty for the dancers is that they have to remember a lot of material and adapt rapidly to changes. Asked about this, Helgi Tomasson, one of NYCB's finest dancers, obviously a perfectionist himself, says that until a work is truly set, he tries never to forget anything Robbins has choreogaphed, in case it may be needed. Tomasson, who relishes all the challenges working with Robbins affords him, simply accepts these demands as a matter of course, as part of his job. Most dancers are like this. But some of them grumble about it.

The thing is that, especially now, Robbins allows himself no easy ways out. For instance, after speaking in marveling tones about Balanchine's brilliance in orchestrating masses of dancers, he says, "It's a struggle for me to work with big groups; I have a *hard* time with that. . . . At rehearsals I lose contact with the individual dancers, and suddenly there are thirty-two of them coming in, and it's too big or too little or too forceful. It gets what I call 'covered with ice,' and I can't get my feelings out into it—I don't mean emotions, but my feelings about the music, or whatever." He says this knowing perfectly well that he can devise dazzling patterns or turn out snappy finales on demand—he's got expertise to burn. He's not talking about solutions, but about perfect solutions.

Talking to Robbins, you get the impression that he is a tense and volatile man who believes in self-control and admires those who are relaxed. Like everyone else, he is amazed at Balanchine's ability to choreograph with people looking on, people laughing around the piano. He says, "I try to make myself do it. When I first started working with the company again, other dancers would just walk in and sit down and watch, and it threw me because it was so hard. Now I'm a little more used to it and when I feel not uptight I let them do it. And sometimes I even try to do it when I *am* uptight—just for the discipline of it."

He is as impatient with his own weaknesses as he is with those of others. But he is generous in every way to artists he admires. On the occasions when he has collaborated with Balanchine, he says he tries to function more as an assistant—trying to get inside Balanchine's head and produce what *he* wants. He has twice gone on in the role of Sigmund Freud in Robert Wilson's amazing twelve-hour theater piece, *The Life and Times of Joseph Stalin.* He calls Wilson "one of the most extraordinary creative artists of our time"; presumably it excites him to get inside such a man's work. (Wilson is one of the many young, experimental artists who have been helped by the Lena Robbins Foundation, set up by the choreographer in tribute to his mother.)

When Robbins talks about dance, his voice warms with excitement and emotion: Balanchine, Baryshnikov, Twyla Tharp, whom he first saw dancing with her group all over the Great Lawn in Central Park in 1969 ("God, what guts! I loved it. In ballet, we're so timid about finding the proper stage. How great! How relieving.").

Robbins has a collector's tireless eye. He looks at books, paintings, dances, people in the streets. He listens to music. And absorbs and assimilates. When he was involved with musicals, he researched the periods and places in which they were set. As he speaks of this, his eyes blaze with pleasure; you can imagine that the moment when he arrives home with an armload of books is not the beginning of tedious research but the start of the creative process.

Sometimes he simply gets curious about something and starts to study it with no end in view. "I guess I have a child's fascination with the new and mysterious," he says thoughtfully. "You digest a thing and it goes into your head somewhere and maybe comes out in a work you don't expect . . . without your even knowing it."

For instance, he became interested in Noh and other Japanese theater forms during the late fifties, read about them, studied them. When he went to Japan to stage *West Side Story,* he probed deeper. The discipline, the limited means, the economy of gesture interested him. Later, at ATL he experimented with what he'd learned. Much later, at the appropriate moment, some of the qualities surfaced and took shape in the sparse, mellow *Watermill.*

Perhaps, after all, it is principally the open-endedness of ballet that drew Robbins back. I mean, when you make dances for a musical, you know what they are and whether they're going to work very quickly— with luck, almost before you make them. But ballets have lives of their own. Robbins quotes a remark Balanchine made to him after a recent premiere: "We," said Balanchine—and it is remarkable that after all these years and all his successes, Robbins can still tremble with pleasure at a "we" that links him with Balanchine—"we dare to go into the world where there are no names for anything . . . we get our hands into that world just a little bit."

Perhaps this is why dance is at the bottom of the cultural totem pole: the unnameable can be terrifying. As Robbins says, the experience of watching a ballet performance—something that exists briefly, ends, and cannot be recaptured—is too like our daily existence: "It reminds people much too poignantly of their own mortality. So they say, 'Books are better—or paintings or sculptures—because they can be touched. Because they will last.' "

A few minutes after he's made these remarks, Robbins leans forward and says in a worried voice, "Look, I hate big statements now, and I felt just then that I got sucked into making big statements about dance. Essentially what I care about is working; that's what I feel my job is. I don't want to fall into profundities and artistry and surround everything with whipped cream. I work, only instead of being a plumber, I'm a choreographer. I like my job."

FINDING ALL THAT GLINTS
IN GLASS

The Village Voice, May 31, 1983
⌄⌄

I wasn't sure I understood what Lincoln Kirstein meant when he wrote that part of the New York City Ballet's mission was to "canonize the New." Until I saw Jerome Robbins's new ballet *Glass Pieces.* Robbins has stitched into the structure of his work many of the things that characterize Philip Glass's music—simple two- or three-note motifs repeated over and over, rhythmic patterns shifting subtly across a vibrating pulse, accumulation, an emphasis on the ensemble—but he has accomplished this with such deft theatricality that even the conservative members of NYCB's audience are not likely to be shocked. In recent years I've seen people storm out of performances by Laura Dean's company and Lucinda Childs's (to name two dissimilar choreographers intrigued by insistent rhythms, repetition, patterning); I doubt that anyone will storm out of the New York State Theater. Even the brave-new-world tumult Glass's music has when it's played by his electronically amplified ensemble becomes domesticated when Robert Irving and the NYCB orchestra take it on. Canonizing the new in this case means making it comprehensible by introducing it in company with the familiar, the known-to-be-beautiful.

Actually Glass's music legitimizes this accommodation. One of the pieces Robbins uses, *Rubric,* seems to be constructed in the reassuring rondo form; in *Facades,* a saxophone sings a Romatic largo above the pushing beat; and an excerpt from the as yet unperformed opera *Akhnaten* roars along with the sonorities of a barbaric march. So in drawing hero/soloists out of the democratic ensemble, in mixing classical steps with pedestrian walks, in employing traditional partnering tactics, Robbins has responded to what he heard in Glass.

In *Rubric,* his astute use of repetition and accumulation keeps the audience on the boil. A horde of dancers (actually only thirty-five) walks across the stage from all directions, the way busy pedestrians cross a plaza—except that a shared rhythm binds this group. In the midst of this, a man and woman in yellow (Helene Alexopoulos and Peter Frame), distant from each other and traveling different paths, begin to wing out their arms, to run, to launch themselves into assemblés that turn them onto new paths. Left alone on stage, they condense space and activity into a brief formal pattern—a salutation of sorts—and exit. Enter the mob. This time they drop something new into their walk—one little stagger, as I recall; and they give birth, in almost exactly the same way, to another pair of soloists (Lourdes Lopez and Joseph Duell). Soloists accumulate—there's one more pair: Lisa Hess and Victor Castelli—in between group strolls that gradually acquire a lift of the arm, a turn, other simple ornaments. Couples number one and number two execute a brief, tidy, quick-stepping quartet with one hint of partner-exchange (akin to "swing your corner"). By the time number three has arrived, we've been able to anticipate a sextet. Exciting the way the stage keeps contracting and expanding like one immense visualization of Glass's almighty pulse. Near the end, several phalanxes of dancers walk and stop at different times; we not only see blocks shifting within a single mass, we feel those shifts in our own pulse.

In the second section—the traditional "adagio movement"—Maria Calegari and Bart Cook stay close together and in one horizontal strip of stage. Sometimes in their calmly amorous embraces, beautiful Calegari is displayed spread out in flight; at other times, she's curled into less classical positions. Behind the pair, a silhouetted stream of women moves steadily across the stage, echoing Glass's rhythms with reiterated phrases made up of small prances, pauses, pliés, sidesteps, circling changes of place in the line. When Cook and Calegari occasionally break out of their twining to stand side by side, our focus slides to the women (which it does anyway, from time to time). When the women—now filling the background—begin a variation of their pattern, it seems like a big event.

Some of Robbins's most stunning effects are accomplished not by the big, variegated ballet moves, but by simple changes in rhythm or direction, or tiny additions to a phrase. The frieze of women in *Facades,* the squads slipping past each other in *Rubric*—ideas like these are the ones that impressed me. But either because of the way Robbins heard the music or an ingrained love of engineering the large-scale changes and long phrases of ballet, he was chary with repetition (probably much to his audience's relief).

The last section, *Akhnaten,* begins promisingly, with squads of men accumulating in constantly traveling patterns; runs, jumps, turns; crisscrossing, merging, separating. But Robbins brings up (albeit subtly) some Latin macho/boy, flirty/girl stereotypes that don't fit (at one point, a unit of guys bob their heads up and down, and we don't think "rite" or "ecstasy," but "samba").

There are those who find Robbins's choreography most fluent in modest, small-scale works. I also like to see him wrestle with forms that are new to him. The resultant ballets are often thrilling, never uninteresting.

MR. B. MINES THE RICHES
OF THE WALTZ

The Village Voice, July 11, 1977

~~

George Balanchine has made waltz ballets before. His new *Vienna Waltzes*, however, is nothing like *La Valse* (Ravel) with its drastic, slightly decadent atmosphere—a ball at which the three fates seem half debutante, half preening cat, and Death appears as a dancing partner. Nor does it have the intimate yet elegant ambience of *Liebeslieder Waltzer* (Brahms), the ardent, searching complexities that characterize the encounters of four couples at a small gathering. *Vienna Waltzes* bears closer structural resemblance to *Union Jack* than to anything else, not simply because it is immense in its sweep and pageantry, but because it shows Balanchine investigating—with love and inexhaustible resourcefulness—The Step.

Vienna Waltzes is about the waltz, the nuances and variations imprinted on it by time, place, and dancers. The music begins; it is Johann Strauss's *Tales from the Vienna Woods.* The curtain goes up and we see a couple, arm in arm, wandering through a glade. He is in a dress uniform, she in a long, full pink gown. Rouben Ter-Arutunian's glade is remarkable. Five delicate tree trunks break up the stage space and sprout a canopy of summer foliage. Through the leafy backdrop, mirrors glint—giving the illusion that the depths of the forest are full of dancers. Perhaps the most ravishing moment is the simplest. The cembalo finishes its distant, tinkling exposition of the theme, and as the orchestra plunges into the same melody, Karin von Aroldingen and Sean Lavery begin to waltz. They are alone on stage; and their long intake of breath together, the arch of her back, the curve of their arms, the way they sink into the three simple steps say all that is possible about the waltz in its most ardent and innocent form. The ten couples who join Lavery and von Aroldingen (I've never seen her so soft and pliant) also seem innocent—playing endless intricate but gentle games of partner changing, making clusters, circles, and lines appear and disappear between the trees. The dance ends as quietly as it began, with Lavery and von Aroldingen exchanging a long, trusting look and strolling off together.

When Patricia McBride, Helgi Tomasson, and eight attendant nymphs speed into the same glade, there is a moment of shock. The women's net skirts, pointe shoes, darting and leaping steps at first seem indecorous by

---

contrast with the first section. Then, by some mysterious process, the woods clearly turn into a stage set of a stage set, and we are watching a divertissement set to Strauss's *Voices of Spring*. Here, Balanchine has woven together all those ballet steps that seem to be kin to the waltz— balancés, chassés, grands jetés en tournant—steps that extend its dip and rise into the air. Here the partners don't dance with each other so much as *for* each other and for the rapture of the dance. McBride and Tomasson are, of course, wonderful.

The glade is invaded briefly by a comical group. The men, led by Bart Cook, are fops with high, stiff collars, tight pants, extravagant pompadours. Their partners (Sara Leland dances with Cook) are flirty cocottes in very short skirts. The costumes make the men look stout; they're spry but not quite fast enough or clever enough to keep up with the women. This romp is set to Strauss's *Explosion Polka,* and when it is over, the glade disappears, as if signaling the end of an era. The trees lift, and what might be dark, ornate roots become the curve of drapery or grillwork that frames a mirrored ballroom. The oval shapes and black tendrils suggest the mystery and decadence of a Beardsley drawing. Perhaps this is Maxim's, because here is Peter Martins, an elegant, slightly despondent officer. (His costume—red pants and a white jacket—is Karinska's only dud in the whole ballet; the way it glares in the follow spot kills the beautiful mauves and acid greens worn by the eight couples who dance in this part). And here is Kay Mazzo, the Merry Widow herself, in black décolleté, boa, outrageous hat. The music is Lehár's *Gold and Silver Waltz*. This chance meeting of old lovers produces a different sort of waltz. Martins holds Mazzo with casual mastery—one hand only placed behind her waist; and she arches extravagantly against his hand, both taunting and taunted. At the end she runs away, as if late for another rendezvous.

In the first section, during a little dance-game, von Aroldingen, trapped in the center of a circle, can't for a second find her partner. Martins loses his (temporarily we're sure) because of some worldy disagreement. But in the last section, this lost partner motif takes on a supernatural, irrevocable quality. The music is now by Richard Strauss—waltzes from *Der Rosenkavalier*. The art nouveau decor changes, and the stage become a vast, mirrored ballroom with chandeliers. In the Martins-Mazzo section, Balanchine presents the kernel of *The Merry Widow*'s plot; in this he suggests the familiar operatic character of the woman who dreams of visitations from an absent or unattainable lover. Suzanne Farrell bows tenderly to an imaginary partner and waltzes alone. A man (Jorge Donn, on loan from Béjart, replacing the injured Bonnefous) keeps appearing and disappearing. Her dance—elaborate and wistful—will take her to the edge of the stage, and he'll appear suddenly behind her and blend his step with hers. She behaves as if he's always there, or perhaps as if she expects him not to be, and the effect is very sad and strange.

But the ballet ends in an icy blaze with all the dancers from all the sections waltzing together. There seem to be hundreds of dancers—the men in black tailcoats with ruffled jabots, the women in white gowns with long trains like Farrell's. This is not the 1868 of Johann Strauss II, it's 1911 and an opulent, less innocent society. The women must hold up their white trains like sails and manipulate them very cleverly in order not to trip. They are not waltzing for the simple amorous pleasure of it but to be exhilarated by the speed, dizzied by the turning. Seeing the wheeling couples, one imagines an entire society careering out of what Roger Shattuck called "the banquet years" into the chilly excitement of the modern world and an era of war.

A GEM REMOUNTED

The Village Voice, December 13, 1983

W hen George Balanchine's *Jewels* was new, in 1966, I succumbed unwillingly to its glitter, its opulent massing of the New York City Ballet's jewels—the dancers. It was a novelty—a full-length ballet with no plot, its three discrete sections set to music by three composers with dissimilar styles and allied only by the gem motif: "Emeralds," "Rubies," "Diamonds." ". . . one of the best examples of Balanchine's applause machines . . . ," wrote Lincoln Kirstein of the final polonaise in "Diamonds," and audiences gladly let themselves be switched on—by this and by the whole of the sporty, flashy "Rubies."

Kirstein also said that those who watch the ballet frequently ". . . find that 'Emeralds' rather than the bouncier 'Rubies' or the panache of 'Diamonds' are indeed the most exquisitely set gems in this particular *parure.*" At every reappearance of *Jewels* in the company repertory, I've come to feel that more strongly. Four years ago, I pinned the words "elegant reverie" to it; watching the current revival, I wonder if the whole ballet isn't being dreamed. The two couples, the trio composed of a man and two women, stroll through an aqueous green landscape of light, through the temporary arbors and avenues formed by ten women of the corps, the Fauré music (from *Pelléas and Mélisande* and *Shylock*) foliating all with a diffuse blur of melody.

It's a very still ballet. At the beginning, the ensemble stands watching, far less active than is customary in Balanchine works. The illusion of drifting is fostered by bourrées, one of the most prominent steps in "Emeralds." When the ten women make two parallel diagonal lines interlace and separate again, one of the principal couples travels along this shifting path; the woman glides with tiny fluid toesteps, drawing her partner along, dipping under his arm, twining around him. Out of music and dancing, Balanchine not only conjured up romance, but a glade for it to happen in.

Balancées hint at the waltzes of a distant ballroom. Occasionally a wide-legged stance or a stamp, surprising in its heartiness, suggest Renaissance dances. In one pas de deux, the woman's arms, later both dancers' legs, lift in a series of quick sharp moves, the way people imagine wings, and the flutter in the music for one woman's solo engenders a tranquilly playful bower of gestures that she, standing still, traces on the air around her. The pas de deux with the "wings" is like a dreamily amorous stroll, the woman walking on pointe, holding her partner's arm, his hand, their path circuitous.

In the seventies Balanchine added a new ending. After the gradual accumulation of dancers and the subtle reprises that seem to be bringing the ballet to a climax, the dance begins to thin out into slow, careful garlands, gleaming gemlike clusters—as if the dream were fading. The three men walk slowly toward one corner, and as they do so, the women disengage themselves gradually, not so much exiting as receding behind the men. Left alone, the men back up and kneel, still watching that empty corner.

The performances I saw were lovely: Maria Calegari in the strolling duet and the susceptible solo Balanchine designed for Violette Verdy, in which the smooth waltzing fragments into quick little sparks of steps; Daniel Duell, smooth and glowing, not a rough edge anywhere; Stephanie Saland, making her dancing seem like a voluptuous sleepwalking in the byways of the music; David Otto a fine, ardent partner for her; Carlo Merlo leading his ladies (Alexia Hess and Shawn Stevens) along, or shadowing one of them with wonderfully alive courtesy, as if he were indeed fortunate to have two such women to dance with.

It's a good thing there's an intermission to wake people from the glowing dream of "Emeralds," before "Rubies" sputters and flashes onto the stage. Stravinsky's *Capriccio for Piano and Orchestra* drew from Balanchine a contentious assembly of his best-known "Stravinsky" steps: the pinup girl poses, the jutting hips, the legs that swing down and up like scythes, the paw-hands, the prances, the big, quick lunges, the flexed feet, the heel-walks. There's more than a trace of show biz in the way the eight women in short red skirts copy the coolly opulent soloist (always played by a tall dancer, in this case Victoria Hall), or in the way four men crowd in (neatly designed, but the effect is still of crowding) to examine, touch, move this beauty's amazing limbs, or the way the ensemble exits in a prowl.

The passages for the two principal dancers seem to be about difficulty, about people who rambunctiously enjoy not getting on to such a degree that they *do* get on very well. One steps forward, hips swinging front; the other steps back; then they reverse. And much of their dancing expresses this contrariety. He'll reach out and grab her hand as she passes, and the two will pull against each other, as if gauging how riskily they can counterbalance. Their relationship is like a brilliant dance exposé of those relationships Balanchine knew well from his days as a musical comedy choreographer: the two people we know are in love who spend most of the book ranting at and about each other. This man has pals too: suddenly, briefly, he leads them in a mischievous chase around the stage; but it's the woman he's interested in. At one point, he stands behind her and they create elaborate tangles with their arms in the air. There's a similar moment in *Symphony in Three Movements,* but in that ballet, the two dancers do seem incompatible, almost uncomprehendingly so; in "Rubies," their tangles are an amorous tease.

The leading female role in "Rubies" was made for Patricia McBride, and she continues to perform it with roguish impetuosity. Ib Andersen seems as yet only intermittently into his role. Eyeing McBride tauntingly, head down, slashing into the dancing, he's going for the virility, the edge of coarseness the role has, but the characterization doesn't fit him easily yet and tends to erode in midphrase.

"Diamonds" is the Tchaikovsky-Petipa spectacle redefined. The edgy, heated asymmetries of "Rubies" give way to brilliant, grand ensemble work that implies symmetry even when it is temporarily out of balance. The women in white with their waltz steps and sweeping developpés remind me very slightly of the dancing snowflakes in *Nutcracker;* their patterns seem to hang in the air when dissolved.

The duet begins after a long pause, a long look at the empty stage. It always reminds me of something—some old Russian story ballet taken out of its mounting and recut. This time, watching Merrill Ashley reach yearningly out to the corners of the stage and Peter Martins gently pulling her back, wrapping his arms around her, domesticating her, I thought this is what it would be like afterward, if *Swan Lake* had a happy ending. She'd be sometimes remembering what it had been like to be a wild swan, and he'd have to remind her that she was a queen now and he loved her. There's a hint of that strangeness in their very formal, fond relationship.

When he kneels, she leans deeply over him in an arabesque and looks into his face, bringing to mind that farewell in *Swan Lake,* Act II. And even though he has a fine solo, and he bursts into a little dancing of his own behind her, his focus, like ours, is on her.

Ashley is not as reckless as Suzanne Farrell, for whom the part was created. She is beautifully fluid and accurate both in the execution of steps and the tone of the emotion, but I find her still just a trifle unyielding in her head and upper body, especially when the dancing speeds up. Martins looks so at ease, so naturally elegant, so fully present in everything he does that it's no wonder the crowd mourns in advance his imminent retirement and rains applause down on him.

Robin Wagner's new set attempts, mistakenly I think, to join the three ballets. A large hanging tiara ("Emeralds") is replaced by a brooch ("Rubies"), and in "Diamonds," both reappear, surmounting a necklace.

APOLLO RADIANT

The Village Voice, May 21, 1979

A ccording to myth, the god Apollo was impulsive and turbulent as a youth. It was only after spending a year at hard labor in the sheepfolds of King Admetus, as punishment for a breach of Olympian protocol, that, according to Robert Graves's paraphrase of Homer, he "preached moderation in all things: the phrases 'Know thyself!' and 'Nothing in excess!' were always on his lips. He brought the Muses down from their home on Mount Helicon to Delphi, tamed their wild frenzy, and led them in formal and decorous dances."

The three muses in George Balanchine's *Apollo* are hardly wild, but they are untamed—green girls. Terpsichore is innocent; Calliope (music of poetic measure) and Polyhymnia (muse of mime) are slightly gauche or overly enthusiastic in their solos to compete for Apollo's favor. And the dances Apollo leads indeed teach formality and decorum, as when he yokes them together, or reaches his arm around all three of them, or courteously allows each a moment of eminence.

The productions of *Apollo* that Balanchine has remounted from time to time measure Balanchine's own "taming," as if each time he has considered the ballet, something else has struck him as excessive or false and in need of pruning. The Greek costumes and set, important to the first Diaghilev production in 1928, have gradually disappeared. Now he has excised the prologue and the stairway that had come to stand for Mount Olympus. If you see the revised *Apollo* at the New York City Ballet, you won't see Leto on a high platform heaving softly in childbirth; you won't see Apollo unwrapped from his swaddling clothes by two handmaidens; he won't open his mouth in a silent, baffled howl, take his first tremulous steps, or receive the mystifying gift of a lute from the handmaidens. Nor, of course, will you hear all of Stravinsky's *Apollon Musagète*. The prologue, which to the color-struck audience of Diaghilev's day must have seemed chaste indeed in terms of drama, now evidently jars Balanchine by its literalness. After fifty years of affirming the power and resilience of classicism to us through his works, he may well feel that we no longer need to see it born to understand it.

Now the curtain rises on Apollo standing confidently, strumming his lyre with great wheeling gestures of one arm. And, since there is no staircase to ascend, the famous moment when the three Muses cling together behind Apollo and open their legs to a sunburst of arabesques has been transposed to the very end of the ballet. Our last image isn't that of an ascending journey, but of Apollo radiant.

Mikhail Baryshnikov now shares the hero's role with Peter Martins, the reigning Apollo of this decade, and his astonishing performance set into this truncated version gives us a wholly new slant on *Apollo*. He begins with grave courtesy, rather subdued. When he supports a Muse with each hand, he looks at neither of them; it's as if he were quietly weighing them and testing his own ability to support them with the most tranquil and succinct use of his muscles. When the three young women parade across the back of the stage, and he whacks each one of them like the fillies they are, the action startles us; it erupts without warning and with immense relish.

What Baryshnikov presents us with is not so much the young reckless Apollo becoming mature—and without the birth scene, why would we suppose this anyhow?—but Dionysius becoming Apollo. He seems in the process to be molding and channeling his own wild pleasure in dancing as much as he is harnessing the Muses. In his solo, when he brushes one leg across himself to the side and swings both arms in the opposite direction, he emphasizes neither the jazzy asymmetry nor the archaic two-dimensionality of the step, but shows with fierce zest how one part of the body is pulling against another. With the Muses, he is tender shepherd and straining horse tamer and companion; he gives us the sense that he is learning his own nature through the course of the dance.

The company has to provide small Muses for Baryshnikov. Heather Watts makes a sharply young Terpsichore; she's assured, but there's a lovely kind of delicacy about the way she dances her solo and her duet with Apollo. Elyse Borne as Polyhymnia and Bonita Borne as Calliope are less satisfactory; they're pert and sweet and accomplished, but not fully *there* in their dancing.

Watching the rest of a particularly fine program—Peter Martins's *Calcium Light Night,* Balanchine's *Duo Concertant* and *Tchaikovsky Piano Concerto No. 2,* I thought that literal gesture has indeed no place in the Balanchine canon any longer. The two soloists in *Calcium Light Night* show us the contentiousness of their eventual relationship principally by the way they continue their own steps while occupying the same space, by the way their actions never quite end in the comfortable or expected way. Even the curious, romantically tender gestures that end *Duo Concertant* do not make you search for a story. And a glisteningly formal choral ballet like the Tchaikovsky shows how Balanchine's "meaning" isn't necessarily revealed by the particular actions of an individual, but can emerge through a large group gesture. I'm remembering the way the ballerina rapidly circles a ring of dancers standing in trios, and how each trio bends as she passes, so you see that her dancing acquires the force of a wind. Or there's the passage in which the man is flanked by women holding hands—six, I think, on each side—and he slowly lashes first one group and then the other back around him, as if he were opening and shutting great gates.

It was an evening of splendid dancing too—Kay Mazzo (looking wonderfully alert and vivid) and Peter Martins in *Duo Concertant,* Merrill Ashley, Sean Lavery, and Kyra Nichols in the Tchaikovsky, Daniel Duell and Heather Watts more interestingly modulated now in Martins's ballet, and, of course, Baryshnikov. *Apollo* redux. I have to accede to Balanchine's desire to keep rebuilding this crucial signature piece. But I deeply miss the older version; I liked being in touch with the 1928 Balanchine.

ZEN AND THE ART OF

DANCE

The Village Voice, January 17, 1977

▼▼

The dance was concerned with fear. . . ." That's what Merce Cunningham once wrote about his 1944 solo, *Root of an Unfocus.* In 1968, queried by Calvin Tompkins for a *New Yorker* profile, Cunningham said of the same dance, "The audience thought it had something to do with fear. It had nothing directly to do with fear . . ." and then went on to emphasize the importance of the time structure he had devised for the dance. I furrow my brow. My husband says reproachfully and with surprise, "Why should you think Merce under any obligation to be consistent?"

Why indeed? On the deepest level everything that Merce Cunningham has made or said or done connects with everything else; but there are paradoxes, ironies, graceful accommodations. For the past few years, Cunningham, unable to find a suitable and affordable theater in Manhattan, has been presenting here, mostly in his Westbeth studio, what he calls Events—intermissionless landscapes of dancing drawn from pieces in his repertory. Economical, challenging to the dancers, irritating, no doubt, to the hordes who couldn't even get on the waiting list to see his weekend performances. But between January 18 and 23, at the Minskoff Theatre, New Yorkers are finally going to be able to see new dances and recent ones that have already delighted, stimulated, and possibly puzzled people all over the United States, Europe, Asia, and South America. Cunningham—who has choreogaphed since 1942, maintained a company since 1953, and changed the way a generation or more of dancers and spectators thinks about dancing—is finally having a Broadway season. He is interested. But unimpressed.

In his late fifties now, Cunningham is still exploring, still taking risks at a point when many choreographers begin to patent and elaborate on what they discovered years before. His dances remain controversial. A critic present at last season's events at the Roundabout Theatre, unable to understand the enthusiastic response, wrote the entire large audience off as a clique of fans. "An acquired taste," said a member of the London press sourly. On the other hand, Merce says that this summer in Europe he found audiences not as puzzled by his work as they used to be, but interested: "I don't mean they *like* it, but they stay with it." Consider, too, the many young French dancers who dropped everything and came to New York to study with Cunningham after seeing the dance he made in 1973 for the Paris Opera Ballet. Said one of them, "After seeing his work, I had no choice."

"Things in life are changing," says Merce. "If people are going to stay alive"—pause for one of the laughs that studs his conversation—"they're going to have to deal with complexity. It's my idea not to shield people from it, but to introduce them to it." This may be what many people still find unsettling about Cunningham's dances, while the rest of us find it brave and thrilling: He discovers interest and even beauty in what we feel threatened by. Although a Cunningham dance is usually dense with activity, he refuses to guide our eyes through it to any reassuring Big Event. For him, a proscenium arch isn't a frame within which events are hierarchically arranged; it's just a convenient boundary to define what we can see of an open field—it holds the dancing the way a microscope slide holds a lively drop of pond water. To add to the complexity, his dances have their own rhythmic structures, independent of the music that is played along with them. The music itself, supplied by some of the most radical contemporary composers—people like Cunningham's longtime friend and collaborator John Cage, Christian Wolff, Morton Feldman, Gordon Mumma, Earle Brown, La Monte Young, to name a few—can have a disquieting, even assaultive effect. The decor, supplied by artists like Robert Rauschenberg, Jasper Johns, Bruce Nauman, and Andy Warhol, also competes with the dancing for the audience's attention or creates obstacle courses for the performers or partially blocks the audience's view of the proceedings. In a harsh Cunningham dance like *Winterbranch,* the lights may not illumine the dancing; they may even glare at the audience. (Cunningham asked Robert Rauschenberg, who created the original *Winterbranch* lighting, for night light—not romantic glow, but light like high-beam headlights striking a rainy highway.)

And, of course, Cunningham presents the fact of dancing unencumbered by story or idea. He doesn't deny the possibility of "meanings" in his dances, but allows people in the audience the right to receive these in their own way. (He was reputedly pleased when a sea captain's wife told him *Winterbranch* made her think of shipwrecks.) It comes to this: We have to make choices. To some, this impartiality, this generosity, is shocking. There are always people who'd rather look *for* something in art, rather than *at* something.

When I go to Westbeth to watch the Cunningham dancers rehearse for their video program (which was aired last week on the Dance in America series), Merce is clearly both busy and a little tired, yet in a few minutes—tagged onto a hello—he manages to plant more ideas in my brain than most people ever do. When something interests Cunningham, he studies it (Russian, knitting, you know . . .): "Several years ago, I had a feeling that, good or bad, there was going to be more dancing on television, and that I had better find out about it." He's found out a lot. That, for instance, time on television can seem longer than stage time, longer than clock time (he cites as an example how interminable a fraction of a minute can seem when, on a news show, there's a delay returning from exterior footage to the announcer in the studio). That side-to-side motion doesn't always register, because it crosses the small screen so quickly. That, because the camera's eye has no muscle, the intensity of a movement tends to dissipate before it reaches the viewer so that what's gentle becomes bland. This last point, he thinks, may be part of the reason for all the violence on TV: It registers. I like picturing Merce studying "Mission Impossible" for clues to the medium's pecularities.

As Cunningham walks into the studio, struggling into the remarkable four-sleeved sweater Rauschenberg designed for the "Bacchus and Cohorts" section of *Antic Meet* (1958), he says with a wry smile, "It's like going back through history." Like many contemporary choreographers, he's dubious about the value (or fun) of maintaining a large repertory or reviving old dances. Perhaps it's not just that the art is essentially impermanent, but that it keeps requiring the participation of the choreographer. What finished canvas requires a reinvestment of the painter's time and energy before it can be shown? Dancing your 1950s self or transferring to other bodies your 1950s thinking is another matter. For the rest of us . . . well, it's wonderful to be able to see on the videotape the range and variety of Cunningham's work over a period of years—from a beautiful quartet in the 1953 *Septet* (Robert Kovich kneeling, lunging, leaning his body lavishly to one side and another, while three women slowly lean on him and gesture elegantly away from him with long, stringent limbs), to a condensation of Merce's extraordinary 1973 animal solo (primal images of old lion licking himself in the sun, of weaving snake, of wary bird of prey) and a section of the recent *Sounddance,* alive with swinging jumping people.

Perhaps because Merce Cunningham and his video cohort, Charles Atlas, have designed the videoscheme and shot practice runs on one half-inch tape, and because "Dance in America" director, Merrill Brockway, wisely honors most of their choices, Cunningham is able to create a sense of flexible space just as he does in his stage dances, by keeping firmly in mind, and in the viewers' minds, the limited space defined by the small rectangular screen. (In this case, the eye is not free to roam.) Dancers fall out of the dance at the bottom of the frame; others enter the same way. Their shadows affirm the floor. The history-erasing peculiarities of the cut are used as such. On most TV dance programs, the dancers drift around in a vacuum as the camera tries hard to make you believe that last part *caused* this new part.

When I come back to talk to Merce a few weeks later, the videotaping is behind him and the Broadway season ahead. He sits serenely on a bench in the company's dressing room, looking like a wise and agile coach, in a clean pair of blue sweatpants and a red zippered sweat jacket with white trim. It occurs to me that the Zen Buddhism he has studied and the yoga he practices have had effects other than the obvious ones of making him seem calmer, saner, and happier than a lot of choreographers. ("That's the way to do it," he instantly amends to "that's the way *we* do it.") For instance, when I talk to him about presenting Events versus presenting repertory, he says that he not only finds Events very practical, since they can be performed almost anywhere—from American college gymnasiums to European plazas—but "liberating from possession." It's a curious phrase for a choreographer, by necessity a dictator of sorts, by tradition self-centered. Events provide an opportunity for Merce to acknowledge—not just to the audience, but to himself and the other dancers—that movement can function differently in different contexts, just as gestures in life acquire meaning from the circumstances in which they occur.

When Merce talks to me like this, quietly and thoughfully, huge avenues for speculation open up. It's been his concern to bring dance more in touch with the riskiness and unevenness that are now part, not only of our daily lives, but of our scientific and philosophic world-picture. Yet, although he has employed chance procedures to get beyond his own habitual patterns, tampered with our expectations of causality, strewn dancers around a field in which their collisions can present an illusion of randomness, his works are always meticulously structured. (Here's *Torse:* sixty-four phrases of movement ranging from one to sixty-four counts in length, the rhythm not metered and each new count activated by a weight change.) Nor has he ever dispensed with "dancing"; it has occurred to him to use everyday movement—the equivalent of John Cage's affirmation of noise as a possible musical component—but it has not interested him very much. You have only to watch Cunningham himself dance—completely possessed by the intensity of the moment—to understand how important and powerful the act of dancing is for him. Certainly he does all he can to avoid presenting it heroically or self-importantly, but his style is superbly civilized and elegant. No imagined blows in the solar plexus fling Cunningham dancers around. Intensely alert to time and space, they are as self-possessed about their weight as animals. Douglas Dunn, who danced with the company for several years, says admiringly, "Merce is dedicated to the image of a decision." Whether the dancers fling a leg into space or raise it slowly, you feel that they are at all times in a position to reverse that plan.

Yet I am moved to see that Cunningham, having created extraordinary dancing, then goes as far as he can to make it risky, to keep himself and the dancers from ever fixing it down, from feeling complacent. As Carolyn Brown, who danced with Cunningham for twenty years, explained in a wonderful essay in the book *Merce Cunningham* (edited by James Klosty), the dancers are the only ones who don't fully share the creative anarchy enjoyed by Cunningham's other collaborators. Occasionally— less commonly now than during the early sixties—the dancers have options they can exercise in performance. But for the most part, comforted with discipline—although never told "how" to perform—they go out and do their stuff, confronted, perhaps for the first time at dress rehearsal, with scenery that blocks their way, sounds that may shock them, lights that may blind them.

Merce worries about this. "Carolyn was absolutely right about the lighting." He knows now that a sudden light change can cause a temporary loss of equilibrium, and he doesn't want to hurt anybody in the cause of new challenges—just "push the possibilities." He keeps doing this, even though he says he risks—in the conventional theatrical sense—a "poor" performance. Awkwardness, in any case, doesn't bother him; absence of vitality does.

"Performing—to me—means that each time you come to something, you have a chance of making that situation come alive in whatever way that will be—even if you thought the last performance was maybe very good, and you should repeat it. Since that's not possible anyway, we try to go the other way as much as we can. In life, if you decide on something, the next minute it has changed. If you count on anything, it doesn't work. So you have to put yourself, it seems to me, in a situation in which you don't count on anything, and then deal with whatever arises."

Merce's hesitance to impose fixed ideas on his students and company members leaves many floundering. (Dancers, hearing I've talked to Merce, ask greedily, "What did he say? He doesn't tell us *anything*.") I ask him about performing, because clearly his dances raid him with significance, fresh for each moment of each performance. He nods firm agreement when I say that surely being open doesn't mean being neutral. "No, but instead of having a particular attitude, you have to have all attitudes." He understands what he's risking by forcing dancers to find their own way into dancing: "It doesn't work every time; I'm under no illusions about that." Then he says with great vigor, "It's dancing that prompts people to dance. Any other reason is silly. But I don't think most people see beyond correctness. If I'm teaching an elementary class, I can say, 'You have it now; you know where your arms and legs are supposed to be in each movement. But that's still an exercise, and it's not the exercise you're interested in. You're interested in the *dancing.* You must be correct, but you must fill it out, make it alive, go beyond where you are. There's a chasm you must jump and you can't intellectualize.' Sometimes I can get students to the point of seeing that chasm . . ." And, laughing again, he quotes John Cage: "Now you have to go a few steps further and make a few mistakes." And he says approvingly of dancers with fine sense of time and rhythm, "Like a cat, they'll always land on their feet."

Whatever private struggles Merce may go through, his dances acknowledge change without regret. Dancers leave companies more frequently than they used to: Merce makes *Changing Steps,* a series of choreographic modules—which all the dancers learn all of—thus acknowledging replaceability as a structural principle. Carolyn Brown, the beautiful, the irreplaceable, leaves the company after twenty years: Merce make no extended duets for himself and a woman. As the age gap inevitably widens between Merce and the other dancers (oddly, he seems not to be growing older; they're just getting younger), he makes a dance like *Rebus,* which seems in some nonspecific way to present him as an older and wiser man who both guards and is guarded by the vibrant young dancers.

If there were any reasonableness to things, a Cunningham dance would command a steep price, like the works of the visual artists who share his concerns and acknowledge his greatness. Merce, however, has opted for impermanence and, I've no doubt, accepts the drawbacks. On one of the brilliant topsy-turvy pages in his book of notes, *Changes,* there is an unevenly typewritten paragraph I take to be his. It says, "you have to love dancing to stick to it. It gives you nothing back, no manuscripts to store away, no painting to show on walls and maybe hang in museums, no poems to be printed and sold, nothing but that fleeting moment when you feel alive. It is not for unsteady souls."

My offhand list of musicians that Cunningham has collaborated with strikes me as peculiar, in that names of two who have been very closely associated with him—David Tudor and David Behrmann—do not appear.

CONFRONTING THE XEROX
WITH HUMAN GRACE

The Village Voice, October 9, 1978

꘏

In a voice glowing with respect, the WNET announcer gave us his "coming on next" blurb for "Merce by Merce by Paik" and then suggested that, if we wanted to derive maximum enjoyment from Merce Cunningham's dancing in videotapes by Charles Atlas and Nam June Paik, we might do well to turn the sound down. The solicitousness is typical of Channel 13: if we have a bad "art experience," we might be discouraged from ever trying "art" again. Since Dick Cavett and Ed Emshwiller had just succeeded in presenting Emshwiller to us as an engaging trickster, a video sleight-of-hand man, we might not be disconcerted by the sight of Merce Cunningham walking in place while a street, shot from a moving car, sped past him—making him the moving-fixed point in a traveling landscape (any dancer who has toured a lot knows what this feels like). But we might not know what to make of the noisy soundtrack, which began with a crackly long-distance telephone conversation between Cunningham and Jasper Johns. To further shield the fainthearted, the station programmed the tapes at midnight and helpfully identified in white type all the important names and voices that appeared.

Which is more productive—to be outraged by WNET's mild censorship, or delighted that Cunningham still frets so many people? Any artist wants to be admired and understood, but surely if everyone loved Cunningham, he ought to worry that he was indeed standing still in a changing landscape. If up at City Center, the frail, sparse climate of *Summerspace* can still after twenty years produce a few restless coughs in an audience, and if a few expensively dressed people have to slip apologetically into their waiting limousines after three out of four dances, I for one feel cheered.

For years, in articles, interviews, and on his "Dance in America" videotape, Cunningham has been encouraging us to take an anarchic view of his dances—to see what we want to see, to look where we want to look. But this can be carried too far; at some point, I begin to feel selfish—self-indulgent at any rate—and want to perceive at least some aspect of the structure or relationships inherent in a work that makes it unlike any other work.

It seems important to me to notice that each of the six dancers in *Sum-*

---

merspace pursues paths that are, for the most part, solitary, with occasional intersections; that the stage is a place they are passing through; that each seems very individual. When *Summerspace* was made, the Merce Cunningham Dance Company was a small group of contemporaries. Now that there are fourteen next-generation dancers in addition to Cunningham himself, works like *Torse* (1976) are bound to emerge— works in which squadrons of quick, leggy dancers move in exacting unison and contrapuntal patterns (characterized in *Torse* by bending, tilting, twisting motions in the dancers' torsos).

Sometimes I need to see a Cunningham dance many times before I unlock some part of its intricate gearwork. Why have I never remarked the skewed archings and twists of Cunningham's back and head in his opening solo in *Sounddance* (1974)? Especially when his phrase, with the awkward back-reaching arms and tapping feet, is frequently picked up in the background by others of the dancers who enter one by one through an opening in Mark Lancaster's low-hung white drape. Suddenly I notice that the space in *Sounddance,* unlike that in most other Cunningham dances, is an arena; once having entered, the dancers stay on until they exit, again one by one, at the end. I notice, too, that much of the exhilarated, almost acrobatic work the dancers do in pairs, trios, quartets involves people being swung around a fixed point, the way a gymnast somersaults over a trapeze. Sometimes the stage seems full of spinning human turnstiles that others can vault over or duck under. If you watch Cunningham himself, you can begin to think of the dance as a parable about his expanding company. Every few seconds another dancer appears, and Cunningham moves among this array of dancing people as if they represented a phenomenon beyond his ability to control, but not beyond his interest to try to cope with. I like to watch him giving a hand to each of a line of jumping men (there are only four of them, but he makes you think there might as well be twenty, and he'll just do this until he's gotten them all on the other side of him). He keeps dancing in the background occasionally scurrying in to join this group or that one, to lift this woman or rearrange that group. There are few pauses in this violent giant of a dance—the light is white hot and the sound shattering. Even though the City Center's speaker system and house acoustics can't give David Tudor's *Toneburst* the rocketing motion it needs, the music is still extraordinary. When, about halfway through the dance, a quick insistent beating drops out of the sound texture, leaving only a cross-fading of differently pitched buzzes and hums, you feel for a few terrifying moments that it's your own heart that has stopped beating.

The Charles Atlas videotape I saw on Channel 13 ended with five differently dressed Merces recapitulating their themes simultaneously.

Looking at *Sounddance* and then at the new *Exchange,* it's easy to imagine that Merce Cunningham is trying to help us to come to terms with cloning—or, let's say, acknowledging the fascination and horror, the inescapable facts, of duplication and undetectable imitation. To another electronic score by Tudor (one that begins with a high twittering on one side and heavy bumpings that seem to be coming from under the stage), Cunningham begins the dance with all the newest members of his company: Meg Eginton, Susan Emery, Lise Friedman, Alan Good, Joseph Lennon, Robert Remley, and Catherine Kerr (who has just returned to the company after a season or so away). At a first viewing, I notice principally the ways in which groups of four or two form, separate, recombine in other ways. The four men work as a group, then the four women. (When the young men bound off into jumps, Cunningham prudently takes his sore feet into a scuffing walk along the back of the stage, and this later becomes a theme for other dancers to reiterate. Four men and four women can be kaleidoscoped ingeniously into two groups of two couples. The men carry the women with serene, almost remote tenderness—the women arching back in blind trust, while the men move with them slowly and carefully, as if trying not to disturb the shapes they have assumed.

Two couples leave; two stay. Then suddenly we're confronted with a new bunch of dancers—the Cunningham veterans Karole Armitage, Louise Burns, Ellen Cornfield, Lisa Fox, Chris Komar, Robert Kovich, and Jim Self. They do not duplicate exactly what the first group did (for one thing, there's an odd number of people now), but they repeat many of the same movements differently. In the first part, for example, Cunningham gets down on the floor, and each of the four women passes him in some way—crawling under, somersaulting over, sidling around. In the second part, Ellen Cornfield does all these things to Chris Komar by herself. Jasper Johns further articulates the not-quite-duplication by dressing the dancers in leotards individually colored in sections of black, grays, and near whites.

Inlets (made in 1977, but only now presented in New York) is a quieter, more private dance with only six people in it. John Cage's score, Morris Graves's set design, Charles Atlas's lighting, Cunningham's choreography all present in some way—all with extreme beauty—an interplay between flux and stasis, between luminous clarity and misty blur. In Cage's sparse score, you can hear water noises and small pungent snappings and cracklings. The dancers work behind a scrim that fogs their outlines. Graves's huge Mylar disk moves imperceptibly across the stage from right to left, marking off the dancing time. Sometimes the disk's surface reflects the dancing in bright, rippled fragments, the way moving water reflects things; sometimes it is a dark bronze glow in the background. Once, for a moment in the middle of the dance, it goes dark, and the dancing, too, undergoes a partial eclipse.

The dancing seems subject to tides. Your eye stalls on dancers marooned in poses, alone or together; the next time you see them, they may be moving again. Do I only imagine them rocking and swaying in response to a current?

I was glad to see Catherine Kerr again—looking meditative and vulnerable in the lovely duet that Cunningham placed after all the cheerful scrimmaging and tossing around in *Squaregame* (1976). In this duet, Cunningham steadies his partner lightly, as if her long slow legs were some kind of liability that renders her unsuited for simple locomotion. I was also glad to see Lisa Fox begin to come alive in Cunningham's choreography; slim and tall, with the imposing chest and upper back and small-featured face of an Edwardian beauty, she looks confident and almost aggressive in her dancing. The greatest surprise was Louise Burns's performing, especially in *Summerspace*. Burns is short, sturdy, cheerful, with the extravagantly strong arching back that you usually see on a larger woman, like Martine van Hamel. Her dancing has none of the silky remoteness that many of Cunningham's current women excel at, but she has the courage to make assertions on the movement—or rather, perhaps, to comprehend and seize on what it feeds her. She's unpredictable, not always in complete control, not always serene—neither is Cunningham—but she has the alertness of time and space that used to be the hallmark of Cunningham dancers. I sometimes wonder if some of Cunningham's beautiful dancers haven't taken too seriously a statement he made many years ago about a dancer being like a "nature puppet" whose discipline and calmness allow whatever primal forces that exist to speak through him or her. Given Cunningham's unwillingness to direct his dancers, I sympathize with them and appreciate their reticence and good taste; at the same time, their timidity infuriates me when it causes them to appear as if the dance were being done *to* them instead of *by* them.

I'M ONLY HERE TO FIX THE FRIEZE

The Village Voice, August 6, 1979

~~~

When the curtain goes up on Merce Cunningham's new dance, *Roadrunners,* we see Chris Komar posed in a lunge—body bending toward the floor, one arm stuck up in the air. Cunningham himself exits after a burst of tight, fidgety dancing. Lise Friedman, the only other person on stage, dances over to Komar and pulls his bent leg. When he doesn't move, she grabs his hand, flips her leg insouciantly over him, and leaves. Two others enter—Catherine Kerr and I forget which man; they haul Komar in opposite directions, but although he flaps a bit, he's still unbudgeable, and they work their hands alternately up his arm the way you draw lots by eeny-meenying up the old ax handle. Eventually, in his own time, Komar joins the dancing.

The audience is surprised to find itself laughing. Surprised perhaps, because Merce Cunningham is a big holy name in dance, and here in Durham at the American Dance Festival many in the audience aren't familiar enough with his work to expect irreverence. Too, the program had begun with *Torse,* a dry-ice dance, a dance celebrating intelligent prowess with squadrons of people (all fourteen company members) executing busy-legged drills of great purity and complexity.

Roadrunners, commissioned by the festival, is probably one of the most accessible pieces Cunningham has ever made. It's full of good temper and good jokes. Along with the electronically bollixed piano and viola of Yasunao Tone's score *Geography and Music,* we hear the composer's voice reciting, in Japanese-accented English, tales that appear to have come from an ancient and fanciful Chinese geography. The voice bounces from one speaker to the other at almost every word: a tennis match for ears. The stories, if you choose to listen to them, are bizarre: The subjects of a certain king tell the enemy king who comes in vengeance that they have no king, only this bronze statue of a king "for educational purposes. We are all bastards."(?) The enemy cuts off the statue's arms and legs, and at the same time, the real king, who has been hiding in a cave, loses his arms and legs.

You can try to listen to this or not, as you choose. Sometimes it intersects fortuitously with the dancing. The constantly changing array of dancers—in white against a black background—often resembles a parade

---

of statuary. They assume two-dimensional poses, innocently antique, with feet pointing one way and body flattened in a twist, perhaps with one arm curved up and the other curved down. Joseph Lennon advances stiffly, wrists and elbows curling. Sometimes the women dash on with something stuffed under one leotard strap; in Lisa Fox's case, the something is a large white beret; in Meg Eginton's, it's a smart black one, and four men toss her up and down in a sitting position while she wears it. Once, it's just pieces of cloth and two women dust two men off the stage with them.

Robert Kovich sticks one leg out in the air and leans sideways until he's horizontal; in front of him a bevy of women kneels, each of them lifting one arm overhead, so that you can almost believe they're hoisting his prone body. The next minute, some of the women leave in haste one by one and spring onto Alan Good until he's balancing a trio of them. While Lisa Fox kites around, Cunningham attempts to dress himself in a pair of white pants and some sneakers. Here she comes, and he hastily stumbles out of her way, one leg in the trousers. These nymphs obviously don't know what weapons their powerful high-swinging legs can be. Here she comes again, and he grabs his remaining sneaker and finds a less busy spot. Finally dressed, a sweater knotted around his neck, he confronts her—briefly and ever so subtly—with one of Nijinsky's faun poses; an elderly satyr dressed for tennis. But whether the images sprout from Thurber or this century's roster of "Greek" dances, the elegant ease and busyness of Cunningham dancing laces through all the sly jokes and angularities, so that they come at top speed, never demanding your appreciation or laughter, simply there to be savored.

These performances at the festival showed that some of the company's newest dancers have begun to penetrate the mysteries of performing Cunningham (mysteries because he will not tell dancers *how* to perform, only what to perform). Susan Emery, Meg Eginton, Lise Friedman in particular look as if some shutters in their comprehension have opened and are letting inner light shine out. In *Rainforest* Eginton danced the role made on Barbara Lloyd (Dilley) with a lovely combination of wary delicacy and strength. As for Robert Kovich, he has attained the kind of transparency Cunningham mentioned in an essay written years ago: he imposes no attitudes, no mannerisns on the dancing, yet whatever images of human behavior or feeling reside in it emerge freely through his performing. Kovich and Chris Komar, Louise Burns and Ellen Cornfield, provide some of the most expertly joyful dancing in *Changing Steps Et Cetera.* In its festival garb, this dance offers, for quite a while, two time zones: the small bustling games of *Changing Steps* in the foreground, performed by dancers in bright jumpsuits, while behind them four dancers in black execute the formal, smooth unfurling leg gestures of *Exercise*

Piece I. This time the interchangeable modules that make up *Changing Steps* have been meted out in such a way that at one point seven couples perform what has always struck me as an intimate duet (in unison) in a circle around Cunningham, who is sitting immobile on a chair at the bemused center of his creation. Pillaging words from my peers at the Critics' Conference, I find the following pleased and abashed descriptions of Cunningham as performer in his dances: "master mechanic," "visitor from Mars," "prisoner," "henpecked." By the end of *Changing Steps,* he isn't in the center; he's barely visible behind a swarm of his extraordinary dancers (Karole Armitage, Robert Remley, Jim Self are the ones I haven't mentioned yet), flipping his wrists around, making mysteriously workaday looping gestures back there. And it's not entirely clear if he's pulling the dance's switches or caught by its unstoppable momentum.

> *Shortly after this article appeared, I found out that everything I said was being done by and to Chris Komar at the beginning of* Roadrunners *was actually done by and to Rob Remley. The next time I saw the work, I noticed that the "pieces of cloth" the women use to swat the men off the stage are their berets. At most subsequent performances, it has been John Cage who reads the text.*

TWELVE FROZEN MINUTES
OF I WANT TO, BUT I CAN'T

The Village Voice, June 13, 1977

꙳

Up at the Lunt-Fontanne Theatre, where Martha Graham's company is performing, things seem to be going subtly haywire. The biggest picture on the front of the theater and in the ads doesn't show Graham dancing; it shows her posing with Nureyev and Fonteyn—all of them wrapped to the gills in mink (last year's Blackglama ad). Some of the dancers appear to have passed beyond the point of self-confidence and begun to play with the choreography—perhaps with Graham's encouragement. Phyllis Gutelius has ideas of her own about some of the rhythms in *El Penitente*; in the same dance, Mario Delamo carries the cross with his right hip stuck out in a decorative curve, and he too has ideas about the rhythm and emphasis of footwork in the final folk dance. The two "other" sisters (Brontë or not) in *Deaths and Entrances*, of whom Margaret Lloyd once wrote, "One is protective, the other peevish," have now been enlarged by Janet Eilber and Diane Gray to the point where they resemble nothing so much as the wicked stepsisters in *Cinderella*. At the end, when the important sister triumphantly places that mysteriously symbolic goblet on the chessboard, the other two lean so far back in horror and surprise that the effect is almost ludicrous. William Carter does double pirouettes in *Deaths and Entrances* (I'll bet at Graham's request). Rudolf Nureyev, touchingly sober and restrained, still can't draw a straight line through the role of the Revivalist in *Appalachian Spring;* in parts he looks like a good little boy, in parts a wooden doll, in parts a madman. The audience seems to love his being there and adores Peggy Lyman, perhaps for the same reasons. Lyman *is* beautiful (she has a face like Graham's—capital-letter features to everyone else's lower-case), and quite balletic. I very much like her breadth and graciousness as the Pioneering Woman in *Appalachian Spring,* but in *Frontier* she tends to look soft and self-preoccupied instead of vigorous.

I don't understand the exaggerations and the changes (like cutting the exit walk in *Primitive Mysteries,* or putting Phyllis Gutelius in an ugly new black dress for *Deaths and Entrances*). But the reason they upset me is that they all, in different ways, have the effect of making Graham's masterpieces less stark or prettier or foggier in intent or more virtuosic or more conventional. Almost everyone grimaces a lot. Sometimes the effect is so overwrought that you might think someone with poor eyesight was directing the dancers.

Between 1943 and 1948, Graham made some remarkable dances about interior warfare—*Deaths and Entrances, Herodiade, Dark Meadow, Cave of the Heart, Errand into the Maze,* and *Night Journey.* (During this period, she also made *Appalachian Spring,* in which the heroine's doubts and fears are more easily laid to rest.) All of these have in some way to do with love as torment. Most involve in a monumentally symbolic way a woman's (and/or an artist's) coming to terms with something inside herself either by accepting it or killing it. The movement—especially for the heroine figures Graham herself once played, which are inevitably more detailed than the other characters—is resolutely unpretty. These women wrench their bodies from side to side, run with tight, blind steps this way and that, shudder, twitch, fall. The dancing shrieks with ambivalence and a kind of fatal reticence. The women press their legs together, cross their hands over their bellies, retreat from what they appear to crave.

They're arduous journeys, these dances, for the audience as well as for the protagonist. *Deaths and Entrances* (1943) demands almost more stamina than the dance-without-tears crowd can muster. You have to be prepared to suffer its length, its intensity, its minutely detailed passions; you have to put up with not understanding its confusing surface. Sometimes I think that the three elegant, frustrated women brooding in this dark house are really all one woman, that the two men who court the women and fight each other are one man. It's not clear what any of them want—only that they are willful, passionate, thwarted, that one of them passes through madness and triumphs. The Three Remembered Children are curious, too. They slip through the dance, bringing in and taking away the props (shell, goblet, vases, bowl) that trigger memories for the heroine; their behavior is furtive—as if they were afraid they were doing something they shouldn't. Each little girl is like one of the three women and executes her distinctive movement patterns, but less emphatically, less distortedly. They join hands and wrangle futilely against each other, just as the grown women do; but once, left alone, they join hands to play.

If *Deaths and Entrances* is about renunciation (of love? for artistry?), *Dark Meadow* (1946) is about acceptance. And about, I think, darkness and light, barrenness and fecundity, winter and spring. In the dance's first section, the central female figure steps out into wide-legged positions—letting her body go and arms fly—pulls in, falls out again. Rarely does a Graham heroine willingly give in to the weight of her body like this; perhaps it signifies her willingness to come to terms with something. In another section, she pulls a gray veil over herself and curls and rolls in and out of it. Finally she yields to a man who is like both a lover and a guide. The five women and three men (They Who Dance Together) seem in some way to have achieved a calm she has not. You could also see them as acting on a ritual level what woman experiences as private, interior changes. In this they resemble She of the Ground, who passes calmly through at appointed times, turning Noguchi's phallic pillars, planting crosses or flowering branches on them, enveloping one with her cloak, showing the troubled heroine a bowl of red cloth (said by some to symbolize the menses). The dancing for the chorus is marvelous, from an intense opening dance for the women, with jutting hips and stamping feet, to a sextet suffused with an eroticism that has a cleansing strength yet is not without gentleness. The man's part confuses me. When the dance was revived in 1968 with Bertram Ross in Erick Hawkins's role, a lot of movement seemed to be missing, as if no one could remember it. I didn't see Ross Parkes in the revival of a few years ago; the man Tim Wengerd plays does a lot of vigorous and ardent dancing, but isn't stern.

In her two new dances, Graham has taken the tension between desire and fear or reticence and pared away everything else—event, character, everything. *O Thou Desire Who Art About To Sing* is like a frozen eternity of "I want to, but I can't." Elisa Monte and Tim Wengerd advance and retreat tensely. Even when he removes her dress, there's no giving in, only entangling. He ends in a costume attached umbilically to a new dress she has put on. But happy? No. In *Shadows*, Diane Gray and Eric Newton—he in a suit, she in a red evening dress—prowl tormentedly, mostly on and around a blue and gold bench (by Frederick Kiesler—made when and for what?). Janet Eilber and Peter Sparling act for the most part like happy young lovers, dressed in what look like stagy versions of Latin American peasant costumes. Each couple exists in its own world; once, I think, the men make contact. Pent-up maturity remembering take-it-easy youth? Maybe. It's like a troubled sketch for a dance rather than a finished work.

Wengerd is dancing wonderfully this season. I like his sturdiness, his unselfconscious buoyant power. Gutelius I thought very fine in *Deaths and Entrances* and Yuriko Kimura in *Dark Meadow*, as if the movement meant something to them. Carter brought his superb understanding of space—both distant and near—to *Appalachian Spring*. Elisa Monte, small, dark, and intensely alert, made a fine debut in *Errand into the Maze*. There are excellent dancers in the company; it's sad to see them looking confused, vain, or demoralized.

The set for Shadows, *posthumously credited to Frederick Kiesler, was part of the set he had designed for Graham's* Canticle for Innocent Comedians *(1952), as an integral part of the choreography, capable of being moved by the dancers during the course of the work.*

WHAT A TRAIL SHE BLAZED

The Village Voice, May 30, 1977

Anyone wanting to understand the modern dance of the thirties in all its shocking incorruptibility ought to see Martha Graham's *Primitive Mysteries*. The strength and purity of the dance transcend even this current ennervated revival.

Those who love, say, the lush, preening movement of Graham's 1976 technique-demonstration *Adorations* (fitted into a Procrustean bed of Baroque music that removes all jagged edges), may find *Primitive Mysteries* arid. And it is—deliberately and passionately so. Like much art and design of the period, it exposes its bone structure unadorned and gleamingly polished. Also, Graham and composer Louis Horst had been to New Mexico, where they had observed not only the religious customs of Mexican Indians but immense, barren landscapes where everything casts a hard shadow, and even the plants are spiky and without suppleness. Horst's simple music for flute, oboe, and piano has a lot of empty spaces in it; the movement Graham designed for herself and her group of women (the number varies—usually around twelve) progresses by single, clear gestures or repeating patterns—so powerful and so focused that they seem to have been distilled rather than invented.

I can see why many people in the thirties found modern dance unbeautiful. There is almost nothing in *Primitive Mysteries* that isn't angular, stiff, tense. The women in their long, plain, dark blue dresses (with a white ruffle added by Graham at the 1964 revival) look sturdy and unyielding. When they bow, they keep their legs and spines straight and fold at the hip joint. Sometimes they bend backward from the knees, keeping their bodies flat and rigid, as if the sky were pressing down on them. The central figure, a woman in a full skirted white dress with sleeves like little capes, moves among them offering the most succinct of blessings—a grave doll-saint in a Spanish church.

In this dance, as in many later ones, Graham was concerned with ritual. But here there are no complications, no struggle, no characters. The three sections contain images associated with virgin birth, crucifixion, resurrection, but this is no passion play. There are no intermediaries between the meditative central figure and the celebrants (just as in the Graham company of the very early '30s, there were no featured players—only Martha and The Group).

The dance is awesomely formal. Before each of its three parts, "Hymn to the Virgin," "Crucifixus," "Hosanna," the women stride onto the stage in ranks and files; at the end of each part they leave the same way. Always just before the end they make a circle around the "virgin." Always they work in unison groups of four, five, six in severe patterns—lines that move back and forth, clusters, circles. Although the women cover a lot of space with their feet, their arms and bodies are held in a position, which creates a friezelike impression: stillness and mobility combined.

The brilliance with which Graham deploys the women or alters the pattern keeps the austerity from being lifeless. A good part of the first section is couched in question-and-answer form. When the figure in white runs in tiny steps from one cluster of women to another, each group responds to her gesture with one of its own, and these terse gestures bloom out of stillness as icons suggesting crowning, praying, rocking a cradle, spreading a ritual meal. In this section the woman in white joins brief dances, leads processions, but in the "Crucifixus" she is set apart. Flanked by two "attendants," each of whom shades her head with a diagonally stretched arm, she advances by tiny increments toward the front of the stage. The rest of the women march in two shoulder-to-shoulder lines. Their heads are up, their arms bent and lifted so that their elbows jut forward on either side of the heads. They advance in weighted lunges, retreat lifting their knees so high that their bodies cave in. The piano strikes single chords, while the oboe sustains a high wail. On an abrupt chord, the woman stretches out her arms, and the others begin to circle her in huge, racking leaps, their bodies bent forward. Even when the leaps accelerate and scale down into runs the effect is terrifying.

During the final "Hosanna," the woman in white supports another woman. Because their bodies never mold to each other they resemble primitive carved figures whose poses suggest greeting, the deposition from the cross, crowning, resurrection, the replacement of one leader by another.

It is one of the best dances in the world.

Graham has now decided to say in the program that the dance is "literally" the celebration of a girl's coming of age. That one reviewer characterized Janet Eilber as a teenager isn't surprising in view of her pretty, drifting performance. Experts claim that the women in the 1964 revival at Connecticut College looked weak in comparison with the vigorous Graham dancers of the '30s. These women now, taken as a whole have about half the strength and fervency of the 1964 cast. Barely enough candlepower to light up the dance, let alone sear your eyeballs for good.

A FISHY CONVERSATION WITH AN OBLIGING GIANT

The Village Voice, April 23, 1979

"Hello, this is Paul Taylor."

Yes, I guess it is. No mistaking that soft, friendly voice, which, when Taylor is embarrassed, tends to slur and drop its *g*s—as if this cultivated man and acknowledged giant of a choreographer were hoping to disappear behind a country-boy facade.

He doesn't exactly agree to be interviewed; he'll take me out to dinner and we'll see what happens, ". . . but I don't want to talk about myself and I don't want to talk about my dances." So what'll we talk about—the food? "Yes, we can talk about the food." And we send each other uneasy chuckles over the wires.

Taylor is, of course, not the only choreographer who doesn't like talking about his dances. ("For one thing," he says with a touch of grimness, "you can't be misquoted.") In another, later telephone conversation, obligingly *trying* to be quotable, he says, "In a lot of primitive societies, people don't call each other by their real names. Everyone has another name for saying out loud, because to say a person's *real* name is unlucky. I'm not superstitious; its just that I don't like talking about something that—beyond its aspect as a craft—is so personal. Like my own pieces . . . I hesitate to call them by their real names."

Obliqueness, oddity of perspective characterize many of the dances that Taylor has been making since the early fifties. Who are those creatures in *Three Epitaphs* (1956), loping around to funereal band music, the taupe leotards that Robert Rauschenberg designed covering even their faces and glinting with mirrors? They look simian with their hanging arms and slouched-over bodies; they have aspirations toward herding. Funny and pathetic . . . perhaps they are us in our jungle suits. (One of the things Taylor tends to notice about us is that we all *have* jungle suits; *Cloven Kingdom* (1976) could be considered as a more elaborate and harsher statement of the same theme: gentlemen in tuxes and fashionable partying ladies letting their goat feet show.) In *Insects and Heroes* (1961) we never know quite what the "insect" is; in his spiny black outfit, he appears sometimes to be a menace, sometimes a clumsy pet, and he is as heroic as the "heroes" are buglike. Or take the second movement of *Esplanade* (1975), in which a group of dancers stands around for a long time making small, wan gestures to each other; in the rush of traveling steps that characterize this work, these people look stalled—as if they could express feeling only through a codified set of slow signals. People marking emotion the way dancers mark movement during tired rehearsals.

Although Taylor's dances have gotten less obviously eccentric as he has become a mature theatrical craftsman, there is still about most of them some element slightly out of kilter, some loose end that makes you wonder or nags you in the night.

Taylor himself—as a man, as the unforgettable dancer he was until he retired about five years ago—creates a similarly enigmatic impression for all his laid-back courtesy, grin and big laugh, frank wit, shy friendliness ("May I please be excused?" he asks his dancers, wishing to duck out of Friday's rehearsal a little early). When George Balanchine created a solo on Taylor in his half of *Episodes* (the 1959 Graham–Balanchine collaboration), Lincoln Kirstein let loose with a bunch of apparently contradictory adjectives and adverbs that described Taylor's stage persona very well: "Outlandishly violent," he wrote, "whimsically anxious, captiously awkward." Martha Graham, in whose company Taylor danced from about 1958 to 1963, cast him in a number of ambivalent, menacing roles—Aegisthus in *Clytemnestra,* The Stranger (i.e., the serpent) in *Embattled Garden,* the implacable fate figure, Tiresias, in *Night Journey*—as well as making use of his athletic build and sunny humor as Hercules in *Alcestis.* And there was something profoundly moving about Taylor, dancing a solo in his own *Aureole* back in 1962 when the work was premiered; it was so contrary to see a man that large and strong dancing with such grave lyricism, as if constantly reeling and unreeling his silky gestures. The image conveyed was one of both freedom and immense reserve.

Not surprisingly, Taylor's house bespeaks the importance of private rooms. The ground floor with clean-swept grate, wood paneling, green-flocked wallpaper, dark pictures that I can't make out without going close to, a long dining table covered with a lace cloth: it all looks as if some large middle-class family had walked out of it sixty years ago and never come back. He only uses it, he explains, when company comes; upstairs is where he really lives.

I feel Taylor's tiredness. He's preparing a new work, reviving old ones, rehearsing repertory for the company's City Center performances (April 18 to 29). His past is burdensome today. So we go to a restaurant, with a friend of his as a buffer, and we have this completely agreeable dinner during which I try very hard not to say anything that ends in a question mark except, "How's the fish?" and yet what happens is very curious.

Somehow Taylor manages to answer most of the questions I might have asked, or have raised over years of seeing and writing about his work.

It seems to puzzle him that anyone (me) should hold up the early *Three Epitaphs* as a masterpiece. Apropos of I forget just what, he says, "We can teach the whole thing in one rehearsal!" And at some other point he says earnestly, "Do you like *Airs*? I hope you like *Airs*." Well, at its premiere in 1978, I found it gorgeous, but not quite as tender as some of Taylor's other fresh-spirited dances to Baroque music. And, speaking to the subtext of our remarks, I tell him that I grew fond of the dance this past summer, and he says that it always takes time for dancers to settle into a work and vice versa.

He asks me if I've seen the Ohio Ballet (I have); they perform *Aureole* (I know). He answers the question I don't think I ask by touching his head and saying that in order for something new to come in the front, something has to go out the back. "A dance is going to change a little, no matter what. And that's not always bad. If you've seen the piece done before by another cast, you're naturally going to make comparisons, but that's a fact of life. And it has to do with the viewer, not the dance or the new cast." He's delighted that other companies want "the old dances," as long as former Taylor dancers like Eileen Cropley can stage them and he can get on with current business.

It's interesting that important ballet dancers like Rudolf Nureyev want to learn Taylor's roles, and that so many ballet companies are eager for his works. A piece like *Aureole* may be formal, serene, musical, like the best sort of ballet, but it's couched in Taylor's highly idiosyncratic style—with parallel feet, loosely swinging arms, jutting hips, scrunchings-in of the whole torso. The weight of the dancing is also peculiar to him: it's spongy, yet buoyant, the gestures like small banners or huge sails fluttering or billowing in response to a gentle wind. Nureyev, who has danced *Aureole, Book of Beasts,* and an abbreviated version of *Big Bertha* (for television), worked at Taylor's choreography with touching humility and attentiveness, but had trouble with the style. As Taylor says, "Ballet dancers are trained to concentrate on making shapes, rather than on what produced the shape." And, of course, that solo in *Aureole* isn't about shapes at all, we agree, but about continuous flow. (I do not ask Taylor whether not performing is painful to him, or relieving. I don't think I even want to know the answer; it's enough to see how, in his dances, he copes with a new leaderless society.)

"I've always been suspicious of crowds. I don't relate very well to huge groups of people," he says. This doesn't just mean that he doesn't enjoy parties. There are several factors at work: he chooses his dancers for their individual luminosity, for their interest in his work, and their agreeableness. The "pretty good track record" he acknowledges to have for keeping dancers with him may have something to do with the value he places on their personal attributes. (He turned his essay in Selma Jeanne Cohen's *The Modern Dance, Seven Statements of Belief* into a brief for the importance of dancers in any choreographer's work, and will say things like "I can give Ruth Andrien a piece of junk, and she'll make it look good. Not many dancers can do that.")

But Taylor's remark about crowds also relates to his worries about the way today's dance companies must use high-powered advertising to lure a crowd, how audiences prepared to respond en masse to a "sunny" work may not be open to a cloudy one. He's also, perhaps, answering a challenge that has occasionally been tossed at him—that, because he began as a maverick, he made an effort at some point to be popular, to appeal to a larger audience. A letter that he fired off in response to the first review of mine *The Voice* published said—among many useful things that I took to heart and never forgot—"If you believe I have 'sold out,' you must say so. If you think I would trade fine work for 'success,' you are just plain crazy . . ." I agree. And I agree with a former Taylor dancer who says that she doesn't think that he has ever thought in terms of what will sell, any more than he meant to antagonize the audience during the period when immobility was a feature of his work, he just does what he has to do, as any serious artist does, and hopes that people will like it.

In this noninterview, Taylor, in bits and pieces, does bring up his past. Admits that, wanting to be a painter, he swam his way through most of college—not because he enjoyed it, but because an athletic scholarship was nothing to sneeze at. He will generously concede anything you like to be "a turning point." Like the summer he was hired to drive a Chrysler touring car at the dance camp run by Angela Sartorio in Bar Harbor, and the car broke down the first day and he spent the summer watching former Ballets Russes luminaries Pierre Vladimiroff and Felia Dubrovska teach ballet and taking class with Anna Istomina (one of Ballet Russe de Monte Carlo's "Russianized" Americans). "Oh yeah," he says, "mention everybody." Mention Ethel Butler in Washington, one of his first teachers. Mention Louis Horst, whose composition class he took at Connecticut College in 1952. Mention Doris Humphrey, in whose revival of *Song of the West* he danced that same summer. Mention José Limón whose company he had a chance to join. Mention Martha Graham, whose company he did join.

Mention Merce Cunningham. Taylor worked with Cuningham, John Cage, Robert Rauschenberg during one of those epochal summers at Black Mountain College, and performed in Cunningham's 1954 season at the Theatre de Lys. Taylor says, deadpan, that he, like all the other dancers, had learned all the sections of Cunningham's indeterminate *Dime a Dance*, "but during that whole week at the de Lys, my number *never* came up." (Taylor says he went to Cunningham to find out if this was the sort of thing he had to learn to deal with, and whether there was an important point at stake that he didn't understand. Predictably, Cunningham would neither explain nor reassure.) Although Taylor didn't stay long with Cunningham, he speaks heatedly of his work—saying he can't figure out why people don't see how much emotion there is in Cunningham's work, how often his dances are, despite his own disclaimers, "about" something, however ambiguous that something is. And the adventurousness of Cunningham, Cage, Rauschenberg (who designed many costumes for Taylor) seems to have sparked Taylor's early work. James Waring, then also considered eccentric, encouraged and sponsored him, too.

Said *Dance Magazine*'s Doris Hering of Taylor in the '50s: "Mr. Taylor weaves his images with that strange blend of humor and detachment that one often finds in children. It is not the humor of dramatic situation, but of visual incongruity." The sensibility hasn't changed, although the methods have varied, the expertise grown. The inscrutable balance of wit, solemnity, tenderness, and cruelty seems to have characterized Taylor's dances from the earliest days through his notable 1957 concert of minimal and pedestrian movement, through the period when a dancerly sensibility gradually replaced a painterly one, to the dazzling dance works he presents now.

Taylor still rehearses in the studio on lower Broadway where he's been since the mid-sixties. It's homey, it's shabby, and it's not large. Several people crowd into one small office to handle the company's business. Packing cases wall one end of the space, and props pile up outside the dressing room. Today, lighting designer Jennifer Tipton has come to see the new work, *Nightshade*. She's embraced and settled down on a chair between Taylor and Bettie de Jong who, armed with clipboard and cigarette, functions as his assistant. Throwing Tipton clues, Taylor shows her a well-thumbed copy of Max Ernst's *La Semaine de Bonté*—a terrifying collection of etchings of opulent, half-naked women in bondage preyed upon by bird-headed or lion-headed gentlemen, violence in railway carriages, whispered conversations and witnessing eyes. The dancers threaten to split the walls apart with their energy as they bring aspects of these pictures to life in amorphous, powerfully disturbing ways. Mysterious dramas appear and dissolve as Elie Chaib, Victoria Uris, Susan McGuire, Ruth Andrien, Monica Morris, Carolyn Adams, Thomas Evert, David Parsons, Christopher Gillis paw at each other, scrabble across the floor, or watch each others' brutality with impassive attentiveness.

Diggity, Taylor's second most recent work, is supposed to be light-hearted. Artist Alex Katz, who frequently collaborates with Taylor, has created a gallery of cut-out dogs (Taylor's clever, good-hearted mongrel was a model for most of them). But *Nightshade* comes from Taylor's darker side. And it reminds me that one of the most remarkable aspects of his work for me has been his rather medieval presentation of evil as an active force. The sweet-sour comedy *From Sea to Shining Sea,* the cocktail party hell that is *Scudorama,* the loveless society coupling in the glossy affluence of *Private Domain,* the macabre *Big Bertha* in which a "typical American family" is brought to violence and incestuous rape by a sinister amusement pier automaton—these and others represent a sardonic yet forgiving view of our society, of lust, depravity, and spiritual blight. They differ, of course, in style, tempo, degree of humor, in the ways Taylor manipulates his vocabulary of big winging, coiling steps. Oddly, it's the same vocabulary (fundamentally) that the dancers in *Aureole* or *Esplanade* use to look so tender, so seraphically unconcerned with grief. Yet the fact that there's wit in his blackest works as well as in his lightest, tenderness in his wickedest dances, dark currents in his blithest is what makes his works linger with me.

This one, says Taylor, has been giving the dancers dreams. And, when Lila York and Linda Kent arrive, the dancers wipe it all away by dancing *Piece Period,* one of Taylor's most engagingly silly works, which hasn't been seen in New York for a long time. They wing it through the parts they don't know yet, laughing and counting feverishy, watched by one of the great all-time comic cats, who sits gravely in the middle of the dancing space.

Even though words are my business, I can understand why Taylor mistrusts them—the generalizations, comparisons, attempts to pin down, sum up, explain the inexplicable. A dance's real name is unsayable on many counts. As I take my turn thumbing through Ernst, I stumble on his famous scrap of dialogue: "What color is water?" "The color of water."

UNDER THE ARCH, OVER THE TRELLIS

The Village Voice, April 29–May 5, 1981

᠁

Arden Court, Paul Taylor's gorgeous new dance, rings every possible change on its ambiguous title. A garden court. Courts of love. Courtly love. Ardent courtship. Ardor. The Forest of Arden. All of which amount to feats of boldness and tender companionships in an idyllic countryside made of dancing and music.

The music is those excerpts from William Boyce's symphonies orchestrated long ago by Constant Lambert for the ballet *The Prospect Before Us.* The English Baroque sound always strikes me as an outdoor one—hunting parties and elegant picnics by the water. The backdrop by Gene Porter features a single enormous pink rose painted on a blue-green cloth.

Here come the men, leaping on a diagonal across the stage, each in a different way. Off they go. Back they come. Elie Chaib, Kenneth Tosti, Thomas Evert, Daniel Ezralow, David Parsons. They hurl themselves into the air and land with reckless speed, without ever losing that elasticity that characterizes Taylor's style. Taylor likes—emphasizes—male brawn and bulk, but all muscles are made to slide on velvet runners. The men dominate *Arden Court,* yet in one of the most perversely lovely passages, they stand close together and begin, one by one, to pour themselves smoothly into slow-growing vines of poses. As they lunge and bend and revolve, their arms reach out in different directions. It's like seeing spears as a bouquet.

Each of five duets shows a different kind of affection. While Chaib moves firmly yet dreamily across the stage—letting his arms and perhaps one leg sail up in a variety of long curves, pressing through air that seems heavy but not oppressive—Carolyn Adams laces around him. He becomes her arbor, her trellis. As his leg lifts, she, squatting decorously, glides under it with tiny steps; as he leans out, she quietly pulls herself onto his back and he, feeling her weight, lifts one leg to the rear to make a precarious curving seat for her.

David Parsons can't keep still. Jumping sunnily, twiddling his feet around, he doesn't notice Lila York watching him as if he were a particularly showy sort of butterfly she'd never seen before. While he kites around, she follows walking, running to keep up, puzzled but obviously entranced. He flies off, and she gets a proper partner, Kenneth Tosti, who behaves as if she were the blossom, he the bee. Sometimes their gestures are the same, but he moves twice as fast, rolling and hovering around her while she stays the sweet, silky centrifuge of all his activity.

These two rest onstage to watch Christopher Gillis and Daniel Ezralow—a couple of roistering comrades of the sort who know the punchlines of each other's jokes. Now they spring in unison, now a clever bit of counterpoint gets one shooting his leg over the other's agile crouch, and vice versa. The last couple, Thomas Evert and Susan McGuire, really dance together—touching hands, arms around each other; experienced lovers, perhaps, they know the same steps and do them harmoniously.

A formal affectionate dance for three couples follows the duets, then the men's slow dance, then more great rocket-bursts of jumping to end the tournament. And storms of applause.

Taylor's dancers look particularly splendid this season: Cathy McCann, Linda Kent, Monica Morris, Ruth Andrien too (Robert Kahn wasn't dancing the night I went). Karla Wolfangle is back. I value their lack of sleekness and superficial glamour, their different sizes and shapes, their bone-deep beauty in dancing.

THARP'S EXPANDING WORLD

The Village Voice, March 2 4, 1 9 8 0

Two young ballet dancers glue their faces to the tiny windows in the door of American Ballet Theatre's studio, watching a seemingly endless procession of people boil and churn past in some terrifically intricate dancing. "I can't even *imagine* doing that!" says the boy, shaking his head in awe.

Inside the studio, while members of Twyla Tharp's company collapse amid a debris of towels, fresh practice clothes, bottles of juice, etc., Tharp shakes her head disgustedly over a couple of possible layouts for ads to promote her company's season at the Winter Garden, March 24 to April 12. Slumping back to her chair to get on with the rehearsal, she mutters that for the thousands of dollars this ad's going to cost she could have made a sizable chunk of dancing.

Not that she would begrudge the money spent if she liked the result.

Tharp, on the brink of her first Broadway season, is frankly curious about the audience. And the first step is getting people to the theater. Tharp has worked on a film (*Hair*), made televison shows, choreographed dances for skater John Curry, and created ballets for ABT and the Joffrey, but her stage appearances with her own company—from the days when she was considered radical and "difficult" to today, when her art is not only richer, but more accessible—have occurred within the protective and supportive "arts environments." But she's been feeling for a long time that ". . . Broadway audiences can sustain much more than they're ordinarily given. And I don't see any reason not to *prove* that and thereby gain a much broader financial base for the company."

Those who knew Tharp's work in the '60s might be surprised at how considerate of her audience she's become, although in some ways, the tough attitude she had then did reflect concern, if somewhat negatively. It was as if she were saying, "Damn it, we're adults and so are you, and we won't insult you by trying to appeal to you." Now, however, she can say of her revamped *Ocean's Motion* (1975) to Chuck Berry songs, "It's a good opener, it relaxes an audience very quickly. They enjoy seeing good unison work. It reassures them that there is righteousness—a right order—someplace. . . ." (Not that there's a lot of unison in *Ocean's Motion;* there's some sophisticated close canon and many passages in which each dancer pursues a private and juicily complicated path.)

The ad raises another interesting point. These days, the company's public image is a handsome one. Alongside photos of the dancers by Richard Avedon or Kenn Duncan, you're likely to see credits for makeup and hair style as well as for clothes. Tharp points out that even in the poverty-stricken old days when she made the costumes herself, she was always concerned with how she was presenting herself. Now, when the stakes are higher, she simply goes where she thinks the greatest expertise is—to the fashion world, "where people study makeup and hair style as thoroughly as we study dancing, and take pride in it. You have to do it; you might as well do it very well."

It galls Tharp that there are people who think that artists shouldn't get involved with this kind of packaging. She sighs. "Yeah, if you don't, somehow that's supposed to mean that you're more involved with your art. Well, I don't buy that. You can be totally involved with your art and *also* concerned about these more superficial elements. Just to throw it all to the winds and say you don't give a fuck how your face or your hair looks does *not* make you a better dancer."

The irony of these fierce remarks when juxtaposed with Tharp's appearance at the moment suddenly comes home, and she cracks up. She's wearing white jazz shoes, a grayed, old white leotard and tights, and over these a pink undershirt, blue knitted tights that are sixty-percent runs, yellow rubber pants with one leg shorter than the other and a large rip at the crotch, and a man's raincoat draped over her to keep the drafts away.

Doing what you have to do very very well is pretty much Tharp's attitude toward everything in life. It means trying to mother eight-year-old Jesse sensibly; it means being as straightforward and clear as possible with me, since I'm here to do a job too. It has to do also, I think, with making every situation in which she finds herself interesting and useful—and possibly enjoyable—for everyone concerned. Therefore she not only has to keep developing her craft, she has to run her company in a craftsmanly way. She speaks with sympathy, but disapproval, of directors who assume they're going to be hated and behave accordingly, or who are so afraid of being caught with their pants down that they keep the performers in the dark about everything as long as possible.

All of the dancers who have been with Tharp for some time have responsibilities beyond their own performing. Jennifer Way takes care of the daily scheduling, for example. Rose Marie Wright teaches pointe class. Today, Raymond Kurshals reports back to Twyla on his telephone attempts to arrange rehearsals for a TV spot she's doing, and Tom Rawe offers to show John Simon, the composer of the new *When We Were Very Young,* a videotape of the last run-through. Tharp's latest idea has been to turn all but the newest company members into rehearsal directors. Since almost all her dances have two casts, a member of one cast may be assigned to supervise the other cast's rehearsals, which makes him/her responsible for the work in a completely different way. Tharp sounds almost as proud of the lack of bickering and pettiness as she does of the dance prowess or the individual gifts of her colleagues.

So today, after she's given a few pointers on characterization to the dancers in *Ocean's Motion,* she asks William Whitener what *he* thought, and the two of them confer briefly on what needs more work. After the run-through of the new *Brahms' Paganini*—which has hair-raising amounts of power, speed, and unexpectedness and reminds me again that Tharp is into advanced calculus where most choreographers are still wrestling with long division—it is Christine Uchida who goes up to Richard Colton, after he's stopped gasping for breath, with a yellow pad of notes and questions on his amazing ten-minute solo. Tharp, watching intently, may ask for a passage to be repeated, ask Jenny to schedule a half-hour rehearsal for someone who needs it. Tomorrow morning, the dancers will look at today's videotape, with Tharp only if she feels additional comment is necessary.

Later, over dinner, she and I try to decide whether George Balanchine would like the *Brahms' Paganini.* She's not sure. She's pretty certain he'd like *Baker's Dozen* (the ravishing full-company piece she presented here last spring). She laughs at my characterization of her lying awake in the night, running her repertory past an imaginary Balanchine: "Yeah, I try to distract myself from my bigger problems with that one!" (Balanchine, without a doubt, is the choreographer Tharp honors most; and, like him in his younger days, she believes in, and enjoys, bringing all the craft and understanding she can muster to everything from ballets to movies to circus acts.)

Actually Tharp appears to have no worries about the Brahms, although she's almost apologetic for tackling the Paganini variations instead of the more difficult-to-get-into Handel ones. As one might expect, it's not only the beautiful weaving and folding of a Brahms adagio that impresses her, but the classical structuring combined with the abrasive power, the downright violence of some of the variations—all of which she has countered in dance terms. (The dancers, she has just discovered, have nicknamed one of the sections "Agony.")

No, it's *When We Were Very Young*—"The New Piece"—that's still puzzling her. As she fumbles to characterize it, I begin to envision it as a large, nice, capricious new pet, whose care and feeding she's still trying to figure out. It's a full-length thing with words by Thomas Babe, music by John Simon, set and costumes by Santo Loquasto. She can drop remarks about it like, "One of the things that makes it so peculiar is that the characters are stronger, in a way, than their drama." But it's changing every day. In it, Tharp plays a role—"Jane"—not so much laying out a new style of performing for herself as defining a new *attitude* toward performing. (In deadpan earnest, "I'm not going to worry about my steps.") She intends the piece to be comic. She also knows it's serious. It felt okay to her today. Tomorrow? Who knows.

Tharp's interest in words was already apparent back in 1971 in *The Bix Pieces:* a narrator, speaking for Twyla, defined the dance's structure and history, and, in so doing, colored our perception of what we were seeing. And she's been nosing around the edges of such theatrical matters as role-playing and acting for some time now, tackling on her own terms elements she once would have avoided. (The onetime Barnard undergraduate who walked away from a dance class when the teacher said, "Make a sunrise," is not completely, utterly wisecracking when she remarks, "These days I'd say, 'How? Show me. I need that.' ")

Tharp may be struggling—with considerable pleasure—to shape this enterprise; the dancers may not be sure what the hell it is yet, but everyone works very hard to define it. Today, she is rehearsing a set of linking passages. In each of these, company members slog on in a tight, noisy pack with variants of step that seems part march, part tantrum. Each time, they recite a different verse of A. A. Milne's poem "Disobedience," keeping up a battery of complicated rhythmic gestures with heads, shoulders, arms, fists, thumbs. "Hey guys," says Tharp on a hunch, "now try double-timing the words against the feet." "JamesJamesMorrisonMorrisonWeatherbyGeorgeDupree" gabble the dancers gamely. Waiaiait a minute . . . , Speed, not anarchy. Tharp sits quietly and lets them figure it out. "Okay," she says firmly, "put your papers away. You know this; you just don't *know* that you know it." And then guffaws as William Whitener turns to go to his place, revealing that he has stuck another copy of the words down the neck of his shirt.

At one point in the rehearsal, Tharp threatens unseriously to revive the "Osgood Hill" series, and the dancers groan in near-perfect unison. This infamous title refers to a fairly recent example of Tharp's ability to be productive and interesting within any given situation. As part of a summer residency that involved the company's teaching classes to students, many of whom Tharp flatly considered overweight and undercommitted, she decreed that everyone, including herself, should run one-and-a-half miles to the top of a hill—before breakfast—and go through this series of calisthenic exercises she developed. She obligingly hitches up her pants and demonstrates, "It's for the back sixteen circles here sixteen circles coming up sixteen of these which is very good for the shoulder joint which is giving Chris Uchida all this trouble for the partnering very useful for that I do this side stretch one of my old favorite side stretches but it's still the best stretch I know for the bottom of the back which is just contracting that part right there nothing else but that this is the best stretch I stole it from Margaret Craske reverse reverse so it goes for fifteen minutes." She drops, pink, back into her seat. *Then,* at pastoral Osgood Hill, they ran one-and-a-half miles down the hill to breakfast and a full day of dancing.

It's good to see that, as Tharp keeps extending her formidable mind toward whatever unexplored aspect of dancing or music or theater she feels ready to deal with, she remains committed to excellence, to intelligent craftsmanship, to considerateness, to hard work—extremely impatient with people who aren't and full of regard for those who are. For her TV spot; part of an update of an old Omnibus Show, "Dance Is A Man's Game" (needless to say, she has a few ideas of her own on that subject), she's designing a sequence for Peter Martins of the New York City Ballet and Lyn Swann, wide receiver for the Pittsburgh Steelers. Even before she speaks of the intriguing difference between the ways in which the two men deploy their weight, she mentions with pleasure their respect for, and courtesy toward, each other.

Or, raging wearily on behalf of John Curry—who graced the Winter Olympics with a new solo she had made for him and was undermined by the late hour, the low camera angle, the "carpet" and debris laid on the ice by a drum and bugle corps—she says, "Working with him is a reaffirmation of the things that one knows, but that so few people comprehend, which is the desire to excel absolutely. With no compromises."

Toward the end of what looks like a twelve-hour day, Tharp starts peeling off her layers of practice clothes and replacing them with something to go (finally!) eat in. Twisting around to call out last-minute instructions and answer last-minute questions, tossing the raincoat to whoever lent it to her, she begins to haul and unroll a white T-shirt down over her chest. Across the front it proclaims, with unarguable accuracy, THIS IS A CHAMPION.

The raincoat that I assumed was part of Tharp's rehearsal studio garb turned out to be an integral part of the costume she wore in the finished work.

THARP AGAINST THE
WHIRLWIND

The Village Voice, September 30 – October 6, 1981

W atch the kamikaze critic attempt the ultimate daredeviltry: nose-diving into Twyla Tharp's *The Catherine Wheel*—a dance-theater piece so huge-scaled, so active, so fierce, so densely layered and cross-referenced that you sit in your seat hardly able to move, unaware of your breathing for the whole of its seventy-eight-minute development. The suite of songs and instrumental pieces written for *The Catherine Wheel* by David Byrne of the Talking Heads, which comes to us via fastidiously engineered tapes, combines Byrne's voice with a variety of instruments and electronically produced effects. But because the percussion instruments usually lay out a strong rock beat and several of the songs seem to whirl around on themselves, the effect is of a powerful, almost ominous storing up of energy that only occasionally relaxes or explodes.

The Catherine Wheel features the same embattled family that populated Tharp's *When We Were Very Young* (1980)—scrappy, ambitious, ineffectual mother (Jennifer Way); feckless, lecherous, charming father (Tom Rawe); bully/baby son (Raymond Kurshals); flouncy, calculating daughter (Katie Glasner). The expanded household includes a flirty maid (Shelley Washington) and a twitchy little "pet" (Christine Uchida in a furry vest). A dreamy poet (John Carrafa) gets mixed up with them—I think because they have this pineapple that he wants. (Wait, better not bring the pineapple up yet.) Then there's a Chorus, of which the family is sometimes part, and a Leader (Sara Rudner). The Chorus expands the family's brawls into full-scale war, echoes or initiates themes—making them more efficiently abrasive—and comments on the action like the chorus in a Greek tragedy. Within the chorus parts, another "play" occurs that has to do with disruption, with the crowd turning against its leader, with nastiness, violence, and, finally, a cleaning up and a restoring of order: all the wrenching, spinning, swaggering, windmilling dancing slotted into balanced contrapuntal patterns between Santo Loquasto's ranks of steel poles.

Then there's the pineapple. Pineapple as forbidden fruit, as object of desire, as confidant. Pineapple as hand grenade. Pineapple as god—plucked golden from a gilt heaven, disguised as a humble pineapple, sometimes ignored or treated disrespectfully, getting larger and more imposing, destroyed, gathered up in pieces, and at last enshrined on a little golden wheel and hung again on that shimmering cluster. Who would have thought, ten years ago, that Twyla Tharp would ever be investigating the uses of symbolism? (Hang in there, Martha Graham, we may be coming full circle.)

Then there are the wheels. Everywhere. Huge bicycle wheels seen in shadow form, carried across the stage. Inscrutable wheeled objects that descend from the flies, like working models of some unfathomable machine (Santo Loquasto as Leonardo da Vinci). A suspended rack with wheels and down-pointing spikes on which Leader and Chorus keep trying to impale the netted bundle of pineapple chunks. It sticks, then with a double clank, the machine drops the load. (It's your burden you keep it. And don't let it touch the ground if you can help it.) A small tacky living room sits briefly on stage in a wheeled cage. And wheels—as velocity, as spinning in place—accumulate in the dancing: cartwheels, pinwheels, dancers spread-eagled overhead (St. Catherine was slated to be broken on the wheel, but it fell apart at her holy touch), dancers as fireworks, spewing stars onto a black sky.

So (don't tell me you don't get it)—Tharp gives us violence and aspiration, death and transfiguration, dance as both demon and dispeller of demons. And everything washing over everything else, so you see the lineaments of one idea through another, just as you see pieces of the action in shadow-play behind Loquasto's gray-white silk curtains, behind the antics of live performers. And in the black depths of the stage are things you can barely see.

Tharp has made the drama ride a ceaseless base of dancing. The performers keep their feet moving, their hips swiveling, their knees pulsing no matter what they are telling each other with their gestures and facial expressions. People trying to settle the affairs of their lives while on a treadmill, on a dance floor, or an erupting world. The first night I wondered if the fluid, ongoing pulse of Tharp's movement mightn't be antithetical to the development of drama. The second-night performance was cleaner and more pointed, and I found my way more easily through the hugger-mugger of scenes like this one: Brother tap dances ineptly (Mother has taught her kids how to do this and pass the hat), Sister vamps, Mother tries to rent Sister out to Poet, and Poet pretends to go along while waiting for his chance to steal Pineapple. In scenes like this you yearn for a few more small sharp gestures.

There are some amazing scenes. "Down, down we go/Fall through, fall through the cracks," growls Byrne; and Washington, as the maid, has some kind of horrifying fit—making big motions of grabbing and uprooting and thrusting away, of sinking down and rising up. And all the time, her face is doing a carefully structured dance of demented grimaces—tongue hanging out, or teeth bared and eyes rolling. Lust too long balked by subservience and frustration finally explodes in a gibber of rage. Or there's the bumbling, farcical mustering of the family for battle. Poet skips lightly around the perimeter. Mother has to point him in the right direction. Wriggly, itchy little Pet aligns herself with Father, then, perhaps remembering his penchant for humping her publicly, knocks him out and bounces delightedly up and down on him. There's the bitter, looping adagio in which the couple, reconciled, attempts to dance together while their children (Orestes in overalls and windbreaker, Electra in a ruffly jumper) try to pry them apart and get in on the cuddling. There's the phenomenal Rudner, first coy and mischievous and jivey, later spinning and leaping in horror (over what she's started?), shaking her head as if she wants it to fall off. Toward the end, she and the black-garbed people with red masks tied over their eyes seem to be wallowing in evil, and there's nothing bumbling about *their* combat. Grab Rudner, turn her upside down, spin her around. And she seems to expect, even crave, this violence. When the curtain first went up, we saw dark silhouettes of the Chorus—leaderless—going through a cyclical, going-no-place pattern of throws, lifts, punches. Maybe they were practicing for this moment.

But as Byrne opens a twang of glowing chords on top of the running beat, and all the blackness lifts to reveal a golden curtain textured like giant bamboo stalks and Jennifer Tipton beams brightness onto the stage, Carrafa, Washington, and Uchida spring into sight—golden athletes in silk clothes. As all the dancers reappear in twos, threes, singly, violence is transmuted into dancing. Dance as battlefield, the dancer as warrior. Not even in the *Brahms' Paganini* has Tharp made dancing as astonishing as this. It flashes, cuts like swords, spins in air. It gleams with fearlessness, with risk, with trust, with glory. You won't ever have seen people so beautiful, so brave, so engaged with the moment and their individual places within the intricate web of exchanging partners, throwing and catching each other. It's Graham's vision of the dancer as celestial acrobat on another level. These dancers cannot pause to affirm self-image: there's the beat of the music to be shattered into twenty intricate motions of legs, body, arms, head; there's a colleague falling from the skies who has to be caught; another leaping high—duck and let him sail over.

Dancers keep pouring onto the stage and flashing away. No posing, no preparing blunt the impetus or stall the twisting, shimmering current. How can William Whitener keep his footing with leaps, twists, and spins so savagely fast and whipping that he is perilously close to being out of control? How can Richard Colton let one leg swing out and down while he's in the middle of a multiple pirouette so that you think one foot will hook around the other and trip him? How can Shelley Washington leap straight up and believe that Kurshals, several feet away and busy with some other phrase, will catch her as she plummets floorward? How can any of them—Mary Ann Kellogg, Shelley Freydont, John Malashock, Keith Young, and all—*do* what they're doing? Those who had roles in the first part bring their characters into this fray, but dissolve their gestures into the virtuosic dancing. In fact, probably every move you've seen all evening is here. Transmuted.

In the program, Tharp lovingly lists each dancer's name for every appearance he or she makes in this "Golden Section": "Way and Carrafa, Young, Rawe; Young; Young, Glasner, Freydont, Colton . . ." Every ten seconds onstage has a lifetime of dancing in it and deserves recognition. As Byrne's "Light Bath" reprises, Uchida begins to dance alone more quietly than anyone has danced for a long time. Several times she throws herself into the wings and arms catch her. The blacking out of lights leaves her held up in mid-wheel, half out of sight. Perhaps our dance will be moving to another part of the universe, irretrievably shattered, sucked into a black hole, expelled somewhere else beyond imagining.

"Twyla Tharp's subject is not your life or hers. . . ." Arlene Croce wrote that in 1971, and it seemed true then. I think Tharp's subject has always been life, only she chose to make the form of her dances embody

---

those concerns rather than doing any deliberate storytelling. The strongest parts of *The Catherine Wheel,* to me, are those in which form and dramatic intent are one—as they are in the paradigmatic "Family Loop" quartet already mentioned—and the weakest those in which costume and mugging have to tell the story because the steps don't. In the first section of *Short Stories* (music by Supertramp), Washington, Kurshals, Whitener, Carrafa, Glasner, and Kellogg can express a novel's worth of emotions about pairing up, eyeing others, quarreling, finding new partners because a ballroom (or prom floor or disco) tidily provides steps, pretext, and structure. In the second section, violence spills over—no more tender dancing, punctuated by wary pauses and brusque gestures—and Kellogg is hurt, raped and killed perhaps, by the three men. The dancing continues. To Springsteen's apocalyptic cries (". . . down in Jungleland") two other couples—Rawe and Way, Rudner and Malashock—accidentally stumble into other pairings, like joggers in the park who bump into contact. Two beautiful, drastic duets promise reconcilaiton, but the dance ends with silent angry conversations, expostulating gestures, bitter shoves. And here we go again. Compared to the smooth blurry dancing in *The Bix Pieces* (1971) the dancing Tharp's making now is like a blade, honed and polished—slashing, jabbing, slicing curly pieces out of the air. Maybe the increasing violence and risk in her work is intended as sympathetic magic. If you can top the whirlwind, will it subside?

ICONOCLASTS OF THE SIXTIES AND SEVENTIES

Douglas Dunn & Dancers in *Echo* (1980), performed at the Kitchen

During the sixties, some of the brightest choreographers in New York were trying to figure out what dance was. That is, what dance was in relation to them, to the times, and to what had come before. What could you do in the name of dance? Walk across a room, sing a song, not show up and send a message? The dancers, artists, and musicians who collaborated under the rubric of Judson Dance Theater during the first half of the sixties presented some astounding work. Their audacity and the glare of their wit often made more conventional concerts around town look dim in comparison. Sometimes they bored us or irritated us, but in so doing they caused us to look a little harder at our cherished traditions. Eventually, they broadened our definitions of "dance" and the "dancer."

By the seventies, the iconoclastic, impetuous, collaborative heyday of Judson was over. Judson luminaries like Deborah Hay, Lucinda Childs, Trisha Brown, Yvonne Rainer, David Gordon, and Steve Paxton became interested in discovering or refining individual approaches to dance. Hay turned for a while to *Circle Dances,* simple, wholesome pieces in which everyone was a performer and no one was a spectator. Paxton developed Contact Improvisation—a two-person art-sport that has been taken up, reinterpreted, turned to new ends all over the world. Remy Charlip, loosely associated with the Judson group during the sixties, devised his "air mail dances"—drawings of dancing figures that could be sent out to dancers to interpret and perform.

In building a style, many of the choreographers—former Judsonites and newcomers like Laura Dean or Senta Driver—began simply, with baby-steps: Trisha Brown's first "accumulations," with their small, plain moves, their add-a-gesture structure; the calm repetitiveness of Lucinda Childs's *Reclining Rondo;* Laura Dean's *Spinning Dance,* one hour of spinning by three women; Senta Driver's *Memorandum,* a solo in which she walked in a circle, reciting with each orbit the name of a famous ballerina. In minimal pieces like these, the integrity was as alluring as any natural beauty; the structural bones were meant to gleam through the skin. And the building blocks turned out to be capable of supporting dances of increasing richness and complexity.

Virtuosity, all but banned in vanguard circles during the early sixties, made its reappearance in new kinds of daring, intellectual as well as physical. Casual demeanor, crucial to the sixties aesthetic, proved a beguiling companion to feats—making the tricky coordinations, the endurance tests, the risky falls, the memorization of complicated systems, or the display of improvisational wit seem all the more amazing for the offhanded way in which the performers approached them.

In 1974, Douglas Dunn presented himself in a "performance exhibit," lying motionless for several hours a day in a structure he had built; by 1976—the earliest year these articles cover—he was beginning to make extremely vigorous and imaginative dancing for a company. By 1976, David Gordon was presenting dazzlingly witty structures of action, speech, song, objects, and slides with his PickUp Company. Meredith Monk and Kenneth King, who had been experimenting with new approaches to narrative in dance since the mid-sixties, premiered major works in 1976; Monk's *Quarry* and King's *Battery* had a tighter dramatic weave than the choreographers' earlier works, although they were just as full of odd, wildly beautiful sights and sounds.

Over the years during which these articles were written, we've seen the gradual acceptance of new forms of dancing by a wider audience and by more traditionally-minded dance companies. Charlip, Childs, Dean, Driver, Dunn, Gordon, Takei, and Wagoner have created works for other companies. It was the Paris Opera, an institution not noted for adventurousness since the 1830s, that commissioned Dunn's *Pulcinella* in 1980. Under the auspices of such organizations as the Brooklyn Academy of Music and the Los Angeles Museum of Art, both Trisha Brown and Lucinda Childs have collaborated with artists and composers of equal stature to produce what might be termed "postmodern spectacles." Yesterday's radicals have become today's mature artists.

RECKLESS AGAIN

The Village Voice, May 22, 1978

Wearing a T-shirt and a pair of loose cotton trousers, Trisha Brown warms up to work on her new solo. This is a two-hour process, "so let me know when you'll be coming." It's January, and Brown doesn't yet know when or where she'll be performing the solo (May 22 to 25 at the Public Theatre's Newman Theatre). Watching her bend and stretch and swing her lanky, capable-looking body around, I think of something she said in a dialogue with Douglas Dunn that was printed in *Performing Arts Journal:* "In the '60s, a trained dancer was a person with a puffed-out ribcage who was designed to project across the footlights of a proscenium arch stage. He or she couldn't necessarily do a natural kind of movement, even a simple one."

She's one of the people who quietly and persistently—and with good humor—eroded that image. Seeing Brown on the street, you wouldn't think, "There goes a dancer!" And her performing manner, like her last name, is plain and unassuming (there *is* a shade of caprice about "Trisha"). Her protective coloring abets her in dealing out surprises. She dances the uncompleted solo. Oh my God. "I have to perform this about ten times before I can calm it down," she says, breathing hard and starting over. Even though you get an impression of the dance as an untamed animal she's riding, there's no strain, hardness, theatrics. Brown dancing creates the illusion of a current inside her that is constantly being channeled and rerouted so it can pour into a leg, a finger, can make her arms drape across her or her head swing back.

Wendy Perron, who's danced with Brown since 1975, marvels over this elusive fluidity. "She was doing some of the movements for 'Branch' (a section of the 1977 *Lineup*), and her arms were . . . just *around* her . . . like water. I couldn't think of the shape of them. When she showed them to us, broke them down, they became identifiable, like any other arm movements, but when she was really revved up and going. . . ! She taught them as a solid but she danced them as a liquid. And she's always moving more body parts than she says she is."

Brown herself, in clarifying her work, has spoken of using neutral transitions, of playing down big movements, of making "radical changes in a mundane way." All of which is true and well said. But as I watch her on her fifth trip through the solo, I realize that her statements don't quite prepare you for dancing in which nothing ends where you might expect it to and nothing prepares you for anything else. Perhaps it's worth remembering that Brown grew up in Aberdeen, Washington, in the forest, where perspectives are always changing. Things that are hidden suddenly flash into view. You never have the whole story.

Jill Johnston, writing in *The Voice* of the rawer Brown of eleven years ago, noted this quality, saying that everything Brown did looked as if "it had never been done before, inventive, spontaneous, and nonchalant." Brown, sitting at the big table in her loft drinking tea (Red Zinger? Camomile? she has them all) remembers that colleagues then always found her timing unusual, and she attempts to convey in words the unruly zest of her early work, "I remember standing, then totally dropping all my energy—shwap! to the floor, and then gathering it in and shooting in the opposite direction with all my might. And then crawling along . . ."

Those who saw her first dances remember other kinds of surprises: in the course of *Skunk Cabbage Salt Grass and Waders* (1967), she dunked herself in a tub of water; in a part of *Target,* she fell over, saying "Oh, no" for three minutes. She says that her early works, beginning with those performed at Yoko Ono's loft in 1961, were structured improvisations, only partly choreographed. "I always kept certain doors open to go through if I had the courage. I wanted to resolve things in performance, to have that open-endedness, that possibility for brilliance times ten."

This brilliance, obviously had nothing to do with conventional virtuosity. Although Brown, like the other dancers involved with Judson Dance Theatre in the sixties—Yvonne Rainer, Deborah Hay, Lucinda Childs, Steve Paxton, et al.—had had conventional dance training. She majored in dance at Mills, made the de rigeur summer treks to Connecticut College to study with Graham and Limón, taught modern dance for two years at Reed College in Oregon. Her own doubts, her inquisitive and challenging students, her encounters with body-awareness people like Laura de Freitas, a summer workshop with Ann (now Anna) Halprin, led her to reject most of what she'd learned about "modern dance." To the artists, musicians, and dancers who collaborated at Judson, a dance came to be any structure in which human beings dealt factually with the rock-bottom elements of dance: space, time, weight—and the ways in which other humans or objects or sounds affected these. A dancer wasn't a courtier or a super-athlete or a suffering hero; a dancer was a person who performed the dances. There was a respect, a love for what Yvonne Rainer called "unenhanced physicality." And the distrust of fanciness that Brown expressed so smartly in the *Drama Review* in 1975: "Traveling steps have always stymied me. Traveling steps are what dancers use to get from Place A to Place B on the stage. I have usually walked. It would embarrass me to hop over there."

People who saw Brown's work only in the late '60s or early '70s mightn't think of her as a remarkable dancer. An architect maybe, an artist certainly. In 1968, after the Judson people had gone their separate ways, Brown began in another way to define the wry edge between risk and safety, between the functional and the illusionistic, between a fantastic task and the matter-of-fact execution of it. She began to climb the walls. But her "equipment pieces" like *Walking on the Wall* (1971) and *The Floor of the Forest* (1970) weren't designed as acrobatic stunts. They wittily disoriented the audience's perceptions and sense of gravity. When, in *Planes* (1968), three women slowly and smoothly climbed over a white wall with holes in it, you couldn't be sure whether you were watching them climb a wall, crawl along the ground, or free-fall past your window. Brown defines these dances as "my response to the limitation of sitting and looking into a box. I wanted to change that radically without moving anybody."

She can't remember now why she got into the equipment pieces, but she remembers clearly why she got out of them: She got tired of dealing with the heavy structures, tired of maintaining the real "chinning-yourself" power it took to perform on them, tired of worrying that someone might get hurt, and, above all, tired of being asked if this was dance. Since 1972, almost all the ingenious structures Brown has been devising to support or generate movement can be carried in her head and on paper. Since 1975, they haven't necessarily been visible in the finished work. A standing-in-place solo she first performed in 1971 and her lying-in-place *Primary Accumulation* (1972) gave the illusion of being built in the presence of the audience. She developed a long sequence of plain, succinct, beautifully chosen movements—usually involving the smooth flexing and rotating of various joints—by an additive process, always returning to the beginning after each addition (e.g., 1, 1-2, 1-2-3, 1-2-3-4). By the 1975 *Pyramid,* the same organizing principle had spawned a complex group work (traveling steps clearly no longer a roadblock). Here, four dancers not only accumulated individual sequences, but de-accumulated. Eventually, since movements began to be lopped off the beginning faster than they were being added at the end, the dance erased itself.

Brown has entered into other witty relationships to performing spaces beside hanging out over them. Like stationing fifteen performers on roof-tops over a ten-block area in lower Manhattan and having them relay a chain of inevitably deteriorating gestures past a roof-sitting audience (*Roof Piece*, 1971) or putting the four performers of *Primary Accumulation* on individual rubber rafts and letting the dance drift around the pond of Minneapolis's Walker Art Center. (These dances were carefully plotted for particular spaces—a fact that often escaped sponsors. Brown, arriving at a campus to perform, would be chagrined to find people thinking any old parking lot would do for her.) She's not doing this kind of work any-more either. "My preoccupation with a given space—a room, a stage, or my end of town—is now internalized. It's in the understructure of my work." An imaginary cube in which she stood graphed the movement for *Locus,* (1975), but the audience couldn't see it. *Lineup* (1977) referred to the edges of the room without using them.

"A bricklayer with a sense of humor." That's how Brown once charac-terized herself in relation to her work. Studios like the one Brown lives and works in reinforce the image of dance-making as something useful and sane to do with your life. A kettle ready for five-minute tea breaks. Cats who'll rub against the ankles of whoever stops dancing for a while. Brown's polite, elderly dog knows, as does her twelve-year-old son, Adam, to skirt the dancing on the way from the entrance to the living quarters.

There are no mirrors or barres in Brown's studio. Beside an exercise mat sits a basket of rubber balls of assorted sizes; the dancers are cur-rently addicted to a technique of muscle relaxation they learned from Elaine Summers, which involves placing the balls under key parts of the body. There's no excess tension in Brown's dances, none in her col-leagues' bodies, and none in her rehearsals.

Brown sits in a chair watching Wendy Perron, Elizabeth Garen, and Mona Sulzman go over some phrases of a new trio. She doesn't say much. In her writings, in her everyday conversation, Brown selects and combines words with the same wit and economy she applies to gesture. (She's one of the few people I know whose converation isn't puddled with "ers" and "ums"; when she can't find the right word, she simply stops talking until it comes to her.) She was one of the most daring conversationalists in the (alas) defunct improvisational Grand Union. Her 1969 *Skymap* ("which I *insisted* was a dance") consisted of Brown asking the audience to lie back and imagine a map of the United States on the ceiling, while she provided an extraordinarily vivid collection of words and phrases with which we could fill in the cities and mountain ranges. And it is words that have gen-erated this new dance. Brown has written instructions for a piece that she says she only half sees. The three dancers have made phrases by following these instructions. Since the words are the same but the dancers interpet them in individual ways, their movements are reminiscent of each others', but never identical. Sometimes you think you're seeing an out-of-whack canon. Brown admits to having been startled by some of the dancers' choices, and often has to resort to a rather Byzantine logic: If a word she has imagined will produce A produces B, then if she wants B again, she has to write A.

These dancers have been working with Brown for about three years. They have absorbed her style and made their own impact on it. The kind of daring and intelligence they have to have, over and above their physical expertise, is a kind of virtuosity undreamed of by the average little girl who plans to be a dancer when she grows up. "I hate my 'mark,' " says Sultzman, taking a rest. "Oh do you?" Garen is pleased. "I hate mine too, it doesn't work for me anymore." (They're talking about the way they've interpreted an instruction to choose a phrase to walk through.) And they're trying to figure out why. Brown says nothing. Although the dancers have produced the movement, it is her wholly mysterious sense of what fits and what doesn't, what must be added and what dropped, what is to be layered or juxtaposed with what that is shaping the dance into an organic whole. She makes a tentative structure, like "Wendy, you do the first part of your phrase A, the second part of your phrase B, and the third part of your A; Elizabeth, you do A, B, C in the same way; Mona, try B, C, A."

They embark on this without batting an eye—pulling the juicy, unexpected phrases into something still more complex. In the notebook, open by Brown's feet, words simmer on the page, "Step right . . . slight keel into a slow turn . . . gallop, wedge . . . go in two directions at once . . . jettison yourself."

Brown once told Rob Baker that, when she took dance composition at Connecticut College, it unnerved her that the instructor (probably Louis Horst) "seemed to want to keep dance from making a compositional first—everything had to be established by the music or by other art forms." Now, it disturbs her that critics are often so beguiled by her unusual compositional structures that they don't deal with the dancing. Which is, I suppose, a bit like defining an important building by talking about its girders instead of the feel of the space it articulates. At any rate, she's working in a different way in these new dances. The forms are more docile; the movement makes its assertions on them rather than vice versa.

Watching the dancing as it pours and spurts and spills around her studio, I think that she has, in some way, circled back to pick up the reckless lust for movement that filled her first dances and is applying to it the luster and formal coherence, the comprehension of simplicity, acquired over years of working at her art.

TWIST THE OPAL—WHAT COLOR NOW?

The Village Voice, November 4–10, 1981

Trisha Brown wears shot silk in *Opal Loop/Cloud Installation #72503.* You see her glinting blue; the next moment the blue has disappeared and she's in mauve; scarcely have you formulated this thought when puddles of blue reappear along the folds. The silk was an inspired choice by costume designer Judith Shea; it's a dandy metaphor both for Brown's dancing and her current compositional processes. Now you see it, now you don't. Watch it under a new light before it ducks, twists, and slips shining into another current.

When Brown dances, a hundred ideas assail her body in the space of a few seconds. Flingshudderscoopupdragtwistreelkickgallop. But none of these is played up. They flood her body—succeeding each other, interrupting each other, happening everywhere at once. So vivid and unusual are some of her fluid gestures that they're like fragments of overheard conversations—something large and complete that has been boiled down, polished, and pulled into silky continuity with a neighbor.

Her new dance, *Son of Gone Fishin',* is the prizewinner for slipperiness. When the curtain goes up on the stage of the Brooklyn Academy of Music's opera house, seven dancers are standing very still in front of a backdrop by Donald Judd—a dark blue cloth dropped halfway down in front of a light blue one. You barely have time to notice that their easygoing dance clothes (Judith Shea again) are made in various combinations of dark blue, light blue, and pale virulent green, before Brown enters in an all-green outfit. As she crosses the front of the stage, the luscious dancing she's spewing out infects whatever dancer she's passing. For a split second that dancer picks up Brown's step-of-the-moment and makes it the first item in his/her own individual phrase. It's like seeing Brown throw off living shadows or functioning as a scanner that makes all it passes bolt into sympathetic action. It's over in a few minutes. Hey, lady, would you mind doing that again, I didn't quite catch your driiiiiiift.

Too late. The stage is a flurry of motion, of quiet dilemmas. Eva Karczag, Lisa Kraus, Diane Madden, Steven Petronio, Vicky Shick, and Randy Warshaw are the intrepid dancers who have to thread their way through this. Everyone is different from everyone else, yet everyone is related: steps you met earlier float to the surface in another corner of the stage, sliding over another person.

All this while there's been musical accompaniment—an almost unheard-of component in a Brown dance. Composer Robert Ashley plays the electric organ; Kurt Munkacsi does some live mixing in the pit. The sound is big and rowdy. A friend said it conjured up a vision of the Yankee Stadium organist on acid. And Beverly Emmons, who has made the stage a luminous field, wittily bathes Ashley with blue and/or green spots, keying him into the color plot. Judd's backcloths start moving. Now we're treated to a pale blue; now to the blue heavy-lidding the green; now to the green alone.

The dancing is full of stumbles and reels; you imagine the floor tilting. Around ten years ago, Brown had dancers walking on walls—roped and pulleyed. What if she's trying to make these dancers *look* as if they're dancing on walls? I wouldn't put it past her. Wrapping their arms around their bodies and swinging them out again (practically at the same time), letting their heads loll and roll, rocketing across the floor into someone else, the dancers look voluptuous, mischievous, and drunk. All at the same time. (I wonder if the drunk look is right. Brown herself always looks alert in her dancing—able to be both purposeful and yielding, taking in the space she's using. Perhaps the complexities of her style tend to make the other dancers focus more narrowly on what their bodies are doing.)

Now watch this. Or try to. There's some doubling up going on. These two people over here are doing the same steps, and those two in the corner, and the guys whipping around in the center. But wait, now one of the upstage people is duplicating one of the downstage people, and everything has shifted. The idea of pairs of dancers separated in space duplicating each others' moves is a thrilling one; your eye has to keep scanning the stage to perceive the teaming up (Twyla Tharp has explored the idea brilliantly too, in her 1969 double quintet, *Group Activities,* and much later in a section of *Ocean's Motion*). Brown keeps changing the pairings, sometimes after the two dancers have done only one move together. Whoops, they've slid apart, if not in space, in their subject matter. Quick, look around the stage and find Karczag's new buddy. There she is in the up left corner! If you peer at the dance intently like this, you can get to feeling pretty proud of yourself. A dance sleuth, by golly. It's more fun, though, to sit back and see the duplications flashing around the stage as if large mirrors were being twisted by invisible hands.

Midway through the dance, Judd's curtains start descending again. And the dance appears to start winding back on itself. Sometimes I thought a perfect retrograde was in operation, other times I wasn't sure. Right at the end, Brown comes back on from where she exited, but she doesn't rewind completely. With an unpredictable splutter and a full stop, the dance ends.

I had been wary about seeing Brown's work in an opera house setting, but her accommodations to a large proscenium stage were impeccable and witty. The quartet *Opal Loop/Cloud Installation #72503* (another essay in doubling, I thought) looked wonderful through its moist billows of sea fog, designed by Fujiko Nakaya. (Brown is from the state of Washington; fog may have been partly responsible for her love for discontinuous visions.) And *Glacial Decoy* (1979) drifted ravishingly in front of its changing array of black-and-white slides by Robert Rauschenberg of familiar things looked at unfamiliarly. When I first saw this dance, I thought only that the dance was too big for the stage frame and that parts of it kept disappearing into the wings. Now I see that the first duet, for Brown and Vicky Shick, shows you only the outside edges of a picture. Brown dances close to the stage-right wings. Shick to stage left. One's appearance usually means the other's disappearance. When Karczag and Kraus jostle about each other in a second duet, we meet the middle. Finally all four dance, and now we see Brown and Shick repeat their opening dance with the missing middle in place. Instead of two women entering and exiting, we see a large picture slipping off the sides of the stage. You could weep with delight.

This time, I even liked Rauschenberg's pleated white tent dresses with bells for sleeves. Emmons's lighting rendered them lighter and more transparent, and the combination of their prettiness with the gentle rambunctiousness of the movement became quite engaging. I remembered being sent off to birthday parties in my organdy dress and coming home with rips in it because I'd tried to follow the boys over the fence.

In the end, the only trouble with seeing Brown's work on a stage like this is not being close enough to see the movement intimately and to cherish the individuality of the performers.

AT HOME IN THE BODY

The Village Voice, January 3, 1977

ᴡᴡ

I never saw Simone Forti during the days when she was also Simone Morris and later Simone Whitman. I've read some of her early dances in her *Handbook of Motion* and tried out a couple of the ones that don't require boards and rope and stuff. I understand her as brainy and playful, but seriously playful like a child, not at all whimsical.

Many years later, here she is, a woman more at home in her body than almost anyone I can think of. Even if I hadn't read her book, I think I'd know that she had gone back—beyond responses learned in childhood—to understand the roots of standing, lying, crawling, to feel her own connections with the ground and the effects of altering the plumb line of her spine.

At the Kitchen last week she didn't dance very much. She sat quietly on the floor watching while Peter Van Riper paced around playing his soprano sax. Tensing his body for the long, tight cries; easing up to play the little shaking notes that cluster around one important tone and then move on to surround another. After he played a thumb piano for a while, Forti moved out into the open space; everything about her looked round and solid—her body, her face (hard to see always behind that pretty, unruly mop of hair). But she's not solid in the sense of unyielding. At the Kitchen she began by rolling. Other people's rolls are dry ghosts of this one. Why couldn't I say for sure where it started? In her right shoulder, I think. And that made her upper back settle into the floor and her head turn to the right. And then her hips responded to the twist in her waist and gently tugged her knees along. I saw her as if I were close beside her, noting with curiosity details like the brief tense scrabble of fingers on floor while she eased into position to roll again. I'd imagine that Forti always indulges fully (never overindulges) in what she does—enjoying her perception of all component parts but never losing the flow of the whole thing.

What else did she do? Sat still—alert, but relaxed. Held two poses—one standing, one crouched, hands reaching out without urgency. Crawled—feeling and showing the soft, strong pull between right-front and left-rear, left-front and right-rear. All the time in the world . . . Once, she took her right hand off the floor, and, as if her weight had been equally distributed between four points, acknowledged the sudden imbalance by toppling over. You could say that not much happened; or you could say that within a few concrete actions, everything happened.

After intermission, she on a trombone, Van Riper on his saxophone played friendly challenges to each other. She very calm, looking amused, while he ran in tiny cartoon-Japanese steps to exchange the sax for an affair made of plumber's pipe—the long, small blown-into part gradually made to end in an immense elbow-joint. He rested it on the floor and created deep, musical farts that undercut her trombone. Then dragged the thing back and exchanged it for the sax, then changed again. Finally, decided to stop: "You've hurt yourself!" said Forti. Yeah, cut his lip on his new monster. So while she watched, he sat cross-legged in front of a mike and gently shook two of those chiming baby rattles—producing by skill and chance a subtle continuum of shifting accents.

TO DRIP, PERCHANCE

TO STEAM

The Village Voice, February 18–24, 1981

▾▾

David Gordon always makes us laugh, doesn't he? We snicker over the sophisticated wordplay that the dancers in his PickUp Co. are so clever at, titter over provocative juxtapositions of music and/or speech and/or movement, chuckle over how shrewdly Gordon pushes things around within the immaculate form of his dances. He can make us believe that anything is something else, that perhaps it's only our perspective that makes events what they seem to be. Those aren't such funny ideas.

Although his new *Profile* (the first of Dance Theatre Workshop's Winter Events) draws, certainly, a nothing-to-sneeze-at amount of hahas and teehees from audiences, it's very serious. More sober in tone than anything I've seen of Gordon's, and—to me—extremely poignant. As usual, Gordon places old material next to new stuff, as if to take stock of the glints one casts on the other. In this case, the sense that rises like mist from the circuitous trails of words and jostling bits of brilliance has to do with leaving and—with luck—coming back home, with love misprized or misunderstood, with people who—despite good intentions—cast others in the role of victim or play the victim themselves.

Gordon himself, looking glum and slow, performs a liquid shambling solo near the beginning of the piece; then, until nearly the end, he stands on the sidelines with other unengaged dancers or blends in with the crowd. This in itself is unusual; usually he seems to be playing, with enormous enjoyment, the role of manipulator and creator, even of star. In *Profile*, he has the air of observing something he has set, willy-nilly, in motion.

Most of the movement in *Profile* consists of dancers doing big, plain actions—lunging, leaning, toppling, walking—or moving to a position, or negotiating some business with another dancer, holding that pose—perhaps commenting on it—and moving on. In "Double Identity," Susan Eschelbach, Margaret Hoeffel, and Keith Marshall stand in a line facing us to announce, one by one, "Susan as Susan," "Keith as Keith," "Margaret as Margaret." Gradually they move into dancerly anonymity: Susan standing in Keith's place *is,* for all practical purposes "Keith." Margaret may eventually have to say, "Margaret as Susan as Keith as Margaret as Susan as Keith." Where you stand determines who you are; what you do announces your role. Pretty soon Margaret, with a hand on each of the other's backs, is saying "Margaret as Mother, as Terra Firma . . ." Then it's "Susan as victim" (and other synonymous objects) slung around by Margaret and Keith. Margaret and Keith can briefly become "Lovers," Susan an "Abandoned Woman," who was a second earlier a "Woman abandoned."

Another less loaded kind of anonymity occurs when the dancers all stand in a big wedge, counting long, unlikely sequences, while "soloists" take turns performing parts of what could be one long, matter-of-fact phrase. And although at the beginning of the evening, each dancer has entered with a swatch of solo material (related, I think, to some prearranged grabbag of solo material, but feathered with individuality), and each has had his or her name projected onto a background, there is a melancholy and sardonic perception of them as interchangeable. Often they function as chorus, conferring mass status on, or adding bulk to, what have earlier been shown as individual gestures. Sometimes they're oddly like the grown children of a large family.

Some of the work's most tender moments involve Valda Setterfield. A telephone rings. "Hello," says Setterfield in her gentle, polite English voice, while diligently working through what amounts to an offbeat ballet adagio. All the dancers except Gordon respond, "Hello." Sitting on the floor around her, one or another of them rises from time to time to support Setterfield, touch her, lift her. When she asks, "What have you been doing?" a long babble of voices responds. When they ask her the same question, she says nothing, only continues patiently dancing, as if that is the only possible answer.

She and Margaret Hoeffel exchange quiet reminiscences about their mothers, while lifting and pulling on each other. Their manner toward each other is solicitous yet workaday, their voices conversational, yet although the activity is intimate, not all of it is comfortable (for example, a couple of times one worms her hands up into the other's armpits to hoist her out of the way). The memories aren't all comfortable either. Love and pride inevitably come up against bafflement and awkwardness as the women talk and move. Hoeffel remembers her mother's flair for making clothes for herself and her many sisters, how people would go to church just to see the family's latest outfits. Setterfield remembers that the austere days of wartime England conditioned her mother never to buy anything not serviceable or built to last, so that new clothes and furniture always looked just like the old ones. They have sadder stories to tell. Both women, improvising this dialogue each night out of some deep and private store, go far beyond interesting performing into something that is moving beyond description.

Gordon joins Setterfield for a final dialogue in which single words metamorphose into other words—"slip," say, into "sleep"—often with quietly punning actions to suit. "I'm glad you're back," they say walking backward until they bump. Occasionally the words eddy into intimate dialogue that is both funny and sad, sparring and peaceful. ("What's an eleven-letter word beginning with W that means . . . ?" says Gordon propped up on one elbow beside Setterfield who, unfailingly polite, is much too sleepy to think of an answer. Is it because we know that Gordon and Setterfield *are* married that they seem so exposed in this? The feelings which in Gordon's previous works have been contained and distanced by the pristine structures and unemphatic performing styles here seem as close to us—and as dangerous—as our own.

STAY IN YOUR FLIGHT
PATTERNS, ANGELS

The Village Voice, December 30 – January 5, 1982

ᴧᴧᴧ

At this season of the year, some people sit around fires and read Dickens and St. Luke aloud; some make their annual pilgrimage to George Balanchine's *The Nutcracker,* ideally holding a four-foot-tall initiate by the hand. These are both good ways of affirming continuity and ignoring the disaster signs all over the place. Others, of a different turn of mind, might have found more comfort in the Lucinda Childs–Jon Gibson–Robert Wilson collaboration, *Relative Calm,* at BAM.

Childs makes dances about order, about perseverance, about knowing your place, about being content with little and turning it into a lot. The eight dancers know their places; in each of the work's three group sections, each dancer has a spot on the floor—a home base to return to after each voyage. Their paths have been plotted with a geometer's care. Their blameless patterns roll on in steady rhythms, through sheafs of steps that, at their most complicated, can make you think of an innocent, underdeveloped form of ballet. They never touch each other or come any closer to each other than their fixed orbits permit; the illusion of allegiances calmly shifting, of changes being made, of groups dividing are all by-products of design, not images of volition.

At the beginning of the piece, the dancers can be seen through a scrim, dressed in white, sitting in their places, knees drawn up, all facing the same corner of the stage. Gibson's music—played live an on tape—is a powerful hum at this point. Wilson sets a crescent moon sliding on the scrim while an unreal universe of stars drifts downward behind the dancers. Scrim up, stars stilled, the dancers muster themselves into the parallel diagonal paths that they will travel on for the whole of this first section, called "Rise." Jumay Chu, Meg Harper, Daniel McCusker, Priscilla Newell, Andé Peck, Garry Reigenborn, Carol Teitelbaum, Tertius Walker. They begin quietly and simply. Walks, small hops and skips that make a lilt in the steady pulse, swings of the arms, turnarounds, rests. Now these four move, now the four, six here, two there, all eight. Matters of gender swim into focus only when four men suddenly move as a unit, four women as another. Your eye travels around and around in the pattern, enjoying the small surprises. Childs's logic isn't leaden; you never can predict exactly who will move next and who will drop out.

Some of the harmonies in Gibson's music—its ringing organ tones rising, smearing, melting, tumbling above the piano's hammered rhythms—make me think of fine old hymn tunes, now iced by repetition into components of an intergalactic anthem. Gradually, the dancers increase the scale of their movements, the density of their phrases, the frequency with which each joins the action. Within their defined limits, they are flying.

When, in "Race," the dancers wear colors, work in pairs that spell each other in quartets, begin to walk in curves, the change seems momentous, although I found this section the least interesting. Wilson beams white circles onto the backdrop in rhythmic patterns. The circles are all made of three not-quite-joined segments, and one of the most striking effects is a timed trip of, I think, five of these; they wink on in sequence, and the last one appears to hit a segmented stick. A sentence appears, telling us that Andé (Peck) is a good man who wouldn't just walk off with someone else's dog. Another sentence tells us that Rose is looking for someone and is distressed. And, in fact, the next time Peck enters dancing, he has a cheerful white dog on a leash; he doesn't look at all sorry to return the dog to a little girl who walks out on stage, reaches out for the leash and takes the dog away.

The dog episode is like a watermark on the dance's surface; it spits a little bit of history at you, makes you wonder about things, briefly undermines the dancer's anonymity and the vision you've begun to have of them as tireless cosmic marathoners. A less pleasant shock occurs near the end of the first section when a light way at the back, and almost out of sight overhead, fizzles out a shower of orange sparks, as if to remind us that the calm is, afer all, only relative.

Child's solo, "Reaches," premiered last spring, is one of the most intriguing I've seen her do. Without any of the light, dry skipping that looks so aloof when she performs it. In this, she travels back and forth on a diagonal path, beginning with only a few steps in each direction before turning back, and, according to private rules, enlarging her scope and pulling it in again. To change directions, she swings her arms, sometimes in big wrenches that could pull her off-balance. The irregularity, the slight, jolting drama of her progress contrasts with Gibson's sustained saxophone notes and the slowly altering wedges of light (shaped like crescendo and decrescendo signs) that now echo, now cross her path.

The last part, "Return" is the most vivid. Wilson's segmented lines and curves almost tweed the backdrop, so dense and active are they. Each of the dancers—now dressed in deep blue jumpsuits by Carol Murashige— has a spot on the stage pricked out by a small circle of light, but each also has a wing to enter from and exit into. So the dancers regularly appear and disappear. They enter walking swiftly backward in curves, or forward; you always know where each will come from and what he/she will be doing, yet the double-tidal pattern is even more full of mild surprises than "Rise": overlaps, empty places, moments when certain dancers will execute a leap a second before certain others and make the stage picture flare.

The audience is divided. Some people have left before the end of the ninety-four-minute, intermissionless piece. Most clap and cheer. A man says, surprised, to his companion, "That's the worst concert I've ever seen!" I feel as if I've been offered a lesson on the beauties of order, and freedom within limits. The night air outside the theater is not more bracing, pure, or burning cold.

WHERE CHANCE AND CHOICE COLLIDE

The Village Voice, June 14, 1976

At one point during a rehearsal of his *Lazy Madge,* Douglas Dunn stares at the dancers who are waiting patiently for instructions. He's been turning out movement at a steady pace for about two hours. Now he deftly shifts the ball to them, asking for three individual activities—like tying a shoe, drinking water. But he doesn't want these pantomimes clear: They're to be sketched out, barely indicated, blurred around the edges. More like thinking about what you're going to do than doing it. I'm interested in the way his instructions gently tug the dancers away from the comfort of their own easy outs. Like many choreographers of his generation, Dunn uses Merce Cunningham as a kind of reference point—accepting as a given that one dances about dancing. But one of the things that makes Dunn one of the most interesting choreographers around is that he shows—Dunn seems particularly interested in showing (on virtuoso dancers and in a noncommittal context)—some of what the human body reveals when it is ill at ease, hesitant, off-guard, making choices.

This has always, I think, been a feature of his solos. (*Lazy Madge* is, in effect, his first substantial group piece.) After seeing *Gestures in Red,* I wrote that Dunn looked like a man you could trust. And then spent a lot of time wondering what I meant by that. I was pretty sure it had only a little to do with his level gaze, his casual demeanor, his lean well-made face and body (he could probably play Robert Redford better than Redford does). Now I think I was responding to the fact that his dancing seems so much a process of testing forces or monitoring space. When he launches into something risky or totally surprising, I still sense it as the product of some decision: "Now, if I shifted my pelvis a little more to the left, what would I have to do if I didn't want to fall?" Unlike some dancers, he doesn't do all his testing in a studio, so that he can ask the audience to accept only a glittering result unencumbered by effort. He doesn't present A Balance (with appropriate fanfare), but a man in the act of balancing. So . . . a man you can trust. Like the butcher who grinds the hamburger where the customer can see it.

Dunn began choreographing five or six years ago—while he was still dancing in Merce Cunningham's company. He's done a lot of different

---

kinds of things, been involved in some provocative collaborations (with Sara Rudner, David Gordon, David Woodberry), continued to work with the Grand Union—the improvisatory group that developed out of Yvonne Rainer's company. He won't allow himself to forget that the point isn't so much to formulate answers as it is to keep asking new questions. Nor is he reluctant to push things to extremes. (At one of the last performances the Grand Union gave in this city, Dunn entered in his underwear and took a good half hour to get dressed and some more time stretching a rope across the performing area and getting people in the audience to hold it or tie it for him. Treating preparation for performance as performance material too.)

What Dunn is doing today is adding a group section to *Lazy Madge* for the performances at 541 Broadway on June 11 to 13 and 18 to 20. "A grand finale?" I ask. He laughs a lot. And says, "Exactly." While we sit in his pleasant, rather Spartan loft (efficient kitchen, bathroom, work table, studio, but only one easy chair plus a few foam mattresses stacked, discouragingly, against the wall), waiting to see what dancers will show up, he shows me a bunch of papers, a score of *Lazy Madge*. You mean a record? No. Jennifer Mascall, one of the dancers in *Lazy Madge*, is making a book of choreographers' private notation systems—drawings, notes, whatever. Dunn had never thought about such things, but he got interested. He gave poet Annabel Levitt some of the little notebooks he jots things down in all the time; she ordered the material into categories (like "death," "choreography," "phone numbers"), and arranged them into poems. Poems whose speculative, adventurously rambling structure is analogous to that of *Lazy Madge:* ". . . first I do it standing, and now I do it taking a shit, now I do it kicking horses . . .") They reveal the contents of Doug's mind, filtered through another sensibility, just as the dance reveals his material through decisions imposed by the dancers. Up to now, Dunn has choreographed material for them one at a time, inevitably zeroing in on their individual energies. He's made a few duets or trios. He doesn't set his own part except for moments of contact in a duet (safety first). The dancers then decide individually in performance what to do when. Every performance has been, will be, different from every other one.

Douglas Dunn didn't begin dancing until his junior year in college. He likes this story: He was staying on the Princeton campus over a vacation to finish an overdue paper, and a friend took him to visit a professor of Chinese literature, a remarkable man—then very ill, dying, they thought—who had embarked on a project which involved studying each of the arts for two years. He said to Doug almost immediately, "Have you ever taken ballet class?" Doug forgot the conversation, but the professor recovered, got Doug to the local ballet school, and that was that. Dunn, hooked, spent one summer at Jacob's Pillow ("Margaret Craske, La Meri, Ted Shawn—I'd never even *heard* of them"), came to New York in the summer of 1968 and by fall was working with Yvonne Rainer. Sometime after that, he began to dance in Merce Cunningham's company, too.

Dunn tuned in instantly, unhesitatingly, to what Cunningham was doing with the very first class he took at the studio. A technique that had clarity and discipline, but room to move around in. Dancing from which every-thing deliberately allusive had been sheared. "It was freeing for me. I wasn't worried about art, I wasn't worried about anything anymore. I just wanted to do that dancing." Dunn admires—as I'd have guessed—the look of Merce Cunningham dancing: the alertness, the upright posture. "It's so . . . civilized," he says—meaning Cunningham's view of the human body. He can remember a time when he identified so closely with Cunningham himself that he said backstage to Carolyn Brown, "I'm not interested in dancing how I am now. I want to dance the way Merce is dancing now. I want to be that old in my dancing." (And he laughs at himself: "Not to mention that skilled, or anything. . . .")

For a long time, Dunn was content just to work at dancing, but even-tually he began to wonder about performing. He had never felt an urge to be up on stage; he had simply wanted to dance, and here he was doing a lot of performing. What was that all about? Finding it made more sense to him to examine the fact of performance "when it didn't have to do with just doing your steps," he began to make dances without much dancing in them. In one of the sections he contributed to a collaborative piece with Rudner in 1971, he lay spread-eagled on the floor while Rudner held three-minute poses on his back. ("Sara *hated* doing it.") Another section had to do with his hanging her up on a block and tackle. And more still-nesses. During the first part of his solo *Time Out*, Dunn—for about a half hour—fitted his body into a corner of the room, checking out all his own joints and bending points, holding each pose. (He says he found himself doing this one day in Paris in a gallery event organized by Robert Wilson. Perhaps it reflected the fact that he was living in a very small hotel room and had nowhere to work.) He set up *Four for Nothing* (1974) so that four performers would have to cope with being in a space with almost nothing to do. An empty space that would, in a way, stay empty, because so much of what was going on was going on inside the performers. Then he went to another kind of extreme in *101*—filled the space of his studio with an astonishing splintery maze and lay in it for four hours almost every day over a period of weeks. On view. Exhibiting himself in the most factual and unequivocal way, and—since he had decided he would not move nor speak nor open his eyes—laying himself open to being treated as an object. Many people spoke to him, although only on the very last day did any kind of hostile teasing or touching occur. He became, in a sense, not only the "performance," but also the audience of our thoughts and our creaking progress.

Like many choreographers today, Dunn hasn't much interest in repertory. If you missed his joint concert with David Gordon in which the two of them batted 200 individually conceived mini-phrases (100 each) back and forth like a conversation, well, you missed it. The same with the straightforward, but wonderfully unusual lifts and carries he and David Woodberry worked out in their collaborative event. His extraordinary *Gestures in Red* is portable, though, and so—decidedly—is *Lazy Madge.* As least for as long as it continues to interest Dunn and his collaborators.

The 2 p.m. "grand finale" rehearsal is amazing to me. Now I understand, almost, something Dunn said earlier about *Lazy Madge,* about "treating the impulse to make a dance as an autonomous impulse—even separate, in a way, from some kind of plan." He's trying to do a minimum of preparation and to keep the dance steadily growing, flowing on. At 2, he sets Jennifer Mascall and Dana Roth, two tall women, inching along the floor on all fours. By about 2:45, he's poured out a long contrapuntal sequence that brings them together, standing shoulder to shoulder. He stares a minute. Christina Grasso-Caprioli and Daniel Press have just come up the stairs and are fiddling with their leg warmers and doing desultory pliés. Okay. Next minute he's got Christina jumping into Jennifer and Dana's arms. Now Dunn has a lot of options: they can set her down, they can . . . but here's Daniel, and now Ellen Webb, too, waiting on the sidelines. He asks them to run in and swoop Christina away from the other two and carry her off like a battering ram. That's the way it goes all afternoon. Jennifer has to leave the rehearsal, so she leaves the dance for the day. Ruth Alpert arrives and walks right into the choreography. When Michael Bloom comes in much later, full of beans, Dunn catapults him into the tired herd with a jump. For four and a half hours, there is only one official break and very few pauses. Dunn is very precise about what he wants ("Lay your hands along a forty-five-degree beveled hill"—I like that one), but not finicky about instant perfection, more attentive to force and direction than to shape. As he thinks, he ruffles his yellow hair, rubs his face pink, slides to the floor, wanders through the dancers making little feints and jabs at the air (at the dance?). Absolutely, and calmly, *refusing* to run dry. Or to fiddle too much with what he's doing. His process demonstrates potently—although it doesn't explain—that however startling his movement, however much it veers from the large to the small, the clear to the sloughed-off, the fast to the slow, the calm to the violent, it never has that self-conscious "what-if-I-scratched-my-nose-now?" look that some post-Cunningham choreographers achieve. It is dance at the moment it is being danced. A pretty sound image of life as it is being lived.

STILL CHANGING THE RULES

The Village Voice, June 15, 1982

Maybe nice isn't the right word to describe how it felt to have Steve Paxton and Douglas Dunn performing on the same weekend. "Satisfying" or "arousing"—or both—might serve better; "nice" seldom is the right word anyway. Why mention them together at all? Because they both danced with Merce Cunningham and cadged from him some useful ideas about what a dance doesn't have to be, and because they performed together in Yvonne Rainer's company and in the Grand Union, where they taught us, and probably themselves, some useful facts about performance. That, for instance, performance is anything you do in front of an audience the minute you begin to do it in front of audience, that the performance "set" is unavoidable for viewers and doers alike, that trying to "perform" what you're already performing can as easily conceal what you're doing as enhance it.

And, for both Paxton and Dunn, coming into dance when they did (reaching good form in the 1960s) and with the intelligence they had, they did not have to coat their dancing with Masculinity as many male dancers of the '50s did. Beginning in the '60s, gender was something you had—like a good turnout or a tendency to sweat a lot. The influence was undeniable, why assert it?

Both choreographers, in these recent concerts, surprised me—did things I hadn't thought to see them do, and did them in striking and thoroughly accomplished ways.

The solo evenings of Paxton's that I've seen in the last few years were composed of a series of improvised sets, very low-keyed. Musician David Moss would play. Paxton would dance, often with an amazing slippery grace and always sensitively tuned to the feel of things (his body in that room on that night with us watching and Moss playing). In these concerts at the Kitchen, Paxton subtly offered connections, themes, emotions in the series of seemingly discrete events he calls *Bound*.

Actually, *Bound* refers to the mix of dancing, which Paxton labels "sinuous/pendular systems," and sound, a recorded array of stuff ranging from traffic and CB static and the explosive pops of hands clapped at a microphone to Bulgarian folk songs and "Napoli" played by a band. But "boundness" is a concept that keeps cropping up. The four pillars at the Kitchen are wrapped in camouflage fabric; a rectangle of the same fabric hangs on the wall just where the image from a slide projector will hit. Does hit, because Paxton walks in, switches it on, and stands framed in the welter of spots it adds to. He's boxed in another way too; suspenders hold a cardboard carton around his hips. As he shambles across the gaudy rectangle of light, or stretches and shifts awkwardly in the cramped space, he fumbles to let down the flaps of the carton and enlarge it.

When he dances, minus the carton, but with a bright green bathing cap (sort of) on his head, he also looks restricted. He keeps twisting and wheeling and lurching, monitoring the state of his balance, keeping things moving smoothly. I know a smooth lurch sounds impossible, but he never quite falls or loses control. Some other part of his body takes over from one that's been too bold, and sends him in another direction. But he keeps his feet stepping closely around each other, and sometimes he lifts his shoulders as if he's trying to make himself narrow in a tight place. The CB sound is abrasive, uncommunicative.

He brings in a large white rocking chair and a white cradle and sits between them. Takes off the green cap and rubs his hair free. Is this the point at which a very slow, mournful Bulgarian song is heard? Perhaps. Anyway, he sits there carefully rocking the cradle, the chair, turning his attention soberly from one to the other. He watches one die down, starts it up, gets the other going. The behavior and the act are curiously at odds: he looks as if he were trying to discover something about rocking, but what that is may be either something so simple he already knows it or something that is unknowable.

Anyway, he does that for a while.

At some point he reappears in white clothes. At some point he removes the camouflage screen, and the projector reveals a splendid picture (could be a Rauschenberg). To a lovely Bulgarian dance tune, he dances. His uncanny softness-in-athleticism is given full play. Bound now by the music, he capers with wild sobriety, capitulating to the beat and the festiveness in ways that are both wise and naïve and make the audience laugh.

But, to end, he puts on another green cap—one that has a cord running through it that's attached to the Kitchen's west and east walls. And he moves east, carefully, sliding along that rope into a small iris of a white light. Those of us sitting near his path receive the full impact of his intent gaze and pale, pale eyes.

In his time, Douglas Dunn has radically varied the amount of movement in his works—none, some, lots—and the amount and degree of compositional control he has wanted to assume. He puts more beautiful and unusual dancing into the hour that *Game Tree* lasts than most choreographers can produce in several years, yet the work doesn't seem at all profuse or busy or aimless. More than in any other piece of his, I was aware of sturdy old compositional techniques being reevaluated and made to serve in timely ways. When Susan Blankensop, Grazia Della-Terza, John McLaughlin, and Deborah Riley first accumulate in one of the corners of St. Mark's Danspace, they're all working with the same parcel of dancing. I don't think they're in strict canon, and they turn every which way in space, but the same held-up fists, wide stances, turns and springs hustle through the group, popping out now here, now there. Dunn and Diane Frank incite the whole group to unison. Much later, there's a great wheel of duets: some of the people progress around the edge of the room. Encountering a partner, they engage in one of several possible patterns. One is fairly calm, a back-to-back leaning and twining; the other can be scrambly, with dancers paddling and crouching on the floor as if this were some game they must try to race each other through. Have you won if you get the other guy neatly draped across your thigh?

There's also a section in which one trio dances closely and energetically, while another rearranges itself in curious tableaux in the corners. The poses don't signify anything obvious, but they're fraught with meaning and your eyes keep sneaking over to them.

While in *Game Tree* Dunn pays unprecedented attention to the niceties of form—to how the space is organized, to how the dancers combine with each other, to how movement motifs are passed around or themes disassembled and remade—nothing is slick or predictable. This may be partly because there's nothing predictable about the movement. As you watch, you begin to believe that you'll never pin this down, that anything *could* occur. There are choreographers (Dan Wagoner is one) who will drop from an elegant movement into a clumsy one and enjoy the jolt. Dunn makes the bodies of his dancers keep graining the movement so that it becomes something else very subtly, and is gone almost before you can pin it down. As you're thinking that perhaps the essence of Dunn's style is long-legged precision, you'll notice how prominent the arm gestures are. You'll see ease and skill, and then someone will deliberately stumble over his own feet. You'll notice that the dancers aren't touching each other, and the next minute Frank and Blankensop will lean on each other, and when they finish that and leave, Dunn and McLaughlin will take turns to dive at each other and be lifted. You'll characterize the dancers as coolly absorbed in the business of dancing these patterns, and then an increase in speed, a ripping gesture of someone's arms, a flung-back head will grip you the way a drama does. I've never known anything like it.

Quite a few of the dancers—all splendid—seemed to tire quickly the night I saw *Game Tree*. They perform more intelligently than many dancers, knowing how and when to show you the effort of turning rather than the image of it, the act of stretching rather than the fact of a stretched leg. But sometimes I feel them shy away from shaping the trajectory of a gesture fully, as if they were afraid that that might lead to an inappropriate finesse.

Patrick O'Rourke filled the space with a clear, white light—uncompromising, but not harsh. Linda Fisher's *Aurora*, realized in performance, created a sparse, but vivid, sound environment. Silence, voices electronically elongated fumbling through words, sharp little explosions like those in a shooting gallery—these are some of the things I remember. During the piece, the dancers, one by one, very gradually add a piece of black clothing to the bright, straightforward practice clothes they're wearing. The adding of black marks off the time of the piece. Grazia Della-Terza is getting into black as the others fall, rise, walk off. She walks out into the center of the space, falls. And doesn't get up. That's the end.

Dunn is a man who uses things up. He had a show in the loft he's leaving. What's there? Empty shelves, polished floor. Words for sale ("Restraint is the graciousness of not crowding the world with all of what one thinks and feels and implies the possibility of choice in action . . .") on scores and scrolls and folded squares. All the dust has been framed. At least I think it has; I've never seen such pretty dust. Thick, soft whorls of it in little for-sale frames look like everything from gray storm clouds to blotched paper. A big, good-looking paste-up on the wall contains all sorts of stuff—a family snapshot, but mostly torsos of women, stone and dug-up or flesh and photographed. Then, beyond the strips of white paper that curtain the front of the loft, a high tilted "bed." Packed into it, invisible as you approach, a man and woman. Partly buried in white cotton, net, satin, he (white) sprawls stiffly in a loincloth, she (black), in a clumsy nightdress, settles with one arm under her head. They're both staring at the ceiling. The goods half unpacked. Post-coital dolls. He will not carry them to his new home.

LIBRARY ST. MARY'S COLLEGE

OUR ONLY DANCING
PHILOSOPHER?

The Village Voice, July 5, 1976

~~~

When I waylay Kenneth King at a pay phone and tell him I want to write about him and his new dance, *Battery, a Tribute to Susanne K. Langer,* he smiles deprecatingly and says that he wishes I'd write something about Susanne Langer instead, that he has been hoping *Battery* would act as a catalyst for more pondering/discussing/honoring the work of Langer ("Maybe," he once wrote me, "our only American sage . . . Why isn't she BEAST-seized with followers?")

Cripes, Kenneth, I'm not equipped to discuss Langer, although I certainly agree that she's one of the few major philosophers to take dance seriously. I can be awed, comforted, and challenged by her theory of art as symbolic form, negotiating insight into the *felt* structure of inner life. (You see, the waters are already closing over my head.)

Kenneth King isn't easy to discuss either. He's our only danseer/wri(gh)ter, our only metapolitical choreographer, the only person I know who's consciously exploring the subtle connections between dancing and linguistics *in performance,* a versatile actor—adept at disguises, and one of the most remarkable dancers around.

He's always been an interesting performer. I remember him when he arrived in New York with a degree in philosophy from Antioch and—between 1964 and 1967 at places like Judson Church and Dance Theatre Workshop—presented fascinating, faintly glamorous dance-theater pieces. Hot subjects coolly dissected and presented with a blankness that was both fashionable and radical. But in 1968, King started laying the groundwork for a different kind of dance theater. Beginning, I think, by spinning, he built his own movement lexicon. He often dances nonstop for long periods of time. His feet runslideskiphopjump with marvelous ease and lightness, he seems to skim the floor. His long, fine body twists and bends, powering his arms and hands to send out small, quick gestures and sketch out curves in the space around him.

However, dancing is usually only one component of a Kenneth King work. For instance, in *Inadmissleable Evidentdance* (1973), he read aloud from Nietzsche, disguised as Pontease Tyak, the Custodian for the TransHimalayan Society for Interplanetary Research (King enjoys this kind of joking)—the noble words coming wryly in a heavy, all-purpose

Slavic accent from behind a huge gray beard topped by dark glasses. In *Ultimate Exposé* (1975), he first appeared as Mater Harry, an androgynous spy in a blond wig, smoking, trembling behind an open fan, and, in a Hungarian voice, muttering tales of corruption.

Whether King reads, or someone else reads, or he switches on a taped voice, his pieces often swarm with words. And since he means those words to be understood on many levels, he sometimes bombards them with extra syllables, blasts them apart, puts them together again in provocative or lustily witty ways, so that they yield up all their implications and reveal facts about their structure. The text for *Metagexis* (1973) consisted of complex speculations on linguistics, read at one point by three people, while King and others danced. The wordplay was dazzling: " 'Isn't it odd that the ID is hid?'/ (('Isn't it OD that is (h)id?')/'THE OD ISN'T AS O D D AS THE ID!!'/ ((This is a (c)ODe to the OD(d) and the (h)ID.))." The texts of *Inadmissleable Evidentdance* and *Ultimate Exposé* dealt with government conspiracies, the devious doing of the NSA and the CIA, who were keeping under wraps inventions like the Master Control Panel, which could revolutionize existing communications media, and Mesmex, a new energy fuel that could eliminate the need for wires to convey electricity.

Now, however, when I want to ask Kenneth about the Telaxic Synapsulator, his metamachine that can cure radioactivity, he says gently, "Please, I think we should talk about Susanne Langer."

But King's concern with langauge *is* related to Langer. "I know dance is nondiscursive," he says, "but we process our perceptions linguistically. Language is bound up with how we see in ways we're not even aware of. And often when I do a movement, words come to mind—not because the movement *means* them, but because the gestures, the act of dancing, become a reflective device." This last certainly relates to ideas Langer put forth in her two volumes of *Mind,* concerning the role of primitive choric dance and work chants in stimulating the frontal lobes of the brain to invent symbolic thought. King uses words like *syntax* and *grammar* when he talks about dance. He profoundly admires Merce Cunningham for his brilliance in mapping out a dance language not burdened by meanings, yet a whole field for meaning. And King's dancing is usually as nonspecific as Cunningham's.

When he puts words *with* his dancing, it's in order to frame it in some way, to make clearer those dance-language connections that intrigue him. Sometimes his texts—certainly *Metagexis,* he acknowledges—are too dense to be picked up on the run by a dance audience. About all you can do then is see his dancing as a symbol for the intricacy of thought and the flow of ideas. In *Ultimate Exposé* he needed clarity, and wisely projected key words before he spoke them.

To King, dancing reflects all the movement of the world (that of tides, ideas, and so on, as well as living things). He says it better: "Naturally dancing is always disclosing hidden confluences, concurrent patterns, corresponding analogies, larger connections, unsuspected configurations—revelations, even—about events . . ." Perhaps this is, in part, what he means when he says "My dancing does contain a seercret code"; and, watching him dance, you can easily believe he transmits and receives messages from who knows where. The function of the dancer as a medium for prophecy is ancient and honorable, but today's danseer has more to reveal than the will of the gods. Our new all-powerful (and capricious) gods live in White Houses and mastermind giant corporations and government agencies. They've spawned demons they can't control. No wonder today's dancing prophet must be a seercret agent, a master of disguise, a dealer in metaphors. The dervishes whirl down blessings: Kenneth predicts Watergate. He did, too—in an early version of *Inadmissleable Evidentdance* presented at a WBAI benefit: "I wasn't sure what I was doing; I just felt certain in myself that the words I was saying were right. And when Watergate broke, two years later, Bill Dunas and Jeff Norwalk knocked on my door at four in the morning and said. "You *were* right!" He sounds amazed still.

The disguises he traffics in are as proper to a man of the theater as to an undercover agent. But King's characters often run through several dances, and they're very close to him. The dancers in *Battery* say that during a rehearsal break when they were gabbing about having kids, Kenneth convulsed them by saying poker-faced that he had two children, both thirty (possibly Mater Harry and Harry Hoodwink).

"Personas allow us to express things we couldn't as ourselves," says K.K. (Parenthetically, I think he's a shy man, and needs to maintain a certain elusiveness. Although he's frank and great fun to talk to, Kenneth doesn't like to be telephoned; you have to leave messages for him at a variety of places and arrange for assignations.) "Personas give us a frame of reference. It's a way of embodying figments—portions of a fantasy—in concrete expressive form." Interestingly, others have played Pontease Tyak while Kenneth played someone else or himself, which suggests that the persona is independent—some part of King that, instead of remaining simply a mental set, has been disembodied and (we're hot on the trail now) re-embodied. And . . .

"Could we get back to Susanne Langer?" I hear you, Kenneth. No personas in *Battery* and not a single word spoken.

It all connects, though. At a rehearsal at Synod House of St. John the Divine, where the piece is to be performed, Kenneth talks to the dancers about clarifying in their gestures whether they are dealing with signs or with signals, denoting or connoting. Much of the dance will involve improvisation: The dancers have a set of options through which they can manipulate a given vocabulary. For instance, in the series of clear, plain arm and body positions which the dancers call "the clocks," King defies as a *code* "all the ways the arms and legs need to be in opposition or together with the pulse, while *patterns* "are uncovered by putting together the coded possibilities." It's these patterns that aren't isolable from the dance, that come into being at the instant they're performed. (Take my word for it: This is thinking Langeresquely.)

Kenneth is gentle, but now and then frustration takes over his voice. Running easily, in his sweatpants, shirt, and the headband he always wears, he calls out, "I'm not warmed up properly. I can't really do it. But *please* don't let the energy drop!" As if he sensed his own function as a kind of transmitter.

For the performance, an immense empty leather chair sits near the audience, the two published volumes of *Mind* on one arm, a small Buddha on the other, a candle and flowers and a small lettered quote on the floor. All honor to our sages. Why should they be denied glamorous presentation or stage-door johnnies? In the warm dimness of the big room, the eleven dancers enter one by one and begin to execute a sequence of arm gestures so slowly that if you pan around the deep space—barely able to see the people on the little stage at the back—you catch them at almost frozen moments, and sometimes a raised arm *does* seem to be signaling "wait," and sometimes it is just a raising arm (and all that can convey). Sometimes, almost, the dancers echo in passing the shapes of the superb art, ancient and modern, glowing from two slide projectors. Some of the dancers feed into a slow horizontal procession, whose peaceful deliberate attitudes suggest a ritual. As the "clocks" appear in their most basic form, six of the dancers revolve a clump of three transparent screens of differing sizes. Although these screens later spread apart to *frame* (aha!) parts of the action, I now see circles everywhere. Four people walking calmly shoulder to shoulder trace a border of immaculate individual circles around the room. For a long time a moving frame of people outlines the space—they're rolling, turning, making Texas Stars, creating a centipede of scalloping paths around each other. The distant vibrating, ebbing, and flowing sound of William Tudor's tape is joined at some point by an insistent changing two-unit phrase played by Pierre Ruiz on his violin. The dancers increase their trajectories through space. They embellish the "clocks" with more small, vibrating "telegraphic" gestures. They begin to jump and run with the movement. Like the spies of his other dances, they clearly transmit and receive, marvelous sensors just for the current of dancing. The first night, Karen Levey is transfigured—all her antennae are out, and King seems everywhere at once—closing in on other dancers, picking up or reinforcing their gestures, dogging their steps. A kind of walking whirlpool of dancers develops, and all the arm gestures we've seen are tossed up on its currents. The dancers spread skeins of movements over the floor—stunningly complex, yet quiet and clear. The light has intensified as the dance gathers power, and together they fade peacefully.

I sense that in *Battery* King has created an act of homage by giving some of Langer's principles visible form. A prism refracting the structures of thought. But I don't know. I've never tried to explain anything about Kenneth King before. I have been stimulated/stupefied/bored/deeply moved by his work, but what I understand of it I've picked out of the air (I've no doubt his mind resonates more powerfully than most). Langer, now in her eighties and at work on a third volume of *Mind*, saw the first part of *Battery* when it was premiered last May. I hope she liked it. She may have many worse exegetes than Kenneth King who has said—and without hubris—"I Am Truth's Dancing Partner."

A friendly letter from Kenneth King and a not-so-friendly one from musician Pierre Ruiz informed me that Ruiz's part in Battery *had not been simply that of an accompanist, but that of a collaborator. I couldn't have known that fact, but I have often been faulted for not being clear about the relationship of dance and music in a particular performance; I'm so busy with my eyes that I forget about my ears.*

MAPPING FIELDS THAT
DON'T STAY STILL

The Village Voice, April 5, 1983

Sometimes I can imagine that Kenneth King has surveyed the vast changing fields that Merce Cunningham's dancers inhabit and mapped them. Watching King's dances, I think not only of maps but of pulsing signals, of the flaring paths of tracer bullets, of the network of afterimages left on the retina by an explosion of fireworks. In *Lucy Alliteration (A conceptual oratorio)*, King, Carter Frank, Shari Cavin, Mary Ann Daniel, and Bryan Hayes might almost be improvising around a set of patterns derived from the basic grammar of Cunningham classwork: they describe arcs on the air with their elite legs, they try out various tilts or twists or bends of their bodies, and with their stretched arms draw other circles and arcs, point out diagonals. If you imagine the light patterns their gestures might leave in the air, these would be long and distant from any center, rather than a bunch of close-in squiggles.

The dancers are ostensibly serene, yet they take fire from each other. As King says in the program for his company's performances at the Kitchen, he generates "programmed movement possibilities," which provide the dancers with options and can make out of any moment something more startling and more complex than he, as choreographer, could have planned. We see the dancers circling, skimming over the floor; without stopping, one will suddenly be part of a pattern that another is making. A gesture will answer, echo another; a spark will leap across the space and ignite something unforeseen. There are rarely collisions though, and were the dancers not so alert, intelligent, excitable, I might be tempted to view them as astral bodies in eccentric orbits.

The mobility of the dancers is supported by Pamela Tait's limber speaking, as she rambles about the space curling her tongue around strings of alliterations: "like light like like like loss like Lucy . . ." (a clumsy paraphrase). Tait's delivery is amazingly clear and thoughtful; she might almost be trying to make sense of all those messages that end with "like Lucy." Messages. The dancers seem to be flashing them too. When a few people simmer around in the little black-curtained alcove visible behind an open door, when they line up behind each other and advance in a ragged canon of whirling arms and plunges away from that line, you can almost see them spitting light. As in the phantasmagorical slides (by William-John Tudor and Christopher Peregoy) that constitute a prologue, *Annexialics,* the dancers seem rimmed by the fire their dancing generates.

Scream at Me Tomorrow is a scream—a dazzle of cosmic one-liners, or as King says, "redemption by nonsense." The dancers move more quirkily now, their feet traveling fast and intricately all the time, their bodies and limbs flourishing about them. And now the dancers talk along with Tait, argumentatively, conspiratorially: "I'll take the Yukon, and you take the Nikon." "No, You take the Nukon, and I'll take the ikon." (Was that the exchange between Frank and Hayes?) King is a talking-dancing standup Nijinsky, body scribbling on the air, voice intense. "An audiovocal soufflé" is what he claims to have made.

A screen (Richard Johnson: computer graphics) reiterates/projects some of the wilder thoughts: "Put elephant genes into a chicken and explode the oven-stuffer" or "God didn't really create the world in 7 days; he jerked off for 6 and then pulled an all-nighter."

Even though I scarcely understand King's program notes, the performance this evening does speak to me of circuitry, of messages crackling through the air, of parallel trajectories, overlapping, intersecting paths, of telepathic communication between dancers, of dancing as a symbolic language with no one-to-one references and a cornucopia of meanings. I'm not sure where *Flextime* leaves off and *Dance Motor* begins; both present a flexible image of time, both are powered by dancing. The dancers' spacesuits—blackhatched, red in front, white in back, or vice versa—make you think they're twice as many. William-John Tudor's electronic score for Synclavier is at first melodious—Bachian sonorities in orbit, grave and noble. But later, the musical space compresses; the utterances become pointier or are reduced to a massive throbbing. Peregoy and Roger Donnelly video the dancing from opposite corners: a row of television sets captures the image—some show it black-and-white and fairly close, others present a more distant colored picture. Moment by moment, before our eyes, the dancers get hotter, stronger, smarter, quicker, more beautiful. Mind animating matter; dancing kindling thought; dancer setting off dancer. Jeffrey McRoberts bathes it all in a red glow of light. I begin to imagine that if everything were to come together in *one* particular way, a way unknowable in advance, even to King, there'd be such a blaze we'd never be the same afterward.

Confused by the battery of equipment and the numerous program credits for this concert of King's, I misattributed the live video work. It was done by Tim Purtell and Debbora Oliver.

DANCING A SONG

The Village Voice, May 20–28, 1981

✦✦✦

I first met Meredith Monk in 1965, when we were both performing in the old Dance Theatre Workshop loft on 20th Street. She was doing her 1964 duet called *Diploid*. She and another woman wore featureless blue-gray masks over their faces and made sporadic quiet, humming noises in order to signal their locations to each other. I (a tradition-bound Modern Dancer) was shocked to find out that they *really* couldn't see, that there weren't cleverly concealed eyeholes in the masks. She was shocked that I was shocked: Why would she want to fake something like that? I decided that she was either crazy or a genius.

Her performance history has confirmed her unique and formidable gifts. People who saw her immense epic theater pieces like *Juice* (1969), *Needlebrain Lloyd and the Systems Kid* (1970), *Vessel* (1971), are always trying to tell those who didn't how rare and beautiful these works were. Billed respectively as "theater cantata," a "live movie," and an "opera epic," they utilized big public spaces, buildings, vehicles, animals, fire, hordes of people and objects, required the audience to journey from one place to another, and hence weren't easily repeatable (although Monk successfully revived *Vessel* last year in Berlin for the Schaubühne am Halleschen Ufer). Her more recent work has been slightly more portable: *Education of the Girlchild* (1972–1973), *Quarry* (1976), *Recent Ruins* (1979); the smaller scale *Plateau Series* (which she terms "landscape pieces"); *Paris, Chacon, Venice/Milan,* the surreal travelogues she created in collaboration with Ping Chong.

Monk's tributary career as a composer and singer has gradually assumed the status of a major current. Not only does she provide music for her theater pieces but she gives concerts and has cut three records. The latest, produced by ECM, will be released here in August. It's a music concert that she and two organists and members of her company, the House, are presenting right now (through May 31) at the downstairs Space at City Center.

In the past, I've compared the structure of Monk's theater pieces to that of a mosaic, of a jigsaw puzzle, of an amphora reassembled from potsherds. None of these fancies is entirely accurate. True, her works, however epic in scale, always appear to be composed of small pieces— tableaux, actions, music, words, film, alone or combined—but these pieces aren't fragments: each is polished, clear, complete in itself. The point is that each of these modules acquires heightened significance or resonance when it's juxtaposed to other events in the work, set in particular contexts, repeated or varied. I still remember with delight how, in *Vessel,* she moved all the Part I people and furniture from her loft to the parking lot where Part III took place, and there was this little living room—rug, lamp, chairs, and all—sitting in the big space like a world embedded in another world.

In Monk's works, a slowing of tempo, an unusual amount of repetition, or a fastidiously controlled degree of exaggeration edge what might seem an ordinary event toward the bizarre. In *Education of the Girlchild,* six women sitting around a table suddenly don spectacles: the effect is both funny and eerie, and because they all do it at about the same time, the question of vision becomes preternaturally important. Sometimes the occurrences themselves are fantastic or dreamlike: Lanny Harrison suspended above the *Quarry* audience at La Mama, gesturing extravagantly and mouthing words—at once the entertainer caged and on display, the dictator haranguing the multitude, the child heroine's mother—a radio singer—seen through a haze of fever as a faraway, unreachable figure.

The structure of Monk's music bears, it seems to me, a kinship to the structure of her theater pieces. It reaches the ear as a chain of tiny modules. Sometimes a ground base of circular links, often repeated many times on an instrument, runs under the vocal part. In her unaccompanied songs, she takes a short motif extremely distinctive in tonal quality and works very subtly at reinforcing it or gradually altering it. Her own astonishing vocal range not only includes extreme highs and lows of pitch in a conventional "good" singing voice, but moans, snarls, whispers, screeches, croons, and all manner of precise and infinitesimal shadings of pitch and timbre that are common in Middle Eastern music but seldom figure in the Western concert repertory. And her songs are as evocative of place and character as her theater pieces are.

April 29. A red-letter day in the life of *Turtle Dreams,* the new composition Monk is premiering at the Space. In her deep, narrow workspace, a rented electric organ sits beside her own—first it's praised for its low price tag, later berated for its thin tone. And here's pianist/composer Julius Eastman to join Steve Lockwood at the keyboards. Live music for the first time.

The first thing you notice about the texture of this rehearsal is that it's like a meeting of collaborators—people who are easy with each other, committed to the work at hand, knowledgeable about all aspects of it. Ready to begin, the singers stand in a line: Paul Langland, Meredith Monk, Robert Een, Andrea Goodman. All are accomplished and versatile performers, interesting to look at and listen to; as Monk admiringly points out, their technique doesn't mask their individuality. The organs start with an insistent repeated figure. The singers wait. Then, in unison, they begin stepping neatly from side to side—step, close, hold; step, close, hold. A skeletal waltz. Small Monk, her hair in two braids, standing very straight, starts to sing in a high, thin voice, "Aaaah, aaaaah, wain to dhe stoh, shoh, stoh . . ." Gradually the other voices join with blurred language or with wordless chants that can layer over each other into counterpoint or stay independent like questions and answers.

This rehearsal is going a little too fast or too slow down a street with synchronized traffic lights. How far can you get before you hit a red one? (Not all the score is written out in the conventional way, and Monk is still making alterations.) At each snag Monk moves to peer over Eastman's or Lockwood's shoulder, to point, explain, twiddle knobs, look back at the others to ask questions or receive confirmation. Often Een or Langland follow her with suggestions. It's one of them, I think, that advocates trying the flute stop on the new organ. ("Oh, *that* sounds better!") Goodman says patient things like "Well, we can try it and see how it works." And they line up again. And again. Making this kind of remark: "Well, we're gettin' it." "Yep." (Sigh, bend over and touch the floor.) "You always have to have at least one rehearsal like this; no other way to do it." "Nope."

Often during an enforced break, one of the performers will go down to the end of the loft and crouch down to look, pleased, into the mock-up of the Space, which designer Yoshio Yabara has made, with four vivid little dressed figures standing on a black island. (Yoshi is the first designer Monk has ever collaborated with, and she says that he is indeed a kindred spirit.)

Back to the line. Over to the organs. Back to the line. Monk works with the others on this project the way you try to fit a stiff new key into a lock—patiently and questioningly jiggling it, moving it a hairsbreadth this way or that, sensing any useful shift in its position, and knowing, without a doubt, the moment at which it clicks into place.

Like any new work by Monk, *Turtle Dreams* takes up new ideas. "My pieces often have a kind of Utopian feeling to them," she says, "but my own everyday reality is that I live in New York City. And I wanted to do a piece in which I did acknowledge that I'm hearing things grating against each other all the time, and that I'm hearing this kind of energy drive all the time. The louds and the softs aren't modulated the way they are in the country." New ideas, new risks. And Meredith, sitting on her couch, pulls her braids straight up and folds them over the top of her head, as if they too need to stretch now and then.

May 6. The living, breathing organ players have become an important fact of life, but Eastman's off earning money today. No one likes having to go back to rehearsing with tape (can't hear the parts, thin texture, no presence!) Seen without stops, *Turtle Dreams* swims into focus and takes on a pronounced, yet mysterious texture. The side-stepping is almost constant, but it encompasses changes of direction and formation. Shifts into couples. Sometimes the organs stop, and the four continue stepping; once they all lie down, quick as an eye-wink, and stay on the floor while the music continues. At times they make fluid gestures with their arms and hands—none alike; these resemble, fugitively, tipping a hat, brushing hair back, wiping at an invisible pane of glass to clear the steam away. In the shifting vocal texture, small lullabies surface and roll under, also denials and questions, cries of alarm. All the sounds are clear; put together, they're often abrasive. Things rub against each other. Disaster looms. When the piece is almost done, Gail Turner appears in a far corner. Nodding her head delicately, like one of those Japanese dolls, she raises her arms as if to waltz with an imaginary partner and advances with tiny, almost mechanical steps on a long diagonal. I remember from Yoshi's mock-up that she'll be wearing a white hoopskirt. The nineteenth century crossing today.

Eventually *Turtle Dreams* will be part of an evening of little acts, "a surrealistic cabaret." The relationship of movement to singing is something Monk's constantly trying to figure out, she says, the different ways they can go together. *I* think that in the process of figuring, she's come upon a new thing: roughly speaking, music-theater in concert form. I've seen her perform her *Songs from the Hill,* and although she stands quietly throughout some of the songs, in others she allows her body to assume the lineaments of the character that's emerging in her voice. For "Mesa," she takes on the stance of a much bigger person, a man perhaps, as she calls to what is palpably a vast, dry Western space, "Hey, heeey, hey, hey, HOOoooh!" For another ("Jade," as I remember), she screws her body up in response to the high old-woman's natter she's making in her mouth. I've never seen a singer do quite this before. And in "Dolmen Music," from *Specimen Days,* which is also being performed at the Space, the six singers sit in a semicircle—Even playing the cello too—and deliver the music as if it were a lifetime of pleasant and animated conversation around a fire; you hear the music as a circuit crisscrossing the group.

One of the things Monk likes about music concerts is their directness. "In theater, I always feel we're one step removed. We create a world, and the audience comes into that world, whereas in a music concert I can say, uh, 'Now I'm going to do this song.' Or 'Now we'll show you a film. Be back in ten minutes.' " The audience can enter a "world," but the door stays open. Also, music is more flexible.

"In songs, you can do three characters in five minutes, but in theater that's hard." She talks of her casting for *Specimen Days,* the big theater piece with Civil War themes she's been working on for a long time: white women will play black men, and so on, which will perhaps keep the audience from falling into stereotyped ways of looking and thinking. But that's still not the kind of fluidity she's talking about. How *can* you achieve that? Why do you always have to start with an "idea" in theater? ("All I'm telling you in this interview is my questions.")

One way *I* think Monk achieves fluidity in both her theater and music pieces has to do with the elusive manner in which she layers time. Like Turner passing through in her hoopskirt. Often Monk seems to regard the present as if it were the past: in the archaeological slides that accompanied *Recent Ruins,* a vacuum cleaner appeared among the clay vases. In the silent, black-and-white film Monk made on Ellis Island, her company moves among the ruins, both evoking and occupying their own ancestry.

In a master class in Philadelphia, she asked everyone to think of a pose, a gesture, a few words to represent each of his/her grandparents. The results were quite extraordinary. The agile young girl settled down into pot-bellied grumpiness. The glossily trained young male dancer on an instant assumed the identity of a spoiled, bitter woman—true enough to stop your laughter before it could start. Generations bloomed around the dank gym.

"I'm always asking myself . . . I'm always trying to figure out . . ." These expressions keep cropping up in Monk's talk. I think everything she does is a profound question about life. And no one can frame questions quite the way she does.

UNDERWATER ALL
ISLANDS CONNECT

The Village Voice, April 26, 1976

∿

As Meredith Monk's remarkable opera, *Quarry,* begins, Monk is lying on the floor at the dead center of La Mama's vast, open performing space, a pillow under her head, a quilt spread over her. Lying motionless, she suddenly cries, "I don't *feel* well!" And in her light, panicky voice repeats the phrase several times. Then, "It's my eyes. It's my eyes. It's my eyes. It's my eyes. It's my skin. . . ." The clarity with which she reproduces the same intonation for every repetition makes the sick child seem both immensely forlorn and yet in some state beyond the easy reach of our pity; her voice is like a bell announcing that the ritual, the performance has begun.

Monk, islanded on her "bed," is surrounded—at some distance—by four other very specific areas of activity: Biblical ancestral figures (Tone Blevins and Daniel Ira Sverdlik) kneel on a mat, he working slowly on a scroll, she with a length of fabric; a gray-haired couple (Lee Nagrin and Pablo Vela) inhabit a fragment of what might be a comfortable study; a woman (Lanny Harrison) in a flowery '40s dress sits at her dressing table with a playscript; three women (Monica Moseley, Gail Turner, and Mary Schultz), in drab clothes that also seem of the '40s, sit around a plain table eating a meal. Imaginary spokes seem to radiate from the child to the four scenes that tremble in some layer of her mind just beneath her delirium.

Perhaps the woman who comes and speaks to her soothingly is her mother; the gray-haired couple might be affluent and gentle European grandparents; the three women could be her visions of herself at later stages. A homey kind of fate figure, a maid (Coco Pekelis), trudges the entire terrain with her broom. She's grumpy and sore-backed, but her broom whacks the floor with insistent rhythms, and it's she who rests on a chair beside Monk and switches on the "radio" that delivers the score— Monk's sweet and eerie singing and piano playing—as well as a few cryptic and nutty fragments of radio drama and weather reporting.

All three sections of *Quarry* ("Lullaby, "March," "Requiem") are composed of small interlocking pieces. The scenes are brief; the music moves in short repetitive modules. Nothing seems to cause anything else, but events gather power from other events until a small snowball has acquired the force of an avalanche. Afterward I couldn't remember exactly what happened when, but while I was watching it, a profound logic seemed to be molding its development. Monk's use of repetition and correspondence is very subtle. Tone Blevins and Daniel Sverdlik repeat a flight they made as the Old Testament couple, but dressed in shabby, dark European city clothes. Nagrin and Blevins, in opposite corners of the room, fold pieces of fabric in the same way. Ping Chong (billed as a Dictator) is the audience when Lanny Harrison appears high up in a glass-walled booth, singing a garish and inaudible song—the unreachable celebrity mother of the sick child, and also, somehow, a terrified captive.

Everywhere, Monk has laid private history against the history of an era and small, specific actions against fantastic and ritualistic ones. The gray-haired man, a Cervantes scholar, complains mildly to his wife about some professional slight offered him by a colleague. Yet people proceed through carrying stiff white clouds or B-17s on the ends of sticks. And Monk and the maid and the inhabitants of those four zones in space and time (Four corners to my bed . . .) don't always behave "naturally." The woman in the flowered dress goes through a rehearsal of a drama and exaggerates it into an ungainly but beautiful dance. Monk puts on eyeglasses and takes off in a galloping, shuddering, shrieking dance around her bed. For a while the maid lumbers after her. But the "grandfather" terminates this bizarre scene by carrying Monk back to bed and asking her quietly if she'd like some milk.

The first part of *Quarry* ends with a gentle and beautiful passage by twenty-seven people in white called "Wash Chorus," whose supple but firm contrapuntal dancing and humming seems indeed to wash over the room like a benediction. In the second part, autobiography begins to merge more and more with the history of nations and races. A child's visions blend with our common nightmares. The World War II images persist. Five bizarre dictators of different sorts (Latin American military, Near Eastern guerrilla chief, intellectual in wheelchair) die off one by one. Around Monk's restless, recumbent figure, hordes of people march and chant, perform endless vigorous calisthenics. This, the climax of the piece, is followed by utter quiet, while your eyes wander over a field of huddled or collapsed bodies, watching their breathing subside. There is a film, too, an amazing film in which piles of rocks, which you imagine to be small boulders, turn out to be gigantic; and tiny white-clad figures on mysterious errands appear and disappear from behind them. And scraps of white material caught on twigs floating in black water turn out to be lifeless people drifting, draped over logs. A reminder of the ironies of scale and distance, of death by hard labor. Also, a metaphor for the digging into time, the sharpest of memories eventually rubbed smooth by the flooding of years.

And the heroic scale of this and the exhausting rally and the final circling requiem chorus of the entire cast is punctuated by the small, chilling moment in which Nagrin and Vela put on their coats, leave their "house," and ceremoniously drop their jewelry and money on the floor. "Your valuables please" (you can imagine the voice). Clink clank—the ring, the watch. At the end, the great chorus gone, the maid in her coat and hat, showing Monk a photograph in a book. Of Hitler.

Of all the pieces Meredith Monk has dreamed up and that she and the House have performed ("realized," her word, is better), *Quarry* is the richest—in part, the mining of the holocaust by an American Jew, sheltered in body, but besieged in spirit.

Since 1976, I've seen Quarry *many times—via the fine film of it made by the New York Public Library's Dance Collection and supervised by Monk. I'm surprised that at first viewing the three women seated around a table struck me as possibly representing "visions of herself [Monk] at later stages." They certainly have the import of images into which Monk has projected herself, but now I see them as people forced to go into hiding, like Anne Frank and her family. Their pent-up dancing, a visitor who brings them food . . . odd that I didn't see it right away.*

PLEASE DRAW ME A DANCE

The Village Voice, October 22–November 4, 1980

"It came about one jet-lag evening in New York. I awoke to a call from Nancy [Lewis] asking if I would do a dance for her. I said yes, and fell back to sleep. Weeks later I met Lucas Hoving in Rotterdam. He said I hear you are doing a dance for Nancy's concert in two weeks. Then I remembered the phone call. Immediately I mailed off a postcard of a woman lying on a couch with her legs and arms akimbo. I wrote, this is the first movement of the dance, if you want more call me in Paris and I'll send the rest . . ."

This is how Remy Charlip—dancer, choreographer, author and illustrator of children's books—described the genesis of his "air mail dances" in a 1976 issue of *Eddy*. At ATL last week, acting as interlocutor for what he called A Conference of Mail Order Dances, Charlip regaled the considerably enthralled audiences with the same story. And other stories.

Since Charlip's 1972 adventure with Nancy Lewis, he has mailed dances to companies and solo dancers all over the world. Scattered over a sheet or so of paper are small dancing people. Sometimes they're stick figures, but more often they're fleshed out, with trousers and a shirt and, intermittently, an eye or two. The people appear to have been stopped by the page in the middle of the most unimaginably lively activity. Seldom are they on balance, rarely are they waiting. They have just—or are just about to—fall over backwards, plunge onto their heads, launch themselves into the air.

How individual dancers see the impetus of those figures determines, in part, the finished dance. Charlip sends very few directives as to sequence or dynamics or floor plan, although he usually works in one way or another with the performers before the dance is put on. It's the dancer who must consider whether a particular eccentric crouch is to be rolled up into from a lying position or whether it's going to crumple down from a bold kick that ran out of juice. Will the gesture depicted be hit boldly or slid into? Will it be tense, or soft and open? Will it simply be a moment to pass through on the way to something else? Turn the paper, make the wall the floor, alter course—just don't stick in any extraneous gestures.

I once told some students about Remy Charlip and showed them his drawings to work on in class. They were delighted, but also, I think, a little shocked. These particular dancers had been brought up to believe that for a dance to be valuable, it had to be dredged up from your soul. This is a pretty good idea. The trouble is that a lot of students of choreography aren't sure exactly where their souls are located or how to go about this interior journey, or how to get out again once they've ventured in.

But the combination of chance and choice, of control and freedom that Charlip's drawings induce takes dancers' minds off the soul-hunt, the search for meaty subjects or undreamed-of forms. And the paradox is that the resultant dances usually look intensely personal and as if they mean something important to the people who're performing them.

In accord with Richard Zelens's interest in eastern religions, Charlip sent him drawings based on gestures associated (as I remember) with certain Japanese ceremonies, and Zelens arranges and performs them with grave power—first clattering a small pile of sticks out onto the floor and gradually arranging them into a triangle of white cloth. (I couldn't quite stay with this one, in part because of the way John Dodd's handsome lighting kept altering drastically.) Barbara Roan turns the manipulation of a red towel into a faintly sinister incantation, as if she, in top hat and tails, with her long hair hanging loose, traveling excruciatingly slowly across the floor to Nino Rota's music, were a magician mesmerized by the power of her own spell. Abelardo Gameche and Eduardo Ramones, two charmingly serious young men from the Taller de Danza Contemporanea of Caracas, also dance with intense control—pressed together, back to front, or occasionally side to side, as the drawings decree. The movements are big—lunges and stretches—but the image is of a boundless unspoken tenderness between two people. The slowness, is broken by sudden spattering passages, and for the second half of *Los Palos Grandes,* the men dance to Haydn's music, each holding out (and regarding intently) a big feather-shaped leaf.

Slowness and soberness don't necessarily proceed from Charlip's drawings. Nancy Lewis strung her thirty-nine *Chinese Attitudes* in long, careless striding garlands—repeating them often. In a costume by Jane Ekman that looks half clown suit, half Grecian tunic, assaulted by Richard Peck's hot music, Lewis resembles some Delsarte lady running through a routine she's half forgotten on a stage fraught with small obstacles. In *Our Lady of the In Between,* Toby Armour undulates with great concentration, her feet scrooching along a blue square of fabric. Occasionally, voices from inside a small cardboard city and a cardboard island (by Shirley Kaplan) mournfully and distantly echo the Bach aria that accompanies her voyage, the island's tiny palm tree quivering.

Only in the jolly piece d'occasion *Happy Happy Happy We,* for an all-star cast (Ronald Dabney, Lance Westergard, Sheila Kaminsky, Phoebe Neville, Tryntje Shapli) does the rhythm of posing dominate. And in the *Twelve Contra Dances* (Beethoven), there are no predetermined shapes whatsoever. Westergard and Dabney enliven the floor patterns Charlip has given them only with walks and runs, a few jumps and leaps, making changes of direction touch off swerves, chases, friendly, even flirtatious competitions to see who can get where fastest. (It's particularly nice to see Westergard, whose virtuosity at making himself into extravagant shapes has been exploited by many choreographers, just *going.*)

Charlip's interest in gesture has several aspects. The large moves a body makes can be construed as gesture—reaching out, curling in, toppling over. Lexicons of attitudes and/or gestures can be used for the purposes of "expression," as in the Delsarte system, or as a language, as in the signs used by the deaf. Charlip gives us that absurd and lovely old song, "Every Little Movement Has a Meaning All Its Own," in two gesture languages. Bruce Hlibok opens the program "singing" it with his hands. Later David Vaughan sings it in a mellifluous voice, helped by Al Carmines at the piano, and then—revealed to us by a spotlight as sandaled, tunicked, and wreathed—runs through a catalogue of Delsarte gestures with heavy and utterly hilarious sincerity.

Some of the dances mire slightly in a single sustained dynamic, several of them seem long. The most splendid to me are *Dance on a Floor* and *Waves.* The first is a solo for Toby Armour, the second a duet for Armour and Charlip. *Dance on a Floor* was conceived for television, shot by WGBH from overhead, while Armour performed on a sheet. I haven't seen the videotape, but stills make it look ravishing; even in the head-on version at ATL, the crouching, lying-down solo has a meditative sensuality. Armour's extraordinary command of dynamics removes the solo from any possibilities of wallowing and allows you to read many subtle shadings of emotion into the way her body suddenly stretches into immobility, then curls into cattish comfort, each turn of her hand, each absorbed placement of her cheek clearly delineated.

I've never seen Armour perform so wonderfully. Her long, lithe, elegant body has acquired an ability to soften movement, to give in to it. And in *Waves*, she and Charlip often sustain each other with roundness. At one point he moves with immense but stoic violence, while behind him she folds her whole body around him to stroke him into calmness. Later he stands behind *her*, caressing the space close to her head with small noddings and bobbings of his head. Armour dances beautifully by any kind of standards you care to apply; Charlip has a peaceful sense of weight and fullness in his gestures, which is also beautiful to see. And it was fine to see dancers who aren't kids (actually almost no one on the program was) dancing as if maturity were something as important to take account of in dance as in any other department of life.

LOOPS OF TEARS

The Village Voice, June 4, 1979

W hat makes Dan Wagoner's new dance, *Seven Tears,* so marvelously engrossing isn't the unaffected musing tenderness of it—although that is an important part of its affect—or the splendid dancing of Wagoner and his associates—although that dancing is indispensable. No, the dance's secret grace is its structure: more visible, more coherent, and more fluid than in many of Wagoner's big arduous fields of dancing.

Yet, although the form is clear and worth thinking about at all times while you're watching the dance, it doesn't impose itself on you as an intellectual exercise. The form of *Seven Tears* functions like a huge inquisitive hand turning the dance gently this way and that so that it becomes, like a tear, prismatic. The music is John Dowland's *Lachrymae,* played, I think, on an ancient organ; the seven melancholy pavanes all sound like variants of the first—an instrumental version of Dowland's ravishing song "Flow My Tears." Wagoner has made some solos, but most of the work's seven sections are for a group of dancers coming and going, happening upon each other, clustering together, herding off on the same course, and then quietly, wanly, splintering and drifting into solitary ways.

It doesn't take long to notice that the same phrases and groupings reappear in other sections, but performed by different dancers or laid out in a new order. Toward the end, Wagoner twists the whole dance in space so that actions once veiled by others now become prominent. The changing of roles doesn't, in this case, suggest fickleness or the interchangeability of company personnel; it makes the dance seem like a series of conditions, existing in tremulous but confident balance, each one of which is always being upheld by one or more people.

Wagoner's style of moving seems more lavish than it once was: deeper bending in the body, more sweeping with the arms, less strident with the legs. (Wagoner himself often bustles around in a curiously stiff, footsore manner and/or flails about with straight arms, looking as if he's suddenly half remembered something he'd forgotten.) I see fewer of the non sequiturs that can be either witty or disturbing. There is less disruption and more following things through.

The dancers make good sense of things too: Heidi Bunting, strong and opulent and extremely sensitive to changes in texture; tall Sally Hess whose arms and legs wrap into movement like parts of a climbing vine—tendrily but insistent; JoAnn Fregalette-Jansen, who always looks alert and searching, yet leans sensuously into the steps. Diann Sichel, blunt and clear in her delivery, can make enormous springs into the air. Christopher Banner is long and flexible, slightly oblique in manner, while Robert Clifford, tall and heavyset, combines blockiness with bouyancy.

The other new work on the company's programs at Judson Church (where ten years ago—can it be?—Wagoner presented his first choreography) was *A Play, with Images and Walls.* Not a play exactly, but plenty of images and imagined walls. It's a rambunctious, countrified piece. The audience adores it, maybe because it's so full of *stuff*; to me, too much evident contriving has gone into it.

All the dancers stay on stage most of the time—the women wearing short calico dresses (by Pat Varney) that they keep tucking up into their underpants in a disarmingly functional manner. Poet George Montgomery moves among them, uttering his warm direct poems, then waiting while some dancing happens. Furniture begins to appear—a chair, a bench, a galvanized tub. In one poem, Montgomery says that he'd like his poems to be so—I forget the exact word—"natural" (maybe), that when people opened their mouths they couldn't help saying them. But as soon as he's finished talking a poem, Natalie Gilbert at the piano begins to play and sing it (sometimes with Milagro Vargas's helping voice)—I mean she sings the song that she has made of it. Her music is fresh and tuneful, sometimes very lovely and gently complicated, and she has a deep, warm, slightly rough voice that I like a lot. But while some of Montgomery's poems can bear being lifted into song—like a lovely one about arms remembering other arms, which occasions one of Gilbert's finest settings, and a caressing duet for Hess and Banner—others are so factual, so like everyday speech, that it's disconcerting to hear them elaborated.

The dancers also follow the sense of the poems, sometimes quite literally as when Wagoner shags like the playful bear Montgomery likens himself to, and Montgomery, copying him, ends up on the floor being tickled. In addition to dancing and watching, the dancers also perform more prosaic acts: Heidi Bunting washes her feet, and at the end three dancers take turns jumping splashily into the tub, like kids told to wash their feet before getting into bed.

The Voice gave Jennifer Tipton an Obie for her lighting. The dance world ought to honor her, too, for her exemplary work on concerts such as Wagoner's.

HOW PRISTINE DARE
YOU GET?

The Village Voice, January 1, 1979

~~~

Four dancers execute fifteen variations of solo dances choreographed by William Dunas in 1978. Seven on film, six live, seven on video. That isn't fifteen? Well, is the flesh-and-blood Naaz Hosseini perhaps doing the same slow-starting solo that Grethe Holby goes through in Robert Megginson's film? Are the real Pat Graf and the filmed Pat Graf dancing the same sequence of smooth, dutiful attitudes, and can they be said to be the same when the eye of Megginson's camera elongates a diagonal that our eyes barely pick up between the pillars of the dimly lit Kitchen? Perhaps Janna Jensen's solo on Marc Levin's videotape is the "same" as the one she dances on film. Perhaps it isn't. At St. Mark's last spring, Holby was the only one to do a sudden fall; this time Jensen gets to do it on tape.

This latest manifestation of Dunas's current project tends to make your mind run on like this—speculate, worry, try to memorize; he forces you either to deal with monotony or leave (unless you are one of those who sits and fumes for the pleasure of exploding later). This luggage of solo material that Dunas keeps repacking, refolding, redraping on his four models is evasively classical in its effect. Not-quite-ballet. Every move the women make is controlled, gentle, attenuated. Usually it is their legs—unfolding into the air, brushing out lightly—that initiate movement; sometimes it is their arms. Their heads and bodies, placid and thoughtful, travel along to supervise. True, some dances stay in one place and some cover ground, some are fairly fast and some are slow; but all are clearly cousins in a family distinguished by pale coloring and mild manners.

Over the course of the evening, we see the same movements many times, repositioned in new sequences by Dunas, given new emphasis by the four different women. An attitude done by Pat Graf's long lean limbs is a complex of curves and angles; Grethe Holby, forthright and sturdy, may make the same move look like a matter of achieving a balance rather than of creating a design. Naaz Hosseini may put a delicately sharp accent on an arm gesture that Janna Jensen swims through. Is it a coincidence that the evening is called *Isle of Wight*? Not only does "wight" mean nimble, but the island is diamond shaped, affording the sea traveler four clear views of its landscape.

While we sit in chairs or sprawl on the floor, Dunas changes the vista of his simple landscape for us in every way he can—freezing it in slides, letting the film and video media impose their viewpoints (cuts, zooms, all that too), sometimes seeing how its rhythms are affected by violinist Susan Korngold's playing of Bach's Partita II in D Minor. The lack of contrast, the sameness of texture must be deliberate, must relate to the subtlety of Martha Boyden's white-on-white painting hanging behind the dancing. I leave, feeling that Dunas has not been trying to show us "dancing" but that he has been attempting to instruct us in a language. Not because he intends to "use" it to refer to something else but because he thinks the process of looking at dance syntactically might interest us.

WHEN THE LION LIES DOWN
WITH THE LAMB

The Village Voice, February 13, 1978

Outside Town Hall, a bundled-up old lady stops to peer at a tacked-up glossy of James Cunningham taken in 1968. Cunningham, staring intently ahead, is standing on his hands, while on either side of him his feet fly past at shoulder height, ready to thunk down ahead of his hands. The old lady puzzles over him for a long time.

Inside on the Town Hall Stage, Jamie Cunningham sits smoking with his limbs spread out around him. Eyeing the space. He still looks like his picture. A swarm of people—his company, his lighting designer, Raymond Dooley, ten or so friends (New York substitutes for the students he incorporates into certain of his pieces during college residencies)—warm up, try things out, pace off the space, hunt for missing props, kibbitz. Offstage, some animal masks are laid out.

In a flickering color film, a man with a fox's head and a woman chase each other around the lawn of what looks like a big house in the Hamptons. His long arms and legs flail the air randily. Treed, she laughs. Games in which you've almost managed to scare each other are perhaps the most delicious of all (James Cunningham and Tina Croll, *Mr. Fox's Garden*, 1967).

The Town Hall Interludes performance (last week) and the upcoming concerts presented by Dance Theatre Workshop at ATL (February 9 to 12, 16 to 19) celebrate the tenth anniversary of Cunningham's company. It's hard to believe. He's one of those rare choreographers who appears on the scene almost full blown. With the possible exception of *Aesop's Fables* (choreographed with Lauren Persichetti and the only work he's made to a single piece of music and someone else's scenario), his dances are like squares in one big crazy quilt. He could stitch a piece he made in 1968 between one made in 1970 and one made in 1974, and you'd hardly know the difference. Except that the recent ones tend to be bigger and shinier.

Ten years of touring, performing, teaching, creating—ten major dances (if you don't count the children's shows and a few pieces d'occasion). All of them assemblages of simple, happy dancing (cavorting you might call it), pop tunes, nursery rhymes, parodies of theater and dance forms, yoga chanting, animal behavior (snarling, barking, howling,) monologues, dialogues, sex, myth, and fairy tale. Cunningham's world is one in which opposites are reconciled and roles are exchanged. (What cannot happen, according to Mary Poppins, in the crack between the first and the last stroke of midnight on New Year's Eve?) It is a world in which a man dressed as a bride forsakes her possible grooms for a woman dressed as Lassie. Said Cunningham in a statement he once prepared for *Dance Magazine* (not printed, no doubt, because of its offhand reference to pleasurable masturbation), "Wasn't Isadora our first lady president? Wasn't Walt Whitman her father and Walt Disney her son?"

Two women with coats over their leotards, carrying purses, walk care-

fully to a door in the wall of the loft. The door opens and out comes a much smaller woman in a short bunchy fur jacket, a purse hanging from her wrist. They all kiss each other gravely and graciously on both cheeks and walk along together. Little girls playing lady (Linda Tarnay, Tina Croll, Lauren Persichetti, *Skating to Siam,* 1968).

Many people all over the country look forward to a performance by the Acme Dance Company the way you look forward to your birthday when you're a child. Others are disappointed that Cunningham's work hasn't Developed Much or has gotten too slick. Still others, in speaking of him, fling the anathema of Self-Indulgence around. Cunningham himself is frank about wanting to make work that pleases him. "When I came to New York and stopped working in the commercial theater," he says, "I stopped feeling that I had to make up *this* kind of a piece or *that* kind of a piece. I think many artists have this in common: there are things that get to you and that you investigate over and over. For instance, I'm always interested in trying to learn how you integrate your mental, physical, and emotional self. And how opposites connect—Shiva and Shakti, Apollo and Dionysius. And in theater that integrates many aspects of performing."

The Swan Queen fixes supper. Von Rothbart, wearing a tiny gold jock-strap, props himself up on his elbows and reads aloud from a porno-graphic novel. Prince Siegfried, knees drawn up, sits and listens. He asks: "Do you identify with Enrique or Maria?" V.R. replies, "With Enrique, I guess." "Oh good!" says the Prince, "because I . . ." Torrents of Tchaikovsky asterisk the scene (Lauren Persichetti, Edward Love, James Cunningham, *The Junior Birdsmen,* 1970).

Jamie says that if I didn't know him well, he'd be sure to tell me that he identifies with Lewis Carroll, especially in the idea of that moment be-tween sleeping and waking when different realities converge. Carroll too was interested in the uses of parody—in taking a poem, a story that has been significant to people and "looking at it in the way that it seems to you now, just turning it slightly."

The Dying Duck hunkers down, waddles backward awkwardly, peer-ing this way and that, and triumphantly lays an egg before expiring (James Cunningham, *The Clue in The Hidden Staircase,* 1971).

What Cunningham is—what he likes to do as a performer—shapes his works. His body is not only amazingly rubbery, with long limbs and slop-ing shoulders, but it is something of a tabula rasa: He can be man, woman, eternal child, shrink into enjoyable savagery, stetch up and grow powerful and noble before your eyes. His voice is equally flexible—capable of yowling, producing clipped and waspish tones, or flowing out with serene and offhand resonance. Only the finest actors have this kind of focus—absolutely centered, all inessentials pared away. Few are as lovable.

You can trace his interest in masks back to his childhood in Toronto (he began to work with the Toronto Children Players at the age of five). "When you put on a mask, you become a medium—except that it's quite unconscious: this other energy actually comes through you. That's what was so vivid to me as a child and made performing so exciting. What I found magical about theater was that you could be anything, a horse, a rose; the mask is the touchstone that allows that to happen." Cunningham's use of costumes and props is also harum-scarum and childlike; the handmade and makeshift mix with the expertly finished (he likens the blend to a picture: Here it's carefully painted, there the canvas shows).

Adam and Eve are matter-of-factly domesticating Eden. They exchange one creature's panther head for a cat's, and his roars dwindle into meows (William Holcomb, Patty Kozono, and the company, *The Clue in The Hidden Staircase,* 1971).

For a while, Cunningham studied in London at the Royal Academy of Music and Dramatic Art (note his abiding interest in all forms of show biz—even though his Mae West wears a cow's head). For a while, he worked at the BBC with the idea of becoming a film director (note the cinematic way in which he splices ideas into the middle of other ideas or fades one image through another). You can attribute some of his relaxed intensity to his studies in the Alexander technique. None of the above of course, can entirely account for the foolish-wise, funny-sad, delicate-vulgar, innocent-sophisticated, messy-controlled, tremendously entertaining rituals he makes.

The Spectre of the Carnation appears to charm and liberate a trained-to-kill soldier. Gently she removes his shoes and socks. Then with the tidiness and speed of a highly recommended nanny, she rolls the socks into a ball and turns the top over (James Cunningham and Ted Striggles, *Dancing With Maisie Paradocks,* 1973).

"Comedy is a very serious business," says Cunningham. He's not so interested in farce, which, as he says, "is more hard hitting and involves broadcasting: 'I'm funny.' Like Mel Brooks. I'm more interested in light and shade. I love what Maggie Smith does: She plays a real character, and she's in it emotionally, but she's also outside of it mentally. The way she moves too comes out of the emotions, but it's tuned up so that you can see it physically."

A rooster pulls along the Goddess Athena who's standing on a little red wagon (Linda Tarnay and Ted Striggles, *Apollo and Dionysius: Cheek to Cheek,* 1974).

Even watching Cunningham and his dancers rehearse for a little while, you can sense how collaborative the process is. Barbara Ellman, Jane Comfort, Olgalyn Jolly, Ric Rease, Michael Schwartz—of these, only Elman has been with Cunningham for a long time. But they are all asked to contribute, improvise, make decisions. Cunningham was lucky when he first started out: he found Tarnay, Striggles, and Persichetti (with whom he developed not only *Aesop's Fables* but the beautiful duet *Lauren's Dream*). "They had trust, and they were so open," he says. "A lot of people looked at you very *strangely* when you asked them to be frogs or whatever." Cunningham loves to work with children during the company's work in the NEA's Artists-in-Schools Program, and he treats them the way he does everyone else, considerately and with respect for their intelligence (some kids from P.S. 3 will appear with the company on special matinees at ATL, on February 12 and 19). But when he works with adult dancers, he'd rather have them be mature artists with their own creative energy: "Then it's much more like grown-up people interacting; otherwise you feel like a tube of toothpaste that's being squeezed out." (He has a fine laugh.)

A man irritably offers us his sole thought on religion: "We should all come into the darkness and stop skulking about in the light" (James Cunningham, *The Zoo at Night,* 1968).

I've always found Cunningham didactic. Up freedom. Peace. Sex is fun. Down aggression. Machismo. Dance that takes itself too seriously. Once the company sent out a flyer/questionnaire with two identical pictures of Lauren Persichetti in her collie suit, one breast half exposed. Said the caption, ONE OF THESE IS GREAT ART. ONE IS PURE FILTH. DO YOU KNOW WHICH IS WHICH? Speaking in his unpublished statement about what he calls "games worth playing," he says, "In *The Junior Birdsmen,* we juxtapose old 'masculine' competitive games such as soccer, where all the men are active and only the ball is passive, with new games where the men are both active and passive with each other: then it's possible to interact. Otherwise, if you're both superactive, it seems inevitable that you shoot each other."

But it seems to me there's a paucity of wily and well-educated imps these days. And it pleases me to re-read this bit of Cunningham prose: "The building is a Greek temple except that across the front someone carved U.S. TREASURY. George Washington was made President in front of it. On May 21, 1971, we reconsecrated the place as a temple. The spirit of Isadora Duncan appeared between huge columns and led us in a dance. Beethoven's Ninth Symphony was heard in Wall Street; also 'Country Road.' Then masked animals danced around the statue of George Washington and massaged his iron calves."

Happy anniversary, Jamie.

The Dying Duck, The Specter of the Carnation—these are my names. Cunningham could have been thinking himself a Swan, a Rose. But something about the askew nature of his visions invites such flights of fancy.

ORDEAL BY LIGHT

The Village Voice, August 24, 1982

▾▾

Kei Takei has been working on *Light* ever since she first came here from Japan in the late 1960s. Almost. It seems so anyway. Last year she showed parts one through fifteen in a marathon performance, but usually the audience gets to see only a few pieces at a time from this great, clumsy, visionary work.

The separate parts can seem to be about ritual, labor, competition, collaboration, but all are full of struggle. The performers, usually wearing some variant of white cotton kimonos, or curious bib-and-diaper wrappings, bend under the weight of burdens, stamp, crouch, collapse, stagger to their feet, push or pull against imagined wind or enemies or helpers. When they "dance," they stamp and clap in stubborn rhythms. You go to see each new part of *Light* wondering what task, what calamity will be occupying Takei's Moving Earth now.

Whatever it is, they'll approach it with utter concentration. What seemed only an occasional feature of the early parts of *Light* has come to be a fundamental issue in the later parts. The people are very primitive— not fully articulate with their bodies; they treat ordinary objects with demented reverence. Sometimes I think we're seeing a wry view of evoluion.

Parts 10 through 13 were the "rock" stanzas of this epic. The dancers used little stones to build circles and paths, to clash together in rhythmic games, to stone an individual. Even their combats were formal encounters. In Part 15 and the new Part 17, the fighting is scrappier and more savage. From the orderly agrarian duets of Part 14, with basket-bearing couples stamping on a white "field," their arms cutting sowing and reaping gestures on the air, we've come to greed and corruption. In Part 15 there's sowing too, but the exhausted, combative dancers stagger under the force of a powerful wind, becoming covered with nasty greenish-brown padded shapes that they stick onto each other when they bump into each other.

In Part 17, they fight over a ragtag array of clothes. As in several of the parts, the performers enter the action gradually. First two are lunging and retreating, eyes locked; by the end of the first section, two individuals each face a string of enemies. People attach themselves to a new direction, a new rival without any apparent reason; a half turn alters the configuration of the battlefield. John Wilson, who was also set apart from the group in Part 15 (beating sticks, stones together, scraping a metal spear on wood, eyeing the "diseased" creatures—trying, perhaps, to produce fire?), opens one of the bundles and with a grin of wild glee displays a shirt. Shirts! They are grabbed, tossed, spread out in three lines of five. Two men staring intently straight ahead walk slowly down one line. Suddenly one grabs a shirt and scrambles into it. Who'll get the next one? The onlookers gibber incoherently and make rigid gestures of excitement. At each line two more contestants are added. Then all unfold bundles and squat down—very cooperatively—to play metal bowls, claves, small drums, and xylophones, in rhythms determined, I guess, by composer Norma Dalby. Wilson sings a solemn wordless chant. His deep voice lifts into a lyrical falsetto. Rested, they begin another clothes game, while John Wilson and Julie Hall play percussion instruments. Before, the people were either spastic—when onlookers—or straight and serious, but awkward—as contestants—or adept—as musicians. Now they simply race back and forth in determined paths, putting on clothes as if time were running out. It's funny of course, this crazed greed, and awful too, as the dancers become more and more encumbered with skirts, petticoats, trousers, trunks, blouses, sweaters, shawls, hats. Some of the outlandish combinations are almost beautiful.

Takei is an astounding performer—like an animal, like a spring, everything full, nothing extra. Sometimes her ten dancers (in addition to Wilson) almost match her fervor; sometimes they overdo the tension and emotions, so that they look as if they're acting, instead of just . . . *doing.*

Part 16 is a solo for Takei. She begins bent over, muttering into the ground, as if praying, an oddly forked stick over her back. Offstage Laz Brezer growls chants adapted from Buddhist ones, and from offstage is tossed a large white wooden radish, a daikon. At first, it seems to hurt her, to stick to her, to weigh her down when she picks it up. But she adores it, scampers around it in an agitated little dance, falls onto it with childish lasciviousness. Gradually, she takes it apart, pulls out its white leaves, finds the wooden pin that holds its two halves together. Now she's happier than ever; she arranges the dismembered radish neatly, picks up her stick, and strides toward the vegetable and away from it swinging her stick in arcs, her knees bent, her body hunched, her breath beginning to come in gasps. She pays scant attention to the daikon with green foliage that someone throws, and none to the storm of daikons that's hurled around her. Some hit her; she doesn't notice. When she abases herself exhausted before her daikon-icon, "real" ones continue to pelt down. There must be 200 there before the lights go out.

Where will these people be by Part 18?

SENTA DRIVER: STOMPING OUT A NICHE FOR HERSELF

The Village Voice, October 22, 1979

I walked into the dimness of Washington Square Methodist Church and saw this dancer I knew, Senta Driver, telling a small boy that all he had to do was to keep saying the multiplication tables in his head. Then she strapped him onto her back in a sling that held him facing away from her, said "I'm ready," to whoever was running the lights, and started striding heavily back and forth across the church on diagonal paths.

The work was called *Melodrama,* and this 1975 dress rehearsal preceded the debut of Driver's company, Harry (pragmatically subtitled "dance and other works"), which will be performing in BAM's LePercq Space from October 24 to 28. *Memorandum,* another dance on that early program, is still the piece that people usually bring up when Driver's name is mentioned. What happened is this: Driver strode on in a dark jumpsuit with a black veil over her face, made a cryptic warding-off gesture toward the direction she'd come from, and began to pace resolutely in a circle. Resolutely and weightily. Driver is a medium-sized woman and long-bodied rather than long-legged; she's not plump, but she gives an impression of solidity and force. Anyway, every time she came past a certain point in her circle, she uttered the name of a famous ballerina. As she inexorably moved up through history, you could learn something about each dancer from Driver's enunciation. "Marie TagliOni," she breathed reverently, while she flashed the name of Fanny Elssler, the legendary sylph's rival, in a way that called up a more vivacious, less ethereal dancer.

I was much taken with Driver's audacity. And by something more unusual. Her sense of history. Clearly she was a minimalist. Clearly she was a conceptual artist. But she was—and is—interested in matters that do not interest choreographers one might otherwise be tempted to link her with—Laura Dean or Lucinda Childs or Trisha Brown. Things, too, like performance styles, personas, dramatic situations treated as "material," not unlike the way in which, in Harald Lander's ballet *Etudes*—a showy paean to virtuosity and ballet training—an excerpt form the story ballet *La Sylphide* is presented as material. (Many choreographers who consider themselves up-to-date would resent being mentioned in the same breath as *Etudes;* Driver understands the point and doesn't seem to mind the comparison.)

During the course of a long conversation, Driver brings up—pertinently and sympathetically—Pheobe Neville, Meredith Monk, Merce Cunningham, Douglas Dunn, Trisha Brown, Laura Dean, Twyla Tharp, Martha Graham, Pearl Lang, Jane Dudley, Grethe Holby, Bill T. Jones, Martine van Hamel, Natalia Makarova, Felia Dubrovska, George Balanchine, Mathilde Kschessinskaya, Anna Pavlova, Marie Taglioni, Peter Anastos. She goes to so many dance performances that people used to take her for a critic. (Although she does refer to a particular critic as "one of the outstanding interesting dummies of the field," she is benign on the subject of critics. Thinks most of us—me in particular—aren't harsh enough and that "people who rail against critics imagine that everyone else in the audience has *humming* going on in his/her head.")

Few choreographers considered radical have spent so much time examining the past they're determined to make a break with. Driver says that she once wrote in a notebook, "History is a nightmare from which I am trying to escape." Now sitting in her apartment, which is very colorful and multifocused compared to her dances—or maybe it's just that it hasn't processed *its* history—she balances a coffee cup, and modifies that outcry: "I am aware of history. I respect it. I'm trying to find where it belongs and how to use it without repeating it." And she adds firmly, "I have never seen any reason to continue unless I could do something that was original."

Driver thinks that she really began her career in the audience, although while a Latin and philosophy major at Bryn Mawr, she started coming into New York and taking a class once a week (which, she says, she naïvely thought was enough). She racked up a couple of summers at the American Dance Festival and, hooked, took off for Ohio State, where she'd heard the training was good, and picked up an M.A. in dance. (She always acknowledges her debt to the head of Ohio's dance department, Helen Alkire, who, she claims, formed her taste and judgment, taught her to be both disciplined and open to whatever came along.)

Her ambition was—had been for some time—to dance with Paul Taylor. She got into his company very soon after she left Columbus, and stayed there from 1967 to 1973, although she characterizes their relationship as "stormy" ("He fired me in 1970, but I wouldn't go"). Taylor once said "Senta talks a lot," and it's her guess that he mistrusts excessively verbal people. Which she is. Most of Driver's best roles in the Taylor company were ones she inherited from other dancers. She remembers Taylor asking her why she didn't want to look like herself in *Aureole* instead of like Sharon Kinney. Driver, typically, felt that she had a commitment to history, to preserving the Taylor style of a certain year by dancing as much as possible like the dancer on whom the role had been made. This stance may have puzzled Taylor; I find it noble.

Finally out of the Taylor company, ordered to rest for several months because of the tendinitis in both her ankles, she read and thought about choreography. "I had to consider, 'what can you do that someone else isn't already doing very well?' I loved the kind of work Paul did. I loved dancing it. And it was important to me, *for me*, not to do anything like that—not to make a career doing the pieces he forgot to do. Since Douglas Dunn had already covered lying still, the only thing I could do was to walk. I'd take three-hour blocks of time in the studio, and since I tended to sleep to avoid doing anything, I made a rule for myself that, if I wasn't dancing, I'd walk continuously, because I *had* to use the time." (She was encouraged to find that Laura Dean had undergone a similar period). When her feet hurt too much to walk, she crawled or rolled. Out of this came *Memorandum* and, after that, *Melodrama*. "The number-one thing I did in the studio was to walk around and around," she says wryly. "And then I had this big breakthrough and began to walk diagonals."

Since the debut of Harry, Driver has made a number of witty and provocative works—many of which, she is aware, have literally provoked, *infuriated*, some members of the audience. Some of the pieces have involved intrepid and pungent juxtapositions of sound and dance: two dancers walking as fast as they can around a five-spoked pattern, while Tom Johnson provides an excited commentary on their supposed competition (*The Star Game*); three deadpan dancers executing phrases of bold, blunt movement while, on tape, lighting designer Tom Skelton calls for a myriad of light and sound cues for a final rehearsal of Jose Limón's *Missa Brevis* (*Board Fade Except*); dancers slouching around dispiritedly while a soprano walks among them singing the lyrics of some Gilbert and Sullivan songs—sweetly and sincerely, as a manifesto instead of a joke (*In*

Which a Position Is Taken and Some Dance). Who but Driver would end a dance with a long kiss between two performers (*Sudden Death*)? Or have a woman, elaborately coiffed and wearing early twentieth-century practice clothes, perform a dramatic solo on point while sitting on a revolving piano stool? (*The Kschessinskaya Variations* is usually performed as part of *Two Dances from Dead Storage*.)

Driver's interest in weight—your own, someone else's and how to deal with it—has surfaced in many of her pieces. Watching a Driver dance, you usually hear the pound, thud, slap of feet against the floor. You notice people carrying each other, people standing on each other. Driver says this isn't meant to look cruel or political, contrary to what some spectators think, it's simply a matter of finding out how much weight you can support, of accepting another person's weight as a burden you must cope with. And the idea that women can be strong, can carry men, has become a major factor in her work. So has its concomitant: that men can be carried, can be presented as sex objects, can do the kind of precise, detailed dancing they're often not expected to do. It may be this skeptical attitude toward conventional gender-deportment that has led her to collaborate on what promises to be a diverting new work with Peter Anastos, formerly one of the directors of the Ballets Trockadero de Monte Carlo, a gifted choreographer and—as the legendary Olga Tchikaboumskaya—no stranger to paradoxes of gender. He too is obsessed by dance history.

I go to Driver's studio—well, only hers for a year, isn't it beautiful, she says enviously—to watch class for the company and a few others. Driver, as is usually the case, is collected, good-humored, and full of energy—not a hair out of place. (I think that she works hard to counteract the impression that might be produced by her soft, round, pretty face—the kind that often seems to go with a more indulgent attitude toward life). Here are the members of Harry. Jeffery Clark, who's tall and long-legged, with an innocent face and the chest and shoulder development of a crack swimmer; Rick Guimond, smaller and thinner, with limber flyaway legs and a way while performing of looking at the others as if they really interested him; Nicole Riché, compact, technically adroit, with unusually powerful and well-defined back and arm muscles for' a small woman; Peg Conner Hewitt, strong too, but softer, with a cheerful face and untidy hair.

It's some class. A few of the long sequences the dancers perform while sitting on the floor have the swinging kind of vitality that's in keeping with Driver's respect for early modern dance, "for what Martha started with in the '30s: weight, simplicity, starkness." Nothing looks usual, everything looks arduous and physically suspenseful: the weighty, fluid arm gestures ("not neat," she calls, "but rich"), the way the dancers can make a leg move by throwing it from the hip joint, the push-ups, the intricate rhythms. Then, while Senta works in a corner with a newcomer, Jeff puts the others through a long combination performed while standing on the head, which ends with a terrifying dismount, in which the dancers topple to the floor in one piece, like trees. "I thought the body would look good up there and have a good time," says Senta, shrugging, and it's true that *I'm* the only one wincing. The dancers are also perfecting what Driver calls "preparation for point-work." Barefoot.

All this turns out to be stuff that's in her new work, *Primer*. And now you can understand why Driver says with a grin, "Marathon running has created an atmosphere in which my work should flourish." It has to do, she says, with finding out what the body can do, with maybe taking it a little farther. She's interested in violence—not in the sense of brutality or sadism, but as a violent expenditure of energy, even to the breaking point. Like the Graham of the '30s, she's scornful of prettiness, "Pretty starts at the ankle and goes all the way out to the toe and that's it." What Graham wrote in 1928 might almost have been written by Driver today: "Virile gestures are evocative of the only true beauty. Ugliness may be actually beautiful if it cries out with the voice of power."

Driver isn't arrogant about her work or inconsiderate of her audience. Of her recent *Theory and Practice,* she says "it turned out to be a two-week workshop. It's my work of that year, but it shouldn't be on the stage." She's begun to think about ways to provide relief from the prevailing intensity of her dances; she's investigating passive movement. Certainly her preoccupation with force and intensity sets her apart from most contemporaries, who are interested in a more laid-back, underplayed style. (Even Driver's casualness is controlled.) So does her way of altering material through stylistic changes—often theatrical ones, too—rather than movement changes. I call her a maverick, and she says with a certain irony, "Am I lucky enough to be in a new slot? After all, I'm hardly the first person to do many of these things."

Driver is getting plenty of recognition these days; the company is doing quite well; she got a Guggenheim last year. She says she has no right to complain. But she does sometimes wonder where she belongs. "People who examine the current generation of choreographers do not examine me. Places that present what I consider my kind of work seldom present me. . . ." I'm touched by her puzzlement. It would be highly unfair if someone as scrupulously concerned as she is with the past, present, and future of dance didn't end up as a chapter, a page, or a very lengthy footnote in the dance histories of the next era.

TWO DIFFERENT WHIRLS

The Village Voice, October 22, 1980

"Oneooreefourfisix, twotworeefourfisix, threetworeefourfisix . . ."
Laura Dean rapidly walks a bunch of dancers through a floor pattern, the absurdity of her speed-crazed gabble breaking the tension of the
rehearsal. Like all dance rehearsals it has its own particular feel. In this
big dreary windowless hall on the fifth floor of City Center, you can sense,
within the basic texture of hard work, little zigzags of curiosity, doubt,
high interest, guardedness.

That's because these aren't Dean's own dancers, but members of the
Joffrey Ballet. The idea of Dean doing a piece for the Joffrey is as intriguing as the prospect, back in 1975, of Twyla Tharp's making something
(*Deuce Coupe,* as it happened) for the company. Dean's dances are always clearly structured, elegantly patterned; so, often, are ballets. But
Dean's movement style is understated, full of little stamps and kicks and
hops; no matter how difficult it is to perform, her dancers attack it with
the unspoiled verve of people dancing for pleasure. And Dean's structures have none of the frequent climaxes and high contrast of dances
made to conventional Western music. Like the scores she writes herself,
her dances tend to repeat patterns over and over. Long sequences of
spinning are a feature of her style, so are geometric patterns, and an emphasis on precise rhythms. No princesses, no soloists, no stunts.

Well, but look here, Laura, these women are on pointe. "Because that's
what their bodies are trained for," then with a smile of pure pleasure,
"and that's what makes them beautiful." The process of accommodation—hers to these dancers, theirs to her—is one of the challenges. Rehearsals have been going on for a week now—five days of two to three
hours a day. Dean-dancer Angela Caponigro, her long red hair a curtain
down her back, sits poring over a fat book of numbers and diagrams.
Dean, spraddled on the floor, a pair of rusty old black pants hitched up
over her tights, is ready to announce first cast and second cast. She makes
a nice, sincere little speech about how important the second cast is, and
how she's going to try to give it as much rehearsal time as she can. Then
she takes a breath and reads off quickly from the paper in her hand:
"First cast:
  Cammy (Cameron Basden)
  Carole (Valleskey)
  Ursula (Burke)

Valmai (Roberts)
Larry (Laurence Blake)
Glenn E. (Edgerton)
Luis (Perez)
Tom (Mossbrucker)
Second Cast:
DeAnn (Duteil)
Lynne C. (Chervony)
Lynn G. (Glauber)
Glenn W. (White)
John (Grensback)
Julian (Montaner)
Carl (Corry)
First cast come forward."

These are *very* well-behaved dancers. They exchange no looks, express neither jubilation nor disappointment. Only as Glenn E. comes forward, the corners of his mouth lift briefly. From now on, the second cast hovers in the background. Their job is to learn the dance without cluttering up the choreographers's perspective or getting in the way of the first cast.

Dean runs a brisk, even-tempered rehearsal with a minimum of gab. "Good!" she says warmly when approval is warranted—perhaps needed. Or: *"Yes!"* Demonstrating a typical Dean step, a rapid little kicking, she even throws an absent-minded "good!" to her own reflection in the mirror. The kicking step doesn't sit well on the dancers; it looks light and pattery. After a few more rehearsal days, Dean will abandon it.

These dancers are used to working with many different choreographers. In each new venture they have to discover as quickly as possible what gets this choreographer's dander up, what working habits please that one. They're still taking Dean's measure.

The women, unsure of which foot they ought to be on, ask no questions. Standing neatly in their places while, behind them, Dean shows something to the men, they hold up fingers and legs at each other and come to some decision among themselves.

Beautiful or not, the pointe shoes create problems new to Dean. The extra length of foot makes it hard for a woman to come down into plié as softly and rapidly as Dean would. Doing the same step as the men, the women look more brittle, less easy.

After a run-through of the material-to-date, Valmai leans panting on the piano, then looks at Laura and laughs apologetically. This dance calls for a marathoner's carefully nursed energy, whereas ballet dancers are more used to working like sprinters—a flat-out effort for not too long, then a built-in rest (or exit) before the next big push. Dean's dances are shaped like communal rites: the dancers begin on stage and don't leave until the pattern is completed. The gradual elaboration and intensification of step and rhythm is one of the things that makes her work mesmerizing. But it's an ordeal—fifteen, maybe twenty minutes of continuous dancing.

Four days later. Mark Goldweber's injury healed faster than anyone thought it would, and since Laura orginally wanted him in the dance, he's here doing his best to catch up. What with the two extra men assigned as covers, Dean seems well-stocked with males (providential, as it turns out).

The big news today (to me) is a long, calm procession that gives the illusion of snaking endlessly from the back of the stage to the front. It's a canon, of about eight different big smooth moves, and the half turns that Dean has built into it make the dancers appear now to beckon the person behind, now to greet the person ahead. Forever and ever. Dean, without changing her approach to form, has adapted herself to these dancers' hard-won skill at making handsome designs with their bodies. Goodbye stamp-kick, hello arabesque? Not quite. But clearly she has created her own variants of the large pristine shapes ballet dancers are comfortable in.

Suddenly Dean rattles off the names of eight dancers and asks them to come stand side by side. As they do so, it becomes apparent that all are first-cast people except for Mark and Lynne C., and that Carole and Tom have *not* been called. Laura and Angela stare at the dancers and the dancers stare at themselves in the mirror, as if trying to see what Dean sees. Earlier today she warned that some cast changes might be announced next Tuesday. Back to rehearsal. "First cast," calls Dean. Carole and Tom come forward as usual; Lynne C. and Mark retreat. Lynne looks as if she'd like to ask a question, but doesn't. You would have had to be watching Carole very closely during all this to notice anything happening to her at all, but on the scale of about one millimeter to the inch, she was clenching up inside. Three days of worrying coming up. (Dean is usually considerate of dancers and their feelings, but at this stage, she admits to wearing blinders, so narrowly and intently is she focusing on the work itself.)

Tuesday. Everyone looks rested after the two-day break. Dean herself is peppy and smiling. And, in the middle of demonstrating something, hitching up her favorite holey pants for the hundredth time, she says casually, "By the way, casting stays the way it is." Today's rehearsal is more relaxed, a tiny bit noisier, perhaps because Dean has set the dancers working by themselves in pairs—each first-cast dancer briefing his/her opposite number on the latest changes in the tricky counts or intricately meshing paths. In a well-run dance company like this, no one does this grudgingly or imperfectly. It's saner to compete with yourself instead of with your friends, pitching your mind and body toward some decided-upon excellence or rising to meet the choreographer's demands.

It seems that Dean plans to begin the ballet by having everyone spin for nearly two minutes. No spotting, heads still, eyes open and lowered. A ballet dancer's nightmare. The women are on pointe. "I talked to them about it. They said they were fine, no problems," says Laura when I seem incredulous. I mean, perched up there on those tiny platforms, spinning! But of course, they wouldn't complain, unless they were dying. "Yeah, I guess so . . . gee, I don't know," she sighs. "I keep asking them." DeAnn, in the second cast, proves it can be done beautifully—lean, tall, very young, she seems to get taller when she turns and to acquire breadth and stability. (The others applaud her.) Then Cammy (looking, as usual, outlandish and glamorous at the same time; a little chiffon skirt worn over warm-up pants and a jewel at her throat) finds a way to pit very fast spinning steps against the slow arm gestures. Can everyone do that? Probably not. (I can see why Laura had to force herself to stop having second thoughts over casting: when DeAnn can turn like a bloody top or Lynne C. makes the "second big six" look gorgeous, or Mark jumps with such resilience. . .)

Robert Joffrey walks in neat as a pin, smelling of good cologne. He doesn't stop the rehearsal or acknowledge the dancers, nor do they pay any attention to him. He sits down and taps his foot energetically to the two-piano music that's throbbing out of the speakers. I don't think he's here to gauge the choreography, but to see how "his" dancers are doing. He's proud of how adaptable and disciplined the five newcomers from the Joffrey II are (have been brought up to be); he's told all the dancers how interesting and broadening it would be for them to work with Dean. Who smiles at him, widens her large brown eyes, and says in a gentle, firm voice, "as long as I have plenty of time to clean."

"Cleaning" is going to be crucial. Once Dean has finished mapping out the dance, she needs to turn it inside out, make sure no one is, say, freezing in poses the way some of them are now, or flattening out the dynamics of a phrase. For instance, with this new phrase, one simple movement becomes a huge stumbling block. The twelve-count phrase is to be performed in canon in a crisscrossing pattern. It's exhilarating, almost hair-raising, as a dancer leaps between two dancers coming the other way, and they love it immediately. But this one little jump after the leap baffles them. She asks for the ballet equivalent. "Assemblé" think most of them. "Cabriole fermé" says Glenn White. But she wants an easy drop of the weight, no big deal, accent down, not up (when she says "down," several of them obligingly jump very high so they can come *very* down). So later when Ursula raises her hand and asks, "On that assemblé, do you want . . . ?" Dean warns, "Don't *think* of it as an assemblé!"

Dean looks cheerful, but as she packs it in for the day, she says she's worried (to anyone who knows her, this is hardly news). They're getting the steps, but when will they get the "soul"? They're so used to being *light!* I notice that they do some of the steps more fluently when they're marking, even when they're kidding around—which they're beginning, discreetly, to do, letting an arm wave turn them momentarily into sirens, a mistake become a hilarious new idea. When they muster themselves to dance though, they get unnaturally pulled-up, programmed for precision. Which may suit many of the choreographers they work with, but Dean's style requires that the rhythmic precision and vigor support a relaxed flow, an openness in the body, but not a set stance.

Friday. One down. Luis is in street clothes, sitting on a chair, pressing his knee gingerly. The doctor says maybe pulled ligaments, maybe cartilage, "but I'm not even going to think about that. I'm planning on doing as much as I can tomorrow." Today he's supposed to rest, but the second Laura starts showing a new step to Mark, his cover, he walks onto the floor to learn it. And to remind himself and everyone else that he's *not* out of this dance.

The dance is almost sketched out. It even has a name: *Night.* But you don't need the title to see the dancers as luminous beings, whirling and interweaving in some cosmic ritual. The long full sleeves they are to wear will emphasize the slightly East Indian look of the flexed hand gestures Dean has given them. Reminiscent of Indian dance forms also is the way the dancers often advance with a complicated pattern and retreat with simple traveling step in order to come forward again. Here are the endless opening spins (Cammy serene and glowing, getting high on it maybe?); here the snaking procession (see how beautifully connected Glenn E. is making it, dig Ursula's intensity). As they drop one by one into a marking time pattern, Valmai, mouthing counts constantly, suddenly figures out how to keep her weight over her heels on a flat-footed chain of turns. Today she's wearing a Joffrey T-shirt that says "I GIVE TO IT." Perfect. (Australian Valmai, bony and delicate, but quietly dogged, will get a step or perish in the attempt.)

The several big crossing canons are full of surprises. For example, the dancers may feed in one by one, but midway through the pattern everyone has somehow acquired a partner. (Those arm waves look weird today— either sloppy or vampy.) "I definitely plan to work on this. A lot," says Laura, watching concentric circles of spinning contract and expand around an invisible center. (Are Tom and I the only ones who think Tom may pass out?) The dance keeps pulling back down to quietness and simplicity and then building up again. Even with all the mistakes, I get the image I often get from Dean's dances—that the dancing is being woven on a huge loom lying on the floor, gradually accumulating the power to lift from the loom and spin up to the sky.

Next Tuesday. Pianists Paul Epstein and Pat Graf (herself an accomplished dancer) arrive to play for rehearsal for the first time. Now more than ever the dance seems like a complicated web of time and space that the dancers have to wriggle into at just the right point. And to top it off, Larry is out; an injury he got last week may turn into a concussion, and Glenn White's dancing for him today. Luis is at the doctor; Mark's dancing for Luis. Carole's toe obviously hurts. The arm waves are gone—just as well. The simple weaving step is back.

Over and over and over, uncomplaining, they start at the beginning of the dance, inching along a little further with each repetition. Two counts have mysteriously disappeared, and in the newly warming rehearsal atmosphere, everyone gets very engrossed in the hunt for them. The dancers, now assessing Dean as a good guy who appreciates intelligent questions, are full of helpful suggestions.

"I get forty-nine," says Angela, "every time." Forty-nine? So be it. Epstein and Graf rock with Dean's churning, repeating phrases of music, the room rings with them; when a section comes out right, the two pianists congratulate each other. You can tell that Dean is itching to get to work on the quality of the dancing and not have to wade through this number-bombardment. But she's reassuring and calm when another count goes haywire and Valmai says "I'm sorry" in a small voice from her place at the back. (The others cheerfully aim imaginary index finger pistols at her; there, but for the grace of God . . .)

At a break, most of the dancers without a word slide to the floor. Later, over salad and beer, Laura marvels, "Don't you think that's very unusual? I had never seen them do that before." The season, the Joffrey's first proper one in New York since 1978, is less than two weeks away. Fewer than forty dancers are rehearsing almost two dozen ballets. The injuries are starting, and what's worse, she's about to have rehearsal hours taken away from her and to start losing more dancers to other rehearsals.

Away from City Center where she comes on like a champion optimist Dean is downright mournful. She'll have no time now to make changes or question her choices. Nor is she thrilled with her use of pointe shoes: "It was so new to me, like ABC; I'm still learning the alphabet. If I had a chance to do another ballet, I'd want to work with a couple of women for a couple of days first just to see what that's about. Joffrey wanted me to go

on tour with the company, just to hang out with them, but *my* time schedule . . ."

And how will the dancers ("just incredibly wonderful kids") hold up?
Will she have time to help them perform *Night* as beautifully as possible?

"But Laura . . ." And the worried perfectionist allows the assured
creator and the old-pro pragmatist to show through. She waves a hand and
grins, "I'll be fine. It'll all work out."

*Ironically, but predictably, the casting of **Dean's** Night had
changed by the première. Perez and Goldweber were both dancing,
and Blake was not. Chervony was in and Valleskey out. The injury
merry-go-round keeps companies like this spinning.*

THE PAST
REKINDLED

Maria Theresa Duncan, photographed in 1979

Whenever aestheticians talk or write about dance, the word "ephemeral" comes up. Not until the twentieth century was a comprehensive system of notation developed, and since few choreographers bothered to learn it, it entailed the expense of a trained notator. Film, another twentieth-century development, required a much larger budget. Only in the past fifteen years have developments in video made some sort of record-keeping affordable.

In the past, works were handed down via word of mouth, skimpy notes, and demonstrations by ballet masters and dancers with good memories. Choreographers not only accepted the fact that their works would disappear or gradually erode, they often took pride in the slippery nature of dance history. Changes made by dancers or a bright new ballet master might keep a particular piece fresh and up-to-date. George Balanchine altered steps in his own ballets to suit new dancers, new discoveries of his. Some of the most adventurous modernists, from Martha Graham on, place such value on new work that they tend to see old works as merely steps in their development and are glad that few of these have survived.

Yet—particularly for historians and critics—the past has a mysterious allure. We don't want everything to be now. We flock to the Met when word comes that American Ballet Theatre has mounted a "lost" Balanchine ballet, *Symphonie Concertante,* a score of which was discovered in the Dance Notation Bureau's files. Controversy boils as to whether it was notated sensitively, taught "correctly," whether it is being performed in the "right" style.

When we see a revival, the main issues seem to be these: have those in charge been accurate as to the steps, but mummified the spirit; or have they made hash of the choreography in an attempt to keep the work from appearing dated? If in the revival of a Mikhail Fokine ballet the dramatic logic he so prized is violated, the work may look foolish where once it seemed powerful. In the case of modern dance, the shape of the choreography may be preserved, but the dynamics that defined the style may have eluded today's performers and rehearsal directors. A work like José Limón's *The Moor's Pavane* (1949) can apparently survive any number of second-rate performances—as long as they're passionate. The Othello story sails through on Limon's beautifully constructed dramatic line; however the larger human conflict between balance and stability on the one hand and risk and disproportion on the other can become invisible if the dancing isn't given its proper weight and thrust. Calmer, subtler works that were once considered great can all but vanish. "What's all the fuss about?" some people wonder after seeing a vapid revival of Graham's *Primitive Mysteries* (1931) or an inexpressive reconstruction from notation of Doris Humphrey's *New Dance* (1935).

For the critic, writing about revivals or reconstructions holds all the terrors of playing hide-and-seek in the dark. Do we simply consider whether the ballet in question "works"? Do we set ourselves up as watchdogs of tradition? And how do we figure out what the tradition in question was like? I well remember the confusion and embarrassment that arose at one of the annual conferences of the Dance Critics Association, when Danish scholar Knud Jurgensen offered convincing evidence that some of the choreography we admire as most charmingly characteristic of the great nineteenth-century Romantic, August Bournonville, is in fact Bournonville altered slightly by ballet master Hans Beck around the turn of the century. Many present were surprised that they found the supposedly authentic Bournonville steps, which had been pieced together by Jurgensen from the master's notes and markings on musical scores, to be more foursquare and less interesting than those performed by the Royal Danish Ballet today. (And who knows what changes have crept in since Beck's day?)

A more fundamental question is, "Would you rather see a bad revival or no revival at all?" My curiosity is too powerful for me to choose the latter, but when I sit through yet another doggy presentation of something I've loved or a bewildering one of something I've always wanted to see, I think about changing my mind. Except in the case of certain classics, like *Giselle* or *Swan Lake*, which have achieved through repetition a kind of existence independent of performance, off-base execution of a dance can write its obituary.

MARIA THERESA: ISADORA'S
LAST DANCING DAUGHTER

The Village Voice, February 26, 1979

᠊ᢦᢦ᠊

I t's like a fairy tale the way she tells it.

She was one of a troupe of children dancing to celebrate the electrification of the theater in Dresden. They carried heart-shaped rackets, she remembers, that lit up when put in contact with places marked on the stage floor. She was nine years old and one of the best dancers—what a disgrace that she, Theresa, should stop dead in the middle of the dance to return the smile of a woman sitting in one of the boxes. But, as she explained later to her mother, this lady looked like an angel, like . . . the statue of Demeter in the park.

The next morning the doorbell rings. There, amid the snowdrifts, in golden sandals and a Greek dress, stands Demeter. "May I come in?" asks the goddess in broken German. The door to the parlor is thrown wide, and she reclines grandly, Greek fashion, golden feet up on the stuffy, red-plush sofa. What does she want? Theresa, of course, to come and live with her and other specially chosen little girls, to be a dancer. And since her name means nothing to them, she offers them tickets to her Dresden performances. The family sees her dance, and that is that.

Theresa Kruger was one of about twenty little girls who left their homes and families in 1905 to go to Isadora Duncan's new school in Grunewald. Later, she was one of the six young women who often performed on Duncan's programs and who—given the undignified nickname of "Isadorables" by a French critic—toured the United States by themselves to great acclaim between 1918 and 1920. And would have toured another season had not Duncan, with the inscrutably harum-scarum mixture of concern and neglect, love and jealousy that characterized her relationship with her "adopted daughters" summoned them to return to her in Europe.

Theresa—or Maria Theresa as she has called herself since she began a career as a soloist in 1921—is now the last dancing daughter of Isadora Duncan. Irma, Lise, and Margot are dead. Erica, who gave up dancing for painting around 1920, is in a convent; Anna, completely blind, lives in an institution. But Theresa of the sturdy legs, beautiful arms, wide, blunt face—the one photographer Edward Steichen considered the most gifted, the one critics praised for rhythmic clarity—endures, and, at eighty-three, likes to think she has quite a few good years of dancing left in her.

She did stop dancing for a while during the '60s when a heart attack and the death of her husband, Stephan Bourgeois, laid her low. And, no doubt, she took some time off from performing when her two sons were born. But she was successful as a soloist, especially during the '20s; in 1934 she danced at the White House; she was giving concerts at Dance Players Studio and Carnegie Recital Hall during the '50s when Duncan dancing was considered old-fashioned, when the modern dancers all interpreted Isadora's legacy of freedom as freedom to deal with their own times in their own way. Now there is a resurgence of interest in Duncan—among dancers, the public, and the rapidly growing group of dance scholars: we are curious to know how she danced and what she danced. We are greedy for more than descriptions, than the photographs of her with round arms raised as if to receive the sky, or drawings of her skipping in Bacchic abandon, head turned to look behind her. And so, in honor of the centennial of Isadora's birth (May 27, 1877), Maria Theresa assembled a company again, and the Isadora Duncan Heritage Group has been giving small-scale performances at the YWCA on Lexington Avenue. (There are performances next on February 24 and 25, again on March 3 and 4.)

I first saw Maria Theresa when she was giving a master class last spring at Marymount Manhattan. I remember her standing in the center of the gym wearing a long, beautifully draped lavender tunic, her dark red hair dressed in ringlets à la Grecque, her legs still strong and shapely poking out of a slit in the dress, her face . . . well, even with good bones, the face of a woman in her eighties looks *used.* She had stopped exhorting the students with a sweeping of her arm; she had stopped yelling encouraging words in a heavy German accent. She was just standing there looking bleak, while around her in a circle skipped a frenzy of young girls—a few good dancers (perhaps a shade too light, too precise), some hardworking, joyless students, and another group high on self-expression, wearing improvised tunics (checked gingham, whatever you've got), cavorting along, oblivious even to the pulse of the music. Maria Theresa looked as if she despaired of controlling what she'd set in motion and didn't much like the look of it.

But she rallied, began to toss her arms like branches in a wind. (Several of her own student assistants would rush forward, arms out, saying "Don't Maria," every time she'd get too active or try to stand on one leg.) Once she leaned close to me, flashed a rueful lipsticked smile, and said, "You should have seen me when I was sixty!"

Isadora wasn't a teacher; she was a pied piper. The little girls she gathered as students went to her body, mind, and soul. Even when left for long periods with Duncan's sister Elizabeth and her gymnastic exercises, even when parked for a cold winter in what Isadora believed to be a château, but which turned out to be the château's stable, with inadequate food and clothing, they remained in love with her. Ruth St. Denis bred some rebels—Martha Graham, Doris Humphrey, Charles Weidman; Duncan bred only disciples. Even when the girls revolted they did so not because they wanted to dance in a different manner but because they wanted to be financially independent, to dance solos, to interpet the great music Isadora had introduced them to. In effect, they preserved and interpeted and taught a concept of dance born at the turn of the century, in part as a reaction against confined, overstuffed, overembellished art and living. It was also a form that expressed woman's freedom—not so much freedom to compete with men in the marketplace but the freedom to put away corsets, take lovers, bear children out of wedlock, and to dance like that kind of a woman (powerful, supple, fecund) instead of like some man's vision of the seductive fairy as an antidote to the respectable wife.

Maria Theresa, who today combines wisdom, innocence, and mischievousness in beguiling proportions, says that she realizes now that Isadora didn't want her girls to grow up. This had to to with the horrifying death of her own two children and the loss of a third shortly after its birth. ("She was always dreaming of children.") It also became clear that Isadora couldn't brook rivals.

A question of mine sets Maria Theresa talking about her last year with Isadora. Her talk is wonderful, and like her dancing, unhasty. When I saw her perform Liszt's *Les Funerailles*—one of the slow pieces she still dances—she walked simply and majestically onto the small Y stage, sank to her knees, and stayed there grieving for quite a while, moving her head a little, perhaps beating a hand against the floor. She used time luxuriously, confidently, allowing every change to flower organically out of her response to the music. When she talks, she keeps saying, "Well, to make a long story short . . ," but that clearly is impossible. She cannot be diverted from a subject or made to jump forward or backward in time. The words roll on like a tide, bearing a flotsam of vivid and revealing images.

She makes you see Isadora as the girls saw her from the boat returning them to Europe—a tiny figure pacing back and forth on the jetty, a white shawl, something blue fluttering from her head. The Nike of Samothrace breasting the wind. She imitates Isadora looking them over disapprovingly and saying, "No dancing for at least a month. I have to fatten you up first; you have to go on a spaghetti tour now. Each of you has to gain five or ten pounds." (Was this only concern for her protégées' health, or did it reflect her unwillingness to appear, in her forties and quite heavy by then, with a bunch of sylphs?) Maria Theresa shows how Isadora used to twitch her mouth around "like a little rabbit" when irritated, amused, or unwilling to answer a pressing question like "When are we going to dance?"

The summer of 1920 slipped into fall; the girls were forced to cancel their American tour, their own money was almost gone; Isadora took them from France to Italy to Greece (so that they could have the "Greek experience" that had so influenced her), but she never rehearsed with them or spoke of performing. More images of Isadora emerge: sitting at table, taunting her pianist Walter Rummel (who was evidently avoiding her bed), "Eat this slab of roast beef, it will make you *strong* and *healthy*. Drink this wine!" Then, Isadora beginning to sense that Rummel and Anna were having an affair, "She had a way of sitting quiet with only her eyes moving . . ." (Maria Theresa leans back, presses her lips together, and flicks her eyes from side to side of the empty Y conference table.)

Theresa was blamed by the other girls for influencing them to leave America, and she depicts herself finally flying into a rage, "I grabbed Isadora, I *shook* her. I said, 'If you don't dance with us tomorrow, I don't know what I'll do.' Suddenly she looks at me and says, 'That's the way I like it. I like it when you are so wild. Tell the girls I'll teach.' " But, although there was a little teaching after that odd summer, and a little performing, the Isadorables began to drop way until only Irma remained to accompany Isadora on her messianic, perhaps desperate, mission to Moscow. Maria Theresa tells of one last conversation. When she asked Isadora what she, Theresa, was to do in Russia: " 'I want you to teach. A thousand children.' 'Oh no!' 'Oh yes.' I was appalled. I was never good at teaching children because of my bad hearing. And Isadora said, 'I don't want anyone else to dance and exploit this art. I want you to teach.' " And presumably those children in turn would be content to teach others so that, in a way, Isadora would be the unique professional, followed by generations of amateurs who would dance only for spiritual and physical enrichment.

Yet, curiously, Isadora did not, in the usual sense, teach; she inspired by music and by her own example. Irma, in her book *Duncan Dancer,* describes a session in which Isadora, asked by her pupils to break down a passage or do it slowly, found herself unable to, and took that as proof that great art couldn't and shouldn't be dissected. Irma was methodical;

Maria Theresa isn't: she stimulates, sketches out general patterns, demonstrates, draws attention to the music, and has little sympathy for the unmusical, the unpoetic would-be dancers. "They should go plant cabbages."

I watch six young women in rehearsal try to feel their way into some dances to Chopin piano pieces. (Maria Theresa is at home; she has a cold, and her daughter-in-law won't let her out of the house, so the rehearsal is handled by her assistant, dance historian Kay Bardsley, once a member of the company Maria Theresa had for ten years.) The women, in a motley assortment of Greek tunics, run smoothly in loops around each other—one, then another, then another joining in. They break out of this idyllic sisterhood of nymphs to laugh and argue about who goes where just like any dancers, but I notice that they'll suddenly drop one dance and proceed to another, as if afraid that they'd lose the spirit if they got things too tidied up all at once, or become too like one another in their response to the music. Jubilea Sebert, one of the most gifted, runs through the Chopin nocturne they call "The Angel" knocking softly on an imaginary grave and pointing the way to heaven; she does it beautifully, and the others clap for her; Bardsley laughs and says something like "Lovely! Too bad we have to be a little more accurate." In other words, instead of learning the steps first and *then* trying to infuse them with meaning, the dancers learn the music, the feeling, the broad shape of the dance and only afterward proceed to the specifics.

For this approach you need more time than anyone has these days. "Isadora would turn in her grave," says Maria Theresa, about the relatively short training and rehearsing period. She also says, "All great art is personality; movements per se are boring." Which may explain why the secrets of Isadora's greatness remain so difficult to unravel, the history of her dancers so hard to trace. Watch Annabelle Gamson perform the solos she learned from Julia Levien who learned them from Irma Duncan. Suddenly some of the pictured poses come to life—the maenad beckons, devours, the oppressed serf wrenches her hands free of the earth and flings them wide—and they come to life, not haphazardly, but set into subtly constructed phrases. Whose phrases? Isadora's or Irma's? Isadora, everyone will tell you, never performed a dance the same way twice. Watch Maria Theresa, watch Julia Levien, whose Isadora Duncan Commemorative Dance Company is also performing this spring, and you see a beautiful sense of weight, a grandeur of spirit, a musicality—but these women are years older than Isadora at the time of her death. Watch lovely Maria Rubinate of Maria Theresa's group; she's very sensitive to the nuances of a Brahms waltz, but in the tiny curving gestures of her arms, the gentle sway of her body you see three shadowy dancers—a young girl imitating an old woman remembering the precepts of a genius who's been dead for over fifty years. And which, if any, of these group patterns were designed by Isadora? Or are even like anything designed by Isadora?

Isadora's vision of "nature," however basic it may have appeared, was a romantic, idealized one, yet it is not entirely anachronistic in a period when so many fear that the world is about to be paved over. Revivals of Duncan's work, or Duncanesque works, can, depending on the circumstances and performance, seem either naïve and precious or profoundly simple and moving. To Maria Theresa, of course, Isadora Duncan is still "the central fire of the universe in the dance—flaming higher than ever!" Slyly, she quoted young Maria Theresa giving herself confidence by saying "Well, if I am only a flame of *her* fire, that still means I must be pretty good." There is something rarified about the life pattern that Isadora set for her back in 1905. Describing with touching wonder that day Isadora first came to her mother's house, she lifts her hands and says, "It was like when Demeter entered the house of Metaneira and touched with her high head the ceiling of the house, and the ceiling was raised."

It only occurred to me years later that what Maria Theresa was saying might not have been, "You should have seen me when I was sixty," but "You should have seen me when I was sixteen." I'm sure she was something at either age.

I'd also like to reinstate a story that had to be left out. Maria Theresa wasn't happy about how Maria Rubinate was performing one of the solos, and told her to make it slower. But how can I do that? Rubinate asked, pointing out that the speed of the taped music was fixed. "Then," said Rubinate, to me, "Maria did it. Slower." Meaning, that the older woman's rich sense of the weight of each gesture created the illusion of slowness.

FAR FROM MANHATTAN

The Village Voice, December 17, 24, 1979

I don't know what they do with garbage in Copenhagen. I never saw any. The streets of the old town are clean; so are the stone and brick houses that are cream, brown, blue, crimson, and a color that's halfway between butter and the flesh of tangerines. The canals that wind through parts of the city are full of clear, bright green water. At the porno supermarket, everything you might want is neatly displayed and labeled. The high taxes support handsome pensions for the aged; I even saw a well-dressed bag lady. Occasional signs of violence—aggressively drunken teenagers, the flash of a knife in the main railway station—come as a shock. "Drunk?" says the tour guide. "perhaps they were Swedes."

It is a pleasure to see the ballets of August Bournonville in this handsome, gentle-mannered, resourceful city where they were made and which they somehow resemble, and it is important to see them in the intimate Royal Opera House (the "new" one, built in 1874 near the site of the old one) where every small activity Bournonville devised is vivid and comprehensible, where capital letters over the proscenium arch spell out NOT FOR PLEASURE ALONE.

However, what seemed like hundreds of foreign balletomanes, critics, and historians appeared to be taking intense and heated pleasure in the week-long festival that ended on November 30, the one hundredth anniversary of Bournonville's death. In the theater's salons and intricate mazes of staircases, people argued over dancers' interpretations, over which director had cut or interpolated what. How had Act II of *Napoli* come to be lost? Why had Hans Beck (ballet master from 1894) made new dances for Act II of *La Sylphide*?

In his memoirs, *My Theatre Life* (now available in English in a splendid translation by Patricia McAndrew), Bournonville writes, "The art of mime encompasses all the feelings of the human soul. The dance, on the other hand, is essentially an expression of joy, a desire to follow the rhythms of the music." It is his adherence to this precept that makes his dramatic ballets like no others you can see today. People in his ballets— and they are people—usually dance from exuberance or excitement or because they're at a party or a festival or entertaining others. The heroine of *A Folk Tale* dances among the trolls to play for time; James dances among the sylphs out of a morbid excitement and perhaps to convince himself that he is finding happiness; the Sea Demon, Golfo, forces the heroine of *Napoli* into a duet, as if by doing so he can convince her they're made for each other. But Bournonville's characters don't dance anguish or despair; when Gennaro in *Napoli* believes that his Teresina has been drowned in a storm, he clutches his head, staggers around, falls to the floor, and in general behaves with the passionateness that Bournonville attributed to Neapolitans.

All the "dancing" is bright-tempered and in control. Judging from Bournonville's own *Konservatoriet*—a memento of his Paris studies with Auguste Vestris from 1824—it would seem that the steps he used were typical of the period (he also includes steps like "jeté Taglioni," "pointes Elssler," "glissade Grisi" in his written lexicon). Typical, too, is the buoyancy, the soft intricate footwork. What's unusual in terms of later ballet is the absence of poses, stops, walks to new positions. The beautifully managed phrases purl along with adroit spatters of quick little footsteps suddenly producing one of those sailing leaps with the back leg bent, or perhaps a pirouette that ends with the dancer not planted in fifth but balanced on one leg and unfolding the other smoothly—a gracious gesture, not a confrontation or a demand for applause (these dancers never break the flow of a work by bowing to the audience anyway). Sometimes you see a perfect balance—the Sylphide poised for a second in arabesque as if the air were still around her—but more often the Danes seem to pass through balances, making comprehensible those caught-in-flight lithographs of the 1830s and '40s.

Dancing is a matter of gentle sweep and momentum, of pleasurably novel changes of direction and rhythm within a phrase. And this is true of the happy bounding solos; the rapid-footed ballet-gypsy stuff; the smooth, coiling, flowering, all-on-one-leg adagios (the few that Beck didn't excise); and the host of spirited national dances that Bournonville loved so well and set so beautifully—the tarantellas, the seguidillas, the waltzes, reels, hornpipes, and stamping Scandinavian couple dances.

Mime is not simply a gestural recitative to link dance passages, it is the lifeblood of the work, And whether we're seeing "dancing" or formal mime or quite natural behavior, it's all meaningful as movement. When someone would ask in intermission, "Not much dancing in that one is there?" I'd be hard put to say.

There simply aren't any crowd scenes like Bournonville's on the stage today. Everyone seems to have a reason for being there and a way of showing that subtly and intelligently. The stage picture is so rich that you can hardly take it in. The quay in Act I of *Napoli* fairly bursts with life— entertainers, artists, tourists, vendors, fishermen. All are played with distinction by children and adults of all ages—not only extras and students but the young dancers of ten, twenty, and thirty years ago now ripened into superb character performers.

Bournonville's grimmer ballets to do with Nordic myth and history have been lost, but his three major "Romantic" ballets tell a lot about his theatricality and his morality. *La Sylphide* (1836), the best known, and slightly atypical, is in two acts because it ends badly. Bournonville's James, clearly in the wrong for leaving his charming fiancée and comfortable life to chase pretty demons, loses everything. Both *Napoli* (1842) and *A Folk Tale* (1854) have festive last acts in which all the troubles of their supernatural second acts are resolved. Gennaro, the fisherman hero of *Napoli,* and Junker Ove, the young nobleman of *A Folk Tale,* traffic with demons, but not because they want to: they're two different versions of the archetypal hero who descends to the underworld to achieve his goal. Armed with a holy medal, Gennaro rows into the Blue Grotto, where his drowned sweetheart has been revived and turned into a Naiad by the demonic Golfo (terrific stunt with a breakaway costume). But Teresina resists the lust of Golfo, and Gennaro doesn't succumb to the Naiads. The power of love plus the power of the medal reform the demon, and the lovers row home rich with sea plunder. As it stands now, this act is a bit numb. Years ago cut to ribbons, recently pieced together by assistant ballet master Kirsten Ralov, its pas de deux have that stagy "now-I-give-you-my-hand" look. The naiads don't tempt much, and they tend to dance in two crisscrossing lines when it would have been more typical of Bournonville, I think, to break them into sisterly trios and quartets.

In the midsummer magic of *A Folk Tale,* Bournonville turns Romantic conventions upside down. The girl who emerges from under a hill and lures the hero with a goblet of flaming liquid appears dangerous, but clearly she's only a pawn of evil. It's Junker Ove's hot-tempered fiancée Birthe who's a fledgling monster. And just as puberty brings out the heroine's longings for light and love and religion, it brings out the troll in Birthe (this is one of those switched-in-the-cradle deals): as she dances elegantly before her mirror and her maids, her demonic and greedy soul begins to emerge in irrepressible twitches and clawings.

But, although there is a bevy of damply pretty elf maidens who whirl the hero into senselessness and insanity, the demonic element in this ballet is a wonderful grotesque society of trolls. "A Biedermeier *Nibelungenlied,*" said a Viennese visitor in delight when the Act II curtain went up on Diderik and Viderik tapping busy rhythms on their anvils (the score by Hartmann and Gade is a really fine one) while small bent-over troll boys pumped huge bellows for them. To a party comes the troll bourgeoisie in full fig. Through the brown rags, crouched stances, the clomping feet, we identify cranky women, brutish husbands, timid wives, shy children, loutish boys, marriageable girls.

In these surly revels, the troll brothers who crave the heroine are presented as opposites: Diderik is foul-tempered, staggering around spraddle-legged, swiping at everyone; Viderik is shy and gentle and keeps his arms and legs pulled in, his gestures tiny, as if he were afraid to take up too much space. The rather passive hero doesn't tame this underworld: he never even really enters it. This ballet's Orpheus is Viderik, who helps the heroine back to earth and tames the human furies by gleefully turning them into head-wagging automatons with his harp-playing.

Here's something else August Bournonville believed: "The beautiful always retain the freshness of novelty while the astonishing soon grows tiresome." Not for Bournonville the spectacular effects Marius Petipa carried off in his salad days, such as the climactic moment of a dance in *King Candaule* in which each dancer's flowery headdress opened to reveal a living child. Bournonville's best surprises come in the way he turns a dance phrase, or in schoolboyish jokes like the sudden bang-bang of muskets we hadn't even noticed in the bustle of *Napoli*'s finale. There is very little in Bournonville's extant ballets of grandeur, glitter, tragedy, or sexuality; perhaps this is why even those who love his ballets—as most of those who made the trip to Denmark for the centenary of his death appeared to—say worriedly to each other, "Of course, Bournonville is not for everyone . . ." or "Isn't it wonderful? It'll never come across at the Met."

But Bournonville is, in his own way, profound. The plot of *A Folk Tale*, perhaps the most fascinating of his surviving ballets, evokes a rich jumble of tales and legends. When we look at the last-act wedding in leafy glade, the girls in their green dresses, the maypole, we can see Hilda not just as a girl who's gotten out of the clutches of trolls, but as Persephone who has emerged from the underworld to bring summer to the land. Even works like *Far From Denmark* or *The King's Volunteers on Amager*, works that Bournonville termed "vaudeville ballets," even uproarious comedies like *Kermesse in Bruges* contain perceptions of human behavior that are sound as a nut. Surely no plot in which a woman puts on a mask to test her husband's fidelity is resolved with as little fuss as it is in *Amager*. Caught out, the man looks at his wife ruefully and very lovingly, and between the two of them, in a nearly motionless moment, everything is understood.

There's a good grain to Bournonville's theatricality. In *A Folk Tale*, he sets up one of those scenes in which maids parade around in their absent mistress's clothes, but he doesn't supply the obvious climax of having the bad-tempered young woman catch them at it; he only lets us understand from their sudden consternation what *would* happen (and maybe has before). When in *Amager* the gentleman musician, Edward (Tommy Frishøi), dresses up to dance a reel with two local boys (Johnny Eliasen and Frank Andersen), the three work in perfect unison, but Andersen and Eliasen dance with happy pride, Frishøi with just the barest trace of condescension. In *Far From Denmark*, we're seldom allowed to forget that it's really Danish sailors (on a ship anchored off Argentina) who are dressing up to perform the outrageously fantastical Eskimo and American Indian dances. (Two principal young cadets are always played by women, so when *they* assume silk tunics and pointe shoes for the pseudo-Chinese dance, they're clearly the stars of shipboard frolics.)

One of Bournonville's deftest practices is that of offering us characters in pairs, so we can observe how differently two superficially similar people behave in the same situation—a sort of mime counterpoint. There are the aforementioned cadets in *Far From Denmark* (and from old lobby photos you can see that one is *always* wigged as dark, the other as fair). There are the two peasant boys in *Amager*—one bluff, one a go-alonger—plus the interesting tangle composed of their two sweethearts, two flirtatious cadets, and *their* sweethearts—all of which gives rise to much remonstrating, pleading, shrugging, and flouncing out of the room. In *A Folk Tale,* we have the bad and good troll brothers, Diderik and Viderik, and the child helper of each is a small echo of his master.

Of the three brothers in *The Kermesse in Bruges,* one is a feisty lout, one a fool, and one the hero. As the lout's girl, Dinna Bjørn cries and wrings her hands a lot worrying over him; the fool's girl (Anne Marie Vessel) is the sort who folds her arms and pulls men around by the ear.

Hans Brenaa has restaged this robust ballet wonderfully—not just drawing lively and tender dance performances from Ib Andersen and Mette-Ida Kirk but shaping the stew of activity so that comedic moments surface enticingly without stopping the flow. The ballet's rather like one long chase, especially the great final scene in which young Carelis saves his two brothers and their alchemist benefactor from the stake by dancing the whole town into a stupor with his magic violin music. Fine ladies, stout burghers, scholars, children, peasants, and monks cavort helplessly, finally agreeing to *anything* if only they can rest.

One of the ballet's most entrancing scenes is one in which the cannily simple brother, wearing a magic ring that makes everyone fall in love with him, is doted on by a fine lady—dressed in silks, fed, and feted, and stared at fondly. Here Niels Kehlet does some of his most inspired acting— spearing one last drumstick as the butler removes the food, getting his feet inexplicably tangled or his arms folded the wrong way, but absolutely delighted and in no way humbled by his good fortune.

Kehlet has always been able to bounce between hero roles and character ones. At forty-one, he still sails through the air as Gennaro in the festive last act of *Napoli,* as well as giving the role and the occasion a gladness no one in the company can quite match. As the surly Diderik in *A Folk Tale,* he is all coarse vigor and shambling twistedness, as pathetic as an ugly and ugly-tempered pet who would nevertheless like to be loved. Bournonville created wonderful roles for men of all ages, roles that good performers can shape to fit them. I have no idea whether Tommy Frishøi can jump high or not; he's a perfect debonair hero for *Far From Denmark* and *Amager* where Spanish dancing and reels and hornpipes are his dance material. Johnny Eliasen, a strong young dancer with an engagingly thuggish face—good at playing boisterous boys or elegant brutes—makes his

Diderik less twisted and more of a confident bully than Kehlet's, Fredbjørn Bjørnsson's Viderik is a marvel of small, shy gestures and painfully stiff dance steps. The company's director, tall, thin Henning Kronstam, who played heroes in the '50s, now shambles slyly around as the lemonade seller in *Napoli,* knees hitting together, laughing and pointing in conniving glee. Niels Bjørn Larsen gets the tiny plum role of the Streetsinger in *Napoli*—an amazing piece of mime: while he silently sings, a sweet quavering trumpet in the pit provides his voice. What's most amazing is that Larsen does it straight and lets the novelty of the concept produce the laughs.

Of the young men, Ib Andersen is the company's virtuoso—boyish and ardent with a beautiful easy lift to his chest, clean beats, and a pirouette that turns an audience to jelly (he gradually retards his multiple whizzes to end in a fifth position that has the composure of a period at the end of a sentence, rather than the exclamation point some dancers make it). Arne Villumsen, a darker bigger man, has a beautiful jump and more somber stage persona; I was surprised how expressive he was in *Napoli,* slightly disappointed in his broody James in a *La Sylphide.* Frank Andersen has come a long way over the past few years; his carriage is easier, his jump bolder, his legwork more incisive, and he continues to be an engaging actor. As Gurn in *La Sylphide,* he's always aware of Effie and aching at every sight of her.

Bournonville's roles for women are a bit less meaty. Still it's a pleasure to watch Kirsten Simone as the amorous widow in *Kermesse;* or Sorella Englund, once admired as the Sylphide, now fine and febrile as the witch Madge in the same ballet; or Solveig Østergaard (the great Swanhilda of the '60s) in blackface doing a wild nineteenth-century guess at African dancing. And Lillian Jensen as the troll matriarch provides a grandly sloppy underworld version of a hostess who gets drunk at her own party. Bournonville's ingenues aren't all alike, but most of the young women dance modestly—airy and soft-footed. One of the problems for company dancers has been to maintain this early-nineteenth-century gentleness and suppleness in the instep without looking weak. It's an uphill battle evidently. Watching the way the children in *Konservatoriet* throw their legs high in the air and let the feet flap I wonder if there's some flaw in the training these days.

Eva Kloborg has very nice feet and a pleasant, unaffected style. Annemarie Dybdal is good at tricky balances. Dinna Bjørn has a beguiling gentleness, but they often seem to lack assurance, to be afraid to impose even a modicum of individual phrasing to the dancing. The audience loved Heidi Ryom, partly because she is vivacious, and Mette-Ida Kirk, who has a robust innocence. Mette Hønningen, on the other hand, has assurance but a disturbing amount of tension; both she and Dybdal turned the last Spanish dance in *La Ventana* into just the hard, hoydenish thing Bournonville was opposed to. Linda Hindberg appeared often during the week—a model of high-bred sensuality as the Argentinian Pepita, nasty as the troll-maiden, delicately musical in the duet from *Flower Festival in Genzano.* She can look oddly awkward, miscalculating impetus, but on the last night gave a ravishingly serene performance of one of the solos in *Napoli.* The up-and-comer is clearly Lis Jeppeson; her Sylphide was, interestingly, rather mad; even in her pliant dancing and beautiful feathery balances she looked deranged, as if trailing after mortals might be considered abnormal behavior for a sylph.

The question of whether Bournonville *is* Bournonville is an endless one. Clearly, one can't blame him for the current second act of *Napoli* (Kirsten Ralov mostly, with a bit of Hans Brenaa and perhaps some Harald Lander, said one source), but other additions and deletions are more elusive. Luckily, Bournonville wears most of them gracefully. In 2005 let's celebrate the 200th anniversary of his birth.

THE PARTNER WE CAN'T REFUSE

The Village Voice, December 28, 1982

▁▂▁

If you ask most people to list the dance works they would include in a pantheon of masterpieces, Kurt Jooss's 1932 *The Green Table* would probably be among them, and those speaking and writing of the ballet often seem to be saying that the greatness of the work rests on its never-out-of-date antiwar message, and the pungency with which Jooss delivered that message to a world poised between two immense wars.

I'm not denying the power of the subject, but there have been quite a few antiwar pieces we commend for their spirit and instantly forget. To me, Jooss's primary theme for *The Green Table* was death, with war providing the pretext and the machinery. It's the profoundness of his vision of death—or Death—that keeps the ballet blazing in memory.

So I was interested to hear Kurt Jooss say to Robert Joffrey, in one of the documentary portions of Dance in America's fine new television show of *The Green Table,* that he had always been fascinated by the medieval dance of death and, long before making *The Green Table,* had planned a ballet on that theme. There are almost no scenes in *The Green Table* that make us feel the horrors of war as powerfully as we sense the inevitability of Death and wonder how and when he will come to each of the characters. When he begins to lead the numb figures of his victims in a long parade, Frederic Cohen's music swells into ironically sweet chords of triumph. We notice that the slippery, sleazy profiteer isn't among them, know that he will try cunning and evasion as usual, and are only satisfied when he who profited by the deaths of others is himself caught by Death, as if by an incorruptible police officer.

The antiwar statement is most pithily articulated in the bookend scenes of the masked diplomats in their black silk suits pounding pompously on the conference table. They're the ones who make us feel outrage as they mince about and gesture effetely to a poisonous little tango, which, played on two pianos like the rest of the score, links their machinations with those of performers in some seedy cabaret. They are the ones who have provided Death with an extraordinary harvest.

Jooss's Death is a terrifying grim reaper. It's not his white-boned face or his get-up as a spectral Roman soldier or the greenish light in which he always appears that makes him frightening, but the sweep of his scything gestures, the way one leg flashes like a knife when he turns it in and then out, the huge amounts of air he gathers with his arms. As the fighting begins, he marches tirelessly in the background, mechanically flexing his biceps like a phantom general exhorting his troops.

Jooss's scenes have the hard-edged succinctness of line drawings, but the flexibility of cinema. We are at a town square, on a battlefield, beside a road, in a brothel, on a hilltop. War, as theme and condition, unifies into a tragic design the various modes of Death, the places he visits.

What makes the ballet so profoundly moving, I think, is the wisdom with which Kurt Jooss delineated the encounters between Death and his prey. To the soldiers performing their highly abstracted maneuvers, he comes simply as the enemy soldier they didn't notice behind them, as one of them. To the captured female partisan who has been signaling boldly with her scarf, who has killed a man, Death is an officer, and will command the firing squad she must always have known to be a possible end. To the distraught and exhausted young girl the profiteer has placed in a brothel, Death appears as one last partner. Each of the soldiers she has been dancing with has his own crudely lusty style—farm boys waltzing drunkenly. Like one of them, Death grabs her by the hips and presses his groin against her, but then he begins a clumsy, yet purposeful dance—

taking big hopping steps and yanking her around him in a circle by one hand. Suddenly it's as if she were caught on the blades of a revolving fan, whirled by an implacable machine. When she falls, he slides down beside her; for one second, the lover getting into bed, before he raises to us an emotionless, unequivocal face.

In one of the most delicate scenes, an old woman—one of a crowd of sorrowing women traveling along a diagonal path—sees Death at the end of the road. At first she is terrified, but then she begins taking tiny, faltering steps toward him on tiptoe, and the music, which has seemed merely mournful, now can be heard clearly as a distant waltz and an even more distant lullaby. Death is a courtly partner to her, and she curtsies bravely. In the end, she goes to him to be picked up like a child and carried out of our sight.

Dance in America's tape features the Joffrey Ballet. Jooss worked with the dancers before his death, and his daughter, Anna Markard, returns from time to time to coach them. The Joffrey production has always been marvelous and the videotape ought to stimulate people to see it (*The Green Table* is being done three times during the company's current season at City Center). Philip Jerry is remarkably strong and clear as Death, and Gary Chryst plays the Profiteer with slimy deviousness.

The Green Table's terseness isn't ideal for television, where, it seems to me, cloudy and amorphous images acquire a voluptuous clarity. On the small screen, the simplicty of the soldiers' marching and fighting with their rhythmic jabs and thrusts becomes almost cartoonlike. The authentic stage lighting doesn't always work on television either. Emile Ardolino's direction features more sudden cutting between medium-close and very long shots than I like, but he lets you see the ballet, and the photographs, film clips, and interview material are marvelous.

DON'T FAULT FOKINE

The Village Voice, January 14–20, 1981

The trouble is that there is no dance form . . . There is only miming and hubbub, and that doesn't keep for 30 years." That's what Edwin Denby wrote about a Ballet Russe de Monte Carlo *Scheherazade* in

1944. And I would guess that the production of Mikhail Fokine's ballet that Frederic Franklin has staged for Dance Theatre of Harlem, and which the dancers are performing with such touching earnestness up at City Center, is less like the ballet that thrilled Paris in 1910 and more like a spiffed-up, streamlined version of the one that trudged through hundreds of one-night American stands during the late '30s and early '40s.

As Denby implies, *Scheherazade* was no choreographic masterpiece. It was created as a vehicle for Ida Rubenstein—big, beautiful, dramatic, and rich, but no ballerina—and the irreplaceable Vaslav Nijinsky. Serge Diaghilev, and Alexandre Benois, who devised the scenario, intended to make the public swoon at the barbarism and opulence of forbidden color combinations, harmonies, gestures. By all accounts, they succeeded wildly. And perhaps the lack of "choreography" was in part responsible. Fokine, in this case, was less interested in making dances than in orchestrating an orgy and a slaughter, in animating Leon Bakst's violently beautiful sets and costumes and Rimsky-Korsakov's luscious music, so that the public—between the quite brief opening and closing of a curtain—could actually gaze into the kind of exotic Eastern dream world that preoccupied so many writers, painters, and designers of the day.

We can't recover the innocence of vision that would allow us to be as shocked as the spectators of 1910 were. Our eyes are used to seeing blue and green together, hot pink against orange. Orgies are commonplace on our stages. How could we find a seated dance for three odalisques as novel as Benois did? And we in 1980 wouldn't be titillated by the mating of a Shah's concubines with African slaves, even if DTH cared to make this racial point.

At the second performance of the DTH *Scheherazade* that I saw, when some of the dancers were beginning to look less baffled by this sexy stew they found themselves in, I felt puzzled that events which had clearly been designed to make hearts beat faster or arouse pity weren't quite doing so. It was as if you could glimpse what must have once been masterful direction and pacing through layers and layers of veiling, or as if the passage of time had slipped things askew.

So much that witnesses of the first performance describe, that photographs show, simply doesn't happen in this production, or happens in such a way that you scarcely notice it. Where is the bite on the breast that André Eglevsky remembers Fokine instructing him always to apply as the Favorite Slave reaches Zobeide?

Where is the clapping that accompanies the Slave at the intoxicated height of the dance, when Cyril Beaumont describes him as springing and spinning along a "human avenue"?

What was it that Leonide Massine found so exhausting about this last dance when he was the Slave? Eddie Shellman spends quite a bit of it standing still while the others circle him.

The build-up to the Slave's first appearance prepares you for a Class A entrance. Virginia Johnson as Zobeide pleads and pleads with the reluctant Chief Eunuch, finally slings her pearls at him as a bribe, leans hot and decorative against the frame of the opened door, while the others roll on their pillows and the music hits a climax. Then what? Well, there's a pause; and then Eddie Shellman sort of runs out looking around eagerly. We ought to be gasping. Why do so many writers recall their excitement at Nijinsky's entrance? "Nijinsky shot out of his room like an arrow from a bow in a mighty parabola which enabled him to cross in one bound a good two-thirds of the width of the stage . . . I do not know whether he took a running leap or not, but the actual effect was as though he leaped from a crouching position . . ." (Cyril Beaumont). "A pause, and suddenly a superb, golden animal jumps up to an incredible height from a crouch and with one movement he possesses her" (Romola Nijinsky). Memories falter, writers exaggerate, we know all that; yet something thrilling must have happened to trigger such prose. Shellman does a single exquisite bound into the air, with his legs bent under him in a diamond, but it comes a moment later and with premeditation.

Shellman, a dancer I admire considerably, gets laughs for a death scene that ought still to be capable of rousing horror. People who saw the original *Scheherazade* invariably remember Nijinsky falling, thrusting quivering legs straight into the air in such a way that he actually seemed to spin on the back of his neck, and then falling limply. This legs-up gesture is just one of a series of agonized acrobatics that Shellman does, and he doesn't spin while doing it, although he later scrabbles around on two feet, with everything else off the floor but his head. Massine did complain of the difficulty of performing "innumerable contorted twists"—was it just a matter of emphasis and believable phrasing that made this single image—"like a fish tossed onto the sand"—so memorable and so horrifying? And where is the chase of the Slave by the guards with scimitars?

The time between the unexpected return of the Shah and his malevolent brother and the massacre of the illicitly partying couples is puzzlingly short. There's no reaction time built in. Then you find in accounts of the original production that, as the orgy began, four eunuchs slipped away (clearly to alert the master, since they accompanied him on this last entrance: Fokine was fastidious about dramatic logic). If the Shah enters expecting to find trouble, the structure makes sense. It's these same four eunuchs who originally strangled the Chief Eunuch; DTH only has two eunuchs, used for window dressing at the very beginning. When you see that three of the sultanas have to carry off the jewel boxes that they've just taken the trouble to bring on, with scarcely a second to grab a jewel or two, you suspect that many details of this ballet have eroded with the years.

Eglevesky remembered in a *Ballet Review* interview how enraged Fokine would get if the lascivious couples didn't structure their improvised lovemaking according to his guidelines: "I don't want to see both bodies sitting up or both bodies lying down." How he would rant at the poor DTH orgiasts! Beaumont, writing in 1938, recalled Enrico Cecchetti's detailed acting in the role of the Chief Eunuch, and added, "Of late there has been a regrettable tendency on the part of certain interpreters to make the Chief Eunuch a comic personage, which detracts from the dramatic balance of the ballet." Yet Joseph Wyatt has been coached by Franklin to waddle and wag his head, and without training in this very European type of character role, how can a dancer look other than comic? Mel Tomlinson, as the Shah's villainous brother, also has difficulty making his role believable. He plays it surly and arrogant, and, in a passage in which he, I think, is supposed to be insinuating in gesture that the harem women are unfaithful, he behaves as if they were dangerous animals about to bite him.

By the second performance I saw, Lowell Smith as the Shah had developed in ease and indolent grace and I believed his love for Zobeide, his grief at having to see her die. Virginia Johnson is a silky, coolly sweet Zobeide, and her slim body suffers most from Carl Michell's ideas about costuming. Geoffrey Guy's set is "after Bakst," but Michell and the company's co-director Karel Shook have both been quoted as saying Bakst's costumes would have made the dancers look unacceptably bulky. Given the possibilities of modern fabrics. I think this was a sad decision. Not that some of Michell's costumes aren't handsome, but they aren't extraordinary in the way that Bakst's were. The original costumes would look more shocking and barbaric today than Michell's skimpy updates. Karsavina, pictured in one version of Bakst's outfit, doesn't look fat, only soft and opulent. Johnson, in a long-sleeved jacket and tailored pants, would make any Shah put her on extra rations.

My point is that I see no reason DTH *Scheherazade* couldn't be vivid and startling; neither Fokine nor altered tastes should be blamed if it isn't.

LET YELLOW RING

The Village Voice, February 23, 1982

In this age of specialization, an artist like Vasily Kandinsky might be an anomaly. Snaking up the ramps of the Guggenheim to observe the splendid Kandinsky in Munich: 1896–1914 (the first of three Kandinsky shows the Guggenheim is mounting), you think there's nothing the man and his contemporaries wouldn't try: furniture, embroidery, jewelry, clothes, posters, calligraphy, book endpapers, vases, and woodcuts, gouaches, water colors, oils. The show presents a milieu in all its complex interactions. Common concerns are everywhere evident—the sinuous, tensile, curving lines of the Jugendstil, the themes from myth and folk tale, the enamel-bright colors, politics, each other. The artists establish militant societies to push new art or open new possibilities for the dissemination of their work. Kandinsky paints Gabrielle Munter painting. Munter paints Kandinsky painting.

In conjunction with the exhibit, the Guggenheim has sponsored the realization of Kandinsky's one-act opera *The Yellow Sound.* In 1982, we have the world premiere of a work first drafted in 1909, published in 1912 in the *Blaue Reiter* almanac, and never performed. Gunther Schuller sensitively orchestrated and fleshed out the extant bits of Thomas de Hartmann's score. Schuller, director Ian Strasfogel, choreographer Hellmut Fricke-Gottschild, and designers Robert Israel and Robert Riddell studied Kandinsky's scenario for instructions and clues.

The production is a beautiful thing—a complex array of marvels and disappointments. Compare the German title *Der Gelbe Klang* with *The Yellow Sound.* It conveys not just a yellow sound but the sound of yellow too. "Klang" has a different sort of resonance; it's more violent, somehow, less mellifluous. Kandinsky was profoundly interested in specific relationships between color and sound, and, since he became acquainted with the ideas of Theosophist Rudolf Steiner around 1909, he may also have been aware of the ways in which the sounds of words convey something beyond literal meaning. I only bring up the Klang/sound comparison because what seems to have evaded the ingenious team of reconstructors is the emotional and spiritual message of the work. In his essay *Concerning the Spiritual in Art,* Kandinsky avowed that if the emotion of the artist in response to the world as he senses it doesn't penetrate the work of art, then that work of art is a sham. The feeling of what he termed "a true work of art" can, he wrote, "deepen and purify the feeling of the spectators."

I wonder what he would say to a production that leaves many spectators wondering whether the five magnificent yet clumsy yellow giants who stand about, desultorily raising arms that are comically both limp and stiff, are figures of evil or of good? They have nightmare heads—one is a real teddy bear with what looks rather like a drum crammed with drumsticks for a hat, but the gigantic "messiah" figure that raises its arms into a cruciform shape just before the final blackout is also robed in yellow. If yellow signified aggression to Kandinsky, as the program suggests, then the mystery deepens. (His scenario does say, cryptically, that none of the brightly cloaked people in Scene 3 is wearing yellow.)

The scenario doesn't say what *The Yellow Sound* is supposed to mean, but, presumably, had Kandinsky and his collaborators been able to mount it, they would have unified the vision that has come down to us in fragments.

The noise of it is exciting: the radical dissonances coming from the Speculum Musicae in the pit—the storms and hiatuses, the vivid emotional coloring of the De Hartmann/Schuller score—the foreboding voices of the unseen Y Chorale, the muttering of the five basses hidden under the giant outfits, a couple of offstage howls in gibberish, the clanging of a little bell in a leaning red tower, the clear, loud voice of the man who calls "silence" to the boy pulling the bell, the anguished, fragmented murmuring of the cloaked figures—"The flowers cover everything." "Cover conception with innocence." "Close your eyes." "Open your eyes."

The appearance of it is always spectacular, but not always stirring. Some of the most splendidly realized ideas are those having to do with light. Theater electricians of Kandinsky's day would have despaired of what Israel and Riddell have managed so smoothly on the stage of Marymount Manhattan (which supposedly has the same dimensions as the Kunstler Theater in Munich). Slim beams of light, colored and white, crisscross the stage as the opera begins; gradually, behind a scrim, a great egg of gold light begins to glow on the deep blue back wall until it's almost too bright to look at. Throughout the work, blackness, blue, red, and yellow light give way to each other; the entire forestage grays down; shadows move on the backdrop; clouds of smoke roll from stage left—on one occasion glowing with an incendiary light, billows of darkness above the red. Watching these colors change with the music gives stirring intimations of the feelings that Kandinsky must have intended to suffuse the work, and which the stage action would amplify.

What puzzles me about such a conscientious attempt to resurrect this lost work are the many ways in which the present collaborators deviate from Kandinsky's scenario. Kandinsky wrote of a wide green hill in the distance; Israel and Riddell have constructed a small fairly narrow mound (very beautiful) that stands slightly upstage of center. They have built a wonderful, luminous, phallic flower that can bloom from the side of the hill, drop back, or wig-wag alternately with another branch (perhaps this is the "trembling" Kandinsky mentioned). But they haven't shown us the parade of "tiny figures" plodding ceaselessly up the hill, faces straight ahead, which is supposed to terrify the cloaked figures. Unless the dim, comblike, moving projection on the hill was supposed to be tiny figures? The people in the jewel-colored velvet cloaks (members of Fricke-Gottschild's Zero Moving Company) don't passionately throw their individual phallic flowers away and move downstage; they move downstage and tidily put their flowers on the floor just behind the scrim. The five yellow giants move their arms in futile gestures occasionally, but I didn't see them tremble much. They "grow" like the Christmas tree in *Nutcracker,* but the yellow messiah doesn't—a detail Kandinsky mentioned in his scenario.

Some of the scenes are very short—the man-boy-bell one is over in a minute or so. The most developed is a bizarre and troubled dance for a group of people in colored tights (more like union suits) and a soloist in white tights (Fricke-Gottschild). Kandinsky envisioned them with painted hair, but here they are hooded.

Constructing this dance must have been the most problematic job in the whole production. Kandinsky had been working with dancer Alexander Sacharoff, and he, presumably, would have been the man in white. Dalcroze-trained, Sacharoff desired to move "naturally" and with powerful emotion. Fricke-Gottschild looked at pictures of him, yet no pose F.-G. strikes has quite the morbid power of one Sacharoff struck for the camera (reproduced in the program). His body is bent almost as if he were sitting on an imaginary chair; everything is narrow and dropping and averted except his raised hands. His head falls forward and sideways so far that you can imagine him collapsing. The picture suggests that bizarre, medieval religiosity that involves frequent fainting in ecstasy.

Fricke-Gottschild's dilemma is that of the man who knows too much. Kandinsky's suggestions of puppetlike behavior, of religious hand gestures (offerings held up), of obsessive, repetitive motions of hands or legs or both together—Sacharoff would have had to interpret these in the year 1913, the same year in which the young Mary Wigman first went to study with Rudolf von Laban. There was no Expressionist tradition in German dance yet, no aesthetic involvement with the machine age. So if Fricke-Gottschild's thoroughly expressive and bizarre gestures—jerking spasmodically, whirling his forearms, crumpling up—make us think more of later Wigman, and even, said some in the audience, of Murray Louis or of the two-dimensional figures in Paul Taylor's *Three Epitaphs*, it may be that neither he nor we have been able to unlearn what we know.

The problem, however, isn't so much one of authenticity but of a failure to communnicate emotions clearly. The people in cloaks never rise to the heights of terrified frenzy Kandinsky outlines. We do not really see the people in tights move from happiness to extreme weariness (although we do see them sit on the floor in the varied postures suggested by Kandinsky); we don't see them gradually beginning to notice the soloist and finally "gawking" at him (because of their placement in relation to him, we can't see their faces when they do "gawk," if they do). Nor does their dancing finally reach a degree of bacchic fervor greater than anything they've done before. The long changes from vigor to lassitude to excitement (or whatever) don't become visible.

One can see the opera's string of cryptic scenes as glowing pictures, all of which express aspects of the struggle from confusion to enlightenment, from darkness to light—with all the dissonances and alogical happenings such a passage entails. Perhaps the five giants are at some intermediate stage of knowledge or spiritual development—as the program says, "alternately menacing and inspiring."

In line with its illuminating decision to submerge us in a whole artistic milieu, the Guggenheim's theater program begins with music Kandinsky admired: Arnold Schönberg's delicately colored and eruptive *Three Piano Pieces*, Opus 11 (1909), which pianist Russell Sherman, who plays them beautifully, characterizes as falling into the "musical and historical limbo of 'pure' atonality"; Alexander Scriabin's tremulous *Tenth Sonata*, Opus 70 (1913); and de Hartmann's *Three Maori Songs (Impressions of Gauguin)*, Opus 15 (1913), settings of poems of Konstantin Balmont. These poignant and delicate love songs (sung in Russian by Beverly Morgan and played by Dennis Helmrich) are receiving their American premiere an astonishing sixty-nine years late.

Given the transience of the performing arts, it is unmitigatedly thrilling to sit in a theater and watch something that we have—as Walter Sorell said in the lobby—"been waiting seventy years to see." All quibbles aside.

Other people tell me that the messiah figure did grow. I can't say for sure whether my perception was a misperception, or whether my definition of "grow" is narrower than it ought to be.

VIEW FROM MOUNT
OLYMPUS

The Village Voice, February 6, 1978

⌁

When Doris Humphrey's *Day on Earth* was first performed in 1947 by José Limón, Letitia Ide, Miriam Pandor, and Melissa Nicolaides, John Martin wrote in the *Times,* "It is almost as if she [Humphrey] had looked from some other planet and seen things telescoped into a simple, arduous pattern of dignity and beauty." This may be the key to *Day on Earth.* It is about the deepest personal relationships—man to wife, parents to child—but, although it is full of feeling, Humphrey's meaning emerges through the congruence or the jostling of patterns and movements rather than through emoting. You could never perceive your own life this way while you were living it. Humphrey's view is serenely idyllic and fatalistic: no small complexities interfere with the simple cycle of work-love, work-loss, work-birth, work-death.

The man works in long, straight diagonal paths with firm pulling and thrusting gestures that suggest plowing and planting. The young girl's dancing is all springy and curving, her energy that of a fountain of water. The man moves over the earth, digs into it, but she spurts into the air and arches down, tantalizingly fresh. He abandons his steady rhythm for her more restless, ecstatic one. But after she has left (to die?), and he has returned to his "work," another woman comes to dance with him, and as soon as we see her strong, confident movements—so like his—we know that they are well-matched. The two of them walk to the box they were all grouped around when the curtain rose, and lift a sheet that covers a child. While she frolics, they resume their themes of planting and plowing. The mother leaves briefly, and father and daughter sustain each other. Eventually, the child leaves (to die? to grow up?); her parents make little fences of their arms, but she gaily ducks under. The mother mourns; the father calms her, gets her back to work, but the work patterns turn quick and jagged, unsatisfying. She moves away, perhaps also to die, and he continues doggedly to work. Then, with slow, final gestures she folds the sheet—letting her whole body lift and curl in, as if she were finishing all the work of their lives to put away forever. At the end of the dance, the child is sitting on the box, and the three adults, lying at her feet, unfold the sheet by tossing it up in the air and letting it billow for a second before they pull it firmly down to cover them.

Day on Earth is an extremely beautiful dance, the best, I think, of the pieces Humphrey made for the Limón company, when the white-hot purity of her big early dances had warmed and softened. And Aaron Copland's Piano Sonata matches the dance in rigor and inevitability.

I saw an interesting revival of *Day on Earth,* performed at Riverside Church by Jim May, Betsy Fisher, Lorry May, Jessica May, and pianist Patricia DeVore. The fact that the fictional man, wife, and child were being played by a real family gave a curious intensity to those parts of the dance where the three dance together. Humphrey's parents' delight in their child perhaps merged with the Mays' own pride in their daughter Jessica's dancing; and their bodies seemed to know each other profoundly. That was exceedingly beautiful.

Jessica May is much younger (seven) than most little girls who have played this part, and her accomplishment is amazing. I don't think she's as good as she will be in a few years. Nine- or ten-year-old girls, such as Humphrey made the part on, begin to have a keen—almost romantic—sense of beauty and fitness and a little more control over slow movements. Six- and seven-year-olds, tend to be scrappy and matter-of-fact. Of course, no one could resist such a tiny cricket of a child doing her part so conscientiously and well.

Many of the dramatic changes in the dance were made clearer than in other performances I've seen. Jim May isn't the weighty, heroic kind of dancer José Limón was; he's slim, almost boyish looking. But his dancing is strong, ardent, and plain—without mannerism or phony tension. Only at the end did he look too hectic—as if the man were throwing his work away instead of letting his grief infuse it. Lorry May didn't have quite the breadth in her dancing that I associate with the role of the woman, but she projected love, pride, happiness, grief with beautiful honesty and lack of sentimentality. And Betsy Fisher is sturdy and merry rather than delicate and erratic, as many who played the role have been. She looks like a lively country girl, and that image worked too.

What was perhaps missing from the performance was that slight sense of distance that Martin marked in the choreography. However, I'd rather have warmth and intelligence than undue solemnity and portentousness.

SHE GAVE A LOVELY LIGHT

The Village Voice, January 11, 1983

"In our present day theatrical scene, I do not know anyone like Anna Pavlova," wrote the critic André Levinson around 1912. "It has been given to her to infuse the abstract and disciplined formulas of the classical dance with an exquisite sensitivity, refinement, and pathos, in keeping with the contemporary spirit." And later in the same article: "Pavlova's line is not only decorative and extraordinarily expressive; it is symbolic. Do we not regard a Pavlova arabesque as the visible expression of something ineffable?"

To the millions of people who saw Anna Pavlova dance in cities and towns of Europe, North and South America, the Far East, Australia, she must have seemed not only ineffable but miraculous. Imagine this swan, this bacchante, this princess with the beautifully arched feet and liquid arms appearing at the Armory in Battle Creek, Michigan, on New Year's Day, 1915, and showing up with her company later that day to perform in Kalamazoo before entraining for Muncie. No wonder so many dancers and balletomanes all over the world have written of a single magical night in their youth when they first saw Anna Pavlova dance and the world was thereafter different.

As Keith Money's impressive, enormous, and expensive book about Anna Pavlova shows, this remarkable woman was quite literally consumed by dancing. He estimates that she logged 400,000 miles of touring before she died in 1931 (still thinking she might go on that night). There were economic reasons for the constant touring, most of it procured through the zeal of her manager/lover (possibly husband), Victor Dandré, but it's obvious that she was addicted to performing.

Money seems to have done painstaking research. Not a Pavlova expert, I can find only a few minor issues to quibble about. He engages in some pioneering speculation about her birth—suggesting, with some cause, that she may have been the product of a liaison between her washerwoman mother and a member of a prominent family of Jewish bankers. Because he documents her career so thoroughly, you often feel as if you are trudging through her life, month by month, sometimes even day by day. This will not distress a true Pavlova freak of course. And through the details of her career, artistic issues surface. For instance, during her days as a student at the Imperial Ballet School and as a young dancer in the company, it was noted that she had little turn-out, that her back was flexible but not strong. (She wisely spent some time off at La Scala studying with the aging Caterina Beretta, in order to develop accuracy and stamina.) Yet despite any technical flaws, her rise through the St. Petersburg company was rapid, and old Marius Petipa kept handing her important parts in his ballets, even remolding *Giselle* to suit her gifts—which leads one to suppose that he too was tiring of the staidly virtuosic stars he had developed and enjoyed Pavlova's expressiveness, fluidity, delicacy, and a certain nascent impulsiveness that the book's many photographs hint at.

Pavlova has been censured by some of her contemporaries and by critics: for not sticking with Diaghilev; for accepting Alfred Butts's contract to perform in London's Palace music hall—one act among many, forced to provide new novelties each week; for filling the repertory of her company with less than superb choreography, notably by Ivan Clustine, who seems to have been able to produce anything, from retread Petipa or Legat, to Greekish pieces vaguely influenced by Isadora Duncan, to exotic and sexy fables in the manner of Ruth St. Denis and Ted Shawn. Money forbears criticizing and offers what he supposes to be Pavlova's reasons for Pavlova's decisions. After all, she did attempt to introduce to music-hall audiences what she considered to be ballet treasures, like *La Fille Mal Gardée* (abridged) and new work, like Mikhail Fokine's *Les Preludes* (1913). The lavish production of Petipa's *The Sleeping Beauty*, which Clustine worked up for her New York Hippodrome appearances in 1916, gave many Americans their first look at this ballet. And when she and Mikhail Mordkin toured America in 1910, most of their audiences had never seen dancing so accomplished. Critics, even those as erudite as Carl Van Vechten, were at a loss to analyze an unfamiliar art that clearly merited serious attention: "Pavlova twirled on her toes. With her left toe pointed out behind her, maintaining her body poised to make a straight line, she leapt backward step by step on her right foot . . ."

It ought to be mentioned that Money writes very well indeed, and that the book is crammed with pictures—the famous ones and the unusual ones. They chart the transformation of the charming nineteenth-century coryphée—slightly sway-backed, with correct, small-scale port de bras and a modish hairdo—into the tragic, wildly fluttering swan, the darting dragonfly. We can see the lovely freedom of arms and upper body that Isadora Duncan inspired her to. We can understand just how sexy some of the Pavlova–Mordkin duets were (wrote a Londoner of their much-repeated *Bacchanale*—which Money attributes to Fokine: "She, light, laughing, and elusive, is the rippling stream wooed by the sun, the brown, strong Mordkin"). In thinking of the artistry of Pavlova's dancing, we easily forget that one thing she brought her audiences was sensuality with class.

Toward the end of the book, the pictures are saddening—the fashionably dressed woman has a slightly bulkier body and utterly exhausted eyes as she capitulates to the apparently endless stream of photographers. Yet here she is at forty-seven in Montevideo, poised on point as the girlish Lise in *La Fille Mal Gardée,* or pressing herself into a two-dimensional nymph-in-flight pose for *Dionysius,* and her beauty seems undiminished.

Anna Pavlova, Her Life and Art is in the best tradition of Knopf's dance books. I could wish for a detailed bibliography, but mooned over an appendix of reviews and quaint articles, including one by "Grace Curnock," who dogged Pavlova on a London shopping expedition.

Money refers bibliography seekers to another work: *Pavlova,* by John and Roberta Lazzarini, a Dance Horizons book published in 1980 by Schirmer Books. The Lazzarinis' *Pavlova* is valuable for other reasons too: it's a sort of catalogue raisonée of her repertory in chronological order, with brief, shrewd remarks on each role and photographs beautifully reproduced in sepia tones and framed in imaginative ways.

I was reading about Pavlova when I made my annual pilgrimage to George Balanchine's *The Nutcracker,* and I thought about her intermittently between delights. Some of the best sugarplums in the ballet are reserved for the audience. The children on stage don't see the Stahlbaum's parlor shoot up, as we do, and the unearthly glittering tree grow to the roof. Mary is asleep when her chaste, ruffled bed begins to glide through a frosted landscape; we imagine for her the perilous joy of looking up from a warm bed into a black winter sky. Two dreaming children, of course, watch the agile comestibles who so graciously perform to reward the heroism of boy and girl, but do the children see in the Sugarplum Fairy and her Cavalier a pattern of courteous love that they might one day emulate, or do we see it for them?

Well, I was thinking this too, but I began to think about Pavlova in connection with these dancers. Maria Calegari as Dewdrop, long legs flashing, hovering luminously above and among the waltzing flower-women; Suzanne Farrell, a touch of wildness about her Sugarplum Fairy that night, leading Adam Luders on with a boldness that was entirely of this earth. These dancers will never have to do themselves in through years of one-night stands. They rarely have to perform third-rate choreography. A New Yorker with time and money can watch Farrell every night she performs and observe the many subtle changes in her dancing, the spontaneity and daring she brings to a role. The time she spent in the company of Maurice Béjart some years ago, dancing works I didn't much care for, only deepened her beauty.

Anna Pavlova hadn't Farrell's options. She could have stayed in the Imperial theaters, probably dancing less often and less adventurously than she craved. She usually hadn't the patience or the spirit of self-sacrifice to wait around while Diaghilev tried to raise money. So it was music-hall seasons and touring, and no taking shelter with a master choreographer. Perhaps she wouldn't have been able to submit to a Balanchine and devote herself to showing us how expressive and how susceptible to an individual's phrasing his choreography is, as Farrell has done.

On the other hand, a dancer with the City Ballet will possibly never know—mercifully, she might well say—what it's like to steam into a strange town, pull on a costume, warm up, and dance for people who may never have seen ballet. And catch a train for the next town. Everyone knows what a ballet is now, thanks to television, and millions of people have seen Suzanne Farrell on Dance in America; for which she produced the equivalent of a single performance's worth of sweat (give or take the extra finagling for camera). But, somewhat like the children in *Nutcracker* who don't see what we see, she doesn't feel in her bones the response of those television viewers. And it was, in part at least, that feverish, almost voluptuous giving and receiving that made Pavlova dance herself to death.

I said in my review of Keith Money's book that I was no Pavlova expert. This came home to roost when Oleg Kerensky wrote to point out that the "pioneering speculation" about Pavlova's parentage, which I had attributed to Money, had first appeared in 1973 in Kerensky's Pavlova biography.

The next time that I went to see George Balanchine's The Nutcracker, I was mortified to note that little Marie does, of course, see the Christmas tree grow. How could I have forgotten? My error may have been triggered by the fact that we do see the event differently from the way she appears to see it. From her perspective, object after object shoots up; while we observe the increasing discrepancy in scale between her and the room she inhabits. Literally, the room is growing; figuratively, she may be shrinking.

FACTS THAT OUTMYTH
FICTION

The Village Voice, August 12–18, 1981

▃▃▃

Ruth St. Denis danced in public for the last time in 1966, two years before her death. What she chose to dance at the age of eighty-seven was *The Incense,* the dance that had opened the very first program she had given as a "serious" interpretive dancer, at New York's Hudson Theater on March 22, 1906. *The Incense* is simple and eloquent in terms of its material, its repetitive structure. A veiled woman in a sari holding a salver enters the stage through an opening in the back curtain. She advances with a smooth walk, her hips swaying slightly from side to side with the rhythms of Harvey Loomis's pseudo-oriental piano music. Scattering incense from her tray onto a brazier, she lets her fingers spiral upward in imitation of the rising smoke, following it with her gaze. After more circling of the stage, more scattering of incense, more rising of fumes, she puts her tray down and begins to ripple her arms with uncanny fluidity, her body settling into opulent S-shaped curves, her face calm and ecstatic. Even when you see two films made of St. Denis performing this solo when she was well over sixty, you can understand what thrilled audiences— both in concert halls and in vaudeville theater—what excited German artists and writers like Hugo von Hofmannsthal when St. Denis visited Berlin in 1906. St. Denis—impressed by the ideas of Ralph Waldo Emerson, Mary Baker Eddy, Swami Vivekananda, trained in the ideas and methods of the French movement theorist François Delsarte—believed that art linked both observer and performer with the divine. Her dancing affirmed that loftiness, but it was also profoundly sensual. St. Denis was a beauty and knew how to use that beauty to appear mysteriously seductive or imperious or hoydenish. Nurtured also on six shows a day in Worth's Dime Museum, a protégée of David Belasco, a variety artist of some repute before she reached the age of sixteen, she had a shrewd understanding of how to create an effect in the theater.

As Suzanne Shelton brings out in *Divine Dancer* (Doubleday, $15.95), her remarkable biography of this remarkable woman, St. Denis was "a genius of lowbrow" who aspired to higher things. This duality may have accounted for her allure and her influence; it also plagued her.

Her career developed in an American society that distrusted art both for its supposed triviality and its odor of immorality, a society that created often blurry or hypocritical distinctions between high art and entertainment. On occasion, St. Denis thought of herself as being forced to do the latter to support the former; sometimes she forgot which was which.

Yet Shelton's fastidious research has revealed how many times St. Denis thought she had failed to develop her gifts. On the occasion of her London appearances with Denishawn—the company she had formed with her husband Ted Shawn—she wrote of the dances ". . . these were not the products of that austere and great beauty of which my soul had dreamed. These were not properly the fruit of twelve (sic) years." And in 1950, she said, "I have become an opportunist for money in place of an artist."

"On the evening of January 27, 1893 Ruth Emma Dennis stood inside the Adamsville School, shrewdly surveying the crowd of neighbors and friends gathering for her production of *The Old Homestead,* a popular play celebrating rural virtues and temperance." From this first description of Ruth St. Denis's mother (one of the few women to earn a medical degree from the University of Michigan in the 1870s), Shelton writes biography with a storyteller's verve. She's earned the right to do so. As the spectacular bibliography reveals, Shelton has plumbed all the available material, including the boxes and boxes of St. Denis's scrawled diaries in the University Research Library at UCLA; she has also turned up a wealth of new information in such places as the Somerville Free Public Library and the Somerset County Courthouse (St. Denis grew up on a farm in Somerville, New Jersey). More important, she has interpreted the gleanings from clippings, diaries, letters, pictures, films, atlases, contracts, books on everything from oriental philosophy to dress reform in lucid and illuminating ways.

Part of Shelton's job has been to separate myth from fact. In 1939, when St. Denis's career was waning, she wrote (with Henriette Buckmaster) her autobiography, *An Unfinished Life,* a work that flits over her career with an understandable vagueness about dates and names and influences. In 1969, her great friend and champion, critic Walter Terry, wrote a biography largely based on the many conversations he had had with St. Denis, a chronicle of events as she remembered them. And only recently, with revivals staged by Klarna Pinska or Marion Rice, with the publication in 1979 of *The Drama of Denishawn Dance,* by Jane Sherman, a former company dancer, have we gotten a very clear idea about those dances that St. Denis and Shawn performed on the vaudeville circuit and on the oriental tour of 1925. Famous Denishawn alumnae like Doris Humphrey and Martha Graham have maintained that they profoundly admired St. Denis, but have said little about her art. Their own work took them in very different directions, and by the 1930s, the new generation of "modern" dancers clearly considered Miss Ruth passé—too concerned with prettiness and exoticism, not in tune with the raw vigor and dynamism of America in the throes of the machine age.

Shelton has rescued St. Denis's career from the aura of kitsch or triviality, to place her with Isadora Duncan as one who related movement and expression in a vital way. She has also untangled facts and myths. Students of dance history have heard the tale of how St. Denis, on tour with Belasco's *Madame Dubarry* in 1904, saw in a shop window in Buffalo a poster advertising Egyptian Deity cigarettes. Shazam! And Ruth was instantly wrenched from a career in commercial theater to the pursuit of high-toned oriental disguises. Certainly the poster was, as Shelton says, "a catalytic icon" for St. Denis and one source of inspiration for the 1910 *Egypta,* but Shelton reminds us that a penchant for exotica and interest in a fabled (and not always authentic) Orient was reflected everywhere in art and popular culture around the turn of the century. As a girl, St. Denis had seen the extravaganza *Egypt Through The Ages* on the Jersey Palisades and "Egyptian" performers at Coney Island. The American Delsarte exponent, Genevieve Stebbins, whose performing impressed young Ruth, included an Eastern Temple Drill in her manual of exercises. Japanese and Chinese literary works were appearing in translation. St. Denis even choreographed a Japanese solo in 1900 when she was in London with *Zaza,* hoping Belasco would allow her to perform it between the acts of his *Madame Butterfly.* And, like many lucky enough to be in Paris in 1900, she visited the exhibits of oriental art, music, and dancing at the Exposition.

What has concerned Shelton throughout the book has been to understand St. Denis as a phenomenon of her times. This diminishes neither her charisma as a performer nor her magnificent unruliness as a person. Shelton's sympathetic but unsentimental view reconciles St. Denis's grandiosity with her practicality, her genuine religiosity with her vulgarity, her imprudence with her savviness, her graciousness with her self-centeredness, her storehouse of plans with her laziness at putting them into execution. The woman who could rouse an audience from polite appreciation to hysteria by breaking into a "cakewalk-cum-tango" *is* the same woman who on the oriental tour gathered her dancers together every Thursday evening and read aloud the new version of a mystical four-dimensional universe set forth in Ouspensky's *Tertium Organum.* (It is perhaps predictable that St. Denis would buy Einstein's Theory of Relativity only if it came redolent of veils, incense, and spiritual uplift.) The woman who posed happily for photographers swathed in silks and jewels *is* the same woman who—also with apparent cheer—worked the graveyard shift at

Douglas Aircraft for $33 a week under the name of Ruth Dennis Shawn for most of 1943.

One of the myths that grew up around St. Denis was her "great romance" with Ted Shawn. Shawn, twelve years younger than St. Denis, came to her as an acolyte and became her partner and her most efficient manager. In their long, tumultuous relationship as soulmates and professional rivals, he subtly committed her to teaching schedules and touring commitments that bored and wearied her, he packaged her solo art into exotic genre pieces, he sought her undivided attention throughout the scads of extramarital affairs that both enjoyed. Although they pursued their careers separately for a while during the 1920s, and ceased living together in 1931, Shawn refused to contemplate a divorce that would shatter their public role as lovers. They continued to advise each other, get together for highly publicized reunions and, when he was fifty-three and she sixty-six, they considered touring together.

Yet the idea that St. Denis was thoroughly impractical and interested only in her own dancing, while Shawn was a good organizer, is another Shelton dispels. True, at the height of Denishawn's prosperity, Shawn built a network of franchised Denishawn schools, coached movie stars, sold dances (and costume designs for them), recorded the music for technique classes and dances for the Ampico Piano Roll Company, and published a magazine. Yet when he planned to use money raised on dates in the South to get the company to London, it was St. Denis who asked that it be used to help their school in California—which was in financial trouble. She objected to having every day planned for her, but the vision of a school, a colony, a community of art was as important to her as it was to him, and at the end of her life when she was making a career out of playing madonnas in churches with her Rhythmic Choir, she was trying to interest backers and poetic young men in a center that would encourage "the Ministry of Beauty . . . the Divinity of the Arts." And passionate entrepreneur though Shawn was, he was as guilty as she of the extravagances that eventually brought Denishawn to financial ruin. As Shelton so trenchantly comments, "Creator and preserver, romantic and realist, they brought together in their diverse points of view the complete creative process of the performing artist. Like the Yin and Yang of the Denishawn emblem, they were complementary halves of a whole, but, tragically, each aspired to become the other."

Divine Dancer is one of the few dance biographies that can be considered superb on every level—the handsome treatment Doubleday has accorded it is a great asset too—but I'm particularly grateful that Shelton deals so sensitively and evocatively with the dances themselves, as well as with the ideas they embodied and the woman who created them.

THE NEW GENERATION

Bill T. Jones and Company in rehearsal

Most of the choreographers represented in this section began to choreograph during the second half of the seventies. Some built on the achievements of innovative choreographers in whose companies they appeared, or whom they admired. You can see the Cunningham lineage in the work of Karole Armitage, although not in the work of Charles Moulton. Marta Renzi, Sara Rudner, and Nina Wiener are clearly Tharp offspring. It's less obvious that Dana Reitz worked with both Tharp and Laura Dean.

Much of the new dancing of the eighties tends to be crisp in its rhythms, pristine in its structures, violent in its energy. The peaceful, fluid look is rarer than it was a decade ago. Compared to the glossy athletes of modern ballet, these people may appear refreshingly homespun, but there's no mistaking the value many of them place on strength, speed, endurance, expertise. They dance as if time were running out. Watching Molissa Fenley, I see an analogue to the millions racing and jogging over America's terrain. Perhaps they are training to deal with the apocalypse; perhaps they are showing the computer a thing or two.

In the eighties, we're seeing a resurgence of interest in narrative, in emotion as content for dance. It has always been the force behind the work of the Japanese Eiko and Koma. The very dissimilar choreographers Bill T. Jones and Johanna Boyce have always been interested in unusual ways of dealing with autobiography in dance. Others, trained to think in the Cunningham mode that dance is its own content, approach the issue guardedly. (Twyla Tharp had been choreographing for almost twenty-five years before she used outright narrative elements in a dance.) The old narrative structures won't do, but neither, perhaps, will the coolness and casualness dancers once so carefully cultivated.

A SHINING EXAMPLE

The Village Voice, March 10, 1980

▗▄▖

The last time I saw Sara Rudner dance was in a warm house on a chilly evening around Christmas. The occasion was a private showing of a new fine film called *Dune Dance* that Carolyn Brown and James Klosty made. Suddenly there was Rudner, alone, sliding down this immense sand bank, black curls flying. In her breathtaking and musical downfall, she twisted, kicked, spun, arched her body and crashed on her face, rolled, sprang up, suspended herself off-kilter and fell again. It is one thing to do your dance on a beach and quite another to collaborate intimately with the sand.

This fearlessness, sensuousness, wholehearted engagement with the issue at hand characterizes Rudner's dancing. She seems always to be exploring, with immense pleasure and total absence of affectation, just how much weight to give a gesture; how abandoned or controlled to be at a given moment; whether bigness is the question, or delicacy, or something in between; how fast fast is. You can call what she does the product of a superb dance intelligence or—as a young student startled me by saying—of divine inspiration.

Although Rudner has worked with several modern dance companies since she graduated from Barnard with a degree in Russian studies, it's not Paul Sanasardo or Pilobolus you associate her with, but Twyla Tharp, with whom she danced from 1966 to 1974, and with whose company she continues to appear now and then, out of respect and love for the work. Only a Rudner would attempt to rehearse her own small company for a tour, choreograph a new piece, learn and tape Yvonne Rainer's seminal *Trio A* for Dance in America, prepare to perform with Tharp in the latter's Broadway season (March 24 to April 12) *and* stand in for Tharp in one of Tharp's new pieces.

Rudner laughs her happy, robust laugh when she tells me that her own new dance is only twenty minutes long—figuring I'll be surprised. This is because one of her finest, *As Is* (1977), was a four-hour marathon for four dancers. "That had a lot to do with wanting to provide myself and others with a different kind of dancing experience—to do it for a long, long time, not really caring what the steps were. I guess it's the athlete in me. Of course," she reconsiders, "the only way you can get *through* one of those long things is to structure it so that it doesn't become blather to you, so you don't get bored or lose the sense of what you're doing."

Rudner's long pieces have seemed to me like chunks of fascinating dance material that she studies, plays with, builds with—her choreographic intelligence and imagination a high-intensity beam illuminating now this aspect of dancing, now that. These days she's just addressing herself to another kind of timing, a tighter compositional structure, to "what I'd call more 'classical' choreography." Sponsors, like those presenting Rudner and her fine ensemble of women around the country this spring, may be relieved by this new interest in brevity. Me, I'm interested in whatever interests her.

During the past few years, Rudner has gone back to performing steadily with Twyla Tharp's company and has not been presenting her own choreography. My title is perennially apt.

THE WOMEN OF THE HOUR

The Village Voice, September 19, 1977

ᵥₐᵥ

The subject is heroism. On Sunday, September 4, four young women danced almost without stopping for over three hours. That's a fact, but not the only important one; after all, Sara Rudner didn't set out to make an ordeal, and anyone—almost anyone—can fill three hours with movement. The heroism grew from the concept and the content as well as from the bravery of the performance.

The skelton of *As Is* consists of nine phrases: Original phrase, Accumulation, Arms and Legs, Tensies, Swimming, Heads Up, 1111.22-22.3333.4444, Shoulders and Running, Positions. The last eight all have roots, however slender, in the Original phrase. Then each of the nine phrases in turn becomes the subject matter of a dance with subsections of its own—choreographed, improvised, a bit of both.

It matters a lot that most of the material is exceedingly beautiful and interesting and that the dancers—Rudner, Jean Churchill, Shana Menaker, Vicki Shick—understand it and display it so wonderfully well.

The audience packed hotly into two small, handsome rooms—the Commissioner's Office of the old Customs House. Some, on a guided tour of the building, had come only to gawk at the ornate ceiling; flocks of these had to be dispersed at the doorway and asked to stop cackling. Rudner politely asked for spectators to squeeze back even more. (She knows her space requirements; the dancers' legs flipped to within inches of the watchers' noses.)

Armed with Rudner's gently didactic program notes, even newcomers to dance began to ferret out variations—to laugh when they realized that Jean Churchill's mat solo was the Tensies theme done lying down instead of standing up—or to see how a few of the Original phrase's head twitches and fleetingly pawed hands could turn into a whole "Zoo Story." Not all the dancers worked every minute. Some collapsed to drink water or pull new blue-grey shirts over their drenched ones, but they also charged back and forth between the main chamber and the antechamber; in the antechamber someone was always improvising on material drawn from all nine themes, and each had to pick up with what the previous person abandoned. It escaped no one in the audience how impeccable everyone's timing must be to accomplish this without music to cement things together.

The dancing was frank and generous. A dancer might stretch a leg luxuriously high, but without the lack of resiliency that the intent to display can produce. Rudner's style forces the dancers often to twist or bend one part of the body against another. This, too, gives them a clever, adaptable look: they ride the current of dancing the way an entrant in a log-rolling contest has to respond to the flux of water. The exception to the easygoing look of things was Tensies. When Rudner first did it as a solo, her muscles tensed until vibrations took possession of her body (odd, she looked the way some dancers try to look all the time—pressured and hard-muscled and ominous). None of the others, except maybe Churchill, could achieve Rudner's horrific rigidity; but, even so, fragments from this theme made the texture of the dancing suddenly snap and snarl interestingly whenever they appeared.

Everything shed light on everything else. Movements acquired new meaning when seen backwards, inverted, slowed down, prone, turning, without accompanying arms, held in poses, doubled with someone else's dancing. In the Accumulation section, the dancers threaded their way through piles of clothing, making gestures related to the shape or feel of the garments; then they put them on. Then Rudner accumulated clothing; then she took it off and went through the movements without the clothing. When she began to dance holding a sweater, I felt faintly exasperated, thinking this an example of the whimsy and exhaustive didacticism (I'm going to show you every single thing I can do with this kick) Rudner occasionally yields to. But as she began to swirl the sweater around her, making it wrap and slide and swing with the dancing, I suddenly saw more deeply into the slipperiness of the phrase and even how the small articulations the body makes in dressing are closer to what Rudner is interested in than are the large, all-at-once gestures of so much theatrical dancing.

Since so much of *As Is* involved controlled improvisation, the dancing revealed almost as much about the dancers' preferences as it did about the material. Shana Menaker in her solo used a lot of the arm, leg, shoulder stuff—giving the impression of a tough balancing act. Vicki Shick, softer and more pliant, let her solo stumble and collapse and roll up again. Churchill, precise and evidently clear-minded, began her solo with material from Original phrase done constantly turning. Rudner, one of the remarkable dancers of this generation, performed with her usual fullness and joyful absorption in the event of dancing, making everything sensible and daring at the same time.

As the dance itself grew bigger and riper and more and more well known, the dancers became wetter and tireder. The afternoon sun got into their eyes, and a prism of light, lengthening on the floor, played tricks with the dimensions of a corner. I began to think how in some forms of dance—certain ballets, say—dancers carefully prepare themselves, hoard their strength for a few minutes of perfect execution and immense effort. A breathtaking sprint. What Rudner created in this dance was more like a marathon. For mind as well as body. Dancers and audience endured together, going through many changes of consciousness and physical states, having to make decisions and revise goals. Both were ennobled. There was no doubt, however, which were the heroes and which the grateful populace. When the dancers finished repeating (differently yet again) the nine phrases for us as a wrap-up, I wanted them to be wreathed in flowers and carried on our shoulders out into the sunset streets.

NINA WIENER: ON HER OWN TRACK

The Village Voice, April 9, 1979

Why should I choreograph the same kind of stuff—even if it's good—as someone else is already doing? I mean, what kind of contribution would that be? How could I justify doing it or asking someone to give me money to do it?"

Nina Wiener's voice, high to begin with, rises in excitement, fervor, and amazement as it spools off my cassette to be transcribed. My husband looks up from his book and asks if she will self-destruct when it's over.

I know what he means, but I doubt it. After dancing for three years with Twyla Tharp, after presenting a couple of concerts of her own work (in 1976–77) that were fine, but not wildly original, Wiener started beating her own track through the brush. My feeling is that anyone who has the nerve, brains, and stamina to do that is going to be okay. Few do, and they tend to be ones history books record. Not that there are any new movements to be discovered, but there are ways of selecting and putting them together that can result in dancing that looks different from anything else.

I first saw Wiener's new work at an earnestly informative, but very stimulating lecture-demonstration in December 1978, in a big, hot gym at Hunter College Campus School. It was already evident that her basic seed material and methods of cultivation and cross-pollination could yield a prolific and seductive crop of dancing. (The organic metaphor is not inappropriate.) Wiener had begun by designing three highly dissimilar patterns for arms alone. One, known to its intimates as "Bugsy," uses, for the most part, big, open motions; the second is tiny and gestural (Wiener thinks it has a "narrative quality"); the third was made lying on the floor but is performed standing up, which gives it a flat look (palms that were pressed on the floor may now be presented to the audience). The three dancers—Timothy Buckley, Bebe Miller, and Alison Pearl—then collaborated with Wiener on what they call "solo translations" of the arm patterns. This involved finding for the legs and/or torsos interesting equivalents of what the arms are doing. Interesting, but precise: no cheating, "hawkeye on the movements." If an arm is flung forward the dancer may fling the corresponding leg forward, or step forward, or lean forward, or perhaps allow the arm's impetus to generate a counterattack and send the performer reeling backward. Wiener may impose additional conditions, like telling Buckley she wanted one of his solos to skim all over the space with big movements and lots of vitality, or telling Miller that hers was to be a jumping solo. The rest of Wiener's job involves suggesting, pointing out options, editing, shaping the dynamic texture, patterning the space.

This is the basic process, the beginning. Manipulated in a surprising variety of ways, it has yielded a rich body of dancing that will be presented as *The Condor Material* at the Brooklyn Academy of Music's LePercq Space April 19 to 22. When I arrive at Wiener's narrow, homey, dirty-white loft on lower Broadway, Wiener and Glenna Hamm are working on a solo translation of "Bugsy." Hamm, fair and sweet-faced, strong as a pony, is a student Wiener met while setting a piece at the University of Illinois. Met, admired, and stole for a semester. "What's that?" asks Wiener, pointing at Glenna's knee and foot nudging at her other knee and foot. Glenna shows how the gesture relates to a brief moment when her arm wraps across her chest toward the opposite shoulder. "Okay." But it's not just circling or thrusting or wrapping gestures that need a leg equivalent, it's nose-wiping and thumb-wiggling and clasped hands scalloping through the steamy air. Pleasant, considerate, but demanding, Wiener puts Hamm through the intricate, active, unpredictable material several times before she assesses the amount of improvement and sweat and moves on.

Tim Buckley and Alison Pearl both have pale skin and straight, raggedly cut black hair; but where he is wiry and prone to sudden, intrepid violence ("there's nothing Tim thinks he can't do"), she is small and silkily precise. Bebe Miller is a black woman with a cropped head, a slightly childlike body, and a meditative quality to her dancing. In silence and in absolute unison, the three of them begin to dance. At one point they work in a tight formation, covering a lot of ground. At intervals, one of them leaks or explodes away on a private excursion and links up again with the other two at a preordained point in time and space. You have a sense of complex dancing, of a unit that gathers power from the impact of individual forces pushing in and out of it.

But now consider, please, how this one small section was made. (Wiener has to draw me a diagram before I understand). Each dancer has made a set of "miniatures"—highly personal variations, comments almost, on a five-count excerpt from his/her own and everyone else's "Bugsy." Are you with me so far? Okay. So all three do Bebe's miniature on her own "Bugsy"; then they do Alison's miniature based on Bebe's "Bugsy"; but while Tim and Alison continue with Tim's "Bebe Bugsy" and move on to the next set of miniatures based on Tim's "Bugsy," Bebe takes off and does her original "Bugsy," arriving to rejoin the group, just before Tim is ready to break out. And so on.

This fastidious and complex structuring—almost invisible, sensed in the finished work as coherence, soundness—may be Wierner's only heritage from Tharp. Certainly Wiener has worked hard to get Tharp out of her body—no mean feat after three years of dancing with, talking with, traveling with, and eating breakfast-lunch-dinner with someone that distinctive.

Wiener, tall and thin, with short, curly hair and a pretty, small-featured face, isn't dancing today. She's sitting on a chair, leaning forward, her legs (in red sweat pants) crossed, her arms folded in. She says I make her nervous. She wonders aloud about "presenting material" versus "making dances." But if at this point her "material" is fascinating dancing, what more does she want?

By the way, why arms? Why start with the top half of the body? She shrugs. "I've studied dancing for a long time, a lot of different kinds of dancing, and it's always been *bottoms*. You go to ballet class and you have *bottoms*. In Limón technique, the top is always a result of what the *bottoms* are doing. Also, I didn't want people to associate my work with some other technique, to have them think things like [she narrows her eyes appraisingly] 'she's holding a bad arabesque.' And I didn't want narrative associations. The emotions I'm dealing with—if I'm dealing with emotions—are subtle. Like . . . well, when you've done with a day, you have a certain feeling about that day and the subtleties of emotion that went into it." (With a droll, rapid-fire agenda of what she would consider a bad day, she makes it clear that she's not talking about the events, the plot-line of a day, but the rhythms, textures, atmosphere of it.) So far there's no touching, no two dancers sharing a single pattern. Maybe that'll come later. Right now, Wiener says she thinks of the dance as a series of private statements and the interchange of these.

Nina puts Bebe through a little killer of a solo, nicknamed "Mary Novak," after the girl who performed it in Illinois. (The material Wiener made during her residency at the University of Illinois is being incorporated into the Brooklyn performances.) When you watch gentle Bebe plunge and ricochet off the floor and coil around on a tight path, you understand what Wiener means when she says "I try to get the dancers to succumb to the movement—not in a sloppy way, but so that they're using their potential and their bodies and the movement's potential and the movement's body. So that they can define the thing that comes after by the thing that comes before." Today she tells Bebe that she wants the arms and upper body to look wild, pulling the legs along. Bebe is supposed to know what the legs are doing, but she doesn't have to make a big deal out of showing us. Bebe mops her face, nods, and hurls herself into it again. This time, Nina yells, "That's the idea! Yes." And decides that Bebe should rest.

We retire to the kitchen so that Glenna and Alison can tidy up a section they're not ready to show *anyone* yet. The kitchen table appears to be a standard sheet of plywood on such a high base that anyone sitting at it feels ten years old. Perhaps that's why Wiener—again mentioning nervousness—sits beside me, rather than choosing to have us face each other across the enormous table like two little girls who've been told to play nicely together.

Wiener didn't have to convince her parents that being a dancer was important. Her father, only nineteen when she was born, stage-managed the Lester Horton Company in Los Angeles for a while. Bella Lewitsky was one of Nina's first teachers. The family moved around a lot—her father was primarily an engineer—but "I had good parents," she says, "and they made sure I got to dance class if I wanted to go to dance class." They must have known good teachers from bad ones, too. In 1969, she was one of what seemed like hundreds of performers in Twyla Tharp's lawn piece, *Medley,* and Meredith Monk's *Juice* (that was the year of the now legendary giant-space dances). She made a little money dancing with The Merrygorounders, the children's company that over the years sustained many modern dancers, and for a while she worked for a time-sharing firm. After you learn how intricately her dancing is organized, it's easy to understand why she'd be good at a job that involved going into offices and showing the people there how to computerize as many of their procedures as possible. When the firm folded, giving her a year of unemployment, she took classes by the dozen and made it into Tharp's company.

Now that Wiener's on her own, money is an even bigger problem: "With the amount of work we put in in a day, I can't hold down a night job and make work and dance and get my dancers better. There's barely enough time in the day as it is." She says frankly, "money gives you possibilities. You have to become fiscally responsible. I'm not interested in sort of sitting in my back office doing my little dances. I want to reach out as far as I can." (Her voice is on the rise again.)

This year—she breathes a sigh of pleasure—the National Endowment for the Arts gave her a $2,500 grant. That means that she can give the dancers $25 a week for rehearsing and pay them decently for the performances in Brooklyn. And she voices the same sentiments, deprecating and gallant, that dancers have been sustaining themselves with for years, "$25 is nothing. But it makes them feel that they're real." Also, luckily for all of them, Wiener is a CETA artist this year, given a weeky salary to take dance out into the community. This has brought in not only money, but new audiences, who also helped resolve a niggling doubt in Wiener's mind: "I used to worry that the work was too cliquish, that it was so complex that people—you know, *normal* people—weren't going to be able to understand it, but it wasn't so. They liked it."

As the afternoon darkens and the interview dribbles away, Wiener suddenly mentions the world outside her loft, the possibility of war and how that frightens her. We talk about how hard it is for dancers to keep in touch with everything that's going on in the world, to remember "that you're still part of the populace." Then—tired, a tiny bit more relaxed, still very intense—she says, "If you choose to do dance, that's no less important than choosing to be a politician—as long as you're really *trying*." The quality of the effort matters a lot to her. When I point out that there are many young choreographers who are content to make dances in traditional molds, she turns away and says, "That's their problem." Then she says, almost as if she were sorry for them, "I mean, that's not much of a quest."

MERCE'S PROGENY

The Village Voice, March 11–17, 1981

⌄⌄⌄

Merce Cunningham has never, I think, taught others to choreograph, except by example. Most of those who have danced in his company and then gone on to choreograph have absorbed his lucidity, his sense of dancing itself as an immensely engrossing activity. Many have chosen to work without the collaborative varnishings of sound and sets that Cunningham himself favors. Some have taken his interest in discontinuity as an imprimatur to make no connection whatever.

Two Cunningham alumni and one company member have presented their own concerts this month—four, if you stretch a bit to include Robert Kovich's vibrant, high-intensity Cunningham binge in late January. The three—Charles Moulton, Meg Harper, and Karole Armitage—all showed their most recent work on Dance Theater Workshop's winter series, and Moulton's *Opposite Arch* was the first piece commissioned by DTW under a grant from the Jerome Foundation.

Boy, are these choreographers unlike. Moulton has been making up ball games—real ones, involving three teams and two balls—since 1977; Armitage keeps any tendencies toward order and ruliness in heavy disguise; persistent, delicate Harper looks as if she'd crumple if you threw a ball at her.

Moulton's dances seem to me to be more about rhythm than about athletic prowess, although they're certainly vigorous, in a sprinting, good-tempered way. The kind of rhythm that interests him, I think, is the kind that is built on exchange—with one person, or group of people, supplementing, contradicting, enlivening someone else's contribution. So it really *is* like good ball playing. For instance, in *Motor Fantasy* Moulton wears tap shoes while Barbara Allen skids around in treated-to-squeak sneakers. Sometimes you can see that they are doing the same steps adapted to the capabilities of their shoes, sometimes they're working in counterpoint that you can both see and hear. As in all of the works Moulton showed, A. Leroy provides a steady electronic beat for the dancers (and him) to decorate and punctuate. At one point, Moulton stands in place, every so often dropping a precise little roll of steps into the texture that Allen and Leroy are working out.

Moulton performs all his dances as serious but not unpleasurable essays in give-and-take. He and the others walk out, take their places. They look at the audience, each other, the space with calm concentration, neither trying to be ingratiating nor ignoring our presence. Occasionally they grin. Especially Allen, Moulton, and Chase Winton when they've just about made it through the intricacies of *Three-Person Precision Ball-Passing*. For this diabolical activity, the three march out, each holding a ball. One's red, one's orange, one's yellow. We can at least *try* to follow their progress. Well! the dancers plunge and sprint, stamp, and twist to stamp in the other direction; they leap and turn and so on. But the core of the game is a repeated passage in which the three cozy up and start passing the balls. Over. Under. Through. Again, it's rhythm that guides the rapid interchanges. Impossible to figure out where the balls are coming from and going to; what you see is a basket of arms weaving in and out industriously, and then suddenly, just when you've about got it, altering the pattern. Each person looks where he or she is giving (not at his own receiving hand—I did figure that much out), and the intent turning of heads increases our sense of this as a demanding pastime—a cat's-cradle for superbrains.

The game in its three-man version involves tossing too, catching on the run. But the players in the nine-man variant line up in three tiers of three each—sitting, standing, standing on a platform. Now we get to see the three-man passing in canon, to see contrapuntal themes added, to see trios—shifting the facing of the whole group to a diagonal. In one half-time pattern, people in the top and bottom rows reach way down and up to each other, while within the smoothly pumping cage of their arms, the middle group busily slips its balls around.

The new *Opposite Arch* also involves rhythmic interchanges, passings over and under—this time of people. Did I forget to say how subtle and complex Moulton's rhythms are? They're clear but not obstinate, full of bright syncopations that tease our expectations. And the rhythms support the interplay between large-scale movements and smaller, tighter ones, foster the quick changes of direction Moulton favors. He is a dancer easy in his body, neither unduly tense nor floppy—a solidly built man who moves confidently and boldly, as if his muscles were always warm and well oiled, his tendons like greased springs. His colleagues in *Opposite Arch*—Allen and Winton, Beatrice Bogorad, Keith Marshall—rise superbly to meet his daring. Two people hoist a third under the armpits. By the midpoint of the dance, people are hoisting another while someone else dives underneath. The dancers keep returning to vary and expand their initial striding counterpoint, and by the end, they're rolling and rising and running to jump over someone else who's rolling and rising and running to jump over someone else who's . . . and we couldn't get enough of it.

Some people said Karole Armitage shocked them. Wasn't she trashing her heritage? I didn't think so. I thought that she and her colleagues were being fondly and gleefully naughty about Cunningham-dance and ballet and a lot of other things too. After all, she called the thing *Drastic Classicism*.

The musicians, too, I thought, were playing being *bad*. Yet never was there a more accommodating bunch than Rhys Chatham and his group (Nina Canal, Scott Johnson, David Linton, Ned Sublette). The dancers stare them down, check their kneecaps, practice great thrashing arabesques holding onto their shoulders, use them as supports to push off from, even grab stray guitars to add to the stridency. And the musicians glare obligingly or shrug away or ignore the dancers with perfect equanimity.

The whole thing is an immense din. Chatham doesn't fret his guitar; as he strums it hard and fast, he twiddles the tuning pegs to produce howling dissonances. What he and his colleagues achieve is like rock music without words or melody or harmony—rock reduced to rhythmic noise and decorum. Charles Atlas has created a kind of visual din with his design for the piece. Of course, there are amplifiers and the drum set and taped-down wires all over. There's an object, a kind of baffle maybe, hanging over Chatham and another further upstage; for the first half of the piece, these are bundled in black cloth, for the second they're revealed as mirrored surfaces. For the first half of the piece, the dancers wear black-and-white clothes with sweaters and scarves that they can rip off and hurl sulkily into the corners. For the second half they wear outlandish out-fits—Armitage in a big ball of a royal blue tutu over blue trousers with matching pouf perched in her punky crew-chop; Deborah Riley, part of the time in a sort of tacky Maria Montez outfit with a long ill-matching braid attached to her own hair.

Anyway, you know you're in for irreverence when the dancers first hurtle on, arms and legs winging around, and Armitage runs Chris Komar's feet right up the far wall and Michael Bloom jumps into Riley's arms. Occasionally these four join hands and execute little rapid brushes with their feet—things like that; but all have different ideas about which foot to use, which count to be on, so they yank each other around a little. Bloom wears his best crosspatch look, Armitage stares rather wildly around, Komar goes all out for vigor, and Riley moves through everything with sweet firmness. Nathalie Richard and Joseph Lennon join them and the pace seems to increase. All the deep lunges and high leg gestures and deliberate arm positions that they've been bred on get hurled and slammed and messed up with gusto. Often a dancer'll make a big move—step out on one leg and hike up the other, say—and then add a jolt of the body, a throw of one arm, as if Armitage wanted everything to sputter.

The second half of the dance is the same as the first, except that the costumes alter the look, and there are a couple of interpolations: two mu-sicians dancing madly in the background for a second or two; in one cor-ner, two dressed-up little girls with a camera snapping and being snapped with some of these charming, expert, bad-guy dancers. The performers laugh more the second time around, as if it were impossible to keep a straight face any longer.

If Armitage wanted to toss her heritage around the room a few times and see how it bounced, Harper chose to show us the skeleton of dance, how it would look with almost all the flesh stripped, the blood drained away. In a series of duets and trios, a quartet, a quintet, all of which are subtle variations on the same or similar placid material, the dancers mark out steps as routine for them as a ballet barre—tendu, close, tendu, close, tombé, pas de bourrée, turn into effacé, close. That sort of thing—quiet and precise of foot, unmoving of body, with arms that balance what the feet are doing or occasionally swirl around the dancers' bodies with a re-lieving breath and spaciousness. Jumps enter the picture in the duet for Daniel McCusker and Viviane Serry, reappear on a polite scale when Nancy Nasworthy, David Lusby, and Karen Booth are dancing together. But, for the most part, you have the sense that you are seeing the same decorous movements over and over and over, with minimal alterations in sequence, direction, personnel. People don't so much dance together as occupy a pattern at the same time, or occupy the space at the same time, barely aware of the contrapuntal meshing of their material.

The music that intermittently accompanies the dance is very gracious and melodious—vaguely Baroque in style and inflection. Oddly, neither the choreography nor the dancing yields to composer-pianist Beth Eisenberg's musicality. Everyone except Nancy Nasworthy—even Harper herself—seems to be restraining any impulse to shape the movement or really dance to the music, so that, although the work is sweet and gentle, it's also dry. Airless.

WREATHS FOR THOSE WHO
STICK THEIR NECKS OUT

The Village Voice, November 26, 1979

W atching Marta Renzi's concert at ATL, I decided I was going crazy, losing my grip. Was this the choreographer I had characterized, only last spring, as brainy and belligerent, dancing and choreographing as if sensuality were a trap waiting for her?

Now, Renzi, in two old dances, and a new one, reveals that she *can* yield her weight to another dancer, can sink comfortably into a step before she shoots out of it, can let her head roll with her dancing instead of appearing to scrutinize it. Without losing her acute sense of form, or the cutting edge that defines her fluent, twisty footwork, she seems to have admitted to warmth. And it turns out to be no trap at all.

I didn't see *Artichoke for Two* in 1977; now, as performed very nicely and robustly by John McLaughlin and Cathy Zimmerman, it's a gracious and sportive dance for two individuals. Each dancer has a pattern and variants of that pattern that repeat over and over, but the relationship of the two people in space and time keeps altering. So that not only does the movement have a swooping, tumbling quality, the patterns themselves seem to be tumbling over each other, chasing and overlapping. The dancers hold onto each other some of the time, but even when apart they seem to be folding around each other.

Renzi's *Wrinkle* (1978) looks like a different dance now. She says, in the talking that she does during the dance, that *Wrinkle* is kind of yardstick for her, but, of course, one that grows and changes with her. I still see a futile bravery in Renzi's determination to talk with the audience during pauses in this rich, complicated, vigorous solo. She finds the barriers between audience and performer arbitrary perhaps, artificial, yet there she is brightly lit and working hard, while we sit in the darkness appraising her. This time, however, she's relaxed about talking, and it's someone in the audience who sounds mildly aggressive. (Asks her if she's ever realized . . . something, I forget what. Renzi: "I never thought about it." Spectator: "Well, think about it." The implication being, don't put yourself on the spot if you're not prepared to show you're smart?)

Renzi's new dance, *Hold Me,* unlike the other two dances, is set to music. The opening for a group of eight unfolds to an excerpt from *The Magic Flute;* it's a lovely, immensely accomplished dance in which individuals fall out of and back into an ongoing phrase that sweeps around the space. (Here's where I thought suddenly of how many concerts I've noticed Susan Eschelbach in, of how serene she is, yet how bold). But it's in two duets that Renzi crawls most courageously out on a limb, possibly risking her reputation as a recognizable post-Tharpian toughy—breezy and smart and unsentimental. One duet (to Fontella Bass's "Rescue Me") for Valerie Bergman and Keith Young is genuinely sexy—not flashy or cliché-ridden—just a skillfully made and performed dance about two warm people working close together, as if enjoying the ways their bodies mold to each other, slip apart, and touch again. The second duet, wonderfully performed by Renzi and Young, is even riskier. While Otis Redding sings crustily, "I Been Lovin' You Too Long," the two let a weary anger simmer up through their dancing. Without stopping the dance their feet are doing, they thrust fists up and lean into each other, spin away, and fall together again. In their performing—restrained, yet superbly full—there isn't a trace of phoniness, nor is there in the choreography. Emotional content is something the brightest of the new choreographers have been understandably reticent about dealing with: several generations of corn hang over their heads. Someone give this woman a Purple Heart.

CALLIGRAPHER IN DANCE

The Village Voice, March 10, 1980

ww

Twentieth-century American dance has been remarkable for the number of gifted dancer-choreographers who have wanted to throw everything out and start over. Not, in most cases, that they couldn't "do" traditional dancing; they couldn't do it and *believe* in it. When Dana Reitz says that at one time, "reaching behind me was hard, turning around was impossible . . ." she's not speaking of physical incapacity (after all, she danced with Twyla Tharp for part of 1970–71 and then toured Europe with Laura Dean's company), she means that certain ways of moving didn't seem to belong to her, that she couldn't yet understand them or justify performing them.

In the program for her *Phrase Collection* (1978) were printed ten simple, fluid drawings—a calligraphy that mapped out the energy flow for each of ten phrases. On these, and within limits and a structure defined by Reitz, the dancers improvised. The scale was small—not a lot of dashing through space—with many quiet looping hand gestures close to the body. But in this engrossing, subtly rich dance, Reitz certainly achieved one of the things she's after—dancing that is created during performance, that is personal and spontaneous, yet has the firmness of choreography .

Drawing is Reitz's accomplice. "When I did *Journey, Moves 1–7,* three years ago, I was biting my nails a lot, and I couldn't figure out how to define all this stuff I was doing in the studio. So I started trying to visualize what I was doing from the outside." And she realized how confined she felt, afraid to blast out, censoring her every move. Sitting at her kitchen table, Reitz scribbles harsh zigzags on a piece of paper, recreating that moment when her pencil began to dash off into long, increasingly confident loops. All at once, she had the beginnings of a method, a tool that could allow her to focus on impetus, flow, rhythm, rather than worrying about steps. Her hand could stroke many small variations of the same basic calligraphy; her dancing could encompass subtle changes and shadings with each repetition of a pattern. One day she'd start in the studio, the next day by drawing.

For *Four Scores,* which she, Deborah Gladstein, and Robin Hertlein will be performing at American Theatre Lab, March 20 to 23, she has (grin) bought larger paper. This time she wants to cover space. "Also I wanted to start broadly and then home in and find the core of what I was doing." She maps the generously scalloping pattern the dancers can perform in unison—steps, rhythms and all. She blows up a detail: "Then I can take this section, say, and magnify it—deal with it rhythmically or temperamentally or spatially."

Her two colleagues, she says, want to tell me how hard it is. Like the good jazz musicians Reitz admires, they have to improvise comfortably and confidently, learning to treat Reitz's imaginative structures as if they were old familiar songs. Hard. But exciting.

MINING ONE CLEAR VIEW

The Village Voice, May 18, 1982

▀▀▀

One of the many new choreographic options that surfaced during the crack-it-all-open sixties was that of continuing to work a single idea or set of ideas. Instead of functioning like entertainers charged with presenting a variegated evening in the theater, some choreographers began to think like painters—or miners: if you stumble onto a potentially rich lode, you'd be a fool to move on before you've dug it over thoroughly. Of course, the value of this kind of ore is set not by an assayer, but by the miner/choreographer, who may spend years gloatingly bringing up stuff that others don't consider precious at all.

Dana Reitz has struck, I think, a small vein of true gold. Perhaps not every dancegoer would find her work as beautiful as I do, but surely most people, watching her, would sense that something valuable and unusual was happening. Her solo, *Steps,* is improvised, but improvised around such a controlled structure that it appears to have been choreographed. She always starts facing the audience, working quietly on a fluid hand pattern—one hand lifting as the other sinks—and these first, and often repeated, gestures almost resemble daily actions like winding, stroking, pouring, but aren't really like any of these. She keeps shifting her weight from one foot to the other, and gradually she expands the pattern, becoming more vigorous or covering more ground or increasing the scale of her gestures. But often she pulls everything in again, and she is never rowdy. The essence of her style is an uninhibited elegance, like that of a deer or a horse: her feet, shoulders, haunches, limbs, neck roll and stretch and curl with calm, unindulgent sensuality. Unusual and complex movements look subtle and natural.

Another remarkable aspect of her performing is its expressiveness. Her dancing is never officially *about* anything but dancing, yet it fugitively refers to the human condition. Now you see her as wary and tentative, now fiercely positive, now moving from puzzlement to certainty—all because of the way she modulates the speed or weight or focus of a gesture.

At the Kitchen recently, she also showed her latest work, *Quintet Project.* In this too, the dancers are making in-performance decisions, based on choreographic scores. The underpinning seems to be a long, loose rhythmic pattern of steps. In the course of an hour we see it many, many times, but it never looks quite the same. Reitz begins with some of the *Steps* material. The other women stand against one or the other side wall and watch. Then one steps out and joins her. As the dance progresses, it begins to seem like a river; the flow never stops. Dancers step into it, explore it for a while, and perhaps, as it nears one wall, step out to rest and watch. Usually there are two or three people dancing; by the end all five are working together.

But while they are doing the same basic "steps" in a common rhythm, they aren't at all alike, because they all have options they can exercise. One woman may take three steps in a curve and one larger step; another may be in perfect unison with her for the three steps but sink to one knee for the fourth; a third may insert a skip or two without breaking pace. Sometimes the individual variations are bold, other times they manifest themselves as the subtlest of stylistic discrepancies—the fall of an arm, the direction of the eyes.

The women aren't alike to begin with, and Charles Atlas has costumed them all differently—in simple, becoming outfits that seem based on Reitz's preferred attire: culottes and a loose-sleeved blouse. Robin Hertlein is the tallest and moves with sunny strength and confidence. Maria Cutrona is softer, rounder; she's liable to swing her legs higher than the others do, as if she enjoyed her flexibility. Julie Lifton and Sarah Skaggs are dryer and lighter than the others—Lifton at first almost brusque with the movement, Skaggs delicate and careful. But as the dance tumbles along, all the women begin to seem wonderful in their own ways. You begin to understand the dance, and therefore honor the bravery or wit of their choices, appreciate the way they acclimate to Reitz's ideas. The evening becomes a gentle sermon in praise of human ingenuity and of the uniqueness of the individual.

CRAWLING INTO A WOMB

OF RICE

The Village Voice, February 22, 1983

~~~

While we were retrieving our coats and shoes from the cloakroom of the new Kampo Cultural Center on Bond Street, someone I know said, "Well. When you go to a performance by Eiko and Koma, you know for sure you're not going to be seeing an evening of 'American Modern Dance.'" For sure.

Whatever idea Eiko and Koma may be working with—and I'm not always sure exactly what that is—the idea seizes and transforms their bodies. They never seem to have "made up a dance"; their works are carefully conceived, but they always appear as people in the grip of powerful instincts or tides that pull them along.

When the audience enters the deep, narrow performance space, Eiko and Koma are sprawled far apart, face down, naked, on a white platform less than a foot high that almost fills the room. We watch that while the house gradually fills up. Blackout. And in the darkness we hear the dry spattering sound of seeds falling. No, when the lights come up, we can see that it's rice and remember that the work's title is *Grain.* Afterward, pondering the slow, beautiful, violent, shocking images we can understand them all as aspects of fecundity, of nourishment. "Wild rice growing on an unmarked grave . . ." says the press release; the corpse fertilizes the crops that feed ensuing generations—symbolically, if not actually.

Koma is lying on a white mat close to us. Eiko stands at the rear of the platform. Both are now dressed. While he slowly, slowly rolls over, knees in the air, until he is crouching, rump up, face down, like an awkward newborn, she weaves her body and arms delicately in the air, twisting and bending. From her hands, sleeves, from inside her short kimono, rice rattles down onto the platform. At some point, he makes his way to her and pulls her, still waving her arms, onto the lap he makes by squatting.

Blackouts mark off the work. In a black-and-white film of a video by Jeff Bush and Celia Ipiotis, veiled limbs, seen in extreme closeup, tangle gently; a back looks like a ridged desert landscape. Eiko, alone on the white mat, does the same agonizingly slow roll Koma did at the beginning. Crouching, she folds up her body in ways both beautiful and grotesque; one groping leg slides past her ear. She could be a fantastic insect, an unfledged bird, a plant sending out roots and tendrils. Slyly, she picks up one corner of the mat; there's more rice under it. Koma, wearing a colored blouse, dances along. Earlier, he hurled himself to the floor, making the platform bang. But now he's quiet—solid, but fluid; his upper body, arms, head ripple and wobble gently as his feet slide him into deep lunges and kneebends.

The several times they come together, it is to mate. Again he drags her backward to his groin, and they fold up together. He puts a necklace around her neck. In all these encounters, she arches and stretches herself into accommodating positions like an animal in heat. He enters with a little tray of candles and cooked rice. She crawls, and he nuzzles his head into her crotch from behind. While he pulls her back onto him again, she crams the fluffy white rice into her mouth.

These images of being filled, of spewing seed, bloom before our eyes, grave and elemental. Among Eiko and Koma's remarkable works, *Grain* is particularly beautiful.

A MOUTHFUL OF FLOWERS

The Village Voice, March 30, 1982

Johanna Boyce has a refreshingly unsmug way of using loaded material to ask questions instead of to propose solutions. In her *Incidents (in coming of age)*, Bob Gober sometimes reads aloud material on the effects of gender on personal development; some of the bland cultural stereotyping horrifies the 1980s audience. But the material is from accepted texts, and Boyce presents it without obvious rancor. She lets us hear a woman chatting about a life of luncheons, shopping expeditions, picking children up from school: her mother. She shows slides of a soldier in Viet Nam, lets us hear his matter-of-fact voice tell of shooting whatever moved on the river after dark—". . . probably a fisherman, but he was breaking the curfew, so shame on him!"—of his increasing desire for a "round-eyed piece of ass." This is Boyce's brother Gordy.

Seriously, but always fairmindedly, Boyce investigates the ideas and events that shaped her childhood. We see her tomboyishness. In the slides it's baby Johanna who isn't afraid of the huge dog that terrified visitors (it was replaced by an airedale and poodles her mother put bows on). We see her and two friends (Margot Perron and Robbyn Scott) tumble boisterously around (in mismatched shirts and pants, all floral prints) and attempt a ball game. I say "attempt" because they're playing with a ball of yarn, a Kleenex box, and a grapefruit—all of which seem more suitably employed when they stop to wind one, wipe with the other, and cut the third.

There's a lot of dressing and undressing, trying things on and taking them off, fitting them clumsily over other clothes. They gallop around with branches stuck into furry holsters like absurd penises, frail but jaunty. But in all the movements Boyce does or has her colleagues do, you see the matter-of-fact vigor and zest that many young people share—boys or girls. The extremes the texts emphasize—the ladylike and the tough—barely appear, or appear as superficial actions (while Gober reads one of Gordy's raunchier letters to his brother, the three women sit on the floor by lamps with big shades and groom themselves absorbedly). Just before the end, the three remove all clothing but shorts and pass a flower to each other without using hands. This tenderness and eroticism have no discernible role-playing or stereotyped associations with gender. The flower is caught in the crook of an elbow and passed to a bent neck, dropped onto a groin and picked up in a mouth. And after this slow, warm adventure, the women put on mismatched plaid shirts and pants, and take real balls in hand for a fast, precise, exhausting rite of leap, swing, turn, pass, and toss. Art's ability to exorcise and to investigate are both here vindicated, and life's less pleasing aspects presented with a tolerance and grace that ring truer than denunciation.

PERFORMING IS REAL TOO

The Village Voice, March 19, 1980

᠁

I can hardly imagine two dancers more different from each other than Sheryl Sutton and Bill T. Jones. (The only obvious thing they have in common is that they're among the few black artists interested in unconventional dance forms.) I like them both a lot. Sutton is frail, and her dancing has a flyaway beauty. Little about her is fixed down; all the small adjustments and compromises our bodies make in daily life are visible in her movement. She hasn't smoothed the waywardness out of her dancing the way most dancers have. When she does her solo, *Three, Four, and Six,* it barely dawns on me that she's following the same path and doing nearly the same material several times in several different ways. She can step meditatively through her pattern or scamper through it, but she is wonderfully undidactic about the distinctions.

Now Jones is a tall, muscular man. And he's not a quiet dancer like Sutton is. He's juicily precise, powerful, and interested in expending a lot of energy one way or another. He's also one of the few performers I've ever seen who presents a relaxed persona. That is, he's not just Bill Jones dancing for you in today's fashionably unpretentious way. He has theatricalized his casualness—but without phoniness. What he's doing isn't unlike what the old hoofers do. He damn well *knows* he's a performer performing and is at home in that role. His *Addition* (subtitled "a note to Senta Driver") is a brainy accumulating series of gestures. These can range from the small and deft—like putting two fingers of one hand to his eyes—to the vigorous—like a push-up. Through this he grunts accompaniment, grins occasionally, improvises bits of tall tales. Sometimes he seems to be making increasingly more movement fit into the same time span.

The night I went to see Sutton and Jones, a very little girl found him irresistibly funny, got high, in fact, on laughing. Her mother didn't discourage her. So Jones faced the child, said "Psst!", and, when he had gotten her attention, ran through the pattern, staring at her in a not unfriendly way. "This is what I'm doing," he seemed to be saying, "What's so funny about it?" and he went on without a break. She simmered down almost immediately. Now that's ease for you.

The Jones-Sutton duet, *Circle in Distance,* begins with their voices in darkness, prowling the balcony. Jones asks Sutton where she's been traveling this year. She tells him. He adds each new place name to a list he's accumulating: "England, France, Italy, France, Italy, Greece . . . then where?" It's a neat way of coding the accumulation process for an audience—and the idea of backtracking. During the duet, they also take turns reading accounts of what sound like circular journeys through the streets of Manhattan. Chairs and objects that Sutton keeps bringing in map islands in the space. Jones has a phrase that ends with a plunge off a chair; when Sutton brings a large pillow, it cushions and elaborates his plunge each time it recurs. His pliés and other in-place footwork are firmed up in space and then distorted when she brings him something to hold onto, a big animal cage to lean back on. A gesture he makes with his arm, while squatting in one corner of the area, makes sense when she puts a vessel there; suddenly he looks as if he's drawing something out of the pot, and next time around he *does* pull a rope out. It's as if she were filling in the background for him so that on each trip through the places of his dance, the experience could be richer for him.

A SLACK STRING WON'T RESONATE, A TIGHT ONE MAY SNAP

The Village Voice, February 4 – 10, 1981

S omeone sent me an article from *Voices,* a journal of art and psycho-therapy. The guy who wrote the article, Stanley Kelemen, said that twenty years ago the connections between behavioral states, personality, and the body were easier to perceive. People who had been brought up to repress certain instincts in the interests of genteel conduct tended to be tight, inflexible, rigid to the point of spasm. Now he sees people who are not only loose, but apathetic, unable or unwilling to mobilize their strength.

The vanguard of dance, it seems to me, very quickly reflects how we as people feel about our bodies. The choreographers of the '60s complained about the puffed-out ribcages and rigid spines of trained dancers, even as the flower children fled from what they saw as inflated and rigid military and social conventions.

But the warm, casual, grounded dancing that so many of us respond to—the skids and tumbles and twists and never-before-seen sequences—has a low point that is jello: dancers who would rather slough off a move if it looks at all like being strong or clear, perhaps believing that stretching a leg could so easily be construed as corny or vain that you'd better slop through it, if you have to do it at all. The opposite pole is hyperactivity—in dance as in life—unrelated to a clearly discernible goal. Perhaps, as Kelemen says, there's a kind of passivity that ". . . can't bear the buildup of excitation without disassociation."

I couldn't stay at the Symphony Space long enough to see all the important and interesting dancer-choreographers who contributed their services to a benefit for Movement Research, Inc., but what I saw started me thinking again about the dance-bodies that have become our new norm. At one extreme: Kenneth King and a highly active, dense work—the dancers skimming, darting, jabbing their limbs, their bodies taut and agile. There are meetings and congruences, but few relationships as such. The pattern involved isn't the kind you can discern easily, so it's the volatile energy and speed you remember. Whereas the group Freelance (Danny Lepkoff, Steve Paxton, Nancy Stark Smith, Christina Svane, and Lisa Nelson) is all soft, almost to the point of flaccidity. All of these performers can be wonderful, and there was a terrific spatter of energy when the clump that was Stark Smith, Lepkoff, and Paxton first hit the stage to intrude on the quieter, leaning, holding moves of Svane and Nelson. But they devoted a lot of time to walking clumsily with arms around each other, rolling their heads and turning and leaning. And instead of looking relaxed and rich and uninhibited, it looked over-indulgent and babyish, and, in some way, unhealthy, and I surprised myself by thinking this.

On the other hand, Dana Reitz, who had the difficult job of opening this all-star program, danced her *Steps,* a solo improvised around certain ground rules, lavishly—more daring in space, more committed to her decisions, more full in range than I've ever seen her. And the audience was thrilled. And they were thrilled by Bill T. Jones and Arnie Zane, in an excerpt from their new work, *Study for Valley Cottage,* because, I think, of the air of intellectual engagement and purposeful physical vitality the men generated, as well as the structural cleverness and true warmth with which relations between them were expressed.

Robert Kovich works at the top end of the energy spectrum. A man on a hot floor. Most of the dancing that he presented in a concert at Lucinda Childs's loft was so highly strung that I kept expecting to hear a snap and see a dancer crumple. Kovich was until recently one of the most adventurous dancers in Merce Cunningham's company, and his choreography shows the influence of that experience in the busy-footed phrases, the elongated look of the body, the density and irregularity of the compositional texture.

Certainly Kovich is imaginative and clever, well begun on a career in choreography, but what struck me most about this concert was its unaccountably high intensity (particularly noticeable in close quarters). The dancers begin quietly, standing in a clump, stretching their arms, in various directions, looking, bending; they might be dreamily trying out individual codes of signaling. You can identify them: Sally Gardner, Kovich, Anne Lall, Ken Pierce, Ton Simons, Ellen van Schuylenburch. You can admire the curious outfits Suzanne Joelson has dressed them in—pants and shorts of various cuts, slashed open along certain seams to reveal other bright colors underneath. Then, bam, they explode in all directions. They leap and jump and run and kick and stride. They fling their arms or slash them. They bend from side to side. They do all of these at the same time. Turning. Their feet are deliberately noisy on the floor. The movement is extremely fast and difficult; simply to accomplish it in good time takes everything the dancers have. And although there is a kind of rabid elegance to the movement, they execute it with an inelegance that looks deliberate—part of the style.

Kovich rarely mixes slow and fast within a phrase. He makes slow passages to alternate with the fast ones, or, occasionally, to provide a counterpoint. And to refresh the dancers, who, panting, now revolve slowly in attitude, now slide into deep lunges. The dancers come and go, rarely in unison; most often, each pursues an independent course, occasionally collaborating briefly with another. The piece uncannily illustrates one of Kelemen's remarks: the degree of excitation is great, so is the amount of disassociation—the dancers from their bodies, from each other, the parts from the whole.

Obstacle Course/Handicap is almost an endearing parody of the same phenomenon. We're clued to the humor by the dancers' batty outfits (bronzed sneakers, ski caps, etc.) and the clumpy way they land stiff-legged from jumps; but otherwise they do a lot of very fast difficult dancing just as they did in *Nuweiba Reef.* Ton Simons gets small Vivianne Serry (Serry and Kate Nesbitt dance in this) coiled around his waist where she clings staring at his gaudy shoes, while he treats her as a piece of cumbersome athletic equipment. It's odd how jokes like this stick in your mind, not just because they *are* jokes, but because we see purpose, collaboration, and energy used functionally.

David Appel's choreography (or maybe it's improvising) is about as far from Kovich's as you can get. He begins his solo concert at ATL sitting on the floor gingerly probing his own muscles and stretching a bit. He's a small, mild-looking man, without a look one could call dancerly. Almost everything he does is as soft and slippery as butter. Every now and then an unexpected twist, a suspension, a fall will create an unforseen beauty. But Appel never repeats anything, just keeps spooling it out, looking as if the activity were about as interesting to him as taking a shower. It's quite a paradox. Here's this guy dancing all alone in front of an audience for forty-five minutes or so—think of the work, energy, money, self-assurance that takes. And then look at Appel disappearing into the woodwork. Once he barks, sharply, at us. Wake up everybody.

"Leslie's waltz" he announces diffidently, and this time as he noodles around, he begins to sing. "Blackbird singing in the dead of night . . ." His singing is just like his dancing, barely audible—words and rhythms pulled out or squeezed together as he wills—all connections, meaning, rhythmic sense purposely severed.

Just because Pauline Koner has retired as a dancer doesn't mean that she has retired from dancing. On one of the programs on her company's recent series at Riverside Church, she spoke about the precepts of her mentor, Doris Humphrey, and demonstrated her own ideas about gesture and choreographic motivation in relation to her *The Farewell* and *Solitary Songs.*

Koner began nervously, twisting her hands, unconvincingly delivering stock lines I keep hoping never to hear again—about the stage being a magic place and all. But then her body started to get wonderfully busy amplifying what her voice was saying. Koner is a beauty—small, dark, and vivid with huge eyes and strong cheekbones. Beauty has always been important in her dancing, too. I don't mean that she's a vain performer. I mean that she has a romanticist's perspective on the fall of a leaf, or rain in the night, and a flair for creating designs that are meant to be beautiful and full of emotion.

Koner is not far from her seventieth birthday, and she may not have the stamina for sustained performing. But there she was—expanding herself into huge, proud stances, swinging a leg in a big scallop that made her long pink skirt froth up, etching little dithery gestures around her face. Like modern dancers of the early days, she's not afraid to use awkwardness when emotional stress warrants it. She dangles along in helplessly jerky bouncing steps, like a doll, in response to the jangling sounds of a bell.

It all took me back to the days when I danced her dances and we would work for what seemed like hours on the exact density of the air that we should feel on the backs of our hands as we made small polite circles with them. "Oh, Pauline," we would say wearily, "we see." But we didn't really. I kept thinking that even dancers who in no way share her particular aesthetic (except for those to whom phrasing is taboo) could learn from her fastidious attentiveness to the way in which dancing is performed. She understands all the gradations of attack, how to shade a gesture into quietness, how to let it get weak at midpoint and bloom again at the end, without any noticeable break in flow. She has a sense of just how much weight a gesture needs, how much illusory space it should fill. The texture keeps modulating before your eyes.

For all the high degree of artifice in her style, there's a candor in her dancing. Looking at some performers today, I find myself thinking. "So you don't want to look vain or polished, I can understand that. But, really . . . !" Or, conversely, "It doesn't take all *that* energy to do those steps. Stop blazing!" What unnerving changes in the cosmic force fields are our bodies responding to?

MODERN, TRADITIONAL, AND VERY POPULAR

Mikhail Baryshnikov in Eliot Feld's *Variations on America*

LIBRARY ST. MARY'S COLLEGE

Before the so-called "modern" dance was very old, certain parties began to wonder whether its destiny might not lie in bonding with ballet. Modern dance elements could invigorate ballet, update its fairy tales; ballet could fix up the plain-Jane modern dance by judicious loans of glamour, virtuosity, spectacle.

By the mid-fifties, modern dancers were flocking to ballet class, and a few ballet dancers (Robert Joffrey, for instance) studied modern dance. At that time, Glen Tetley could have been considered the prototype for the dancer who was adept at any style. In the High School of Performing Arts and the Dance Department of the Juilliard School of Music, dancers were obliged to study ballet and modern dance. Robert Joffrey's commission of *Deuce Coupe* from Twyla Tharp in 1973 was considered risky. Since then, many ballet companies have presented works by choreographers who are considered not only modern, but vanguardist.

Inevitably some hybridization took place, but it didn't sweep aside all the old distinctions. Frederick Ashton remains a classical choreographer; any contemporaneity in his ballets is achieved in his own way: in *Monotones* through purity and aloofness; in a period drama like *A Month in the Country* through the wise and mature way in which he treats human emotion. Choreographers like Alwin Nikolais or Erick Hawkins who had been at pains at define a personal aesthetic did not balleticize it. That Murray Louis has been in demand as a choreographer for ballet dancers—Rudolf Nureyev among them—is, I think, because his movement style is so intriguingly *unlike* ballet, while his ideas tend to be light and entertaining.

On the other hand, choreographers ostensibly "modern," like Alvin Ailey, as well as some who come out of ballet, like Maurice Béjart, quite often blend elements of both traditions. The hybridization process isn't always seamless. Virtuosity has always been an accepted part of ballet, but modern dance traditionally eschewed display and subordinated everything to the central image or thrust of the work. In Doris Humphrey's *With My Red Fires* (1936), a young woman elopes with a man her mother disapproves of. Watching the film of a revival, seeing him lift her down from her "window" and steal away with her—gently turning her head toward the road before them when she tries to look back——I've often thought how many choreographers would sacrifice the dramatic integrity for a showy, ecstatic pas de deux. (Antony Tudor, alone of the many choreographers who have tackled *Romeo and Juliet,* keeps his protagonists separated during the balcony scene.)

I've seen dances as heavy with psychological overtones as any post-thirties Martha Graham work, except that the dancers' bodies behaved in apparent contradiction to their supposed state of mind. The man going insane stretches into a beautifully placed high développé; the woman who's just been gang-raped emits a barrage of smooth, strong pirouettes before collapsing again. No matter how agonized the dancers' faces, the message is obscured. No one, it is assumed, wants to see real ugliness or loss of control on stage, with the disquieting result that violence can be made to seem rational and seductively beautiful.

Sometimes balletomodern dances are frankly out-to-thrill spectacles in which dancers are hurtling through the air, spinning like tops, rolling on the floor. The turned-out, elongated line associated with ballet has been beefed up by modern dance's emphasis on effort, on showing the pull of gravity in order to dramatize the overcoming of it. Ballet and modern dancers alike train for huge-scale dancing. Once, an arabesque might be slightly more than hip-high; in some companies today, the lifted leg is likely to shoot up to twelve-o'clock-high. A double pirouette is baby stuff these days; students aim for six or more. Some of the modern ballet spectacles strike me as pop manifestations of the current interest in the super-body. Like the sleek-formed, well-muscled new beauties who glow in the ads and fashion magazines, like the increasing numbers of driven people who spend their lives training for triathlons, they reflect our current infatuation with expertise, with endurance, with prowess.

MAN, THE MARVELOUS
MECHANISM

The Village Voice, October 19, 1982

It was almost fifty years ago when Alwin Nikolais saw Mary Wigman perform on one of her three tours of the U.S. and decided to go into dance. It was about thirty years ago, with *Masks, Props, and Mobiles* (1953), that he began to create the kind of luminous theater pieces he's famous for all over the world—dances of sorcery or carnival in which the dancers may be engulfed by an entranced landscape of light, jitter on the edges of a fragmenting universe, disappear, metamorphose, be imprinted with whirling patterns.

In the archive office of the roomy quarters the Nikolais Dance Theatre shares with the Murray Louis Dance Company, cardboard boxes of clippings, notes, photos, whatever, are stacked in neat towers to the ceiling. One box per dance. His first dance-box is as distant in the space of this room as it is in time: I can't even read the label. As I sit talking to him, I imagine that if the boxes were in one of his dances, they'd begin to jiggle imperceptibly, then perhaps sway shyly in time to the electronic music he composes. Letters would slide off one box and onto another; *Grotto* (1973) could bleed onto *Scrolls* (1974), *Imago* (1963) onto *Sanctum* (1964). In the end, all the boxes would crash to the floor. Maybe they'd turn out to be empty.

My scenario isn't a great one ("shitty," Nik might agree cheerfully), but it shorthands the bewitching mixture of mysterious illusions, witty games, and cataclysmic endings that characterize most of my favorite Nikolais pieces. Take *Count Down* (1979), being revived for the company's current season (through October 24) at City Center. At first all you see are five fat pillars, bathed with luscious changing colors by a squadron of slide projectors. Ominous music. The pillars begin to sway slightly. A man strides between them, intent, wary; he senses a mysterious power, but doesn't seem to know where it's coming from. Curious games begin.

The man and his companions are swallowed by the pillars as they pass behind them; sometimes they reemerge immediately, sometimes they disappear for a long time, sometimes they come out transformed into other dancers. The columnar totems/hatcheries become a little less ominous once they're turned so that we can see the dancers who man them. Now they're a harmless background for ritual dance-games, or they're hiding places from which one dancer can hurl a partner into the air and yank him/her back. The effect is not unlike a hot pan of popcorn entering the final stages, but the zest is entirely human. And then? The columns reassert their power, whirling around the stage, grabbing dancers, beginning to topple one by one. Just a jumble of cardboard. Not a living thing in sight.

The image of forces beyond our control, of rites to appease those forces appears in many garbs in Nikolais's most profound works, like *Tent* (1968), in which a dazzling fabric tent, capable of assuming many shapes, is ceremoniously erected by the dancers, and in the end plummets down on top of them. Even a work full of visual and kinetic gags, like *Gallery* (1978), can turn apocalyptic, with pieces of the dancers' faces apparently shot away as they pop their heads up from behind a wall. But in a Nikolais piece, the dancers don't stand apart agonizing over their fates or contemplating solutions, they make the play of forces visible by their kinetic machinations within the environment.

It's curious to me that Nikolais studied dance with people like Humphrey and Graham, with Wigman pupil Truda Kaschmann in Hartford, and with the great Wigman disciple and pedagogue Hanya Holm. They were, in their individual ways, into what he calls "psycho-dramatic" dance, while his interest in abstraction, in the play of forms, in the reduction of gesture to its essence as motion links him much more closely to Wigman's contemporary Oskar Schlemmer, director of the Bauhaus Theater in Germany, who experimented with sculptured costumes and light on moving shapes in the 1920s and 1930s. Nikolais never knew Schlemmer, but he says that Schlemmer's widow, Tut, wanted him to take some of the original costumes and remount a piece. It figures that she would recognize Nikolais as artistic kin.

"Life has become so mechanized, thanks to machines and a technology which our senses cannot possibly ignore," wrote Schlemmer in 1922, "that we are intensely aware of man as a machine and the body as a mechanism." Nikolais in his subtle choreographic manipulations of joints and muscles has developed instruments far more precisely calibrated than the pick-up dancers and bulky art students with whom Schlemmer worked, yet it is interesting to consider Nik in relation to others who have practiced or considered abstract theater: Kandinsky, Schlemmer, Gordon

Craig. The fact is, for all the charges of "dehumanization" that have annoyed Nikolais so over the years, the crucial point with him, as with these other innovators, is that man is always somehow the measure. His screens and scrolls move by human agency in ways they could never be moved by wires alone; without the living dancers the environments would have no point. And the dancers, of course, can be altered to fit. "I didn't want dancers maimed by having the costumes stop here," Nik points to his wrist as he describes some of his early experiments. "I designed *into* the hand, *into* the face so that the thing was one whole piece. I like the body as a whole piece." He also remembers a solo he worked on with Murray Louis, back in the good-bad old days when no one got paid and time was all you had plenty of: "I put stripes on his face and I'd watch very carefully. I could see the face fragment in a particular kind of light. The idea was not to fragment the body, but to see a little more of the inside by destroying the outside."

Like Schlemmer and Craig, Kandinsky and others, Nikolais was—is—fascinated by marionettes and once ran a puppet theater. But for all these men, what the puppet offered was a way of presenting the human condition in some universal and noble way without the distractions of the performer's personality. Nikolais learned from his puppets the idea that "it's the motion that speaks. For instance, the puppet has no nerves, has no sensations at all. The illusion of these is transmitted through motion. I used to perform sometimes in the park for 7,000 people with two-foot-high marionettes, and people would come back and ask me how I'd managed to make their faces change. The value of a gesture has always fascinated me . . . the idea of the qualitative motion that speaks so vividly on its own terms that one needs nothing else. This is what the art's about, I think. I'd throw out the slides and . . ." He trails away. ("I never have enough time to explore . . ." he sighs, remembering to touch wood gratefully for all the touring.)

Puppet images crop up in his dances: the skittering, bagged traffic-people in the "Boulevard" section of *Imago* (1963) resemble hand puppets; in the nimble solos Nik used to compose on Murray Louis, Louis often resembled a clever and antic marionette in control of invisible strings that connected knee with elbow, hand with head. In *Guignol* (1977), two dancers are manipulated into jerky courtship by others, and Gerald Otte is pulled into bizarre dancing by strings attached to sticks wielded by two impassive and slightly sinister men. The metaphor, for Nikolais, may have to do with control, with the illusion(?) that it is we who are determining our own destiny.

Gordon Craig, in his later years, said he never meant the marionette to replace the living actor; he only meant that actors should become more transparent. Nikolais uses living dancers, handsome and gifted ones, and despite his interest in abstraction, occasionally enjoys a frank showing off of their accomplishments. His new suite, *Mechanical Organ, Part II,* presents tall Jessica Sayre as Miss Elastic; Gerald Otte as an antic charmer sliding gestures around his superbly articulate body, padding in the space; Joy Hintz and Timothy Harling as a shy couple jittering on separate stools; Jung Auyang and Raul Trujillo, in a comradely duet laced with nonchalant acrobatics. And in his *Cross-Fade* (1974), photographs of the dancers, nude or patterned with light, keep flashing onto the backdrop so that living dancers can cast shadows on their identically posed images, can have their photos pasted onto their bodies. Nikolais's quiet, quizzical voice (the text is a new addition) ponders ourselves, our shadows, and time, trailing every few sentences into free association: "end of time, no time, time to go, there'll be a hot time in the old town tonight"—that's a paraphrase.

I remember finding it odd when I visited Connecticut College one summer during the '50s that Graham and Limón and their dancers seemed in their work very concerned with individual human emotions, but were distant and often frosty with their students, whereas Nikolais's people, who—as far as I knew them—spent their days being blobs and blips, were cordial and fun to be with. The atmosphere around Nikolais still radiates cheerfulness. At a run-through of his new *Pond* in his fully equipped studio theater, he tells the assembled audience of board members, friends, photographers, reporters, former company members, etc. that *Pond* is an "à la Walden sort of divertissement—a little on the romantic side. I thought I could afford that at this time of life." And cheers, chuckles, and encouraging jokes ring out from the back row. Our little audience, indeed, gasps approval all through *Pond* and cheers itself blue at the end. It's a short work, extremely, deliberately beautiful. The slide projectors beam a pattern that looks like an abstraction of clear drops of water bubbling on a blue-green pond. At first the waving arms and legs of dancers look like fronds of water plants. All the performers are on little, scarcely visible wheeled platforms, so that they can scud over the surface of the floor, eddy around each other languidly, pair up (on one level you see joining organisms, on another, embracing men and women spinning gently in some fluid dream). At the end, connected, I guess, by a cord that appears by magic, the dancers are pulled offstage in a long, calmly seated line.

I'm touched by the fact that the watching dancers let Nik know how much they like his work, and let those of us not "in the family" know what extra-good stuff we're watching. There's a kind of benevolence about the company, and good humor and protectiveness. So Nik can warn Gerald Otte, posing for Lois Greenfield, "She's taking them. Watch out, don't scratch your ass *now.*" And then while Nik is beaming for the camera from inside one of the *Count Down* scrolls, Otte calls out softly to him, and touches his own head to alert Nik to a wisp of white hair that ought to be smoothed back.

We could probably talk for a long time. Nikolais has a lot to say about everything: about the good days with Holm when eight or ten eager people (Glen Tetley, Annabelle Lyon among them) would work all morning, go up to Hanya's apartment and fry some eggs for lunch, go back down to the studio and work through the afternoon. Holm's technique was less rooted in personal style, he thinks, than the Graham or Humphrey–Weidman techniques; she was thorough, she tried to throw people on their own. He has warm words to say in praise of Murray Louis and his choreography. He has a bunch of wryly funny stories about the old days when he and his company were in residence on the Lower East Side at the Henry Street Playhouse. He has hot, unhappy things to say about the mess support for the arts is in; about the government's apparent drift away from subsidy; about the endless quest for money ("We're so required to raise funds all the time that we become mountebanks for wealthy people, and this is very degrading. The gala is one of the shittiest affairs ever invented"); about the fact that arts organizations can get funds more easily than artists ("And I wish I had the money they're giving in grants to study whether they should be giving grants to me or anybody else"); about the need to fund worthy young companies ("They're the roots of the profession. You can't put manure on the flowers. You have to put it on the roots").

He sounds troubled, but not sour. And I don't suppose anything can keep him down. "I am a compulsive creator," he once wrote. "If you give me a schnauzer, two Armenian chastity belts, and a nineteenth-century dishpan—I would attempt to create something with them."

DOES HEROISM DEFINE
A HERO?

The Village Voice, October 22–28, 1980

᷍᷍

Murray Louis is the antithesis of modern dance's early heroes. The Louis–Nikolais style (in effect built by Alwin Nikolais on Louis's phenomenal body and subjected to further modeling by Louis himself) was hailed in the early fifties as a welcome alternative to the prevailing mythico-poetico-dramatico sludge. The dancers didn't dump on us; they were luminous, flexible, feathery, now-you-see-'em-now-you-don't. When they coupled, teasingly beautiful new organisms appeared; their bodies cracked one joke after another. The man Louis plays on stage would never stand unflinching to meet the blows of fate; instead, deftly, nimbly, he'd slip under the raised spear.

That Louis, going on fifty-four, can perform a solo, *Chimera,* that he made when he was a kid of thirty-nine, with undiminished power and zest is a testament to the rewards of wit and dodginess. From slithering along as a bemused, stripey bugbear that doesn't scare *me,* to pattering around drumming his forehead with agile fingers as if he's forgotten some vital rules of successful elfhood, to taking delighted stock of a body that has unlimited resources for rhythmic play in space. Louis is the *echt* theatrical antihero. When the charming and engrossing solo begins to wear a little, when the wily figure makes yet another entrance from his grotto, I admire him still—thinking that Oedipus would have been dead long before this.

The denizens of his new *The City* are also a peaceful lot. So successfully do they adapt to the invisible shapes and pressures around them that they, as much as the projections by Alwin Nikolais, *are* the city. Nikolais's set is vivid and restless; the designs projected on the jagged hanging shapes change many times before the dance even begins. At one almost dire point, the "sky" below turns red and throws a wall of fire up at them. David Darling's music (scored for cello, voice, French horn, keyboard, and bass) is also restless. The dancers do a lot of moving around in this bright, slightly dangerous playground, but they don't fight it.

As a choreographer, Louis can interest you for a long time in the mild permutations of a very simple pattern. At the very beginning of the dance, Danial Shapiro and Joanie Smith take turns walking under the arches they make with their bodies by bending over and curving out their arms. As the six other dancers gradually join, the simple act becomes a structure that

grows and subdivides, seeming elastic enough to build forever. This kind
of thing, or the arresting little design Louis can make out of runs and
stops, pleases me more than the kinetic jokes he pulls out of a tight lineup
of dancers (hint of subway). The dancers (Michael Ballard, Janis Brenner,
Anne McLeod, William Holahan, Betsy Fisher, Robert McWilliams, Shapiro and Smith)—whether sitting to survey alertly a possibly threatening
atmosphere, or breathing percussively, or embracing a partner, or jostling
against each other—have an airy ability to evade obstacles and turn possible confrontations into jokes for arms and legs.

Louis more directly hymns the image of physical and emotional buoyancy in *November Dances,* a new duet that can be performed by any of
three pairs of dancers. I saw Brenner and Ballard, both of whom excel at
giving Louis's eccentric curvets of movements a soft sweep of breath.
Brenner is looking wonderful these days; a very small, quick dancer, she's
adept at giving everything she does an intelligible shape: she dances sentences rather than word lists. The duet is structured like a classical grand
pas de deux—duet, solo, solo, duet—and cracks a few jokes about manners and elegance. These jokes of Louis's, which never fail to delight the
audience, are what I like least about his style. The amount of calculated
head-nodding these two dancers have to get through is staggering; a joint
nod is even the ungracious punchline to the agreeably breezy work.

HARMONY'S FERVENT
APOSTLE

The Village Voice, September 23–29, 1981

Quite a few years have passed since the last time I saw Erick Hawkins's work. His company, touring busily, plays New York infre-
quently, and I missed its last appearance. Seeing his three latest dances in
concert at Alice Tully Hall, I was struck all over again by how different the
ideas of this now magisterial figure are from those of most of his contemporaries, although someone years ago—I believe it was the critic Robert
Sabin—linked Hawkins loosely with Murray Louis, perceiving their common interest in serious playfulness of body, in fluidity, in subtle dynamic
shifts.

Certainly Hawkins's work isn't much like that of Martha Graham, with whom he danced between 1938 and 1951, although he too is interested in ritual, in the uses of formality, in the single vivid image. But the concept Graham began to articulate explicitly in the late '40s—the dancer not only as suffering hero, but as divine acrobat—is, clearly, far from Hawkins's vision. Striving, ardent, mortifying the flesh, achieving more than human feats of strength and daring: that's not how Hawkins sees the dancer. The eight men and women in his company move with idyllic peacefulness as if they've entered into a compact with the force of gravity—promising to tease it only in brief delighted forays into flight, disequilibrium, or accumulating momentum.

It's possible to apply a variety of viewpoints to "nature." Hawkins's contemporary Merce Cunningham emphasizes its chanciness, the limitations of predictability; Hawkins prefers to bring out what is cyclical, constant, and harmonious. Nature allows both interpretations: we can never be sure whether next Thursday will be rainy or fair, yet we can say with assurance that if snow is falling it isn't summer. Hawkins, like Isadora Duncan, believes in waves, in a profoundly orderly current uniting man and the universe, but he doesn't stress grandeur the way she did. His dancers—Cathy Ward, Rand Howard, Douglas Andresen, Cynthia Reynolds, Craig Nazor, Helen Pelton, Jesse Duranceau, Laura Pettibone—rarely focus on the space they're dancing in, or on each other. Instead, they seem raptly to be sensing the caress of air as they waft fluidly through it, the response of the floor to their feet, the poetic inner pulse of motion. The words "sensing," "sensuous," "sensitive" have been often used of Hawkins's style and technique, by Hawkins himself and by others. The dancers don't simply act; they are intensely aware of the impact of each act on their own bodies. It is perhaps this quality of making their own sensations manifest that makes them appear so beautifully and innocently hedonistic to some viewers and so self-centered to others.

The three dances on the Alice Tully Hall program—*Agathlon* (premiered at the Nervi Festival in 1979), *Death Is the Hunter* (1975), and the new *Heyoka*—present the dancers in similar ways. They move much of the time in flocks, all doing the same step, all facing in the same direction. Occasionally one or two or three perform alone or in counterpoint; occasionally a phrase spatters into canon. From time to time, they acknowledge the audience's presence. When men dance with women, you may see four pairs, all gently embracing in the same way. There is something very classical about Hawkins's viewpoint: his dancers no more particularize human responses or movement patterns than Petipa-Ivanov swan-maidens mirror the unruly winging of real swans or the variegated responses imaginary enchanted maidens might be capable of. Hawkins dancers are a cluster of individuals collectively representing a quality.

Dorrance Stalvey's score for *Agathlon* suggests the wind-tongued spaces of Monument Valley that inspired the dance. The dance itself is limpid, but not at all stark or monumental. In front of Ralph Dorazio's bright sculpture—a green gash balanced on top of what might be seen as a letter A—the dancers pulse. As some drop suddenly into a wide-legged plié, others shoot up, stretching one arm like a plume; it's a quintessential Hawkins idea to encapsulate in this simple pair of gestures the rearing up of natural stele through centuries of erosion by fall of rain. Some extremely beautiful moments bud unexpectedly in this dance: a single dancer is launched out of the curving, turning group as thinly and straightly as an arrow. Cathy Ward makes her hands revolve and flower like those of a dancer from Bali or Cambodia. Lifted from behind to leap, now to one side, now to the other of a partner, she hovers for a second then lets her body acquiesce to the lure of the ground. It's a curious and almost indescribable articulation of weight. Ward's solo and a solo for Rand Howard show Hawkins at his most inventive in terms of steps, timing, changes of spirit.

Heyoka begins with laughter. Hawkins is a rare comedian when he chooses to be (as anyone will remember who saw him as an inept squash in his *Eight Clear Places*). Two clownish masked fellows (Andresen and Duranceau) chase each other onto the stage; one immediately trips and falls. They're lumbering fellows with rattling chains and little red balls trailing from their ankles. One tears a big sheet of black paper in half and clumsily but gleefully flaps offstage. His less clever sidekick whacks his head through his paper, doesn't quite get the knack of flight. To the audience's intense delight, they do it all over again—with minor comical differences. Ross Lee Finney's score, commissioned by Hawkins, is full of brassy little fanfares, flirtings with important messages. The dancers enter singly and in small groups over a Dorazio-designed threshold, but although you could at first imagine them circus acrobats, they are simply here to dance. The clowns don't reappear. Hawkins's program note likens them to the clowns ("heyoka") that Sioux Indians send in to "open the people to the poetry of the dance to come." At the very end, a gentle maelstrom of jumping subsides, and a single dancer stands, arm raised; as the lights fade, he seems ready to begin another phase of the entertainment, which we're destined not to see.

Hawkins himself appeared only in *Death Is the Hunter*, swathed in a vivid purple robe (costumes: Willa Kim), decked in long black hair and a frightening all-white mask by Ralph Lee—part skeleton, part paper doll, part cat. His slow inexorable advances, his watchful stares through Dorazio's metal thicket, the menacing way he raises his curved bow make him by far the most arresting figure on stage, even though he moves little. The dancers ceremoniously enter and don identical bland masks which they take off only to "die." In the moment before they pillow their heads on the tiny stony boats Dorazio has designed, they appear more individually human than in the pale-faced chorus a moment before.

Many of Hawkins's costumes are leotards with clear slashes of contrasting color sewn into them. In *Agathlon,* the dancers change midway through, as if in response to seasonal light. The costumes are extraordinary objects, although not always becoming (in *Heyoka,* dancers with black patches look, from a distance, as if someone has bitten a hole in them). A musical ensemble under the direction of Peter Leonard plays the Stalvey and Finney scores meticulously, as well as Wallingford Riegger's *Study in Sonorities.* The dancers are some of the finest Hawkins has had. The dances themselves affect me like a drink of water from a celebrated well, offered in a silver cup. Delight at the sweetness of the gesture, at the intensity (both real and imagined) of the flavor wrangles with thirst.

TAKING ON NEW SHAPES

The Village Voice, August 22, 1977

Pilobolus continues to thrive; its seductive designs and locker-room humor bewitch every audience I've been part of. Occasionally I meet people—quite a few at the American Dance Festival performances—who're appalled by the heartless beauty of the company's jointly made dances or by the violence implicit in many of the four-man knots, chains, and flying adhesions (a Pilobolus specialty). Pilobolus pokes lewd fun at deformity, and on one level the funny or decorative lifts look like cruel and unusual punishment. There's something medieval about the group's sensibility: at best the dances evoke Hieronymous Bosch; at worst, a world of bear-baiting and pet dwarves.

When Pilobolus consisted of four men, the dances seemed all about intriguing shapes of kinetic jokes. Shortly after Martha Clarke and Alison Chase became part of the group, Pilobolus began to develop the allusive possibilities of its tricks (the wonderful three-man structures in *Monks-hood's Farewell*—flexible arrangements of horse, knight, and lance). In the fin-de-siècle Freudian nightmare, *Untitled,* the company brought off its first short story. In *The Eve of Samhain,* they've attempted, for the first time, I think, to assign a character—a clearly individual role—to each performer.

This time the company's joint-choreography approach may have made the project difficult. *The Eve of Samhain* looks as if, rather than starting with a plot or anything like that, each of the five performers (Clarke isn't in it) chose his or her own role, and then together they sat down to plan possible encounters.

The pseudo-scholarly program notes set the tone with references to the Paps of Anu, the "knelling of the dryshod," and other bits of Celtic lore—real or Pilobolese. Jonathan Wolken is an undaunted professor of antiquities who is set upon on Halloween by assorted figures from pre-Christian mythology. They rush in, faceless in hooded robes, and grab the bells from the professor's trunk to peal in the once-a-year revels. Later uncloaked, they turn out to be a husky, goat-legged creature (Robby Barnett), a gibbering blind seer (Moses Pendleton), a coolly lascivious young woman (Alison Chase), and her lover (Michael Tracy). These mix it up in various ways. As Wolken stands appalled, Pendleton, unseeing, clambers up his body to perch on his head, then, afraid of the height, gropes his way down again. The professor, much taken with the minx, dances her decorously around; her lover does bereaved back-flips and cartwheels. The nature of the idea keeps all the funny, scary moments from working together; structurally, *The Eve of Samhain* is a kinetic version of wouldn't-it-be-fun-to-have-Mozart-Helen-of-Troy-and-Babe-Ruth-to dinner? (Probably not.)

There is something both frightening and alluring about the idea of transformation, and I am most impressed when Pilobolus's work touches on this mystery, instead of making virtuosic jokes about it. Perhaps the trouble with Alison Chase's solo, *Lost in Fauna,* is that it's drawn-out and, in some way, so didactic that the mystery is dispelled. Here is Chase, first a mound of ragged pink, then a pair of pink legs and hips protruding from a pink blossom. Once, she makes the audience laugh by pausing to show a royal blue smile. The image she presents is terrifying and unpleasant—a woman struggling to free herself from a monstrous sea anemone or, worse yet, a woman with a vagina where her head ought to be. At the very end, she turns herself inside out (or right-side up) and stands serenely, bare back to the audience, wearing a blue silk gown. Chase falls into one of the traps inherent in the Pilobolus aesthetic: at some point the dance stops being about . . . whatever it's about . . . and becomes a dance about the ninety-five beguiling things you can do with a pink skirt on your head.

There's something not entirely Pilobolese about Martha Clarke; she's a naturalized citizen who retains a faint foreign accent. *Pagliaccio* is the second solo she's made about the vulnerability of the performer on stage, about the pathos of disguises. In most Pilobolus dances, the performers choose a way of holding themselves or moving and stick with it; Clarke seems more interested in changing, in revealing thought processes and motivations. Her *Pagliaccio* is a woebegone androgynous creature, private but also on display. She's dressed like a commedia dell'arte Pierrot, soaking her feet in two pails. She can walk, sort of, in the pails; when she removes her feet, they're in smaller pails. The dance begins to impress upon you futile images of spilling and containment, of filling and emptying. He/she squats over one of the larger tubs and "tinkles" (there is a bell concealed in the tub) while staring at the audience with embarrassment and defiance. By the end of the dance she has attempted escape (or creation?) by climbing a tower of pails; as the curtain falls, she is balancing on one foot. The sensibility of Pilobolus is inevitably male; it interests me to see how, in their own pieces, Chase and Clarke combat this and comply with it.

AND PEARL REMEMBERED
TO BRING DRUMMERS

The Village Voice, December 18, 1978

A colleague once advised me not to cry at dance concerts, or, if I did, not to mention it in print, but the Alvin Ailey twentieth-anniversary gala was engineered—superbly—to get all our juices flowing. Not a glittery fundraising evening, but a this-is-where-we-stand one, a we-made-it-guys one—an evening of pride and nostalgia, celebration and regret, laughter and tears, applause and roses.

"My God, it's Jimmy—James Truitte!" shrieked one dancer in the audience to another a second after the curtain went up on the last dance, *Revelations.* And it was Jimmy, white-haired now, in the center of the group for "I Been 'Buked," where he used to stand during his eight years with the company—his arms unfolding and hovering above the group with a tenderness no other Ailey dancer has been able to duplicate. That's how it had been all evening. Present company members danced with fairly recent alumni like Linda Kent, John Parks, Kenneth Pearl, Kelvin Rotardier, and Hector Mercado, with those who haven't been around for nearly ten years, like Miguel Godreau, George Faison, Loretta Abbott, Alma Robinson, William Louther, Hope Clarke, and Sylvia Waters, with those who were with Ailey during the lean, early years—Charles and Ella Thompson Moore, Lucinda Ransom, Altovise Gore Davis, Dorene Richardson, Carmen de Lavallade, James Truitte, and Brother John Sellers. Oh, and Alvin Ailey, who—minus a lot of the extra weight he's been carrying around since he stopped dancing in 1965—showed more than a hint of his old soft tigerishness with beautiful Hope Clarke in the "Backwater Blues" of *Blues Suite*.

And—how could I forget?—at the end of a ceremony honoring Katherine Dunham, Beryl McBurney, and Pearl Primus, Primus beckoned to drummers she had thought to bring along and danced—a round, merry little woman now, a bundle of bright robes and turbans, covering an unbelievable amount of space in a blaze of energy and humor.

Some of the former Ailey dancers looked better than ever: Miguel Godreau, in Ailey's works and his own solo, *Paz*, danced with the vividness I remember, but, in spite of the whizzing turns and high leaps, he didn't look flashy—just very clear and with that complete absorption in the moment that the best dancers have. Carmen de Lavallade, performing John Butler's *Portrait of Billie* with the excellent Ulysses Dove, not only *danced* it as well as she used to, but brought even more depth and more poignancy to her role.

The Ailey company has always emphasized eloquent performing and roles that demand intense pitches of emotion or white-hot physical involvement. At the gala, we could watch Judith Jamison ablaze with joy in the last section of *Cry*, William Louther in a fury of religious torment in *Hermit Songs*, Mari Kajiwara and Clive Thompson twining in virtuosic eroticism in the duet from *Hidden Rites*.

Even in a more meditative work like *Reflections in D*, exquisitely performed by Dudley Williams, Ailey shows his predilection for lush, fullbodied movement. The style he developed pulls the dancers' bodies into great back-arching positions, tautly stretched arm gestures, and suddenly lets them shoot off into leaps or collapse into falls. For his cooler, vernacular stuff, he reins that powerful impulse in the torso and lets it erupt slyly into sways, struts, wiggles. Ailey's style, compounded of modern dance and jazz, has been seminal (along with that of Tailey Beatty and Donald McKayle) in defining the black dancer's image, an image the next generation copies or rebels against—mostly copies. The image is an ingratiating one: the dancers come off as powerful, aggressive, but supple and not reticent about showing either emotion or their joy in dancing for an audience; playful and comical too, at times.

Ailey always wanted to be popular, to be entertaining, and he has succeeded in that. (His most popular works, *Revelations* and *Blues Suite,* are my favorites too.) But a mass audience isn't a very discriminating audience, and Ailey's work suffers from this—his choreography, his direction of the dancers—and, I think, from his passionate admiration of virtuosity (it's another extreme, another example of the body working toward a passionate peak). Ailey dancing, like Graham dancing, has gotten increasingly more display-oriented and less subtle in performance shadings. It was interesting to see how almost improvisational some of the gestures in "Move, Members, Move" and "Rocka My Soul" seemed when the older Ailey dancers did them at the gala and how more "set," also more exaggerated, less cool they seem now that relays of dancers have had to count them out and pass them on.

Ailey's audience loves everything as long as it's intense and/or colorful and not too murky. At the gala, George Faison and the adorable Marilyn Banks got an ovation for their mugging in Faison's *Suite Otis;* their performing struck me almost as a caricature of the more subtly funny and believable carryings-on in the last part of *Blues Suite.* Talley Beatty's finely crafted, hard-driving *Toccata* got less applause than his *The Road of the Phoebe Snow,* which—especially as it is now staged and performed—strikes me as not only hokey but incoherent. (The dancers suffer a lot, look beautiful, dance hard—who could ask for anything more?) It must be hard for the current Ailey dancers—many of them splendid— to keep steady. Gorgeous Donna Wood can do many things wonderfully, but she can't, for some reason, round her back, which I think robs her of some of her potential power and maturity (the coil-in that powers the stretch-out). At the gala, Dudley Williams gave one of the most remarkably sensitive and musical performances of *Reflections in D* I've ever seen, but I've also heard cheers for him on nights when he simply did a competent professional job with the solo. If the intelligent and gifted Mari Kajiwara gets cheers (and possibly the approval of Ailey and the company) for her high extensions, will she ever have the nerve *not* to use them throughout "Fix Me Jesus"—where they seem out of place, except for the beautiful arching-toward-heaven arabesque that ends the duet?

Once I walked into a rehearsal where Ailey was rehearsing "I Been 'Buked" with about sixteen dancers, and, without stopping the rehearsal, he yelled at me from across the room, "I know, I know what you're going to say: it was better with eight dancers. But this is for the Palais des Nations and it has to read in a huge space!" He's made his choices, and *Revelations* is a wonderful dance anyway you slice it, and we all know that not everything was good about the good old days, that the Ailey company continues to be an American phenomenon. I have twenty years worth of respect, rage, exasperation, and love for Alvin, and I look forward to at least that many more.

And I gotta report that through the tears I am not supposed to tell you I was shedding, the double finale of *Revelations* was a knockout—the celebrated alumni (impeccably costumed) giving way to current company members for the second time around. And then hugs and flowers taking over.

FREEDOM TO RISK ALL

The Village Voice, July 17, 1978

S ince jazz music is rooted in black culture and traditions, and since so many of its greatest exponents have been black, it seems logical that black dancers and choreographers would have been interested in similar forms and techniques. Well, they have and they haven't. They've excelled at "hoofing," or vernacular jazz dancing, and now they excel at "jazz dance," a high-powered blend of modern dance, traditional jazz, and virtuosic feats. Many black modern dancers were, I think, in search of a suitable dance hero or heroine—an image of the Dancer that would be projected regardless of the nature of a particular role or work, something that would correspond, say, to the white male ballet dancer's classical image of a Prince, elegantly linear, erect, essentially nonviolent, polite. You could watch the black image being defined in the sixties, not so much by Alvin Ailey, Talley Beatty, Donald McKayle, or Eleo Pomare as by the young people who showed dances at places like Clark Center, by what they chose to do and not to do, by what they imitated from these experienced choreographers and what they ignored. The new heroes emerged as lithe and flexible in the torso and hips, very intense in the way their bodies arched and coiled in response to emotion, tough and impudent. Now it's a style.

It's never really been Rod Rodgers's style, although he's made use of it. His individual touch is lighter, with more emphasis on subtle dynamic shading, as in *Rhythm Ritual* (1972), which he showed on his company's recent season at St. Mark's Playhouse or his new *Soft Days . . . secret dreams,* a solo to Keith Jarrett music for Jeanne Moss, a small, strong woman who knows how to surprise you with a float that acquires a slash along the way. Now he's gotten interested in the jazz process; his new experiment, *Jazz Fusion,* involves the collaboration of Jimmy Owens and his splendid associates, Jimmy Ponder (guitar), Chris White (bass), and Brian Brake (drums). It also involves a fine actress (Barbara Montgomery) reading poetry, but Rodgers couldn't fully integrate her.

So Rodgers plans a suite of choreographed dance to improvised music, improvised dance to composed music, improvised dance to improvised music, and both dance and musical structures with indeterminate "free spaces." The prospects are exhilarating, but in this first version, the dancers are somehow hampered by their backgrounds in "jazz dance," by some of the archetypes they once worked to create. Sometimes, Owens and his group play sweet-and-easy accessible music, but sometimes they make their instruments howl and quake and produce timbres unlike anything you'd dream of, and the dancers find no equivalent daring with their bodies. The musicians use techniques and traditions as a springboard and take risks (the old-time jazz dancers can do this within limits), but Rodgers's dancers look as if they think the secret of good, improvised dancing is to create something no one would know is improvised. A strained "love dance" (choreographed by Noel Hall and performed by Hall and Shirley Rushing)—tense and unhappy and full of balletic lifts and partnering, seems out of place. Rodgers explains to the audience that he has deliberately incorporated typical black-dance figures—like three women in flashy dresses (Tamara Guillebeaux, Shirley Rushing, and Laura Hausmann) who flounce on chairs and stare competively at each other—without really explaining *why* he feels the need of doing this. (I guess I'd accept it more happily if it had an individual slant or didn't seem watered down.) John Parks is an elegant, lean dancer without much force or mobility in his torso; occasionally, in his own solo, *Ra,* a hint of Watusi steps shows his birdlike grace and wingspread. But in much of *Ra,* as in his solo in *Jazz Fusion,* he seems to be forcing himself into a style that doesn't fit his body or dance temperament.

The terrific music, the pleasure of the audience, the dancers' skill and verve and eagerness made me yearn for more from them—more rhythmic intrepidness, more freedom. I warmed to a certain awkward daring in the *Open Moods* section, loved it when Randy Thomas got that "I never tried this before, but here goes" glee in a men's trio. And suddenly, near the end of the dance, Noel Hall cut loose for a second and did something that looked all his, born of the moment, his feet splayed into a wild position a dance teacher would have been shocked by. And that was it. Or at least, that struck me as a beginning—making the sound, the energy, of jazz become visible, instead of dancing *to* jazz.

BÉJART LANDS: PREPARE
FOR ECSTASY

The Village Voice, April 11, 1977
▁▂▁

Like the play directors who look for ways to put zing into the classics (*Titus Andronicus* as a bikers' war . . .), Maurice Béjart takes venerable themes and plots and slathers them with fashionable significance. *Faust* as a black mass; *Renard* as a twenties farce about three gays and an intruding bitch; *Firebird* as a saga about all-male partisans; *La Bayadère* as a virility rite by desert spirits; Isadora Duncan as Maya Plisetskaya. The passion for transformation invades his work in all particulars: Faust and Mephistopheles exchange appearances via an oily tango; and while Satan (I think) attempts to rouse Faust (by blowing on him) after the Walpurgis Night revels, four women run through a few exercises from Martha Graham's famous floorwork (meaning a dancer always has to wake up for class no matter *what* he's been doing the night before?).

The first section of *Golestan/The Rose Garden*, like the earlier *Rite of Spring*, strikes me as a good example of what Béjart is mostly about: abrupt and savage energy, hard-edged designs, hazy symbolism, and a crowd of terrific-looking young men. *Golestan* does begin like *Bayadère*, with a long line of men (thirty-two of them) in billowing white trousers and shirts snaking back and forth with a single repeating phrase. Later these "men of the desert" remove their shirts, squat in a semicircle and yell and clap while some take turns showing off and competing in leaping and whirling for their pals, the "traveler" seeking something (Micha Van Hoecke), and us. It was exciting, and, as someone more forthright than I said, Béjart copped out by not raffling the dancers off afterwards.

I would have liked seeing Maya Plisetskaya as Maya Plisetskaya—just rippling her beautiful arms and looking grand and important. As herself, she probably could still have nodded at the onstage pianist (Elisabeth Cooper) to start playing; probably she could have also received the bouquets bestowed on her by a chorus of tiny girls in tunics. She could, in fact, have done an entire dance about taking bows and how to keep stirring up applause with beguiling gestures. She's one of the world's most charismatic performers, but it was unnerving to see her at fifty-one playing Isadora Duncan as an ingenue—her shoes (shoes!) making light pattering sounds, her face and body too often conveying an awareness of how pretty, how decorative, her dancing was.

Béjart, aiming to appeal to a mass audience while retaining the trappings of "culture," appeals to me when he is most vigorously and unabashedly spectacular. But audiences seem to love his use of important music (for *Faust,* Bach's B-Minor Mass, intercut with tangos), his solemn, heaving-with-portent rituals, his quotes from literature and philosophy. *Notre Faust,* which is pretty entertaining, is typical of Béjart in that it is elaborate without being elegant; muddled but never complex; dramatic in tone, but with very little specific action or characterization. It begins with Béjart as the old Faust intoning Goethe into a microphone (with a long cord that he twitches along behind him like a tail) while young men in tights execute a canon of flat patterns—alone, in pairs, in trios. The dance is noisy—full of talking and yelling and screaming and writing on blackboards. The style is an eccentric blend of styles—sauté en arabesque yields to a turned-in shambling step to hear-no-evil-see-no-evil gestures to jazzy stomps. Everything is huge and abrupt. Béjart has a habit of stopping the dancing in its tracks every now and then, as if waiting for slow readers in the audience to catch up. Fallen angels parade about in gorgeous church vestments. Jorge Donn puts on bat wings and flies up.

A charge of prudishness or snobbery is often leveled at those who don't adore Béjart. My distaste may stem from something even more fundamental and inescapable. I'm a woman, and Béjart's choreography is savagely antifemale. Not only are the women in his company almost invisible, but they're usually either being mauled or being bitch goddesses. At the end of *Ce Que L'Amour Me Dit,* La Scala ballerina Luciana Savignano (sharp and dark, an ideal predator for Béjart) gives a lot of dance orders to Jorge Donn and then points out a handsome boy (his own lost innocence? his son? a more appropriate lover?), and protectively embraces Donn while he embraces the boy. The Walpurgis Night in *Notre Faust* is an all-male affair (push-ups, stiff-legged walks—the hard-on style of dancing); when Marguerite runs in, she is played with roughly and then thrown away. Faust (Yann Le Gac) dances with neither Marguerite (Monet Robier) nor with Helen (Shonach Mirk—the opposite of the bitch-goddess, weakly innocent). Instead he dances with Mephistopheles

(Béjart), disguised as these women, in a mask and a robe, mincing like a Japanese actor. When Béjart rolls out from under Maguy Marin's skirt, there's no mistaking the message: evil lurks within all women, women breed evil.

I'm not even sure why Béjart needs women in his company. One of the features of his style is that his men often perform movements related to those considered feminine in traditional dancing. In *Notre Faust*, Patrice Touron, a lithe, boyish dancer—perhaps a natural successor to Paolo Bortoluzzi—performs a sharp-footed solo that doesn't expand much in space but requires him to emphasize a lot of small up-and-down actions like those of a woman going on and off pointe. The "jazz" the men do in the same ballet often looks like the hands-folded, knees-together, ass-stuck-out-stuff that Broadway girls used to do. The fierce guys in *Golestan* pulse forward, legs bent and wide apart; with every step they lift their arms and pull them down like powerful wings. Yet they break the line at the wrist to create a decorative hand gesture—surely the last thing a battle-ready warrior with any savvy would do.

Lar Lubovitch has done a piece for ten dancers in Béjart's Ballet of the 20th Century and in this context it's hard not to see it as ennervated Béjart. I think *Marimba* is more than that. It shows people moving always as a group, back and forth in simple repetitive patterns, circling, turning. There are no sex roles, no confrontations, few large gestures, lots of footsteps. The dancers are supposed to maintain a tranced awareness of inner space while the patterns flow over the stage. Except that these dancers, unused to flowing or murmuring, used to thinking of dance as loud, separated gestures, can't give the piece the clarity it needs. Lubovitch hasn't the musical astuteness to bring out the changing inner patterning of Steve Reich's music the way Laura Dean has in her collaborations with Reich; he emphasizes only the basic pulse. Still, I'd like to see *Marimba* again.

Not having seen all the star-laden attractions Béjart brought to the Uris, I can't comment on new trends or developments in his choreography. I don't *think* there are any. He just does what he does—seriously, splashily, well or badly. With and for some splendid dancers. In the past, I've tried to analyze the ingredients of his appeal; but my goodwill has eroded. I understand what some men friends of mine see in his stuff to identify with, but that's, in the end, no help.

Apparently it did no good to mention in this review the charges of prudishness or snobbery that are leveled at Béjart's critics by his admirers. A letter written by a woman shortly after this review was published suggested that I was shocked to see "men express sensuality and emotion" because American men (according to her) are self-conscious about such things. She went on to say of Béjart's men that, "Their energy penetrated your workaday shell and made you uneasy, stimulating feelings that you aren't use to expressing." Hmm. I've liked some of Béjart's recent work much better than I liked what he was making in 1977, but I think that's because elements I value have become stronger in his choreography, not because I'm more in the swing—sensually speaking—than I used to be.

MARTINE VAN HAMEL

FEASTS ON DANCING

The Village Voice, January 10, 1977

It's no more and no less than any important dancer does: you dance the hell out of the Swan Queen, and the next morning you're in a 10 a.m. class like this one—with Maggie Black's friendly, piercing voice telling you, "Pull up your seat, Martine!" Even in a morning workout, Martine van Hamel displays the exemplary simplicity and musicality that won her rabid admirers while a good part of American Ballet Theatre's audience was still in the Martine-*who?* stage. She doesn't fuss, she doesn't preen; she simply makes every movement as full and clear as possible. When she stretches into an arabesque, you're aware not just of her legs lifting behind her, but of her back pressing forward, of her whole body lengthening.

During the ABT season, which begins on January 5, van Hamel will make her debut both as Giselle and as Coppelia. "You know how it is," she says with equanimity and a grin, "either you're in love with three people at once, or you don't know anybody." Van Hamel is happy enough now not to want to talk about her underdog days, but it must have been trying to come to New York after six years as a soloist with the National Ballet of Canada, after winning medals at the Varna competition, and then spend six months as a nearly invisible member of the Joffrey Ballet before finally accepting a job in the corps de ballet of ABT and working her way back up to roles she'd played years before. (The management cautiously unveiled her as Odette-Odile in 1973, three years after she joined the company, at a Wednesday matinee.)

Van Hamel is willing to shoulder some of the blame for those first shadowy years in America. She says rather sadly. "I wasn't really anybody, anyway. I was . . . wishy washy. And it's probably a mistake to expect a ballet company to be like a parent. I couldn't understand why the people in charge wouldn't either try to make you into their vision of you, or else just not accept you." And she admits that she didn't know how to communicate sensibly with management. "I thought I didn't need to talk; I thought I could prove who I am, what I felt, through dancing." She shrugs. "My own stupidity. I'm learning."

Too, van Hamel has had to combat stereotypical ideas about the heroines of classical ballet being slim, frail child-women. She's tall. All her gestures have an almost regal amplitude. Like many generously built dancers, she's rarely brittle; there's a suppleness to her sharpest and strongest motions. On the other hand, she's never vulgar or flashy unless a part requires her to be. When she wiggles onto the stage in Twyla Tharp's *Push Comes to Shove,* she looks very brassy for a minute in a bare-backed silk party dress with her chestnut curls tossing, but Tharp, astutely, kept van Hamel a princess—just turned her into a playful, pampered Scott Fitzgerald one. In *Giselle,* she's an ideal Myrtha—a village maiden frozen by death into a remorseless spirit Queen. But it's not so easy for an artistic director to envision her as Giselle, a girl who's been warned not to dance because of a weak heart.

When van Hamel was being considered for *La Sylphide* in Canada, company director Celia Franca said (van Hamel makes her vowels more cozily Canadian to tell this) well, if she wanted to have a crack at the role she could, but that she, Franca, doubted if Martine could pull it off. Same with *Giselle* now: "Lucia Chase said, 'If you want to do it, you can, but my image of Giselle is not you.' She didn't say it nastily, just truthfully; and, in view of that, her letting me do it is a tremendous compliment." Van Hamel rose to the challenge of *La Sylphide:* it forced her, an adagio dancer by nature, to learn to keep her footwork precise while moving fast. She'll find her way into *Giselle,* I have no doubt.

After van Hamel's morning class, we go to ABT and sit on a studio floor drinking coffee (I eat, she doesn't) and talk about how she works on a role. I like listening to her because she has an abundance of the pragmatic, yet imaginative intelligence that characterizes many fine dancers. Van Hamel neither intellectualizes or theorizes. I'm not surprised that in preparing for Giselle, she hasn't, say, researched the ballet's history or that—although she makes her debut in this extremely difficult role on January 29—she has, as yet, no fixed concept of who Giselle is. "I wait until I get the dancing into a kind of shape before I attach myself to who she is. I just feel things out as I work, and the role develops by itself. When I work with Dimitri Romanoff, he doesn't impose anything on me—he just teaches me the exact steps or the responses that are definitely choreographed. At this point, Giselle is still someone else's vision." Coppelia, which she dances for the first time on January 8, she's hardly had time to develop yet, what with rehearsing and performing all her old roles for ABT's Kennedy Center season in Washington, but she muses, "She's not delicate. I don't think a sensitive girl would be so cruel to a good old man. Maybe that's a clue . . . I don't know. I do know the second act has to be special, somehow. Anyone can be a doll, but you have to be, you know, a *good* doll."

In other words, the movement, once fully understood and realized, tells her all she needs to know about a character or a ballet. Her performing, like that of many I find extraordinary—Mikhail Baryshnikov, Merce Cunningham, Sara Rudner—is in some way transparent. Because it's not that she "does things" to dancing, but that dancing does things to her. At one point in her career, she says, she started to try to "act" Odette-Odile in *Swan Lake* and the whole thing got away from her: "Everything must be expressed physically—or you fall down and you don't understand why."

Like, take this part of *Sleeping Beauty,* she says. "You're dancing around, and Carabosse's mice come on stage. You can't see them immediately and react; if you do, you may mess up the rest of the solo, or else start the audience wondering what kind of a dope you are to continue dancing at a time like that. So, either you try not to see the mice until you finish, or else you see them right away and cut the rest of the solo."

Van Hamel gets up and starts to run through another *Sleeping Beauty* solo, explaining some of the decisions she's made. It's the confident one Aurora does just after she's gotten through the difficult Rose Adagio with those four prospective suitors. "In Aurora's first solo ('It's my birthday! It's my birthday!'), you don't have much choice with the steps—except to be able to do them. But this one is very . . . dry. It has to be done properly. It's plain, but there's a lot to work with." She launches herself into bold steady piqué arabesques: "In the first place, the feeling is circular. You're surrounded by people." The second step is a long chain of hops on pointe. "I'm not a good hopper," she says. "Of course, you can find a way to do it, but then when it goes on and on . . . well, at some point in rehearsal you *have* to say to yourself, what am I going to do with this?" And van Hamel turns the hops into a gradual crescendo of gracious excitement by the how-nice-to-see-you-all arm gestures and head inclinations she adds to them. Backing up in a little prancing step that looks like a happy release, she says, "Yes, it should look free; but if I did it this way [whee!—she falls back] it wouldn't work." She jabs her toes into the floor, sighing, "It's a strange step; if you don't believe in it, it gets to be a kind of sore. I get that a lot in *Sleeping Beauty*. The steps aren't really physical, and I have to work to attach importance to them." After shaking her head over an odd break in the rhythm that makes a sudden exclamation point of a pirouette extremely hard to stabilize, she takes off in a chain of bourrées instead of the usual scampery precipités, grinning. "That's a step I simply had to change." She generously shows me her precipités; they look fine to me, although they're clearly a small person's step, but she squints down at them sour-faced, and says that she couldn't make them musical without a tempo change. Gliding back and forth, she acknowledges imaginary princes. "I'm not trying to pick a mate the way the prince in *Swan Lake* is. I'm flattered by the attention. No big number; I'm just being charming to them." She sketches out a last circle of jumps and folds up on the floor beside her coffee again.

So here's Martine, feasting on dancing, after a fairly long period of skimping. In the past few seasons, the ABT management has begun to take chances with her. The general public has begun to understand what critics and connoisseurs see in her. She's made a successful guest appearance with the Pennsylvania Ballet and is about to do a *Nutcracker* with the Eglevsky Ballet. *She'll* never complain about dancing three times a night; as long as she's dancing enough, she doesn't feel hunger or pain. She's even being carefully paired with a partner, instead of being shunted from one suitably tall man to another. (One hopes that the talented Clark Tippett—coping with Siegfried, Albrecht, Florimund, and Franz all at once—will be able to keep his head above water.)

What more does she want? "Tudor knows I'd like to do *Pillar of Fire*, but I'd never ask him. He has to do things in his own way." What she really, really wants is to have ABT commission or get a ballet just for her. It wouldn't have to be *big*. She makes self-deprecating little faces and says she knows this isn't important, perhaps. "I want it because . . . it's just a nice thing. And it's exciting to learn something directly from a choreographer instead of being in the third cast and having to pick it up on the side. I might feel as if I were contributing. Although probably I'd just let him tell me what to do."

Maybe it's because Martine came to where she is now the hard way that she can speak so feelingly of the morale problem among the women in ABT's corps de ballet. "It can be heartbreaking to see people who are really talented when they join the company start to get bad. Some take hold of themselves and work; some never do." Revealingly, touchingly, she changes from "they": "Then you have to hope that if, after three

years, you've gotten it together, someone will notice—to hope that everyone hasn't gotten too used to you to *see* you anymore."

She's made it. Maybe the climate ahead will be more benign.

KNOCKING ABOUT IN THE
JUNGLE

The Village Voice, May 11, 1982

▾▾

Amerian Ballet Theatre's spring season at the Met opened with the
usual adroit complement of glitter, sound choreography, fine dancing, and dubious novelty. The opening parade of "shades" in Petipa's *La
Bayadère* was as pale and interminably beautiful as one could want, the
three solo Shadows (Cheryl Yeager, Kristine Elliot, and Susan Jaffe) limpid and strong, Martine van Hamel superbly bold, yet withdrawn into
ghostliness, and Alexander Godunov looking more stretched out and resil-
ient than I've yet seen him. Cynthia Gregory and Fernando Bujones
gleamed with rather more worldly sparkle in the Act III pas de deux from
The Sleeping Beauty.

In between these two classics came Kenneth MacMillan's *The Wild
Boy* (wild music by Gordon Crosse). The piece was made as a vehicle for
Mikhail Baryshnikov, although it was danced by Robert LaFosse. You'd
think by now that Baryshnikov would have developed a sixth sense for
avoiding choreographers who think we'll relish seeing one of the world's
greatest dancers hurled around, spread-eagled, walked on, and humil-
iated. *The Wild Boy* is a joyride for sadists, disguised as a moral tale about
corruption and the loss of innocence. Here's how it goes: in a vine-draped
jungle we see a slinky woman (Lise Houlton) preening. (How did she get
there? What is she doing there? You think anybody concerned knows the
answer?) On come two violent, ragged men (Kevin McKenzie and Brian
Adams). They share her. That is, one holds her foot and the other her
armpits while they twist her around lasciviously. The program says they
are "her husband" and "his friend," but the ballet doesn't trouble to clarify which is which. (Do you suppose the husband's the one who puts his
hands between her legs more often?) They leave. (Why?) On come some

tiger fellows who crouch and lunge, roll and and leap; some have even learned pirouettes for the occasion. Here is the "wild" boy, a terrific jumper; he's especially notable at those savage one-leg-bent-one-leg-straight side-zoomers like the one Balanchine devised for *The Prodigal Son.* Suddenly on rush the horrid threesome with a net and snare the kid. (Where did all the tigers go?) They beat him and beat him and beat him and beat him. Then the men leave without securing the victim, and the woman stays and she and the boy copulate. (Instinctively he knows the missionary position; no tiger *he.*) The men return and they and the woman start to beat up on the boy some more. Suddenly he bangs the two men's heads together. The three collapse. The hero leaves and returns swigging from a bottle. (Where did he . . . ? Forget it.) The animals crawl in, ignoring the recumbent louts, and sniff sadly at their now debased friend and retreat. He has Lost All.

MacMillan's sense of theater seems to have left him at the scent of this ballet. While he can express the men's boisterous camaraderie through adroit close canon, the sex duet starts at fever pitch and stays there. I think that audiences can and sometimes should be shocked by violence: but I don't like being stroked by it.

ENTER THE ROYAL
(GASP, SNARL)

The Village Voice, May 10, 1976

La Bayadère, Act IV, is really what it's all about, isn't it? By "it," I guess I mean not only what we call "classical" ballet but also the Romantic imagination. There is a single hero who in a dream pursues his unattainable beloved (unattainable because dead). There is that remarkable very long, slow procession of white ghost-girls, entering one by one, repeating the same deliberate phrase; they all but arrest your sense of time, yet, by the time they have finished, the dark, featureless stage has been defined by their crisscrossing paths and orderly ranks.

One of the reasons that the corps de ballet's unison dancing is so thrilling is that it's not vigorous, sharp stuff (like that the Rockettes are celebrated for), nor is it all simple and square. The phrases that Marius Petipa devised for them are often melting and full of épaulement, so that you rarely see the women head on, but curving or twisting gently in order to direct their eyes or the motion of their limbs to different points in space. In dancing so prismatic, you could be surprised by a dancer's leg suddenly swinging through to point at the floor in front of her: Imagine the effect of twenty-eight legs exclaiming together.

The corps women, rarely off the stage, often have to echo—almost to muse upon—the dances of the soloists they frame. And the dancing of the three principal "shades," of the heroine Nikiya, and of the dreamer Solor are not orderly at all. The chorus's unison murmur confers order on everything, but the solo and duet passages themselves are ardent, even quietly extravagant—full of sudden pressures, shifts of direction, changes of speed that make them very vivid. The three solo "shadows" dance happily—one is even bubbling—as if they're pleased to inhabit an Underworld where there's so much good dancing.

I'm addicted to the Royal Ballet's production, revived by Rudolf Nureyev after the 1877 original, not only because of superb soloists like Anthony Dowell, Merle Park, Ria Peri, Monica Mason, and Vergie Derman, but because of the almost miraculous precision-in-fluidity of the corps. Some discerning person made sure they got a communal basket of roses. They deserved at least a dozen apiece.

For its second week at the Met, the Royal—having presumably sated for a while this city's full-length-classic fans—began to trot out some of its latest acquisitions: ex-director Frederick Ashton's *A Month in the Country* and current director Kenneth MacMillan's *Rituals*. The first is certainly to be celebrated; since it shows Ashton in terrific form doing what he does better than almost anyone else: working with literary plot and characterization in dance. He can make you accept movement as a metaphor for conversation without confusing you or making the dancing look inhibited and ridiculous. And he's a master of the business of creating solos and duets that fulfill the function of arias in opera, without stalling the momentum of the drama. Perhaps this is because these "arias" tell you something new and vital about the characters instead of frilling what you already know.

A Month In the Country, like Ashton's earlier masterpiece, *The Enigma Variations,* has a calm, well-bred atmosphere, but its mellowness is troubled by sudden breathless eruptions of passion. Julia Trevelyan Oman has designed a luxurious drawing room of a set—brocade furniture, a piano, blue-and-cream-colored paneling and great windows flung open on a Russian summer. The characters are drawn from the Turgenev play, of course: the elderly, absent-minded Yslaev, (Alexander Grant); his wife, Natalia Petrovna (Lynn Seymour); her pretty young ward (Denise Nunn); her faithful, stodgy admirer, Rakitin (Derek Rencher); her young son, Kolia (Wayne Sleep); Kolia's tutor, Beliaev (Anthony Dowell); a pretty maid-servant (Marguerite Porter); and a footman (Anthony Conway). These people stroll in and out of the drawing room as if suspended in a great, golden expanse of Chekhovian time. The texture of their day is spare and leisurely. Rarely do they all gather together. The handsome tutor acts as a storm center: he loves Natalia Petrovna and she him; young Vera loves him too and jealously provokes a family confrontation; Rakitin tactfully leaves, persuading Beliaev to go with him. The household goes on, ostensibly as before, buttressed by tact and decorum; but crosscurrents of chilly wind have blown into it.

The "dances"—all solos, or duets—arise out of a superbly engineered texture of casualness: Looks, entrances and exits, single clear gestures tell you almost everything. Ashton's intuition as to when fully developed dance passages are needed and when they're not is unerring. For instance, Yslaev reveals his muddleheadedness with an outraged "I've-lost-my-keys" gesture, and the search gradually involves the entire household rushing importantly here and there, poking into things, bumping into each other. It's very funny, but only slightly exaggerated.

In this extraordinarily succinct ballet, few unrevealing motions or forms appear. The first of several pieces of Chopin music to which the ballet is performed is the seldom heard set of variations on the Mozart aria, "La ci darem la mano." Natalia dances first—a fast, dithery solo; she's slightly flamboyant with her gestures, erratic, reckless in the way she launches into space. You can tell she's a woman who starts things she has no idea how to finish. A few seconds later, she watches while her young ward holds forth, and Ashton, very cleverly, has given Vera almost exactly the same phrases as her guardian. Not only does this point up her youth (she has a very shy restrained way with the dancing), but tells us how much she admires this woman and wants to be like her. Which makes her later anger and disillusionment all the more poignant.

Beliaev is delineated principally through three differing pas de deux. With the impulsive young girl he feels innocent pleasure and perhaps the force of her ardor. (When he carefully lifts her, her feet shiver in the air as if her spine had been stroked.) They dance sweetly hand-in-hand; he'd like to kiss her, but thinks better of it. When he dances with the pretty maidservant, he launches into some boisterous arm-in-arm folk-dance steps—perhaps the constant maintenance of intellectuality and upper-class decorum is beginning to be a strain. But his pas de deux with the lady of the house conveys the combination of near-swoons and furtive starts appropriate to high-class clandestine affairs. There is a beautifully sensual passage in which she bourrées forward, her feet making a wandering little path, her body yielding while he follows close behind, holding her. She looks as if she were turning to jelly with passion. As the curtain falls, she is doing the same step—alone, stiff, quaking.

All the dancers are splendid. Wayne Sleep executes his ferociously nimble solo with insouciant ease. Seymour dances with a wonderful abandon, a generosity of feeling. Dowell has the rare gift of being able to fill out movement completely without ever seeming flamboyant or overindulgent or strained. Perhaps this is what makes his dancing both sensual and decorous.

And then we come to Kenneth MacMillan's *Rituals,* which perplexes me. I've seen plenty of bad ballets or ballets I haven't liked, but very few in which all the highly professional people involved seem to have so completely failed to bring off what I *think* they were attempting. Anything further from the rituals of Japanese theater than this snarl of bodies, color, fabric, and music would be hard to imagine. MacMillan's choice of Bartók's hurtling Sonata for Two Pianos and Orchestra induced hurtling, non-stop motion, which in turn cheapened the Bartók and made it sound annoyingly dense in the first movement, where two spry athletes (Wayne Eagling and Stephen Beagley) practice balleticized wrestling and T'ai Chi with a superbly bulky Grand Master (David Drew). Yolanda Sonnabend's scanty, stripy, no-two-alike costumes add more confusion to the picture. The movement is vigorous all right, but the leaps and crouches and high kicks don't quite ring true as combat exercises. No pauses, small feints, moments of going limp, of walking away. An anthology of big bangs.

In the second movement, MacMillan took off after Bunraku, the puppet theater of Japan. Here Sonnabend chose to costume the traditionally black-clad puppeteers (it takes three to manipulate a principal puppet) in white—thus making them highly visible, especially with the ubiquitous follow-spot that makes everyone important paler than everyone else. MacMillan also dispensed with the Japanese custom of keeping the puppeteers behind the puppets, so I could never catch more than a glimpse of what the puppets (Vergie Derman and David Wall) were trying to do, what with all those grabbing hands and the flurry of white robes. A pas de deux, I think. And they looked sad, I think.

The third movement is sort of Kabuki. A lot of lunging and flexed-footed-strutting and flailing of fists. Over what? I'm not sure because what I took to be a sexy little bitch (Seymour) and her soul sister (Monica Mason) turned out to be (says the program) The Mother and The Midwife.

I found *Rituals* infuriating and I can't imagine what was going on in the minds of those responsible—except the dancers who always do what they

---

have to do very valiantly. I expect some of the key thoughts were: "vigorous," "lot of strong dancing for the men," "exotic," "colorful," "contemporary." Arrggh.

Having seen Ashton's A Month in the Country *on film several times, I have to admit that, in this review, I sometimes got the spirit right, but twisted the facts. Natalia Petrovna's young ward does not echo the older woman's phrases in her solo; in keeping with the Theme and Variations form of the music, her solo is a variation of material in Natalia's solo. It has the effect I noted, of suggesting Vera's admiration for Natalia, their similarities, and their differences.*

There are two duets for Beliaev and Natalia—the second passionate, the first decorous, almost conversational, as if anyone from the household could walk in on it and not be shocked.

In the duet between Vera and Beliaev, the tutor does, in fact, kiss her—a quick, almost brotherly kiss to get her off his back. It's when she immediately blocks his way and puts her face up again that he realizes he's in trouble and, on guard, but tempted, dances with her.

UNREELING THE IMAGES—

LINE TAUT

The Village Voice, April 20–26, 1980

I'm confident that at a guess-the-choreographer contest I'd be able to pick out Eliot Feld's ballets, but I'm not sure why that's so. Perhaps the way his dancers so often keep their arms wreathing close to their own bodies would be a giveaway. Perhaps it would be the fact that once he establishes a style or a character, he rarely betrays it—no Petipa-style supported pirouettes in the middle of a tale of tenement life. Perhaps his current preference for gesture over unfettered, quick-footed dancing would betray him, or a certain reticence about exploiting his material.

This is all odd, because, coupled with an unmistakable, personal style and approach to dance, Feld frequently has a way of making ballets that strike sparks off ballets by other choreographers. It's not that Feld appears to be imitating, either consciously or unconsciously (he's too smart for that), but that he's commenting on or disputing or scribbling notes in the margin of or adding a footnote to others' ballets, the way philosophers go to work on each other as a springboard for their own thoughts. Of the two premieres and one very new dance that Feld's company presented at the Center for the Arts at Purchase, *Anatomic Balm* gave off argumentative resonances of Twyla Tharp, Murray Louis, and Act IV of Petipa's *La Bayadère; Scenes for the Theatre* brought to mind Kurt Jooss's *The Big City*, Jerome Robbins's *Fancy Free*, Doris Humphrey's *Day On Earth; Circa* evoked Balanchine's *Apollo*, Nijinsky's *Afternoon of a Faun*, and, for a surprising few minutes, Glen Tetley's work.

I find this intriguing but also disturbing, perhaps because it goes against the high value we place on originality these days. And because I think of Feld as extraordinarily gifted, one of the few who have brought the terms *ballet* and *contemporary* together in meaningful ways.

Anatomic Balm is set to an arrangement (by Robert Dennis and Paul Zukofsky) of lovely slippery ragtime melodies, and played with extreme delicacy by Zukofsky on the violin and Peter Longiaru on the piano. Its tone is almost always elegantly understated, clear, and supple. The company's twelve women dance it with a meditative kind of eroticism, stretching soft as cats, rarely directing a look or a gesture to the audience.

Christine Sarry begins it alone, and the phrase she shapes so superbly—with its slow hip swivels, stretches and lunges, soft, lazily bouncy footsteps, rhythmic intricacy—becomes the material for a long canon, which the women feed into in groups of three. It's extremely lovely—especially when the groups infiltrate each other's ranks, so that you see one part of the phrase being passed through another. The women exit in a line backward, every other woman on the right foot, those between on the left, as if the dancing were being realigned and rolled up for another day's use.

Most of the group sections have the same smooth deliberateness, the same structural formality, and even more repetitiveness. A couple or more times, the women slip in behind Sarry, retreat, and then unfold the same pattern again. They often work in such close canon or do such similar steps that the effect is almost deliberately blurred (rare in Feld's work). In "Sleepy Hollow," they gradually make a simple phrase, with a leg-shake keyed to the music's tremolo, move away from the audience by stepping side to side in a pack (one line right, one line left) while retreating imperceptibly. It's all like seeing an endless procession of the shades of chorines, sleepwalking through the grooves of an old record.

In a contrasting section, Nancy Thuesen, hair down, throws herself around in some kind of fit, while others race past her, fingers menacingly clawed, like babydoll harpies. Megan Murphy's solo to "Pleasant Moments" is full of silky dancing and prudish gestures of innocence (the big-eyed silent-movie virgin who thrives on being threatened). Sarry has a gleeful second solo, faster and with impudent, elastic wiggles of shoulder, hips, head.

One of Feld's weaknesses as a choreographer is evident in *Anatomic Balm*. He makes phrases in which a great many intricate changes of position, direction, and shape happen while advancing the dancer very little through space. Too much of this, and you begin to wish he would ease up a little and let someone just tear around for a minute. Sometimes a new phrase of music cries out to be acknowledged, strutted out on, but Feld, concerned with subtlety, will keep moiling the dancers around, carefully controlling and developing his idea.

When the curtain goes up on *Scenes for the Theatre,* various city types stand frozen under Willa Kim's set of rusty El girders: a cop, two kids playing marbles, a newsboy, a gentleman and his wife pushing a pram, their poodle. When they begin to move, some do so naturalistically; others, like the newsboy (Jeff Satinoff) or the dog (Mary Randolph), have brief signature themes or characteristic stylized gaits.

Feld seems to have wanted not to tell stories but to create characters and fragmentary incidents that might, by implication, add up to something. Aaron Copland's 1925 *Music for the Theatre* has the same air of fugitive eventfulness, and the setting and costumes bring to mind Reginald Marsh's sketches of street life.

One extended passage is a duet for Feld, as a sharp streetwise charmer who doesn't want to run into the cop, and Traci Owen as a pretty, not unwilling pickup. Another is a bar scene with a pair of collapsing marathon dancers, a sparky couple, a woman rubbing herself all over one of the tables, and three guys drinking at the bar. These vignettes all seem to be couched in different styles; some of the people don't go much beyond what they'd do in public—although the men drink in unison like the sailors in Robbins's *Fancy Free*—while others, like the Lonely Lady, are enlarging a physical restlessness into dance. perhaps Feld *is* deliberately referring to several other ballets or plays.

There's also a burlesque act performed for an imaginary audience (at the back of the stage) in which a happily raunchy clown (John Sowinski) mixes it up with a stripper (Nancy Thuesen) and ends with her head stuck inside his pants.

The subtler thread that idles through these incidents has to do with the Depression. We notice right off that one man (Gregory Mitchell) who seems to belong to one of the intently playing children (Marcus Felix and Julian Green—real children and excellent) hasn't got much money; he has trouble finding a coin to pay for his newspaper. In an angry solo, he imitates the thrusting, digging theme of three workers we've seen earlier; the implication is that he'd like a job, but can't get one. At the end, in the ages-old theater cliché, he sadly pulls his pockets inside out to show us his poverty.

Scenes for the Theatre is an unnerving ballet: you keep waiting, for something bigger to happen. Yet it's fascinating to see Feld attempting to humanize stereotypes without losing their stereotypical stringency. In some sense, he's subjected drama to the slight freeze-drying he applied to the flow of dancing in *Anatomic Balm*: add fluid and they might wash you away.

Circa, to a selection of Hindemith pieces, gives Feld's talent for the pictorial full play. I remember images from it rather than movement. It presents a sober faun (Richard Fein) and three attendant nymphs whom he reins in and lets pull him along, without erotic overtones. Into this fastidious archaic world, three men carry a Venus (Gloria Brisbin). While Feld may have meant simply to convey the image of Venus borne by waves and enfolded in a shell, what you see seems suddenly to be in a different choreographic style and era—the predatory sex goddess borne aloft and manipulated by her muscle men, an image dear to '70s balleto-modern choreographers. Yet the courtship and copulation of the couple is again hieratic and two-dimensional.

Feld's company, with twenty-three dancers, is now larger than it's ever been, and everyone performs with the attentiveness to dynamics and focus and the lack of flamboyance Feld requires. They look wonderful. I quarrel with the way John H. Paull III lights them; they appear colorful, but featureless, which I hope isn't what Feld is aiming for.

DANCERS SHOT FROM GUNS

The Village Voice, November 11, 1980

❧

"**I**n a few years" says my husband, "dancers are going to have four legs. Now, as a critic, are you going to be up there, or are you going to be at the back of the pack?" Yes. Well, no.

This was after the opening night of the Joffrey Ballet's first regular season in New York since 1978. Like the company's fans, I was happy and excited about it. But unprepared. When the curtain went up on Gerald Arpino's *Suite Saint-Saëns,* and twenty dancers started hurtling across the stage, I felt as if I were watching a new racial strain—bred for stamina, strength, and extravagance of gesture, as unreal in their beauty as any sylphide. Some of the men, like Glenn Dufford, have the high leg extensions that used to be seen only on women. The women's legs seem preternaturally large—I don't mean heavy, but important—great baroquely arched instruments that swing and stretch and fold up with a thunderous resonance. Their erect backs, small, neat heads, fluid arms, and gracious demeanor seem delicate compared with those legs.

They don't look like this in many of the ballets in the company's finely variegated repertory, but it's obvious that this is the way Arpino wants them to look, because his choreography emphasizes their athleticism. In *Kettentanz,* men toss women into the air and catch them in a number of dazzling ways. In *Suite Saint-Saëns,* an unusually hectic and florid piece, the dancers keep spinning and leaping and doing splits and flinging their legs into the air and running off. And running on and spinning and leaping and doing splits and flinging their legs into the air and running off. (Except that women are more often carried off.) The personnel keep changing, but there's very little shape to the dancing, because there's no real quietness, delicacy, simplicity, smallness to contrast to the lavish and busy flood of huge steps.

The superdancer idea isn't unique to the Joffrey. It's a trend. Some audiences seem to crave a vision of sleek power and tireless momentum that's almost erotic: the dancer as rocket penetrating space. That the countertrend persists—dancers plainly dressed doing quite ordinary things—only affirms the prevalence of this alluring dangerousness. We have upped our prescribed (and needed) dose of virtuosity, and the side-effects are only beginning to be felt.

The Joffrey Ballet started out as a modest ensemble directed by a talented young choreographer (Robert Joffrey). The splendid photos in the City Center's gallery document the stages in its development. Not only the dancers, but the style of photography gets glossier and sexier. Lisa Bradley, considered phenomenal in the '60s, looks fragile and reticent compared to Ann Marie de Angelo, calmly planted on one pointe and hoisting the toe of her other leg up behind her until her body, arm and lifted leg form a circle. Francesca Corkle is perhaps the prototype. In a class, wearing a soft slipper, she could spin so beautifully centered, and with such an upward tendency, that at the end of, say, six pirouettes, she'd have pulled herself up onto the tip of her toe. (I remember that she used to wear a pink undershirt over her leotard and that one day a young student dancer appeared in class in a similar undershirt and her friend said to her, "Think that'll make your turns better?") But I've always found Corkle thrilling. Now with the Pittsburgh Ballet, she returned to dance her old role in *Kettentanz,* displaying a kind of phrasing and musicality that distinguishes her from even one of the finest of Joffrey's current dancers—Denise Jackson.

Yet it seems to me that the Joffrey dancers have precisely the problems I'd expect them to have, it's hard for some of them to be subtle or precise about certain kinds of timing. And one of the most impressive things about the company is that Robert Joffrey continues to remount unusual ballets from the past and to commission works from new, even radically new, choreographers. You can't fault the dancers on commitment or the desire to achieve a given style. Sometimes they succeed wonderfully: Tharp and Robbins are two choreographers whose works they seem to have understood thoroughly. If they have responded splendidly to Laura Dean, perhaps it's because of the simplicity and clarity of her style, and the kind of concentration required to do it. Having observed so many rehearsals, I can't yet see *Night* clearly; but I thought it looked extremely beautiful on stage. (What an anachronism after such an egalitarian dance, to see bouquets handed out to the women only!)

But Agnes de Mille's *Rodeo* looks just a little off right now. The dancers seem to see what the *whole* thing is about, the large shape of it, their positions as cowboys or frontier women, but they often muff the weight or timing of a particular moment or gesture. Beatriz Rodriguez has the character of the spunky but forlorn tomboy heroine down pat, with no overacting, but blurs many of De Mille's wise comic points by mistiming a reaction or a gesture, enlarging and complicating some (like a pants-hitching one), making certain moves—like an awkward crumpled fall—into something more comfortable.

Frederick Ashton's ballets, of which the company has several, demand even more subtlety and control. And elegance. I like to see the dancers work at his ballets, not only because I like most of the ballets, but because I think they educate dancers in certain horse-and-buggy aspects of their craft. *Illuminations* is the new acquisition. Made for the New York City Ballet in 1950, it's unusually cloudy for an Ashton ballet. Perhaps because he built it on an intersection of images from the violent life of the poet Arthur Rimbaud, from his poems, and, I think, from his drug-induced dreams.

Cecil Beaton's beautiful but inscrutable costumes present the poet's visions as a flurry of white Pierrots. You have to look closely to discern Pierrot-as-gendarme, Pierrot-as-Arab. It's unnerving but fascinating the way Ashton, too, blends his images. While the singer (Thomas Bogdan) renders Benjamin Britten's setting of one of Rimbaud's loveliest "phrases"—"I have stretched ropes from steeple to steeple; garlands from window to window; golden chains from star to star, and I dance"— the poet, in his tight black jacket and striped pants, pantomimes pulling ropes and hanging stars, but ends by drawing his hand between his legs and flinging a handful of confetti in the air—not dancing, but poeticizing orgasm.

We see the poet always searching for something in a carnival of unnaturally stiff or floppy figures. The only others with his range of movement or expressiveness are a dandy (Glenn Dufford) who does a snappy, nimble-footed solo; a white-faced muse (Patricia Miller) who is identified as Sacred Love; and a hoyden with one bare foot (Beatriz Rodriguez) who represents Profane Love. We see curious incidents: a crowned couple (the woman, Sacred Love) with train bearers, made briefly royal by their love; the poet knocking the man's crown off and hugging it to him; the muse tarnished by a group of rough Pierrots (not rough enough) who carry her and manipulate her pale legs; the poet savaged by these and others; the poet accused by Profane Love and shot in the arm. It is all terrifying in a peculiarly delicate and confusing way. But at this point, the acting is as black-and-white as the costumes. Gregory Huffman plays the poet at a constant pitch of strained suffering; it's an ambitious performance, but without modulation.

One particularly outstanding—and subtle—performance in the season to date: Starr Danias—all frail bewilderment over her evident undesirability—in the "Wallflower Waltz" in Ruthanna Boris's engaging *Cakewalk*.

DOES EVERY COMPANY
HAVE A GOH?

The Village Voice, November 12–18, 1980

꙳

You often hear people wondering what the New York City Ballet would be without Balanchine. The Ballet of the 20th Century would undoubtedly founder without Maurice Béjart and the Eliot Feld Ballet without Feld. But ballet companies generally don't rise and fall with one choreographer the way most modern dance companies do, and the problem of ballet companies all over the U.S. is building a decent repertory.

Perhaps this is why any choreographer who can produce a lively, attractive, and coherent work suitable for a fairly conservative audience is considered gifted, and one with a trace of originality as well is touted as a genius—sometimes deservedly, sometimes not. Jerome Robbins in 1943, Gerald Arpino in 1961, Eliot Feld in 1967 established immense reputations with their very first ballet(s). Peter Martins and Daniel Levans are a couple of the most recent golden boys.

But the most prolific and the most wanted ballet choreographer now on the scene seems to be Choo San Goh, Chinese, born in Singapore and nurtured in European ballet companies, who began to make dances in 1973. There's a Goh ballet in Boston; there's a Goh in Houston; there are a couple in Philadlephia—I forget where else. Dance Theatre of Harlem performs *Introducing.* This season the Joffrey ballet gets *Momentum* and a brand new Goh called *Helena.* Most of Goh's work in the U.S., however—about fifteen ballets in four years—has been done for the Washington Ballet, which brought three Gohs to show at its performance at the Brooklyn Center for the Performing Arts.

Goh is known to be a fine teacher, a lovable guy, a choreographer who makes ballet that dancers enjoy dancing. When he came to D.C. in 1976, the Washington Ballet was a semiprofessional group working out of Mary Day's highly respected Washington School of Ballet. It's partly because of his skill and growing reputation that the company, of which he's assistant artistic director, has grown in accomplishment and professional status.

On the basis of the handful of Goh's I've seen, I'd say that one of his most striking characteristics is the way he handles personnel. For instance, at one point during his *Double Contrasts,* two couples are fixed in space, performing a supported adagio in canon with each other, while two "free" women spatter around on the edges of the stage or dart back and forth across it. Later in the same dance, a group of women circles while two couples create small orbits outside the circle.

In Goh's first ballet, *Untitled,* which he taught to a picked bunch of students at Jacob's Pillow this past summer, the counterpoint was as clear and elementary as an exercise. In his more recent work, the counterpoint is a trifle less inflexible—gustier maybe. It's simple enough at first to follow a canon that he passes back and forth between two cadres of three women each (this is in *Double Contrasts* again), but then he teases you a bit by compressing one group's part or extending the other's, so that all of a sudden they're in unison for a minute or two. In *Helena* big single moves in canon happen with such speed and force that they churn the stage into waves. Goh has also learned how to suck a little mystery out of compositional irregularity. In *Birds of Paradise* you see a man standing with his feet pointing sideways and body twisted front, Egyptian-frieze style; a bunch of women perch sitting on one hip on the floor, one arm straight, the other angled overhead. Two men (or is it three?) hustle in carrying another man and drop him into the same waiting-Pharaoh pose; they pick one of the women from the floor and sling her onto the first man so that she can wrap her legs around him and hang there. Then they get another woman for the other man. Then each of the hoisters, all in one move, grabs a woman for himself and yanks her into the same formal cop-ulatory position. The action isn't so interesting, but the implications are: some can do for themselves what others have to have done for them (you can switch the "can do" and the "have to have done" around in that sentence too); and it's fascinating to see that message conveyed purely through a formal device.

I find Goh very musical, and he often sets his dances to powerful and dense contemporary scores—a Bloch Concerto Grosso for *Fives* (which I haven't seen); Poulenc's Concerto in D Minor for Orchestra and Two Pianos for *Double Contrasts;* Ginastera's Concerto para Arpa y Orquesta for *Birds of Paradise* and his Piano Concerto No. 1 for *Helena.* He works closely, but not slavishly, with the musical phrases; although he achieves one of his most pleasing effects in *Birds of Paradise* by repeating almost the entire opening fluttering and swarming of women when the music re-peats its first statement. Looking at some of Goh's musical and structural devices, you can believe that he got some of his expertise from the Balan-chine ballets he performed while with the Dutch National Ballet.

But if his patterns stay with you, his movement does not. Or rather, the movements that do tend to be single, eye-catching gestures, usually done with the arms or hands. All that is detectable as a strong stylistic thread is that he likes the dancers to top conventional ballet steps with a torso that's used very flexibly. The dancers seem to bend and arch more often and more deeply in the course of a phrase than they do in most ballets, which gives an effect of lusciousness. Feet aren't exactly underemployed in Goh's ballets, but they don't call attention to them-selves either.

As for the gestures, they're what I like least about Goh's work. Not only do they usually seem tacked-on, but many of them are coarse or silly—old showbiz clichés for oh-how-deliciously-horny-I-am, or aren't-I-cute? In the rather cool and chastely sparkling *Double Contrasts*, these don't appear (although once the dancers stare at the audience with a dis-concerting insolent flirtatiousness); some rather oriental hand positions stand out only because they come from nowhere. If *Helena* looks like a more mature ballet, it may be in part because there are fewer decorative fillips in it.

The sexy stances don't vulgarize Goh's ballets to the extent they would in some choreographers' hands, although, God knows, they're vulgar enough. There's a moment in the perfectly serious *Casella 1, 2, 3,* which the Pennsylvania Ballet performs, in which the men turn their backs to the audience, grab their buttocks with both hands, and give themselves a little hoist. Although *Birds of Paradise* has its darts and soars and flutters, it's really more like a showy and eclectic mating rite, in which that semi-Egyptian sequence appears after some hard-eyed, hip-thrusting poses more reminiscent of Little Egypt. And at one point near the end, the men regard the women hotly and shimmy their shoulders. If all this is more odd than offensive, it may be because Goh uses these gestures fairly sparingly and with a baffling innocence, as if he actually thinks they're pretty, or fun.

Goh's ballets don't *tend* toward anything. He's not interested in story ballets, but I sense that he has schemes that don't emerge clearly. His endings often leave me with a surprised "oh!" and then "oh??" Half the dancers in *Double Concerto* wear black, the other half white. Naturally Goh makes much of this—setting black off against white or letting one spell the other onstage or mingling them: it's a series of stylish and attractive interchanges, but the ballet doesn't leave you with a powerful impression of overall shape. Worse, his formal devices can seem wedged in for display, like those gestures, rather than used to shape a whole: once in *Double Contrasts,* the dancers line up for a quick pass-the-arm-swing-along deal, like the Radio City Music Hall ballet company used to do so spectacularly (with a follow spot hitting each girl as she picked up the gesture); once they make a big Texas Star, and the effect is so splashy that you have to strain to relate it to some of the more subtle orbiting images that I think Goh is playing with.

One of the things that puzzles me is how unaffecting Goh's ballets seem. This, too, may have to do with the way he piles on effects, as if he didn't trust any of them enough to stay with them a while. He doesn't, for instance, extract the potential tenderness from a lovely part in *Double Contrasts,* in which a man gently pushes a bourréeing woman away from him, and, when she bourrées back, gently pushes her again—not in rejection, but as if he were guiding and encouraging her toward independence; later it's done for an even briefer time with a flock of women. I wouldn't want to see such a passage belabored, but Goh almost hides it. There's some mysterious lack of ease or fullness in the way he presents images.

Goh obviously likes dancers to be passionate and excited: the more inexperienced they are, the more forced they appear. The women in the

Washington company look fine. Tall, firm Joanne Zimmerman, and two small, expansive blondes, Amanda McKerrow and Lynn Cote, dance with particular clarity. But Goh seems to have encourged rather mannered performing from the men. John Goding, in the title role of Lambros Lambrou's *Othello,* is excellent in the appropriate, teeth-gnashing balletics, and Simon J. Dow struts villainously as Iago. But in Goh's less dramatic pieces, Dow and Goding add extra flourishes, perhaps flinging their heads back on a leap further than the lift of their chest warrants or giving an emphatic lift of the chin every time they pose holding a woman.

The more adept dancers in the Joffrey add some ease and breadth to Goh's work, and in *Helena,* Goh wrings some vivid images out of the exchanges between four women and a double set of male partners, without ever stopping that high-energy rushing-about he favors. *Helena* has the same ritualistic fervor as *Birds of Paradise,* minus the lewd hips and sexy activities, but it has some quiet moments (as does the lovely Ginastera score). I saw the ballet at an inevitably rocky first orchestra rehearsal, with the dancers marking some parts, but even so it was possible to see that the solos for the principal couple (Beatriz Rodriguez and Gregory Huffman) are richer in nuances of timing, flow, breath, and direction than Goh's previous work, and these dancers can make them look intelligent and sensitive, instead of merely energetic. I even began to be very interested in these two, feel something for them, until the ending—"oh??"

TRADITIONS OF
OTHER COUNTRIES

The Performing Arts Company of the People's Republic of China

As a catchall term, "ethnic dance" carries a heavy load of condescension. In America, it's often used to mean "other"—in other words, not part of the predominantly white mainstream of Western theatrical dance. I've heard the term applied indiscriminately to an elaborate form like India's Bharata Natyam; to the laundered folk-spectacles of Russia's Moiseyev and similar companies; to the festivities at a Polish wedding in New Jersey. Even though I can see that, to a non-Westerner, ballet and contra dancing might appear to have much in common, wouldn't we be surprised to hear a critic in Nairobi lump them together under the rubric of "ethnic"?

In writing about dancing that is not ballet and not modern dance in one of its various guises, the Western critic often feels not up to the job. Is what we're seeing a village ritual or a highly evolved theater form? Or both? Is it "authentic"? And, if so, is it therefore good, beyond criticism?

It's possible to be too reverent. I've known critics to describe an event as if they'd seen it with their own eyes, when in fact, although it was mentioned in the program notes, it was dropped from the plan somewhere between, say, Kerala and New York. On the other hand, we critics—often unknowingly—use our own traditions as a yardstick. In 1977, a gifted twelve-year-old in a Balinese company was inappropriately touted in London as a "barefoot Nureyev." And while no one is so unsophisticated as to wonder why a Kabuki performer doesn't point his toe, we may apply our Western sense of theatrical pacing to an Asian performance—to the detriment of the latter—or dismiss as foolish a dance/drama with alien conventions of impersonation and dramatic action. When a Bhutanese villain attempts to shoot a holy man and his arrow is turned back on himself, what we actually see is a henchman taking the arrow, running toward the sage, turning, running back where he came from, and sticking the arrow through his master's hat. Would someone in Bhutan find this comical? Awe-inspiring? Both?

In the midst of such critical dilemmas, all we can do is keep our eyes and minds open. Folk or classical dances of other cultures are rooted in tradition, often in a sacred tradition. There may be no choreographer, or, if there is, he/she is not seeking outright innovation as much as subtle rearrangement of conventional steps and gestures. Inevitably movement, costumes, music reflect culture and even landscape. The female impersonator in Kabuki theater never stretches his/her legs apart. This is not a technical weakness; the small, twisting, padding steps are prescribed both by decorum and by the long, narrow kimono. When you see Balinese dancing, you can almost imagine what the light is like on such an island: the intricate ringing of the *gamelan,* the myriad tiny quivers and flicks of the dancers' fingers and eyes suggest the constant motion of sun glinting on water, or wind blowing lush vegetation. The male flamenco singer is not just an accompanist to the female dancer. The compressed trill of his voice may comment on her, tell us of her feelings, caress her, converse with her.

Afraid of misinterpreting, of seeming to patronize, I nevertheless find in writing about traditions that are alien to me an exhilaration akin to that mountain climbers must feel: if you look and listen hard and put your foot in the right places, the views are extraordinary.

CONSIDER THE ETHNIC
DANCER

The Village Voice, February 7, 1977

▼▼

A long time ago I toured the West under the name of Toguri. There were four of us in the dance program, *Legends of Cambodia:* Mara, the boss, a clever and witty Russian who had not only studied extensively in the Orient but had audited Doris Humphrey's choreography classes at Juilliard; Cha'o Li Chi, a Chinese expert in martial arts with a degree from NYU; Edna Evans, billed as Eavana, a remarkably gifted performer in both the Bharata Natyan and Kathakali styles of India; and me, Toguri— stage manager, principal driver, understudy to the star, courtier, peasant, demon. We'd arrive at some tiny town in our blue jeans and boots—except for Mara, who always wore jodhpurs—unload our boxes of masks and gold crowns and brocade jackets and jewelry, block out our low-slung eyebrows with a mortar made of talcum powder and greasepaint, and draw new ones that slanted from nose to hairline, give an authentically eclectic performance (which may have been pretty damn good), clean up, sign our fancy names on the programs of wide-eyed kids, pack the car, and then go off in search of booze and steaks and, maybe, cowboys to dance with.

In those days, I knew a lot of the so-called ethnic dancers trying to earn their way in New York, knew the specific problems that plagued them. The Indian dancers—especially those who weren't Indian and/or couldn't afford frequent trips to India—always had trouble finding music; live veena and tabla players were rare and expensive. Unscrupulous hangers-on would sneak tape recorders into imported Carnegie Hall performances and then whisper news of pirated *tillanas* and *alarippus* for sale. And, of course, I knew the real names of the Americans—the Sam Schwartzes and Rosemary Johnsons who, successfully and unsuccessfully, were disguising themselves as Shalaram or Maria Dolorosa. (Spanish and Indian seemed to be the favored styles, although I knew Americans adept in Japanese, Javanese, and Burmese.)

The name changing by Americans going in for non-American dance styles was (and to a degree still is) as endemic as the Russianizing of names that went on during the Ballet Russe days. Sometimes the change reflects a desire for a completely new identity. Sometimes it's born of a justifiable insecurity or forced on dancers by managers (would you hire, sight unseen, an Indian soloist named Edna Evans?). La Meri, the great Texas-born dance scholar, teacher, and performer, received her name, they say, from an adoring Mexican public and press, who considered Russell Meriwether Hughes a name suitable neither for prolonged bravos nor headlines.

A year ago last fall at American Theatre Laboratory, La Meri, a beautiful, articulate woman, now in her seventies, reminisced about her career for an audience studded with admirers and former students and company members. (What nerve she must have had and how good she must have been to have successfully presented Spanish dances in Spain. Javanese dances in Java. Indian dances in India!) After she had spoken fervently and provocatively about the possibility of being authentic without being traditional, of knowing a style well enough to be creative within it, I was surprised how little the audience's questions had to do with either La Meri's career or with piquant aesthetic points. Why, the audience wanted to know, was ethnic dance always at the bottom of the dance heap in the eyes of critics, sponsors, and granting institutions? Why were people still so obtuse about the distinction between folk dancing and complex dance-theater forms? Hadn't Clive Barnes admitted in a review of the Pavel Virsky folk troupe that he found *all* ethnic dance boring? And why were Americans working in foreign styles regarded with such suspicion—as if by not becoming modern dancers or ballet dancers, they were turning their backs on their own heritage and/or contemporary life?

There are no easy answers. Most ethnic styles are so ancient, so bound up with a people's history, religion, climate, that it's hard not to believe that *anyone* born in India has the built-in know-how to become a better exponent of Indian dance styles than someone not born there. But there are plenty of third-rate dancers in and from India. And who's to say that the superbly skilled Nala Najan, for example, isn't in some profound sense Indian? That his family background is primarily Russian and Puerto Rican doesn't matter when he dances. Of course, there are many mediocre ethnic dancers born and working here, and it's hard not to think of them as exploitative—parlaying a meager stock of knowledge into a career.

Some of the Americans who take up ethnic forms are, frankly, ballet rejects. That's not a bad thing in itself. A dancer who starts late (say, at seventeen) and doesn't have extraordinary arches or ear-high extensions will never get a scholarship at the Joffrey for sure. But with sensitivity, five or more years of study and daily practice, a constant soaking up of musical forms and general culture, he or she *might* make it in one of the ethnic styles. That is, if he doesn't drop out when he discovers that, for example, a continuously crescendoing roll on the castanets is as difficult as a tour en l'air, although the virtuosity involved is less obvious. The phenomenal Indian dancer Ritha Devi lost quite a few NYU dance students from her classes at first: They simply didn't have the stamina to stay in a plié and stamp for that long.

You might call Tamar Rogoff a dropout from the American dance system. "After going to the High School of Performing Arts, which, to me, was like factory, it meant so much to be the only student of a teacher— working in India, with him, for the sake of the art. *In this country I never really knew what 'the art' was.*" She tells me clearly and movingly what it feels like to make a performance good—not for personal glory but so that it will not dishonor, and *perhaps* even add to, an ancient tradition. She speaks of performing for audiences who don't examine dancing with distant objectivity but who devour it as a form of sustenance. I understand that completely.

Some Americans study the ethnic dance forms that are part of their own ancestry. The movement to understand and appreciate black roots has made it easy for Chuck Davis to interest the young dancers in his company in African dance. A few pursue ethnic dance as a sideline: William Carter of American Ballet Theatre has performed as a guest artist with Teodoro Morca's Spanish dance company. Lee Connor, whom Ritha Devi is proud to consider her American pupil, has included Kuchipudi pieces on his modern dance concerts: They fit right in with his bold, vigorous, line-conscious approach to dance. For him, and for Carter, it's an affinity for a style, a way of moving, that set things in motion, I suspect.

I don't even think I had a particular affinity for Cambodian dance; I was recruited because I was in the right place at the right time, the right height, and a quick study (I even made it into the company sooner than a Rumanian who looked terrifically Indian but had never learned to count music). I found the movement beautiful and difficult. My strong, mature, Anglo-Saxon fingers wouldn't bend backward properly; I was plagued with shooting pains in my forearms. And the necessary degree of control maddened me. I was a big Californian: my inclination was toward swinging, thrusting gestures aimed all the way from L.A. to the San Bernardino Mountains. Not for downcast eyes, and a smooth, unaccented flow of tiny steps and slow balances meant to suggest an angel in well-behaved flight.

One high point of my career was being told by Ted Shawn that, although I was the most outsized oriental dancer he had ever seen, I had a mean way with those brass demon fingernails. Another was getting to go on for the star, Mara, and do her ritual fire dance in the all-blue light with the rest of the company watching from the wings with crossed fingers, worried that I might singe my armpits twirling those bowls of flaming alcohol. I have good memories of those days and a swell demi-plié as a keepsake; but, although at some point I allowed myself to be billed as Toguri (for reasons too bizarre to go into here), I *knew*—at least I think I knew—that I was Deborah Jowitt and that some day I'd have to find out how *I* danced.

But a few ethnic dancers seem to be people with no self-identity trying to create a new lifestyle and a more intriguing persona. Even the name-changing business can have odd aspects. Mariano Parra, lucky enough to be born with a perfectly good Spanish name, says shrewdly, "I wonder if, psychologically, they're always ready for that change. Are they together enough inside to sustain the image that goes with that new name?" Are apartments draped in saris and watched over by Buddhas any guarantee of a rich inner life? Or, for that matter, of success in dance?

Some expert dancers are still self-conscious over their lack of bona-fide origins. The uptightness seeps into their dancing in subtle ways. Take one Spanish dancer—his technique is impeccable, he has the stern strong-boned face of an Escudero; but his heelwork reminds me of a typewriter—precise, resonant, and hardly more alive. Does the reason he can't loosen up a little, ever, have something to do with the fact that he's a Hungarian Jew and afraid to take liberties with the steps? Just the opposite is a woman who was once the most elegant of Spanish dancers; as soon as she struck out on her own, she began to coarsen her style in Flamenco, to shrug her shoulders up around her ears, spread her legs, emphasize the thrust of her hips and the provocativeness of her sneers. She's still terrific, but the exaggerated street-gypsy role has taken over.

Perhaps it's our fault, with our stereotyped ideas. Mariano Parra and his dancer-sisters, Inez and Mariana, were born here of Spanish parents. Parra himself has a long, elegant line, considerable restraint, fair skin, a round face, and crisp, prematurely gray hair. Considering his knowledge of many forms of Spanish dance and his twelve-year career, no wonder he's by turns defiant, defensive, and bitterly funny when accused of not looking Spanish enough.

At Camp Beaupré, where Carola Goya and Matteo used to teach Spanish and Indian dance, I used to love to watch baby ballet dancers with a few yards of Bloomingdale's dimity pleated around them and Christmas bells jingling on rubber bands around their ankles, or teenagers with ruffled skirts and high heels, relishing a foretaste of self-assured womanhood. Every now and then, one would look stunning, but few took up

Spanish or Indian as a career. What *career*? Indian émigrés to New York, like Ritha Devi or Maya Kulkarni, often present themselves at the Cubiculo or the Kitchen or somebody's loft, just like the modern dancers. There's a week at Jacob's Pillow in the summer, if you can cut it, plus assorted music festivals, international fairs, kids' shows, and nightclub acts. Dance departments at universities usually book touring companies that are more contemporary and less traditional. Columbia Artists, one of the few outfits still booking community concerts, puts together reputedly hair-raising twelve-week tours of one-night stands that zigzag from Texas to Ohio and back to Texas.

La Meri once said that modern dancers and ethnic dancers have two things in common: They all want to be choreographers and they all want to be soloists. So, perhaps, it's not only lack of money or interested management that makes large American-based ethnic companies uncommon. Matteo's successful Ethno-American Dance Company ordinarily features only one mature soloist, himself, and even so he keeps losing the gifted young dancers he's spent years training.

The performance problems are so damned complex. No mutters of "olé!", no war whoops, no drift of incense can quite create the ambience of a Spanish café, a dusty village, a temple. There's no way an interested American audience in a nicely equipped auditorium can grasp the embellishments that cultural style and personal artistry make on an incident from the *Mahabarata,* the way they'd dig a new version of the old Cain-Abel routine. Well, that's the breaks; but I wonder if the sourness of many "ethnic" dancers stems from trying to keep in touch with an honored tradition, while playing to audiences that see them inevitably as "exotic" and "colorful." I remember that when I was Toguri, polite, awed little girls from small towns in Wyoming would come backstage to stare and ask us how we moved our heads from side to side. At some point it began to bother me a lot—even me, the uncommitted pseudo-ethnic. How much worse for those who devote their lives to these forms. Suppose a ballerina had just danced *La Sylphide,* and all people said to her afterward was, "How do they get the wings to fall off?"

In the course of setting me straight on a fact—that William Carter had appeared with Teodoro Morca in a joint concert, rather than as a guest artist—Morca took me to task for not making it clear that dancers might take up a particular "ethnic" dance style, not because they were "ballet rejects" or "modern dance rejects," but because "they might crave that particular facet of dance." He's right. One can have an affinity for certain ways of moving and so find great satisfaction in identifiable styles that embody these.

Consider the Ethnic Dancer

Anna Istomina (Mrs. Serge Ismailoff) is not a "Russianized American." She was born Audree Thomas in Vancouver, B.C.

Interestingly, Tamar Rogoff has not been performing Indian dance for the past couple of years; she has been trying to develop her own choreographic style.

YOU TELL ME YOUR DREAMS

The Village Voice, July 29 – August 4, 1981

▼▼▼

It is a day of anomalies—clear and bright. By 6 p.m., grownups, children, and dogs have begun to occupy the sandy slope at Battery Park City landfill, with or without blankets, bottles, thermoses, cameras, leashes. The artworks that (courtesy of Creative Time, Inc.) stud the man-made beach have the air of relics from a vanished civilization—ours. People lounge in the chairs set under the Cinzano umbrellas that are part of Gina Wendkos's *The Contest;* people climb Donald Lipsky's red stairway to nowhere (called *Progress* and linked by wires to the World Trade Center); people peer down the corridor of wooden cubicles that form the heart of Alice Aycock's *Large Scale Dis/Integration of Microelectric Memories (A New Revised Shantytown),* or try to climb into what looks like the half-finished second floor of an apartment building designed by a deranged architect. ("How do you get up there?" say the children. "You don't," say the parents firmly.)

Our tribe understands art like this. Nothing is sacred to us. Tim Watkins's twelve "vertical twirlees" standing on the hill guard nothing. The small broken plaster figure of a swimmer (yellow hair, red torso, blue legs) lying half buried in the sand beside Wendkos's work doesn't indicate a shrine defaced; it's been artfully placed to suggest destruction, although there's no place for it in the border of similar swimmers that runs around Wendkos's "pool."

What will the Aboriginal Artists from Australia make of it? We're waiting here to see them dance. While they wait in a yellow school bus parked on West Street. At every window of the bus is a dark face intricately painted with white spots and lines. Meanwhile, big cars drive up; and men in suits and ties, women in flowered dresses and white shoes make their way gamely across the sand. (Must be a party afterward.) They sit on wooden chairs reserved for them. Australian diplomatic sorts? Two elegantly dressed women have been sitting placidly in the hot sun for a long time. ("Oh fat white woman whom nobody loves/Why do you walk through the field in gloves?")

At 6:20 a couple of young New York choreographers and their entourage spread a blanket right in front of what has been tacitly accepted as the front row for half an hour now. The front row moves defensively forward. After a few minutes a man comes to a microphone and asks the front row to move back at least six feet. At 6:30, David, a baby already locked into a supremely destructive relationship with his mother, drops his bottle (*again*) near another baby. For the tenth time, unfairly, his mother slaps him and tells him (*again*) not to throw things. As she turns away with the bottle, he quickly throws two tiny fistfuls of sand on the other baby, who is having a small private tantrum over not being allowed to climb the hill and get a better look at Watkins's bright, seductive vanes. No mother sees this act of defiance or notes the slight increase in flow of Baby Number 2's tears. Both babies are puzzled by the lack of adult response. At 6:35, Clive Barnes, in a blue suit, is escorted deferentially over the sand and ensconced on a folding chair. Our tribe has assembled.

At 6:45, an Australian gentleman drinking cold beer with his wife turns to me and inquires politely if I come here often. This is a surprisingly difficult question to answer. Fortunately the speeches have begun: the thanks to the National Endowment (hearty take-note-Reagan cheers), to the New York State Council (more cheers), to the Mobil Oil Corporation (uneasy, ambivalent hisses), a string of others. Nandjiwarra Amagula, chairman of the Executive Aboriginal Cultural Foundation, explains the difference between public-sacred art—which we may see—and secret-sacred art—which we may not; he attempts to help us understand a complex social order in which art may be owned by a cult, a clan, an individual, and no one may just get up and perform a dance owned by another group. Twice he says ruefully that this trip to America has made the Aboriginals feel that the world is too big. And now, here they come, over the hill in back of us. We hear a distant, nasal chant, the clacking of two sticks together, and a deep windy hooting that turns out to be made by a didjeridu, a thick pole at least four feet long. A shocked dog barks and lunges as the small parade appears—body paint, smears of gray, feathers, loincloths or grass skirts.

The group from northeastern Arnhem Land has the didjeridu player and a male chanter with two sticks. The dances are named for creatures the men hunt: pelican, turtle, fish, jungle-fowl, octopus, dove; for things they do, like fighting with stone knives; for myths from the Dreamtime, when the travels of heroes formed the topography of the earth. Amazing, their feet upon the ground. The three men, thin-legged, hit the earth so sharply with the soles of their feet that you expect it to boom. They keep their knees bent, feet spread a little apart, and inch forward stamping one or both feet very tersely on the beat. In a few of the dances, the three women wearing black blouses and brown skirts who follow the men in a line or stand side by side at a slight distance from the men, stamp in a very different manner—smaller in scale; they lift their feet on the beat and stamp afterward. Often the dancers have the wary gaze and stance of hunters stalking their prey; occasionally they dance as if they *were* the animal—a lot of their dancing looks birdlike to me, like emus or sharp-eyed herons. Members of the Cape York contingent wear grass skirts, feathered headgear, many white spots on their bodies. They clap to emphasize the chanting of Annie Maiikompa Kalkeeyorta. (Photographers run this way and that, hurl themselves on the sand in front of us. A young woman keeps shoving a microphone under Mrs. Kalkeeyorta's chin. The performers watch a jet sail overhead.) Some of their items are succinct stories. An old woman doesn't want to nurse her baby (breasts too sore) and tosses it around the campfire to other women; what we actually see is two dancing men (the Kalkeeyortas: father and son) tossing a small log to each other every time a verse ends. The group, barking and on all fours, suddenly becomes dingoes surrounding a hunter. An old man keeps falling under the weight of a fat fish he's carrying home; his young companion has to pick him up over and over. Two lovers die in a torrent, pierced by the yam-stick they hold onto (two men dancing side by side holding one long stick under their arms).

Stylistic distinctions between the two groups are hard for a foreigner to pick out. The Cape York people hold long, long sticks, but both groups make spear-throwing gestures. The Cape Yorkers do a lot of standing in place, feet apart, jerking both knees in and out, but the Arnhem Landers do some of this too. Everything seems terse and limited in scale: not much space covered, a few repeated movements in each dance, a few close-together descending notes in each song, very short songs (some under a minute). Sometimes a shriek or a birdlike ululation by the singer indicates that only two beats remain. These short song/dances can be repeated or varied, I think, and strung together to make a longer piece. But the rhythm and performance energy is dropped in between repeats; performers shift around, look at each other, mutter. Will they do more? Maybe yes, maybe no.

The photographers swarm off to the side. Here come the dancers and songmen from the northern desert, led by imposing-bellied Maurice Jupurrula Luther M.B.E. (Like the other group leaders, Gawirrin Gumana and Clive Karwoppa Yunkaporta, he is a board member of the Aboriginal Cultural Foundation.) Their dance, dreamed in 1967 by Liddie Nakamarra, concerns the pursuit of a transgressor by four ancestral warriors. While Luther and two musicians clatter boomerangs together, the warriors, their body paint in fuzzy relief and their heads elongated into great bulbous headdresses (pineapple men, someone called them), surround and escort their victim, who is making them follow him to Jundu, where he wishes to die. Sometimes he stops and kneels, sometimes he lies flat. At the end, hunters and hunted huddle up to the musicians.

The setting sun reddens the windows of the skyscrapers. The dancers wanted to perform at night, by firelight; the Parks Department wouldn't hear of it. On real sand and rocks, placed here by human agency, surrounded by wires and lenses, backed up by the Empire State Building uptown, the Aboriginal Artists perform for an enthusiastic and uncomprehending audience. Surrounded by contemporary American artworks that we understand—all having to do with disintegration, with incompleteness, with aborted goals—they perform works about wholeness. The dancing, songs, body painting, preserve the myths. All seem cryptic. (At a workshop the next day at NYU—aboriginal Australians in Sassoon T-shirts—again garlanded with wires and flashed by cameras, various officials and spokespersons indicate, I think, that the art sometimes functions as a practical mnemonic aid, passing down information about topography and any number of events and customs. In a book on Aboriginal music, what looks like a drawing of a spoked wheel is identified as men sitting in a circle striking sticks on the ground.)

At about 8 p.m., the distinguished outlandish visitors ride off across the sands in the direction of their school bus followed by our cheers, mystification, cameras. After they've gone, children beg again to climb on Aycock's finished/never-to-be-finished building and are again refused. The sun sinking behind New Jersey makes lovers want to kiss. Two yachts and a three-masted ship under full sail go up the Hudson. Another jet passes. Two helicopters play tag. The Aboriginals, I hear, cope with things like water faucets by making songs about them. Why not New York?

Artist Gina Wendkos wrote to correct my impression that the broken plaster swimmer had been "artfully placed to suggest destruction." Actually, what I saw were the relics of Wendkos's performance art work, The Contest, *which had involved eighty live performers and three hundred little swimmers. "These were not artfully placed," wrote Wendkos, "but instead are the survivors of the attack by 'James Dean.' " After he "thrashed about in destruction to the tune of 'Rebel Without A Cause,' the audience collected all the fragments." Maybe it was kids who reorganized the residue. It's interesting to note that the more I learn about her work, the more it supports my notion that disintegration was a characteristic theme of the art works in this exhibition.*

COMBAT WITH THE
INVISIBLE

The Village Voice, October 5, 1982

What is *duende?* No one defines it easily. In his speech *Teoría y Juego del Duende,* Federico García Lorca tried to lure it out into words. Something that certain artists, certain works of art possess, something that certain aspects of the world now and then reflect. Music that has "dark tones" has *duende.* This somber, potent spirit doesn't always engender beautiful sights and sounds in art; it raises a chill along the beholder's spine, sets the heart beating fast. Unlike the inspiration that muses and angels bring to the poet, the dancer, the singer, said Lorca, *duende* doesn't come from the outside, it must be awakened in "las últimas habitaciones"—the deepest, most remote dwelling places, the last abodes—of the blood. And it awakens most readily when, in the middle of life, the presence of death is felt.

The dancer Pilar Rioja, now being presented by the Repertorio Espanol, names her program after Lorca's famous lecture. Actors Carmen Cuesta and Francisco G. Rivela sit in one corner of the tiny, high old stage of the Gramercy Arts Theater and read the lecture, interspersed with some of Lorca's poems. The way they sharpen the "y" and "ll" sounds into "j" adds a harsh power to the melodious current of Spanish. Death flowers in knives, roses, rivers, bells; it calls to dreaming maidens, rides with dark horsemen, waits in the bullring.

Rioja is a woman neither young nor old, tall nor short, thin nor fat, beautiful nor homely. Her costumes aren't stunning, neither are they unattractive. She presents herself simply; occasionally in her lighter dances she smiles at the audience as she strides past the front of the stage; more often her face—broad with fine, high cheekbones and a thin mouth—is still, as if she were listening to the dance as it emerges through her feet, arms, body. Sometimes I watch her with interest and pleasure; sometimes, for no reason that I can understand, the air around me feels absolutely still, and my eyes fill with tears.

She dances in the classical Bolero style—in short, full skirts and ballet slippers. The airy steps and neat beats of nineteenth-century ballet blend with little stamps, with castanet rhythms, and the curving arm gestures that swirl those rhythms through the air around her. Her sounds are delicate, subtle traceries on the Bach and Corelli she dances to. Paganini's *Moto Perpetuo,* preceded by Lorca's poem about the castanet—"sonorous black beetle"—incites her to a bolder, virtuosic cascade of trills. The jewel of this part of the program is a long dance to Boccherini, *Grave assai y Fandango.* Now Rioja adds heelwork—building amazing crescendos and decrescendos of sound, keeping the dance threading inexorably around and through the music.

A nearly invisible pianist, Pablo Zinger, and a grave singer in a black dress, Maria Luisa Trevino, appear to perform a couple of songs—one set by Lorca to an ancient tune, and Rioja turns to Flamenco style—long dress, fan, sultry pauses. She ends with a decorous, but spirited *Sevillanas del Siglo XVIII,* to a Lorca song ("Ay, river of Seville,/how fine you look/full of white sails/and green branches").

The second half of the program is all Flamenco, with two guitarists, José Negrete and Emilio Perujo, and a singer, Pedro Angel. The music is splendid. Angel's quivering, nasal voice, the throbbing guitars seem to darken the air on stage. In male attire, Rioja dances a *Farruca* with bold and dazzling footwork, but her most wonderful dancing comes in the *Tangos del Piyayo*—a long, brooding, sensual piece. Her hips swing almost menacingly, her arms snake around her head and body; now her feet drive a rhythm fiercely into the floor beneath her; then suddenly everything lightens, and she skims almost soundlessly over the small, dimly lit stage. It's like a combat with an invisible force, and she is at once savage, meditative, and intoxicated by what she's doing. At one point there seems to be almost no motion on stage, except the quick fingers of the guitarists, and the dancer's feet. In the darkness, the pale faces of the actors and musicians watch Rioja's still, intent face and the force rising through her body, and the tension is almost unbearable.

At the end, death is brought onto the stage. The actors read the poet Antonio Machado's outraged lament for his friend Lorca, killed in 1937 by the fascist government, while Rioja dances a somber *Siguiriya* in a black dress. It's the first time she's used a long train all evening, and it becomes a rustling snake to step over, a long, dark emptiness that follows her offstage.

Seeing this performance reminded me how much I admire fine Spanish dancing and how little I see of it these days. Economics or fashion or I don't know what have done away with big companies that specialize in Spanish dance like those I remember most nostalgically: the Ximenez-Vargas company, the one headed by Teresa and Luisillo. Curious, because audiences I've been part of respond to it with tremendous fervor. To be sure, it's the sexual tension lurking in Flamenco that seems to fire up spectators the most. That's why, forced to make a choice, they'd pick the vulgar dancer over the too-refined one. Yet in the case of great Spanish dancers, it's the image of passion controlled that's so thrilling. When Dolores Serral danced the Bolero and the Cachucha in Paris in the 1830s, Theophile Gautier clearly felt something of this: ". . . She is never indecent," he explained. "She is full of passion and voluptuousness, and true voluptuousness is always chaste." Sometimes you feel—are supposed to feel—that the dancer's restraint will break, but it never quite does, even in the most explosive burst of heelwork, the closest and most heated circling of partners.

I think, perhaps, that the truest element in Spanish dance, the one we respond to most deeply, is not its sexiness or its virtuosic quality but its combativeness, even found at times in the lightness and gaiety of the Bolero. In couple dances, the man and woman strut, circle each other tauntingly, start to leave, wheel around suddenly, like wild birds proving their mettle on the mating ground. For the dancer alone, the adversary is . . . what? The space, the rhythms that must be mastered? The greatest performers can make you believe by their concentration, their fierceness, their force, that the invisible antagonist is death, who must be held temporarily at bay with a display of life. Here too, the end—not shown on stage—will be compliance.

This review was originally part of a column that also dealt with the Spanish dancer, Maria Benitez. Parts of it have been rearranged and edited.

TEMPO WILL TELL

The Village Voice, April 8–14, 1981

If you're dismayed by the impoverished rhythms of disco and the idea that this might be all we've got going these days in the way of a beat to stomp, you should have been up at the Beacon Theater to see the National Dance Company of Senegal. The dancers and drummers work as if the earth must be beaten at all times, the air constantly reminded of the even pulse of our breathing. But what subtle games they play around that pulse, that deceptively steady kneading of the ground. Nine drummers, with tam-tams, split drum, big boss boomer, agree and spat, top each other's patterns. Suddenly, over an agreeable swaying rhythm made by hands patting the hide, sticks will crack a fast higher-pitched nattering against another drum, insisting that what you thought were offbeats are *the* big item. The rhythmic counterpoint is complex, the din gorgeous.

What the drummers' hands can do, the dancers' feet can do. No, not really. You hear their feet on the floor, the soft, elastic thudding that can build to terrific speeds, but counterpoint is seen more than heard. It's provided by nodding heads, rolling shoulders, hands patting the air, hips churning. And/or. It's hard to tell where any rhythm begins or ends. I imagine the dancers take their bodies apart at night before sleeping and put a pat of butter in every joint.

As with every African company I've ever seen, I notice the ability of the dancers to fold at the hip and knee. It is my impression that the faster Europeans want to move, the smaller and closer to the ground they need to keep their feet, but these dancers seem to spread out in space as their speed increases. When they're dug in, skating their feet on the floor at improbable speeds, their opposite knees lift so high you'd swear you see spoked wheels spinning instead of thighs and calves. Two acrobats use their ability to fold up for a variety of uncanny feats. They're both big men in draped trousers with whistles on chains around their necks, which they wheet, wheet on to tell us when the going is tough. They wear rings on every finger, so when they whack the big halved gourds they carry, the noise is sharp and metallic (I think the gourds have some kind of metal spring inside them too). Anyway, these guys do things like arranging themselves in lotus position and then whipping off a chain of back somersaults. One (standing) sticks his head and one foot into his gourd and flips over and over with the help of his free hand and foot.

When I saw this company years and years ago, they were interested in the "village life" effect, with kibitzers and simulated dailiness. Now, most of the time, they present themselves with a more matter-of-fact theatricality. You hear a noise of feet and voices, and a procession of young women and/or men dance on, arrange themselves neatly spaced out, and dance. I liked the fact that the front row in one dance might be the back row in the next, giving us a chance to admire now the tall, cool beauty, now the grinning digger-in. The garb is as polyrhythmic as the dancing: clanking shells at ankle, flailing grass skirts at hip, horns on head for the men, say; wrapped cloth on hips, bare breasts crossed by beads, elaborate corn-rowing or feathery headdresses for the women.

The skimpy program notes aren't much help. This marimba thing worn around the neck must be a Balafon (typically, the man who plays it sings, high and harsh, in a rhythm opposed to the one his hands are playing). Is this remarkable instrument—gourd resonator and stem with a rain of strings to be plucked stretching between—a Dan? Maybe. Is this nimble, masked creature meant to be the animal the young men are hunting in an initiate's dance? This living haystack with a stick leaning out near his peak, this haystack who can spin at an angle, what spirit is he? In the one "drama," is this nimble, masked stiltman a jealous god or the protector of the sacred antelope, Singal? (The woman who plays Singal—maybe—has an amazing death scene; as she lies there, her limbs begin to vibrate so rigidly, so rapidly that you can't believe the movements aren't involuntary.) Which dancer, which drummer is which?

The program mustn't have been well publicized. The gloomy Beacon is barely half full. After intermission, a lot of young Afro-Americans move down front, some in African dress. They start whooping and waving and jumping out of their seats. The Senegalese respond happily. A contest of brainy and sexy improvisation turns this new, hot audience on. Oh yes. The drummer gets so close to one woman, now really shaking her butt at us, laughing and breathing hard, that they seem to rub sparks off each other's rhythms and proximity. Whooee! Where were you?

CAN A DOLL DRINK WATER?

The Village Voice, September 17–23, 1980

~

Puppetry and mime work their illusions in opposite ways. The skilled puppeteer makes his doll of wood or clay or paper take on the semblance of human life, even the gestures and habits of a specific character, while the mime often attempts to transcend the limits of his individual body in order to suggest the growth of a flower, the action of a machine, an archetypal character. The accomplished mime can make the invisible visible; the accomplished puppeteer makes the visible all but invisible. Yet in both cases, the audience's pleasure comes from the simultaneous perception of illusion and the reality. The artist who pantomimes a tug of war delights us because we know there's no rope and no opponent, yet we "see" them. A puppet drinks water, and we marvel at this ordinary act because we know that an extraordinarily dextrous finger on a string or concealed within a tiny sleeve is producing it.

All that's needed to induce such speculation is a week in which the Fujian Hand Puppets from the People's Republic of China perform at the Museum of Natural History (courtesy of the Asia Society) and DTW's New Mime series begins at ATL.

When a small velvet curtain zips open and we see a plucky servant with a head the size of a medium egg pushing a tiny laden cart, we all laugh. By a forward-leaning stance and a repeated thrust of his left shoulder, the fellow let us know the cart is *heavy.* The aristocratic young scholar, his master, has a more refined gait. The puppets are astonishingly life-like, the heads beautifully carved and painted, the robes hanging elegantly, the hair black and silky. With the sound of gongs, cymbals, drums making emphatic comment or raising shivery climaxes, with the high-pitched or growling voices coming from back there somewhere, we might be spending a night at the Peking Opera. Except that we are always, subtly, aware of the shape and limitations of the human hand. The characters have very flat or arched backs, and those without padded costumes have no shoulders. We understand immediately and with joy that a human being our size has developed the skill and sensitivity to condense all his or her knowledge of human movement until it can be expressed by the index finger, the middle finger, and the thumb.

Such skill is so refined that it almost makes you shudder. The point about a treasured Japanese bonsai, I believe, isn't simply that it's a miniature tree, but that it's a hundred-year-old maple tree deformed by artistry.

Watching the Fujian puppets, we're particularly thrilled by what we sense must be difficult for the puppeteers to achieve. A servant pours wine from a vessel into a goblet his pompous master holds; the master drinks and shakes out the glass. A tiny drop of liquid falls onto the stage. A juggler catches a dollar-sized plate on a stick and twirls it. A scholar dips a brush in ink and writes on a little scroll. Combatants dodge each others' blows with scarcely believable rapidity.

The puppeteers make gentle jokes about their own skill. A male puppet's skinny leg, occasionally hoisted by the puppeteer's other hand, always draws audience laughter. A fantastic tiger, with snaggly teeth in a disproportionately large maw, scratches himself in a realistic manner, but he also (via the puppeteer's second hand) whirls his tail in circles. An amazed official's wig spins around on his head. A brave warrior vaults onto a balcony; and the puppet is actually thrown into the air and caught again on his master's index finger.

The repertory of this southern school of Fujian puppetry goes back 400 years or more, but it was reformed during the 1950s to make it more universally comprehensible. The "official" language of China replaced dialects. The "national" style of music (with Western influences) replaced the older folk or operatic material. The pavilion stage was traded in for the miniature, curtained proscenium stage. Five-hour performances were pared down to two hours. The art form, suppressed in China during the Cultural Revolution, was reapproved in 1970, and further pruning and pointing up has evidently been done for touring abroad. (They have heard, in Peking, that we like Bruce Lee.)

One excerpt from a cycle called *All Men Are Brothers* shows rebels penetrating a citadel by disguising themselves as entertainers to deceive the self-important, waddling official at the gates. In another story from the same cycle, a brave hunter kills a tiger that was menacing a student and his servant; then the hunter, his niece, and his helper polish off—with many acrobatic flourishes—a wicked innkeeper and his wicked servants who plan to murder the scholar. In another, a man obliged to sell his beloved horse fights a slew of upper-class baddies who're bent on getting the horse without paying for it.

In these prolonged essays in violence and comeuppance, characters are, on occasion, literally beaten out of their outer garments. Whish! A minuscule silk robe flies through the air. One tale, *The Devil Paints a Woman,* gives a hint of what the puppeteers can achieve in the way of poetic sensuality: the devil, disguised as a woman, almost succeeds in seducing a young scholar, and our eyes strain to see, in miniature, the subtle and gradual yielding of decorum.

But whether the story is active or meditative, the five puppeteers—

Yang Feng, Chen Jintag, Zhuang Zhenhua, Zhu Yalai, and Xu Lina (three men and two women)—convey it not only through gesture, but through rhythm. The puppets may quiver in rage and fear, suddenly freeze, slowly turn to confront an opponent. Their cloth bodies seem to tense with reluctance or determination. It is almost shocking afterward to go backstage and be shown a flat, limp doll with its head dangling.

In its original form, this article also commented on the United Mime Workers, one of the companies on the DTW mime series.

FRAGRANCE CLINGS TO THE SLEEVE

The Village Voice, November 25–December 1, 1981

You would not, perhaps, expect issues of gender to be raised at a performance by the Court Dance Theater company of Okinawa. Or perhaps you would. In Okinawa, as in China and Japan—the powerful neighbors who have stomped around in Okinawa over the centuries—men and women dance differently from each other. The four women who glide onto the Asia Society's stage to perform *Winagu Kuti Bushi* resemble hovering butterflies: they lift their arms delicately and their sleeves spread bright, patterned wings from their shoulders to their hips. The women dance slowly and gravely, rising and falling with small, soft steps that make them revolve this way and that. When they move away from the audience, backs to us, we can't see their feet at all; when they bend their knees, they appear to be shrinking. Sometimes they slide one foot in its cloth "tabi" out to the side, toes crooked up. That's about as bold as they get below the waist, although their arms or hands, fingers pressed lightly together, trace leisurely curlicues of various sizes on the air. In *Yutsidaki,* eight women wear large, lightweight "flower hats" that accentuate the fragile way their heads sit on their necks. In all the women's dances, you can see—barely—infinitesimal rearrangements of the head that make you think of blossoms nodding slightly in the breeze. The women in this dance wield bamboo clappers, but never chatter with them.

The most subtle woman's dance of all is the slow, barely moving *Shudun*, a solo, performed on alternate days by Sanae Miyagi and Hiroko Koja. It is a winter night. The music sighs and snarls. "You and I sharing a pillow . . . it is but a dream . . ." For a long time, the dancer simply stands looking from one side to another, scarcely moving her head. Where is he? Not coming ever again. You have to pare down your Western sensibility to see grief and longing in the small rockings and twistings, the empty-handed gestures. The style resembles Noh almost more than Kabuki; its poignancy is directly related to its control, its elegance, its miniature scale.

The men, of course, are allowed to be bolder—to spread their legs, squat, lift one knee high, set their feet more emphatically on the floor. In Karate, an Okinawan native form, they can jump explosively, crouch, lunge, and whirl weapons around alarmingly. But the warriors in this *Karate Dance* are women. Now wearing no-nonsense black-and-white outfits, the same women who minced and swayed so gently through the court dances lash their long black hair around, and bundle themselves tigerishly for great springs into the air. They hasten offstage (all entrances and exits happen in the up right corner); some return with short swords; then others with the two sticks joined by thongs which can break an opponent's arm; finally one undertakes vicious figure-eights with a spear. The contemporary Okinawan female dancer is obviously no longer restricted to "female" forms, and these women exhibit terrific ferocity and glee.

In *Zei*, women play young boys, as young boys once played women. But the odd thing here is the boys they are playing are as elegant as women, even though their movements are slightly larger and more vehement, the breaks in rhythm stronger. Most of the dances on these programs date from the seventeenth-century banquets given whenever Chinese envoys arrived to crown a new Okinawan king (an ancient custom). All performers were male then, the most desirable dancers being elaborately gowned and coiffed young boys. Indeed, the plot of the charming and touching dance-drama, *Nido Tichiuchi*, hinges on the point that two brothers seeking to revenge their father's death pose as dancing boys to charm the villain. "Boys so beautiful we mistake them for flowers!" sighs one of the evil lord's followers.

The actors chant their own lines—the boys (played on the night I went to Asia House, by Sonomi Miyagi and Sanae Miyagi, one of the troupe's most accomplished women) always singing the same sweet, whining tune, which ascends by microtones, repeats one note for perhaps three beats, and then climbs obliquely down. Their enemy, Amaui, is played by the company's director, Minoru Miyagi, an actor-dancer of immense skill. Lunging, gesturing with a butterfly-shaped fan, sneering and widening his eyes and spitting out his words, he tells us how he killed Lord Gusamaru, the only man who stood in his way. Later, picnicking by the roadside, bedazzled by the pretty boys and fuddled by the wine they keep pouring for him, he gives them his sword, then his vest and sash. Finally, dancing tipsily with them, he hauls off his kimono too. His servants leave, the boys chase him offstage, kill him, and return to dance and sing gaily.

The little play, for all its elegant stylizations, is simple, comprehensible, and beautifully done; the conflict between the greedy old warrior and the lovely implacable boys is more resonant and touching than one would suppose.

The superb musicians who accompany everything sit at the back of the stage. Two sing and pluck the Chinese-derived sanshin; one plays a kutu (koto); one bows a tiny standing fiddle; one blows a flute; one drums. Two other drummers join in the last free-for-all song and dance, which has a folk dance flavor and vigor, but was choreographed by an islander of Kurushima in the early twentieth century. Yoshitake Kamiya and Susuma Taira stage a drum competition. One, a merry, bounding fellow, whacks a drum so deep-toned that you feel it in the pit of your stomach; the other punishes a couple of drums on a stand with cross-handed blows. Everyone dances and sings in this—the two drummers, the women, Minoru Miyagi, the men who've been playing servants or manipulating a hairy, big-mouthed, adorable lion. For the first time, we see men and women dancing together—stamping, smiling, swinging their hips as well as sweeping their hands around, flirting, challenging each other, the women as bold as the men. While they dance they sing a rousing song about festivals, boat races, crabs that can nip you with big pincers, cats who keep the mice down, luscious amounts of rain, and other matters of import to islanders. And the evening ends not with courtiers weeping beautifuly and privately into their sleeves but on this raucous vernacular note. "Iya, iya," they cry and "Sassa!" in high happy voices. In other words, whoopee.

LIBRARY ST. MARY'S COLLEGE

SOME OTHER VISTAS

Les Ballets Trockadero de Monte Carlo in Roy Fialkow's *The Lamentation of Jane Eyre*

W hose vistas? The title for this section is deliberately ambiguous— meant to cover such apparently unrelated items as the view of dance that a novelist might have and the unaccustomed mode of viewing and responding that a particular style of performance might demand. Take the tap performance described. Some of the performers were old masters of the art and deserved to be treated with respect; yet the performance itself was full of unexpected improvisation, irreverent wit, and a good-humored brand of the competitiveness that sparked evenings at the Savoy Ballroom years ago. At such an event, the air between performers and audience heats up in a way it doesn't at the Metropolitan Opera, and the critic who keeps his/her eyes glued on the expert feet may miss a lot.

A frankly political group, like the Wallflower Order, forces you to consider not just the quality of the dancing, but how effectively that dancing delivers a message, and what messages are suitable to the medium. When you watch performances by the travesty company, Les Ballets Trocadero de Monte Carlo, you are seeing a kind of palimpsest: the work before you reveals the inconsistencies, lurking absurdities (and many of the beauties) of the event it parodies. The brawny vampire Wilis of the Troc's *Giselle*, with their black fingernails and lips, move in the same formations as the docile, wan corps de ballet women in conventional productions; in retrospect we realize how much the pretty gestures *do* resemble clawing.

It's also interesting to think about something from another viewpoint: to interview Phyllis Lamhut on the economics of dance, instead of focusing only on her choreography; to probe the impact of Twyla Tharp's choreography on ice skating and vice versa; to look at a parade as if it were a dance.

One of the many things spawned during the dance revolution of the sixties was a willingness on the part of many to accept (or at any rate to consider) as dance anything that was put before us. "If it moves, I'll write about it," I said. Before long, I was promising to write about it even if it *didn't* move, as long as it didn't move by way of making a statement about motion. The anti-elitism of the period was salutary in that it firmly reconnected dancing with its origins in human gesture. As with Leonardo da

Vinci and the mold spots in which he found art-like forms, it became possible to frame anything as dancing. I would not argue that the British ceremony of The Trooping of the Colour is dance, but it is intriguing to think about it in terms of rhythms, space patterns, form. By such critical ploys we refresh our tired vision.

A LIFETIME OF ART ON
THE LEFT

The Village Voice, July 6, 1982

~

The day of the disarmament march, I was in Colorado. I did what I could: considered the Rockies' great age, talked to people, wore my Dancers for Disarmament T-shirt, and reread the notes from my talk with Edith Segal.

I'll bet that Segal—dancer, choreographer, teacher, poet, activist— never had to ask herself the questions being raised today by dancers who suddenly feel the need to create political art. (Do you make a piece *fast* and send it out while it's timely, even though it may not be the most original thing you've done? What role can/should words play? In the case of street theater, how do you deal with questions and responses from spectators?) For Segal, art and politics have gone together almost from the start—maybe, she guesses, from the days when she got her first job as a stenographer, at sixteen, one block uptown from the Rand School of Social Science. She took two courses there: dance and the fundamentals of socialism.

Edith Segal was sixteen around the time World War I was ending, and—judging from her files of letters, clippings, snapshots, her seven books of poetry—I'd say that every year of her life since then has been packed with activity. Clearly, solid left-wing causes act on her the way vitamins do on others. When I go to her Brooklyn apartment to interview her, she settles herself on a little couch that she says is easy on her back, but keeps springing up to locate a photo she wants to show me, or to ask her third husband, painter Samuel Kamen, for a name she can't remember, or to hustle to the piano and perform one of the many songs she wrote for Ethel and Julius Rosenberg. If it weren't for my being here, she'd be commenting on the poem that little Nancy, the new super's daughter, has written (Nancy rings the bell twice while I'm there, anxious for her friend's opinion).

I guess you've noticed I got off the subject. That's what an afternoon with Edith Segal is like. Her memories are so vivid, and she's such an irrepressible performer and storyteller that every question triggers more responses and more questions than either of us can keep track of. Take the scrapbook. It commemorates a program that former students and associates put on a few years ago as a tribute to her. The pasted-in letters from those who couldn't make it to NYU's Loeb Center that day include ones signed by people reminding her that they were her students years ago at Camp Kinderland (a "progressive, secular, Jewish camp," where she taught for thirty years), by old comrades-in-arms like Pete Seeger and Herbert Aptheker, by people who danced under her direction in companies like the Red Dancers. There are letters of appreciation written on the stationery of the Abraham Lincoln Brigade and from the committee that is still working to establish the Rosenbergs' innocence.

How do you unravel a life like this in one afternoon? Maybe you begin at the beginning. On East Broadway. "My father was a cigar maker; he belonged to Sam Gompers's union. My mother was a hairdresser and made wigs for religious ladies." Edith took gymnastics at the Educational Alliance, one block from home: "I wore my sister's gym suit, which was dark blue bloomers and a blouse and flat, black, laced dancing shoes. We did stuff with wands, and the song the pianist always played was called 'Pink Lady.' "

At twelve, she was one of the lucky ones picked out of a dancing class at the Henry Street Settlement House to attend the Neighborhood Playhouse (in the building now known as the Henry Street Playhouse). Lord Dunsany came to the playhouse in those days, and Galsworthy and Michio Ito and Yvette Guilbert. The six adopted daughters of Isadora Duncan caused an epidemic of drapery and liberated dancing among Edith and her friends. She stayed at the playhouse until 1924, and she recollects everything: plays she was in—Whitman's *Salut au Monde, The Dybbuk, Burmese Pwe;* improvisations Maria Ouspenskaya gave in acting class; dancing lessons with Blanche Talmud; speech with Laura Elliott ("Be BOLD! Be BOLD! . . . the things you remember!")

I wonder where she acquired her liberated spirit. Certainly one of her older sisters was shocked to find snapshots little Edith and some friends at Henry Street had taken of each other, nude, as the Three Graces. Certainly her whole family was upset when she ran off with a young man to Niagara Falls, bearing as a talisman a costume Isadora Duncan had supposedly worn: "We weren't going to be married because we didn't believe in it like Isadora didn't believe in it." The pair did relent and go through a traditional wedding ceremony, but then—causing further commotion, I dare say—they hitchhiked to California.

The first real coming together of the left-wing politics her parents dis-approved of with the dancing they also disapproved of came during a stop-over in Chicago. Lenin had died, and the Communist Party was holding a memorial meeting in Ashland Auditorium. An idea came to Segal for a dance, a solo. She'd perform to "The Workers' Funeral March," a mourner, wearing a red tunic covered with a black drape; then she'd rip the drape away and dance to the "Internationale." She found a pianist and got permission from a sympathetic party official. But he wasn't there when she arrived to perform. An outraged man in charge told her she'd dance over his dead body—unless, he said, she could get permission from Fos-ter or Ruthenberg (and, surely, two founders of the American Communist Party wouldn't have any truck with a *dancer*). "Well," says Edith softly, "that didn't faze me at all. I knew what I had to do was right, and I was going to do it." She got to Ruthenberg—"beautiful, handsome, tall, blond man." In her Brooklyn living room, she draws herself up, lays her hand on an imagined young Edith's shoulder, and says gravely, "Com-rade, if you feel you have something to contribute to this meeting, you go right ahead." And I believe the earth still trembles for her when she tells this story.

Do I have to tell you that the dance caused a sensation? Of course not. Segal shows me a little notebook of preliminary sketches for the much-expanded version she staged for the Lenin Pageant in Madison Square Garden in 1928. In one, a horde of stick figures swarms cross one corner of the platform ("Revolution"); in another, they're neatly spaced out in small groups, doing what appear to be contrapuntal work themes ("Re-construction"). Here they are, forming a huge hammer and sickle while the "Internationale" is sung. There was a chorus and an orchestra (one section of the dance was performed to "The Ride of the Valkyries") and scenes from a play about Lenin's life were interwoven with Segal's dances. An ambitious spectacle. Segal worked with at least fifty dancers, augmenting members of the Jewish theater group, ARTEF, with working people pressed into service: "I sat in the cafeteria in the same building as the CP headquarters, and anyone I looked at who walked well, I got."

She had a gift, a former colleague says, for whipping nondancers into creditable shape and making them look good. Moisseye Olgin, writing in *The Daily Worker* on January 26, 1928, spoke of the dancers' ". . . vigor-ous gestures . . . their flashlike rush . . . their turmoil at once harmonic and chaotic like the revolution itself." He approved the fact that "art, here as everywhere, was whipping human potentialities, class potentiali-ties into living form." A letter to the paper saluted the pageant as "the first mass cultural expression of the American worker."

In the pictures that spill out of Segal's files, you can trace her gradual progress toward "modernism" in dance. Here she is at sixteen, Duncanish on the lawn. Here's her first publicity photo; it shows a sturdy young woman, draped in white, with a broad face and bold, handsome features ("They wanted a picture right away, so I went to a passport photo place on 14th Street. I didn't have a costume yet; I just took my white muffler and pinned it to my bra in front and put a string around my waist. There was nothing in back.") Here are some smiling young women at Unity House, the ILGWU summer camp where Segal taught exercises, swimming, and dance; they're wearing drapes over their bathing suits. But the slender young students in the Nature Friends Dance Group, posed as Nazi soldiers about to shoot, are grouped in a simple, bold formation. And you can tell Segal took classes with Martha Graham as soon as you see her in black, contracting on the floor—the lynch victim of several fierce and angular young women who represent the Ku Klux Klan.

By the 1929 crash, almost all the important modern dancers were concerned with themes that exposed—however obliquely—the evils of society. After all, a responsiveness to the state of the world was to be one of the many criteria that distinguished the new dance from ballet. In the 1930s, politically oriented dance groups proliferated. A program the Workers' Dance League put on in 1935 gives a good idea of the current issues: *Forces in Opposition; Anti-War Trilogy; Two Pioneer Marches* (Theater Dance Union); *Red Workers Marching; Kinde, Kirche, Küche; 'Cause I'm a Nigger* (Nature Friends Dance Group, directed at the time by Edith Segal); *Sell-Out* and *Black and White* (Red Dancers, also directed by Segal). Among the New Dance Group's three contributions were *Van der Lubbe's Head,* which had won the First Annual Dance Spartakiad in 1933.

The critics, John Martin of the *Times* as well as writers on the left, juggled praise and criticism a bit awkwardly when reviewing shared concerts like this one. That some of the works were truly proletarian affairs must have added to the aesthetic confusion. Some of the dancers were accomplished young professionals—like Anna Sokolow, Lily Mehlman, or Sophie Maslow. Others were less seasoned—many of Segal's Red Dancers were girls cold from classes she taught in the Jewish afterschool schools. However, the choreographers were, most of them, very young and very ardent; that in itself, thought the critics, was a fine thing. You couldn't quarrel with their social awareness, their rage on behalf of the downtrodden.

Quite a few of the political dance groups seem to have distilled their ideas so that they could be presented as pure action. "Martha [Graham] always said the motion must carry the *emotion.*" Segal's *Red, Yellow, and Black,* created for the Freiheit jubilee at Madison Square Garden, translated the struggles and temporary alliances of communists, socialists, and imperialists into the rising, falling, joining, splitting of dancers dressed in the appropriate color. Eva Schlosser, who worked with Segal and admires her greatly, wants to be sure I understand that, with her, "it wasn't all clenched fists, bent knees, heads held high," but that these were "real dances" with lyrical moments, and that some of them were thrilling. At the height of 1930s agitprop dance, the critics did rebuke choreographers regularly for being too wordy, or too literal, or too simplistic, but, clearly, many of the dances succeeded both as art and propaganda.

As the '30s ended and the war came, some of the choreographers began to move away from making overtly political dances to expand their concert careers. Segal didn't. She had never drawn a line between dances performed for an audience of peers and dances performed in workers' clubs or at rallies. She did her best, period. Yet she seems to have placed the highest value on communicating her ideas. Two of her proudest memories aren't of praise by the dance world. In her 1930 *The Belt Goes Red*, a double line of workers in white passed dancers in black (representing parts) down their assembly line to form a big "machine" at the back. Then through this belt line came a bolt of red fabric, which the workers wove around the machine they had created. At the Madison Square Garden performance, a man holding a red flag ran up out of the audience and got into the formation: "It was so close to this worker that he felt he could do it." *That* moved her. And here's what happened when she performed her solo *Third Degree* ("Where do your comrades live? And he never said a mumblin' word") in an old Polish hall in Toms River, New Jersey, where a strike had been going on. Some of the young fellows in the audience were a bit unruly, and one of the strike organizers made a speech. (Edith's paraphrase is a full-scale performance): "You guys don't know nuttin'. We didn't tell you what they done to us in that jail, but this lady *showed* you what they done to us, and now you know. And if you don't shut up, she ain't gonna do another dance!" They shut up. And she danced the "Internationale."

I don't have space to tell you all she did in Detroit, where she went in 1936 (she did end up acting and choreographing for the Federal Theater Project there). You'll have to imagine her 1940s dance, *The Magic Fountain*, about the battle and rebuilding of what was then Stalingrad. I won't be able to sing you the song about the Spanish Civil War she sang to me.

Since she wrote her first poem—the song that won first prize for best camp song at the summer camp run by Henry Street Settlement—she's written hundreds: poems for kids, poems on love, aging, McCarthy (she got by on her wits . . . stood on the Fifth; it's quite a story but I haven't time), the Rosenbergs, Morty Sobell, Paul Robeson, Little Rock, Angela Davis, Chile, El Salvador, the children of Atlanta, and now nuclear weapons. Benjamin Spock has praised her poems, so have Langston Hughes and other important liberal artists. The publishing houses are small ones; her husband contributes the pictures; she does most of the distribution herself. Some of the poems are wry observations ("I feel like an unmade bed she said/that's been slept in/and wept in/for days"); others are simple and rhythmic, intended to be chanted or sung. Meridel LeSueur, reviewing her latest volume in *The Daily World* this spring, praises her as "a singer of the people."

I ran into Edith Segal and Samuel Kamen at one of the Dancers for Disarmament programs. They'd had a busy weekend: she'd read her antinuclear poems at a Brooklyn meeting; they'd been to St. Patrick's to hear speeches and music offered in support of disarmament. At P.S. 122, they bought a T-shirt, offered me a ride home without determining whether it was on their way, and chatted about the concert. A great span of years and changes in art separate Segal from people like Eiko and Koma or Johanna Boyce and the others, but she got the drift, was thrilled by the commitment and had a fine time. She probably went home and wrote a poem about it. She keeps a clipboard under her bed to write on if she wakes up. She can write in the dark, thank God.

SO HOW'S BY YOU,
SIEGFRIED?

The Village Voice, July 5, 1983

Jerome Robbins is one of several major choreographers to rate a parody from the outrageously clever travesty company, Les Ballets Trockadero de Monte Carlo. Peter Anastos's *Yes, Virginia, Another Piano Ballet*—which alludes principally to Robbins's *Dances at a Gathering*—has for some years been a treasure of the repertory. It was fun, all over again, to attend one of the company's programs at City Center and see the subtle opening solo, with Adam Baum as the Boy in Blue roving energetically over the stage, self-consciously embellishing his dancing with the occasional slavic touch and staring uneasily at a large grand piano which is apparently playing itself.

The Trocks' wit takes several forms. They parody specific ballets or styles of dance through subtle—and not so subtle—alterations in the original choreography. They parody the act of performing by doing it badly (although many among them are now very good dancers), by coming out of character, and by interpolating nutty jokes. And, of course, the sight of them is in itself cause for hilarity: men, all of them flat-chested, many of them large and brawny, gotten up as ballet girls.

When the company "does" *Swan Lake*, Act II, by Betteanne Terrell after Ivanov, Von Rothbart (Ashley Romanoff-Titwillow—I don't have to explain about the names, do I?) pauses down center amid his ominous flappings to adjust his lace cuffs. The Prince's friend, Benno (Zamarina Zamarkova en travesti), helps out in the duet, just as he did years ago in St. Petersburg, only this Odette keeps shooing him away. She also nearly gets impaled on the bow of Prince Siegfried in the course of one impetuous penché arabesque. This Siegfried (Alexis Ivanovitch Lermontov) is a sweet dolt and a dancer of moderate capability in minor skills. His solo is a tour de force of nonvirtuosity, and Odette has a hard time getting the "don't shoot" idea firmly fixed in his mind. Odette is played by Tamara Boumdiyeva, a most accomplished dancer with remarkably lovely legs and arched points. The program *says* she's the "Stalingrad spitfire," but her patience, her practicality, manifested in "what can you do?" shrugs and rolled-up eyes, her endearing glee and surprise at her accomplishments, suggest the Lower East Side girl who's made good.

The Trocks are knowledgeable at spoofing ballet. Terrell's version of the Bolshoi's *Spring Waters* mocks that circusy, sling-the-ballerina-around crowd pleaser most astutely, bringing out all its gleaming coarseness—as do little Fifi Chang and big Lavrenti "Biff" Stroganoff. In *Pas de Quatre* (also by Terrell) four ballerinas mock the manners and style of nineteenth-century stars Lucille Grahn, Fanny Cerrito, Carlotta Grisi, and Marie Taglioni. The cast I saw, Anastasia Romanoff, Fifi Chang, Ludmila Beaulemova, and Zamarina Zamarkova, performed splendidly, with Zamarkova particularly, shall we say, affecting, at rendering the aging Taglioni's elegantly creaky walk.

I'm glad to see the company has again turned its sharp eyes on modern dance. Roy Fialkow has contributed several new numbers, of which I was only able to see *The Lamentations of Jane Eyre*, a parody of Martha Graham's *Deaths and Entrances* (and more), starring, the day I attended, Fialkow (sorry, Agrippina Proboskovna), Yurika Sakitumi, and Sonia Leftova. Fialkow knows his Graham steps all right, and her mode of conveying drama via impassioned soliloquy. He doesn't capture quite so well the ardent dynamics of her style. Every time the dancers used their muscles forcefully, the audience howled, which ought to give Fialkow a clue. The beginning, in particular, is so vaporous and low in energy that I wondered for an moment if Proboskovna was pretending to be Graham dancing in her seventies; if so, she can't quite bring it off. Another more serious flaw that prevents this potentially devastating number from being as apt as it could be is Fialkow's choice of score. Prokofiev is too sweet, too European for Graham who, during the period Fialkow is parodying, used scores by contemporary American composers and who has usually favored dissonance and storminess to accompany dilemma dances.

The season of Les Ballets Trockadero de Monte Carlo comes at just the right time to refresh the dancegoer exhausted from breasting the dance floods of spring. Directors Natch Taylor and Betteanne Terrell present awful ballets that are constructed better than many ballets supposed to be wonderful. And they offer us the salutary experience of laughing at what usually makes us feel depressed as hell.

LONDON LETTERS

The Village Voice, June 25 – July 1, 1980

▼▼▼

To see the Trooping of the Colour on the Horseguards' parade ground is to understand why British audiences didn't take to George Balanchine's *Union Jack*. The ceremony has been performed on the official birthday of the reigning monarch since the eighteenth century, and every year it is rehearsed to a fare-thee-well and rendered with conviction. The soldiers taking part may feel thankful as well as honored, since men in other battalions of these same regiments are less happily engaged in Northern Ireland or Rhodesia.

The grandstands are full for the dress rehearsal, even though a chill, steady rain is falling on the umbrellas and plastic hats of the spectators. The sight of the Footguards and the Massed Bands marching down the road and onto the parade ground induces that sudden unreasoning thrill that comes from seeing a great many people performing the same action in perfect accord. It's a spectacle both grand and terrifying, as I'm sure it's meant to be. Seen in the distance, the smartly swinging left arms of the marching guardsmen look like a single great fringe blowing in a metrical wind. Especially after long periods of silence and immobility, hundreds of men moving one foot into an at-ease stance reverberates like a jolt of thunder; a mass presentation of arms can make the hairs on the back of your neck bristle. An impressive helmeted officer sits absolutely motionless on his absolutely motionless horse, except when various officers approach him on foot, presumably to say the official equivalent of "we're here"; then his right arm shoots up and salutes as if someone had pressed a lever in his back.

Everything is precisely spaced and timed. An interval of 150 yards is prescribed between the Blues and Royals and—oh glory!—the Massed Mounted Bands of the Household Cavalry, with the drummers riding endearingly wise and stolid draft horses and the riders playing on the march, guiding their mounts with reins wrapped around their ankles.

We, of course, don't see the Queen, only a woman in black riding sidesaddle, who is standing in for her and is so anxious not to appear presumptuous that she sits meekly roundshouldered, looking neither to right nor left. We would be expected to stand for the Queen, but now we simply sit huddled under our dripping umbrellas ("Could you lower that a little, please? We can't see").

The marching is spectacularly lucid. The lines of men turn corners without ever employing a curving path; by moving into precisely calibrated diagonals, a unit eventually completes a ninety-degree change of direction. The Massed Bands wheel as a tight cluster without ever relinquishing their vision of straight lines. They parade to a selection of tunes designated as quick marches or slow marches. Since the Irish Guard is trooping its color this year (walking its flag around and around to receive our homage), most of the tunes are Irish, although we're also treated to other marches and a striking band arrangement of "Non Più Andrai" from Mozart's *Marriage of Figaro*. The quick march is 120 paces per minute, says the man sitting next to me (he was in the Rifle Brigade, whose march is a rousing 180, probably designed to get them into the thick of things first). A slow march clocks out at 60 by my watch, and it's beautiful: the foot about to step moves slowly to the front, with a slight, but jaunty turned-out thrust added at the end. The pipers of the Scots Guards, with kilts and gaiters, look particularly elegant doing it. To mark time in a slow march, they lift their knees very high, as in a sober slow motion cancan; the change from this into marching again is curiously affecting. It has the power of a plunge, rather than a step.

I hope they all got tots of rum afterward. The man next to me said he was certain they would.

WHY DO THE USHERS WEAR
TAP SHOES?

The Village Voice, March 13, 1978

❦

Jane Goldberg was a very good dance critic before she gave it all up to become a tap dancer. Our loss is our gain. The simmering audiences who packed Elaine Summers's loft to see *It's about Time* (which Goldberg produced) had the time of their lives watching Goldberg, Andrea Levine, virtuoso hoofers Charles Cook, Albert Gibson, Jazz Richardson, and unannounced guests.

It was wonderful to see virtuosity without slickness, theatricality delivered with a natural glee, dancing that was like a flexible idiom used with loving resourcefulness by superb linguists. The days are past when jazz dancers checked out each others' steps and competed at the Hoofers Club. But these men remember them all—Stanley Brown (to whose memory the program was dedicated), Pete Nugent ("a sweet man," said Charles Cook quietly with feeling), Bojangles Robinson. They know who did which step first and who did what variation on it.

What's remarkable about these dancers, about good tap dancing in general, is the fluid, offhand way in which the performers ride the complex footwork. Part of the fun for them and for the audience lies in whipping off an astonishing step—not as if it were nothing, but with a shy pride and delight. It has to *look* easy, while obviously being unusually difficult.

At one performance when Goldberg introduced Charles Cook, Bert Gibson, and Jazz Richardson, up from the audience, reaching out his arms, came Stump (of the comedy team Stump and Stumpy) and he fitted himself right in, dancing the steps he knew, singing, holding hats for people (hats were a big item), doing a wonderful lonesome song while boohooing elaborately into a white handkerchief. He never did go back and sit in the audience. How could he?

Cook, Gibson, and Richardson are terrific comedians, of course, as well as dancers. They insulted each other. They vied with each other to see who could do the most eccentric step. Gibson and Richardson ripped off risqué poems (one guy prudently clapped his hand over the other's mouth, just as the last raunchy word was about to come out). Each has his own style. Richardson, small and spry, did a lot of keep-your-balance arm waving and stiff-legged stumbles. Gibson, with his popping eyes and respectable paunch, has a looser way of dancing; he rolled his hips smoothly around, letting his feet flap wildly for a laugh. Cook has a bold, imperturbable attack, a wonderful sense of what makes one step different from another in terms of loud and soft, big and small, tight and easy. He also has an immensely kind, rather serious performing manner.

Cook in his pink suit and deerstalker hat, Goldberg in tails, top hat, and knickers performed a terrific teacher-pupil duet, full of tricky sounds and pauses. She protested, laughing that she couldn't possibly do a certain step as fast as he could, but she could. Her rhythms aren't quite as nailed down as his, but she has a frank, vigorous style and an easy sensuous way of letting her body fall. Round hips and sturdy calves—a harem girl with true grit. Her performing manners are lovely, very unaffected, modest; she looks tickled to be doing this with these people.

Andrea Levine is sparer and cooler than Goldberg. Her solo was like a virtuosic drum riff (and Chris Braun accompanied her on the drums). She kept her feet working very close to the floor so she could make rapid, tiny changes in rhythm. What she did was elegant and controlled, very different from Cook's sophisticated gusto and the ways in which he created variety in his *Wave* (which he dedicated slyly to Hanya Holm, explaining that when he and his partner, Ernest Brown, were in *Kiss Me Kate,* Holm was always exhorting them to cover more ground than they liked to).

The sociability of the evening was refreshing, too. Braun, pianist Andy Wasserman and sax player Harvey Ray (who collaborated on an intrepid improvised duet with Goldberg) played terrific old tunes for tapping to and the dancers remembered to thank them often. A whole bunch of novices (I'd been wondering why the ushers wore tap shoes) joined in the finale. Stretch Johnson and his sister were lured out of the audience. And then somebody noticed Al Gusto sitting there smiling. He protested that he was wearing loafers, but he started tapping, hushing our applause to stop and think, then saying in a pleased way, "That's getting it now" and making his long skinny legs really fly out from the knees down. While his friends held up their hands for quiet so we could hear the muted flutter of his rhythms—murmuring every now and then, "my!" "mm, yes!" "look at *that!*"

ABANDONING THE IVORY
TOWER

The Village Voice, January 7–13, 1981

Modern dancers have always had a reputation for social consciousness. When music critic Deems Taylor wished to include a satire of
"The Modern Group" in his *Moments Mousical,* this was the aspect he
chose. Walter Kumme's drawing shows phalanxes of well-trained mice in
poses of supplication, while Taylor's text interprets: ". . . At the left,
three figures representing Boyle's Law are wondering how three other figures, representing the housing problem, got into the act." And this book
was published in the late '40s, a pretty quiescent period as far as high-
mindedness went.

The association of modern dance with liberalism and dissent dates from
the '30s, and has traditionally produced several different forms of action.
Prominent choreographers of the period performed at benefits for the International Labor Defense or the American League Against Fascism, just
as the important figures in the Judson Dance Theatre of the '60s offered
their works on programs and rallies that protested American involvement
in Vietnam. Choreographers have also made dances that could be seen as
a response to the political and social climate of the times, however oblique
or abstract those dances might be. Martha Graham's *Chronicle* and Doris
Humphrey's *With My Red Fires,* both made in 1936, were extremely individual, high-level responses to the Spanish Civil War and the rise of fascism in Europe.

Some choreographers have also made unabashedly propagandistic
dances—dances designed to arouse or rally "the people," rather than
simply to stir the dance audience. Beginning in the '60s, quite a few black
choreographers made political dances that were as unshaded and as up-
front in their sentiments as posters. During the early '70s, a group of
NYU students made an antiwar dance that was brief and abstract, but the
fact that they performed it in theater lobbies during intermissions gave it
the status of strong dissent. Taylor's mouse-satire probably derives from
the cruder dance-cartoons of the '30s. Jane Dudley, a notably conscientious dancer herself, has said that despite the laudable sentiments, some
of those works *were* pretty simplistic, that she could remember seeing
dances in which, for example, two thin girls might portray The Hungry
Masses and one stout one The Fascist Threat.

I haven't seen many overtly political dances recently—one, by Sharon Hom, dealt with the cultural dilemma of Chinese-Americans; another, by Susan Griss, dealt with the labor-management hassles that led up to the ghastly fire in the Triangle Shirtwaist Factory early in this century. Griss is the only New York choreographer I know who's committed to dance as a vehicle for social comment.

The influence of the women's movement on dance has been subtle but powerful. Although Graham's company of the '30s, like Twyla Tharp's company of the '60s, was all female, in the '50s it seemed that if you saw a large group of women onstage in a modern dance concert, you could assume they were waiting for the men to come home from the sea. Women could be featured as antagonists, but you rarely saw them touching and supporting each other to the extent that you do now.

When the Wallflower Order Dance Collective from Eugene, Oregon, performed at Larry Richardson's Dance Gallery in early December, I realized how rarely I see any dancing now I'd characterize as agitprop. The five women who make up the group—Nina Fichter, Pamela Gray, Krissy Keefer, Laurel Near, and Lyn Neeley—are rampant about nearly every worthwhile liberal cause you can think of. They are against violence, against the exploitation of small nations by large ones, against the prison system, against abuse of the environment and the endangering of both animal and human species, against the forcing of girl-children into traditional roles against their wishes.

The Wallflower's performing is a blend of the slapdash and the polished. The women keep hustling behind the rear curtain and re-emerging in yet another set of costumes that look as if they'd been pilfering a high school lost-and-found, yet they all sing and dance and act expertly. Their pieces range from a nearly incomprehensible number called *Z Ballet for Z People,* which has the hectic maladroitness of a summer camp charade, to a cool, abstract dance called *Endangered Species,* in which the women, their bent arms poking like damaged wings at the blue skirts they've pulled up to conceal their bodies, turn and squat and stretch and pick their way quietly along a diagonal.

You don't have to like all their numbers to be impressed by their work, by the robustness, wit, and conviction with which they assume even the most obvious of stereotypical stances. In the beginning, they emerge, one by one, from under Near's dress. (She's carried on others' shoulders, her long skirt concealing them and making her look like a giant Mother Goose.) They're all clutching props and ideas that define roles they once held onto—the scholastic overachiever (Keefer), the inebriate of art and poetry (Fichter); the who-cares?, dope-smoking drop-out (Gray); the girl who'd rather play with the boys at recess and who can beat them all (Neeley); the beauty queen (Near). The wry gusto with which these are presented and their obvious relevance to the women makes them transcend the caricatures they might have been, and, in a sense, are meant to be.

Since the Wallflower has performed in prisons and for various kinds of activists' groups, one of their paramount concerns is getting audiences to identify with them and/or get what they're driving at. Sometimes they sit around semicasually and share experiences; everyone gets a chance to talk and dance about their blood sisters. (Hard-driving Keefer came home one night to find a sign on the door of the room she shared with siblings: No Dancers Allowed!) They often accompany songs with a kind of choreography of sign language, which, they feel, helps their words to be comprehended by hearing as well as hearing-impaired audiences. Sometimes they communicate simply by the intensity of their emotion. Keefer performs a trapped, scrabbling solo on the floor while the others softly sing Holly Near's "Hay Una Mujer," and then recites a poem Keefer wrote on the endless nonmoving time of prison life; her sharp tonelessness and the extraordinary broken timing of words and movements give a powerful sense of hysteria mounting but never quite spilling over. Fichter's solo, *Hospital,* is all hysteria—her high breathless shriek and loose flinging limbs telling an almost unbearable story of countless painful operations to cure a birth defect.

The only issue the women soft-pedal at all is lesbianism, which comes up obliquely in a moving but slightly self-righteous poem by Judy Grahn (the accusatory "Have you ever held a woman's hand?" is answered by words like "Yes, I have held the hand of a woman who was dying . . .")

From what I understand from friends in Oregon, Wallflower must have developed significantly in the past year or so. Perhaps Timothy Near, a woman director who has been working with them for the past month as "theatrical advisor," is responsible for some of this. Perhaps the performers have simply matured. Certainly no one could have given them the boldness and zest with which they dance. When they first begin to move, you tend to try to identify their style with one of the major modern dance "techniques"—Limón, Ailey, whatever. What they do is big like those styles, and full-bodied. But their phrasing, their choice of what arm gestures to use with what legs, the way they put steps together make their dancing look distinctive—personal anyway. After a while, you just see these women dancing in nicely composed patterns, not always in unison, but in harmonious canon or counterpoint. And you admire how Fichter can use her long legs that are limber to the point of rubberiness and yet dance comfortably in unison with sturdy, compact Keefer. Neeley dancing alone looks both heroically strong and warm, yet can submerge her individual power into the group. It's been a long time since I've seen women dancers so luxuriantly at ease and yet so purposeful and daring with their bodies.

Since I first saw The Wallflower Order, the interest in dance as a vehicle for political statement has grown. As the earlier article about Edith Segal indicates, Dancers for Disarmament sponsored a series of concerts and workshops at P.S. 122 in the spring of 1982. More recently, American involvement in Central America has prompted artists to march, to contribute works to benefit concerts, or to create new pieces with specific political content. In the summer of 1984, at P.S. 122, a three-part series of concerts was devoted to "Dance and Social Commentary." Once again, as in the thirties and the late sixties, the events of the day are compelling many politically aware artists to take action in the form they know best.

ART ON ICE

The Village Voice, November 29, 1976

If George Balanchine can venture out of the ballet world to choreograph for circus elephants, Twyla Tharp can certainly do it for ice skaters. And for her, I'm sure, it's not a lark but a new challenge. It's easy, too, to see why she wanted to create an ice dance for Olympic Gold Medalist John Curry; his long, elegant line; his remarkable fluidity; his obvious intelligence; and the performing reticence that in a competitive skater is probably considerd tantamount to diffidence.

There were some superb champions and would-be champions performing in Superskates III at Madison Square Garden—Ken Shelley and Jojo Starbuck, Tai Babilonia, Linda Fratianne, for instance. Some remarkable feats and a few beautiful moments. Judi Genovese and Kent Weigle executed an extremely interesting fast dance, full of tricky rhythms and changes of path. But, for the most part, skaters' routines are, of necessity, governed by rules of competitive skating and also, I think, by fashion. For instance, choices in music these days run to pop songs and show tunes with an occasional light classic. (When I was a kid, it was Viennese waltzes, and I'm *sure* all female skaters looked like Superskaters' Barbie

Smith—blonde, brash, and speedy.) "Choreography" is definitely the servant of virtuosity.

Yet I loved the opening of the program, when all the skaters, in unison, soberly ran through the steps that make up their basic vocabulary (is penché arabesque really called a camel?), and then exploded all at once into a display of, I guess, whatever they felt like doing. Tharp's solo for Curry had more in common with this opening than with anything else on the program. Curry, in white satin pants and velour shirt, skated out into a glare of white light (welcome, in a way, after all the hot pink washes and follow spots, but not making it easy to focus on Curry). When he began to dance to an Albinoni trumpet concerto—as if completely alone, pensively trying out steps, not pushing anything to its fullest—I could see that Tharp loved and respected the skater's vocabulary but kept asking, "Why must it always be done this way?" So sometimes, instead of smoothly straightening his legs, he snapped them straight; he let turns die down completely, never speeded them up to a whiz; once, dipping in and out of a deep lunge, he abandoned a lot of skaterly control and really dropped the weight of his body and swung it up again loosely.

The dance, of course, was studded with moments of Tharpian informality (Curry skating hands on hips as if taking a breather), with a few shuddery wiggles, with vehement stops, with ingenious rhythms. At times, I thought she held him in too much by making steps that were clever and crabbed. Yet the way she and he shaped a passage of slow, simple backward skating made it startlingly lovely. And at the end she emphasized the fact that in skating, a movement can continue its trajectory through space, even when the impetus in the dancer's body has ceased: Curry began to sail in a straight line, standing on one foot with the other held trimly beside his ankle, body still, arms hanging down. As he neared the end of the rink, he gave a small twist of the foot he was standing on and veered calmly in another direction. He kept doing this, very serenely, until the dance slowed to its natural end. Albinoni would have adored it; where but on ice could you get a natural decrescendo like that?

Curry didn't really "perform" the dance; he danced it with a care and interest that struck me as heroic.

BALLET NOVELS: YOU'LL
NEVER DANCE AURORA, DEAR

The Village Voice, September 17, 1979

⌁

"He made American ballet and he made New York a capital of world ballet."

"But the dance that was in him, the dance that was his, stayed frozen up."

"Until now."

Or: " 'Dance! My dear Mr. Lazar! If she's lucky she will be able to walk without a noticeable limp . . .' "

During the '70s, and especially since the success of *The Turning Point,* the ballet world has become a desirable purlieu for writers of popular novels. Perhaps more than a purlieu; in almost all of the seven novels I read, or reread this summer, dance itself is the focus of attention—more of a heroine than the ballerinas (just flowering, or hovering nervously at the farther edges of their prime) or the men they love (horny virtuoso defectors from the Kirov; brilliant, ruthless choreographers; doctors; businessmen).

And the tone of the ballet novel tends to be sweeping, melodramatic, full of incident. Typically, writers in this genre adore classroom sweat, performance as an unrivaled high, the drama of injury, peril and fear as the dancer's constant companions. They play cagey games with the names and personas of real figures in the dance world. Most of the novels feature autocratic European teachers—Italian maestri patterned after Cecchetti (there's one of these in Vicki Baum's *Theme for Ballet*) or Russian ex-ballerinas (like "Alexandra Baronova" in Leland Cooley's *The Dancer*). They flick their canes and say to the heroine (and it usually *is* a heroine) things like "Who taught you? . . . Obviously you've had training of a sort—no?" Usually in these books, there's a mature European dancer too, perhaps friendly like Eglanova in Edgar Box's *Death in the Fifth Position,* dispensing tea and salty advice on sex, perhaps unmitigatedly bitchy like Beshanskaia in Tom Murphy's *Ballet!* Almost always there's a choreographer who needs/molds/dominates the heroine and creates at some climactic moment of the book a ballet that will make or break his/her/the company's reputation. There are the impresarios, several of them modeled, apparently, on Lucia Chase. There are the critics—a John

Martin figure for Baum's novel, and two Clive Barneses: "Simon Bridge" in *Ballet!* and the savage parody "Ivor Noble" in Edward Stewart's *Ballerina.*

There's an immense amount of sexual activity and thinking about sexual activity; this has more to do with the demands of pop fiction than life in the dance world. We're always told right away the state of the heroine's tits—sometimes they are "large for a dancer," sometimes beautiful and pert, sometimes, as with Sasha in Catherine Hutter's *A Time To Dance,* endearingly nonexistent.

I devour these novels with unblushing zest; candidly, the genre has yet to find its Dostoevsky. And why is it that so few of the novelists can convince me that the person they tell me is a genius *is* one, that this ballet *is* momentous? The only authors who come anywhere near doing this, who draw the reader into the core of the dance's momentum are Spider and Jeanne Robinson with the maverick science fiction work, *Stardance.*

The oldest of these books, *Death in the Fifth Position* by Edgar Box (AKA Gore Vidal), first appeared in 1952, and it's a crackingly expert murder mystery. You know the kind: B, a prime suspect for the murder of A, is now dead; before he died, he must have told C who really killed A, and now C has been killed. *Who's next?* The narrator is a sanguine young journalist (ex-Harvard, ex-World War II) hired for a PR job with the Grand Petersburg Ballet. When someone takes a pair of shears to the wire that spins bitch-ballerina Ella Sutton aloft at the finale of the new *Eclipse,* the heat's on. Pete, the hero, sleuths cleverly around, beds an up-and-comer, fends off the aggressively amorous premier danseur ("I wondered whether to knee him or not; the towel had fallen off. I decided against it for the good of the company.") Box/Vidal's images of dance are often wise, and he doesn't go all soft in the head over ballet. He maintains with ease the flat, sardonic style of the All-American Mystery Novel ("As I walked by, however, I heard Miles Sutton threatening to kill his wife. It gave me quite a turn. I mean temperament is all very well, but there are times when it can be carried too far").

The spirit of the late '40s flavors the book—female dancers rehearse in black tights and white T-shirts, rubberband their hair into ponytails, and the skinny, nervous, brilliant young American choreographer, Jed Wilbur, might have been patterned partly on Jerome Robbins. The spirit of the times also shapes the plot, and the author lightly, but very firmly, makes red-baiting and the concealing of Communist affiliations moral issues as well as the paraphernalia of murder.

Theme for Ballet was written in 1958, and Vicki Baum is an accomplished best-selling type of novelist. You can tell her book was written in the '50s, not because of ponytails (although rising soloist Joyce Lyman peppers her conversations with a distressing number of goshes and gees), or because the corps of the Manhattan Ballet consists only of sixteen girls and eight boys, but because the heroine has this tremendous conflict between Home Life and Career. Katya Milenkaya is top-notch but forty-five, married to a darling doctor who calls her "Cath," and lives in Princeton with her little orphaned grandson. At the end, she phones her husband and says "I need you, Ted."

It's an entertaining book, though, with many cleverly managed flashbacks to Katya's beginnings as a child dancer in Paris (she, like the heroines of five of these novels, hasn't got a proper family: they were all tragically robbed of one or both parents early on); to her infatuation with a gifted male dancer; to the hideous accident in which he, suffering from an undetected brain tumor, dropped her off a ramp during a ballet and dove after her; to the hospital where her husband-to-be patched her up. The pages drip tragedy (no parents, daughter killed, son dead of polio, idol killed, self almost crippled, husband asking for a divorce), all of it strangely unmoving. The "present" in the novel centers around the premiere of a new ballet, *The Hive*, and Baum builds her climax to an improbable rolling boil with two deaths, several walk-outs, temper tantrums galore, and round-the-clock rehearsing. Enough to make a quiet life in Princeton look very good indeed.

A Time To Dance and *The Dancer* cover almost the same period, the former in Europe the latter in America. *A T. To D.* begins toward the close of the Diaghilev era and ends at the brink of World War II; Leya Marks, the heroine of *The Dancer*, was born in 1919, and the book extends into the '40s, allowing her boyfriends to be torpedoed and captured.

Catherine Hutter, the author of *A T. To D.*, danced, as I recall, with Pavlova's company, and she treads a fine edge between truth and fiction. Sasha meets Pavlova (did she really climb a ladder to chat with an old ballerina-turned-teacher who was mending her studio roof?). Her amour, Dima Sertis, is part of Diaghilev's entourage; Dima's homosexual father is credited with helping the impresario amass the Russian paintings for his epochal exhibit and raising money for his Saisons Russes in Paris. Richard Tauber gropes Sasha's sister, Marina, a cabaret performer in Berlin. The fictional characters mingle almost unnervingly with the real ones. Sasha, a clever, warm, unblinkingly honest heroine, moves through some richly evoked atmospheres: the houses of Russian émigrés in London, English ballet studios, dreary tours, the Berlin of cocky Nazism. The heroine and her two sisters are terrific letterwriters, and that's how we get a lot of our information—colored by individual feeling.

The Dancer is disappointing, although the setup is intriguing. Leya moves from supering in *Aida* during the days when Balanchine and his

American Ballet were at the Met, to modeling for lingerie ads, to dancing in nightclubs (with a small new ballet ensemble), to starring in movies and on Broadway. The unbelievable clincher is that she throws over everything to go back into training at twenty-five or so to see if she can reroute herself toward *Giselle* and *Swan Lake*. The author, Leland Cooley, produced musicals on TV; his wife choreographed. But he doesn't make the gypsy life vivid. The novel is crammed with events; but simply recounted or carried by dialogue, they come only half alive.

Ballet! and *Ballerina* are real *Turning Point* follow-ups. In the latter, the heroine has a corker of a slangy, devious ex-dancer mother, in the former she falls in love with Baryshnikov (flimsily—who cares?—disguised as Dima Lubov). I found *Ballet!* in an airport and enjoyed it a lot. The author, Tom Murphy (a pseudonym, I'm positive, for someone well versed in ballet lore and backstage life), writes ebulliently with a shrewd use of adjectives and adverbs to juice everything up: someone doesn't simply buy a bag of beets, she buys "two fat bags of them." The everlasting use of last names is mannered ("It scared Greg Holden, and Greg Holden was not a man to whom fear came naturally").

Murphy has tacked a murder mystery onto his ballet novel: there's a plot afoot to kill all Russian defectors. But the mystery and the love-career stories never mesh. (The murderer can be guessed early on, and suspense is minimal.) The real story is an agreeable one of rival ballet companies, of Jennifer and Dima and the rough places in their courtship.

Murphy's choreographer, Alex de Lis, is a curiously unBalanchine-like Balanchine. He's had five wives, is witty, elegant, and ruthless. Yet, although we're told he is the greatest and most innovative choreographer in contemporary ballet, all the heroine, Jennifer Hale, ever gets to dance are roles like Giselle and Coppelia. But if Alex de Lis is puzzling, Marius Volmar in *Ballerina* is even more so. He's sort of a cliché Tudor figure—he hasn't made a ballet in thirty years; it's tacitly understood in his company that you have to break dancers in order to make them great. So there's a lot of cruelty, and Stewart, the author, also plays up the drastic climate of ballet with relish—telling who got blood clots from staying on the pill too long, who fell out the open window doing a pirouette in class. The story concentrates on the friendship and rivalry between Stephanie and Chris. Chris is dying of a rare form of something; and although she apparently neither eats nor sleeps, she takes on Stephanie during the fouetté competition in *Graduation Ball* and ends with two doubles and a triple.

The book loses points on believability all along the way. Of the many streams of French ballet terms, some are undoable as presented. Would a young choreographer change a highly successful first ballet for two couples into a pas de trois because the mother of one of the dancers conned him into it? Would the company that bought the ballet as a double duet cheerfully accept it as a trio? Would a company director tell an aging dancer he was fired *before* a performance so that he would come on stage drunk and weepy? And more. And more . . .

The last book is in a class by itself. It begins in Toronto in 1989. The jumpoff is from modern dance, not ballet. Written by a science fiction writer and a dancer, *Stardance* tells of the beginnings of free-fall dancing, a form the audience can receive only via video. In the work of Shara Drummond, the Isadora of zero-g dancing, there is no up or down, there is movement out from her center or through space: the video camera frames her, but that is the camera's structure. Her video partner is the book's narrator, Charles Armstead, a dancer crippled in a mugging; and he takes over after Shara vanishes into far space—he can dance again in a zero-g environment and establishes a small company. There's a plot, but not a hell of a lot of incidents in the book, and it abounds in the technical descriptions that are an important part of sci-fi ("You lower away, effectively increasing the length of your hammer handle and thus your gee force. When you're 'down' far enough, say at half a gee [about 400 meters of line], you . . ."). The Stardancers are called upon by the military and diplomatic establishments to attempt communication, through dance, with some mysterious aliens hovering out around Titan. In a tour de force of science fiction description, the Robinsons take the readers into the consciousness of humans who are in the process of becoming something else. The book is all about weight and time, only here we experience most of it as subjectively as possible—hanging in space, shooting off at improbable speeds, creating a bloom of dance in a global space, experiencing gravity as a load descending on us again to depress our minds and restrict our motion.

Tom Murphy was delighted that I thought his name might be a pseudonym for a dance insider, but not pleased that I classed his novel, Ballet!, *as a "Turning Point followup." He wrote that his novel appeared in hardcover in March, 1978, "almost simultaneously with the release of the film,* The Turning Point." *Furthermore, he had submitted a detailed outline to his publisher in 1976, with no knowledge of the film project.*

PORTRAIT OF THE ARTIST
AS SURVIVOR

The Village Voice, April 26, 1983

᠁

Phyllis Lamhut is a pro. If I want this interview to focus on survival rather than on art making, she'll talk survival—a subject on which she is an expert. Since she's pretty much the same trim, nimble little blonde I met almost twenty-six years ago—feisty, funny, sharp as a tack—it's hard to believe she has been laboring in the concert dance field for thirty-five years now. During that time she's been in, out, up, down, hot, cold, but never stopped dancing and choreographing and showing her work. An object lesson to those who grew up in the '60s believing you had to have a grant before you could take up choreography.

Lamhut motto number one (all mottoes inferred by me): "Never give up momentum. Momentum is very important to survival. . . . Move. Stay active. Stay busy." Whether or not you've got money.

Straddling a stool in Dance Theater Workshop's rehearsal studio, obligingly chronicling the fiscal dramas of her life, Lamhut decides she's always had a survivor's personality. A by-product, perhaps, of growing up in a poor but artistic family in Bed-Stuy. Shortly after beginning to study with Alwin Nikolais at the Henry Street Playhouse in 1948, hell-bent to be a dancer, she wangled a scholarship. That meant "office work, telephone work, cleaning work," plus, when she got out of high school, "luncheonette jobs, cashier jobs, switchboard jobs." Nik had no money then to pay his dancers regularly. The children's shows he wisely began to create might bring the dancers $15 or $25 (meet at dawn, load the truck, drive, set up, perform, eat, drive, unload the truck). In 1955, the *New York Times* critic trekked down to Henry Street and wrote a rave. The audience the company had been slowly building was now swelled by curious visitors from uptown. Bingo. Some weekend runs—maybe five performances for $100.

Dancers like Lamhut, like Murray Louis and Gladys Bailin, were clever enough to know Nik was worth sticking with. It was a tight, happy group. "Nik was always generous with his cooking, and if we ever needed money, he gave us, you know, $5, $2—$2 went a long way then." Luckily she had a $46-a-month apartment. Luckily, she could use the playhouse for free to show her first efforts at choreography. She'd been performing for twenty years before she qualified for unemployment.

Lamhut motto number two: learn to teach well. A gift from Nik: "If you're going to earn your income, you may as well earn it in your profession . . . and you're always kept dancing when you're teaching."

She has a golden reputation as a teacher. In the old days, the proceeds from a big summer teaching job could carry her for six months. You eat, pay the rent, maybe plow money back into the company, help your husband through graduate school. (This summer, she's off to conduct a workshop in Switzerland.)

Mottoes number three and four: get what you can for nothing. Accept all money, however little.

In the early Henry Street days, before Nikolais began to tour extensively, Phyllis and Gladys, pretty, bright-eyed little things, would charm storekeepers on the Lower East Side into giving them stretch jersey and plastic for Nik's costumes. (Those were the days when some of Nik's most magical effects were achieved by dancers wielding flashlights, and he'd choreograph special exits and entrances so dancers could change gels and slides in the middle of a piece.) With this kind of background, Lamhut is horrified that certain choreographers sent back New York State Council grants because the sum was insultingly small: "Not me; I'd take the money, honey, and *do* something."

Motto number five: learn how to run a company. "The minute you begin to raise money or ask for funds, your whole artistic sensibility has to include—in one remote corner of your brain—understanding of how to function on the business end."

Nik's dancers were privy to company finances, learned about fund-raising and incorporation. During the '60s Lamhut performed with Murray Louis's company as well and went through the incorporation bit with him too. By the time she stopped working with both men (1969) and formed her own company, she was already proficient. She'll hire a booker, but a company manager? "I mean, it's like I could do it in my sleep . . . I'm very good at budgets." When I ask if her company's ever been in the red, she squawks, "What do you mean? Deficit? Never! I would *never* go into deficit."

Motto number six: "Never lose an opportunity to perform."

Lamhut even took a break from Nikolais in the early '60s. "I wanted to see what was cooking; I went to auditions; I got in a show right away [*Ballet Ballads,* choreographed by Hanya Holm]; I did *The Ed Sullivan Show;* I think I did some opera choreography somewhere."

These experiences taught her that nothing interested her more than the life of a concert dancer—"because every time you do a movement it's a challenge." But she'd looked around, studied with Merce Cunningham, made contacts. She began to share programs with other not-well-heeled choreographers whether their aesthetic priorities differed or not (Yvonne Rainer, William Davis, Albert Reid, Phyllis Lamhut at tiny Judson Hall on 57th Street). She was one of many choreographers who showed work on Barnard College's Dance Uptown series or Laura Foreman's Choreo concerts at the New School: "On that little two-by-four stage! I would never say no to her; I loved those things. There were 600 people in the audience all the time. An exposure like that? Packed with energy, life! . . ."

Of course, she admits with a sigh of pleasure, it's a treat to dance in a really beautiful theater (she, Annabelle Gamson, and Don Redlich are about to share a season at the Joyce), but she thinks it's a mistake to need a particular environment in order to feel like an artist. "I'm not like haute cuisine," she says, in an impetuously botched metaphor. "I could dance in a studio, on a high-class stage, in the street, or in a gym . . . without letting my aesthetic drop."

Motto number seven: "You are in an erratic business; to assume you're going to have clear sailing all the way is outrageous."

It's easy to be lulled by success. Lamhut can remember when Nik's company enjoyed the glories of weeks on the Steve Allen show, of stints with Camera 3 and CBS Repertory Theater. But it couldn't last forever. In the 1970s, Lamhut became popular, got her first CAPS grant, started getting grants from the New York State Council on the Arts and the National Endowment, in 1974 received a Guggenheim ("a real fluke"). "In all my innocence, I didn't realize that now you're a chosen one, and now you're not. Somebody else is. Word spreads around the business who's hot and who should get it. Total politics." Yet she wasn't all that innocent. During those years when there were tours, teaching residencies under the NEA's Artists in the Schools program, money for production, when she could guarantee her dancers twenty weeks' work, "I told Natasha Simon (who's been with me for fourteen years) and who had a flexible Time-Life job she wanted to quit when we were doing well, I said, 'Don't ever quit the job, because Doomsday will come and you'll need something.' "

She was right. In 1976 or was it 1977? Lamhut was kicked off the NEA's Dance Touring Program—a program under which the NEA paid part of the company's fee, making dance alluringly affordable in many communities and creating work for companies. Lamhut had already cut her company down to six because expenses—plane fares in particular—were going up. She gets this letter: "Dear Miss Lamhut . . ." Something was said about the quality of her work, something about her fiscal standing. She could *almost* bear having her budget criticized, but the quality of her art? "You can like or not like my work, but 'quality' I always had. You know that, Deborah." (Yes.) "I never recovered from the shock of that insult."

Not that she took it lying down. "I said to myself, 'Hold on! Nobody's going to step on *me* like that. I have put in across this country twenty-five years of a lot of work.' " She, and others who'd been excluded, fought to get back on the DTP, maybe to get two weeks of touring a year. But you can't maintain a company on that, and touring tended to dry up for companies without the NEA seal of approval. Lamhut gradually shifted gears: "I said to myself, 'Forget it, Phyllis, with the company.' I'm not going to schlep all over this country. You cannot spot-tour now. It takes more money to get to Hattiesburg, Mississippi, than it costs to get to California. It's so hard . . . I realized I made $900 on touring—profit—a year ago. No *way.*"

She's going into "projects" ("right now I want to work on large chorale kinds of things, you know, wonderful big, huge plastiques . . ."). Her dancers are loyal, enthusiastic enough to rehearse some when pickings are nil; she'll doggedly choreograph around their part-time teaching jobs: "Who can come Tuesday? Two people? Whenever you see my work and you see two people on that stage, those are the people I had Tuesday." When she lays her hands on money and plans a performance, she'll pay the dancers, give them all billing as guest artists.

Lamhut thinks the current politics of art tends to favor the extremes, the national living treasures and the so-called avant-garde, excluding the middle. A little more than two years ago, she wrote an angry, witty letter to New York critics about their injudicious cultivating of the "new" and signed it, "Phyllis Lamhut, a member of the lost generation."

She is fierce on the subject of trendiness ("Lar Lubovitch got so hot he went broke. Now he's doing well, thank God"). Together we remember how Cliff Keuter disbanded his company and went off to California to work, how Elizabeth Keen had to drop her company and Dan Wagoner nearly did ("I called him up and said, 'don't you dare!' "), how Viola Farber found work in Europe and finally got a Guggenheim long after less established choreographers were honored.

Now—touch wood—things have turned around again. Lamhut was stunned and delighted to receive one of the NEA's few three-year choreographic fellowships.

Last motto: "Be flexible, but stick to your guns."

Nope. One more: "Hustle—put that in your article. You want to know something? Managers hustle, but nobody can hustle like a dancer if they know how to do it."

And after more rueful words about the gray and murky period we're in, about how dance as a whole—still not quite an integral part of the American way of life—is probably going to suffer in the blighted economy, she tires of talking about struggle and begins to speak excitedly of the Wigman solos Annabelle Gamson taught her for the Joyce season. Hitching up her black plastic pants, not bothering to warm up again (what the hell, we've known each other how long?), she plops down on the floor, and, suddenly, in the lazy opening gestures of Wigman's *Pastorale*, becomes the artist, completely, beautifully immersed in the moment of performing.

Survival, with honor, of the very damn fit.

INDEX

Fialkow, Roy, 273–274
  Lamentations of Jane Eyre, 273
Faison, George, 211, 212
  Suite Otis, 212
Fichter, Nina, 279, 280
Fiddler on the Roof, (Robbins), 5, 6, 7
Finney, Ross Lee, 207
Firebird, (Béjart), 215
Fisher, Betsy, 156, 205
Fisher, Linda, 88
Fives, (Goh), 235
Flextime, (King), 95
Floor of the Forest, The, (Brown), 69
Flower Festival in Genzano, (Bournonville), 145
Fokine, Mikhail, 131, 147–150
  Bacchanale, 158
  Les Préludes, 158
  Scheherazade, 147–150
Folk Tale, A, (Bournonville), 139, 140–141, 143
Fonteyn, Margot, 39
Foreman, Laura, 290
Forti, Simone, 75–76
Foster, William Z., 269
Four Bagatelles, (Robbins), 12
Four for Nothing, (Dunn), 83
Four Scores, (Reitz), 182–183
Fox, Lisa, 35, 36, 38
Frame, Peter, 17
Franca, Celia, 219
Frank, Carter, 94
Frank, Diane, 87
Franklin, Frederic, 148
Fratianne, Linda, 281
Freelance, 190
Fregalette-Jansen, JoAnn, 107
Freydont, Shelley, 60
Fricke-Gottschild, Hellmut, 151, 153
Friedman, Lise, 35, 37, 38
Frishøi, Tommy, 142, 143
From Sea to Shining Sea, (Taylor), 50
Frontier, (Graham), 40
Fujian Hand Puppets, 257–259
  All Men Are Brothers, 258
  Devil Paints a Woman, The, 258

Gallery, (Nikolais), 200
Galsworthy, John, 268
Gameche, Abelardo, 104
Game Tree, (Dunn), 87–88
Gamson, Annabelle, 137, 290, 292
Gardner, Sally, 190
Garen, Elizabeth, 70, 71
Gautier, Théophile, 254
Gelbe Klang, Der. See Yellow Sound, The.
Geography and Music, (Tone), 37
Gestures in Red, (Dunn), 81, 84
Gibson, Albert, 276–277
Gibson, Jon, 78–80
Gilbert, Natalie, 107
Gillis, Christopher, 49, 52
Giselle, (Coralli), 132, 158, 219–220, 265
Glacial Decoy, (Brown), 74
Gladstein, Deborah, 182
Glasner, Katie, 58, 61
Glassman, William, 14
Glass, Philip, 17, 18

Glass Pieces, (Robbins), 17
Glauber, Lynn, 122
Goding, John, 237
Godreau, Miguel, 211
  Paz, 211
Godunov, Alexander, 222
Goh, Choo San, 234–237
  Birds of Paradise, 235, 236, 237
  Casella 1, 2, 3, 236
  Double Concerto, 236
  Double Contrasts, 234, 235, 236
  Fives, 235
  Helena, 234, 235–236, 237
  Introducing, 234
  Momentum, 234
  Untitled, 234
Gold and Silver Waltz, (Lehár), 20
Goldberg, Jane, 276–277
  It's About Time, 276
Goldberg Variations, The, (Robbins), 5, 12
Goldweber, Mark, 123, 125, 127
Golestan/The Rose Garden, (Béjart), 215, 217
Good, Alan, 35, 38
Goodman, Andrea, 97, 98
Gordon, David, 65, 66, 76–78, 84
  Profile, 76–78
Goya, Carola, 246
Graf, Pat, 108, 109, 126
Graham, Martha, 3, 39–44, 46, 48, 68, 117, 119, 120, 131, 132, 135, 162, 198, 200, 202, 206, 215, 270, 279
  Adorations, 43
  Alcestis, 46
  Appalachian Spring, 40, 42
  Canticle for Innocent Comedians, 42
  Cave of the Heart, 40
  Chronicle, 280
  Clytemnestra, 46
  Dark Meadow, 40, 41, 42
  Deaths and Entrances, 40, 41, 42, 273
  El Penitente, 39–40
  Embattled Garden, 46
  Episodes, 46
  Errand into the Maze, 40, 42
  Frontier, 40
  Herodiade, 40
  Night Journey, 40, 46
  O Thou Desire Who Art About To Sing, 42
  Primitive Mysteries, 40, 42–44, 132
  Shadows, 42
Grahn, Judy, 280
Grahn, Lucille, 273
Grain, (Eiko/Koma), 185
Gramercy Arts Theater, 252
Grand Union, 70, 82
Grant, Alexander, 224
Grasso-Caprioli, Christina, 84
Grave assai y Fandango, (Rioja), 253
Graves, Morris, 35
Graves, Robert, 24
Gray, Diane, 40, 42
Gray, Pamela, 279
Greenfield, Lois, 202
Green, Julian, 230
Green Table, The, (Jooss), 145–147
Gregory, Cynthia, 222